ENDINGTHE
MOTHER WAR

ENDING THE MOTHER WAR

MOTHER WAR

Starting the Workplace Revolution

JAYNE BUXTON

MACMILLAN

First published 1998 by Macmillan

an imprint of Macmillan Publishers Ltd
25 Eccleston Place, London SW1W 9NF
and Basingstoke

Associated companies throughout the world

ISBN 0 333 71968 9

Typeset by SetSystems Ltd, Saffron Walden, Essex
Printed and bound in Great Britain by
Mackays of Chatham plc, Chatham, Kent

To Patrick, Olivia and Joely

CONTENTS

❖

Acknowledgements   ix

Preface   xiii

Introduction: The Mother War   1

Part One Myths from the Superwoman's Briefcase   21

1 The Guilt Thing   23
2 The Myth of the New Father   50
3 The Myth of Managed Mothering   73
4 The Day-care Dream   101

Part Two Myths from the Earthmother's Kitchen   135

5 The Myth of the Earthmother, the Perfect Family
   and the End of Crime   137
6 Everyone's an Earthmother at Heart   167
7 The Myth of the Few Short Years   189

Part Three No More Myths   205

8 The Family-friendly Workplace: How Far Have
   We Got?   207
9 Beyond Family-friendly Policies: The Case for a
   Workplace Revolution   249
10 The Organizational Change Agenda   298
11 Starting from Where We Are   345

References   379
Bibliography   396
Index   401

ACKNOWLEDGEMENTS

✧

THERE ARE MANY without whose help I could not have written this book.

I am indebted to Jane Bradish Ellames at Curtis Brown for having first spotted the potential in what was initially a very rough draft manuscript, and for her unceasing support during all stages of writing. To Catherine Hurley, my editor, I also owe huge thanks, for both the quality of her professional advice and her support and enthusiasm. Those in Macmillan's editorial services, publicity and marketing departments who supported the book so wholeheartedly also deserve my thanks.

The following people took time out from busy schedules to grant me interviews or provide me with valuable information: Irene Allen of Listawood; Annabel Allott; Kirstie Axtens at Parents at Work; Liz Bargh and Lucy Daniels of WFD; Sally Bevan; Tracy Camilleri of WMC Communications; Christine Camp at Midland Bank; Fiona Cannon and Anne Jenkins at Lloyds TSB; Ted Childs and Maria Ferris at IBM; Sheila Cook and Dorothy May of the BBC; Shirley Dex of Cambridge University; Joanna Foster of the BT Forum; Ellen Galinsky and Arlene Johnson at the Families and Work Institute in New York; Jonathon Gershuny at the Economic and Social Research Council at Essex University; Marie Gill at Asda; Diana Good and Caroline Stroud at Linklater's and Paines; Linda Haas; Gay Haines and John Stuart of hat pin; Valerie Hammond at the Roffey Park Management Institute; Maeve Haran; Christine Hill, of Christine Hill Associates; Margaret Hodge MP; Dr Juliet Hopkins at the Tavistock Clinic; Dr Philip Hwang; Bruce Macdonald and Sheila West at The Royal Borough of Kingston; Roz Morris of TV News London; Brandon McDonagh at the Industrial Society; Peter McGuffin of the University of Wales College of Medicine;

Rosa Monckton; Peter Moss from the Thomas Coram Research Unit; Pat Nazemetz at Xerox; Martin Neville at Lilly Industries; Anne Marie Piper; Susie Orbach; Eliza Parker of The Gotham Group; Rhona Rapoport; Carole Reay; Dr Ian Roberts at the Institute of Child Health; Gerry Robinson, Peter Coleridge, Roger Maverty and Stephanie Monk at Granada; Carole Savage; Mrs Steve Shirley at the FI Group; Hilary Simpson, Peter Clark and David Sibbert at Oxfordshire County Council; Ruth Tait; and Peter Wilson of Young Minds. I would also like to thank the dozens of women who granted me interviews but preferred to remain anonymous, as well as the friends and colleagues who allowed me to make reference to stories recounted to me during conversations over the past several years.

I am especially grateful to journalists and authors Maureen Freely and Yvonne Roberts. In addition to granting me interviews, during which they shared stories and insights that greatly informed the book, they proved to be enthusiastic supporters of both me and the book within the public arena.

Special thanks also go to the following people: Roger and Leonie Bannister, the use of whose kitchen table enabled me to complete a first draft in relative peace and seclusion; Janet Hull, chairwoman of the Women of the Year Lunch, who secured me interviews with several women associated with the lunch: Roz Morris, Carole Reay and Anne Marie Piper. Adrian Stacey and Laura King at Gemini Consulting's Information Centre for their tireless and cheerful fulfilment of my many requests for information; Linda Drury, Mary Hay Jahans, Jaspa de Pastor and Louise Marks, Gemini personal assistants who have all, at various times, assisted me in carrying out the administrative tasks associated with the book's completion.

Gemini itself warrants special mention. The firm as a whole has shown itself to be remarkably accommodating and flexible as regards mine and other working mothers' needs. The firm's philosophy centres on the principle of achieving results through people, and its ability to capture the hearts, minds and energy of people within client organizations is a key reason for its success, and something that distinguishes it from many other consulting firms. To my mind, Gemini's willingness to invest in its own people – as evidenced by its recent commitment to embarking on a project to improve the

Acknowledgements

work–life balance for all consultants, as well as a host of other practices and policies, represents an extension of this philosophy. Two people at Gemini have been especially supportive of me, at all stages of my career, but particularly during the time I spent writing this book. John Bateson, my mentor for over five years, encouraged me to devote the time to the book, and to further pursue my interest in the work–life field. Steve Beck has consistently expressed interest in my work, and in seeing it brought to bear for the benefit of Gemini's consultants and clients.

Last but not least, I would like to thank my family: my mother, who despite having devoted all of her time as a young mother to raising her daughters, has never once been defensive or condemning of my decision not to do so; my father, who has always encouraged me in my ambitions, even when they have lead me down paths which are the opposite to the ones he might have chosen; my sister, Cal, for her unswerving support and encouragement; and my husband Patrick and our two girls, Olivia and Joely, both for giving me a personal reason to write this book, and for putting up with me while I did so.

PREFACE

❖

THIS BOOK EMERGED out of frustration with the ongoing debate about mothers and work in Britain, a debate in which the question 'Should mothers work?' is repeatedly posed, and a familiar duo, the full-time housewife and the full-time working mother, are set against one another, like the poor beleaguered contestants in a cockfight, to answer it. It emerged, also, out of anger at the many lies that are told by both sides in this debate, and out of a desire to tell the truth about mothers, work and children.

Perhaps more importantly, the book was also born of a positive conviction that there is an alternative third angle within this tired debate, one which offers hope of a release from the stalemate and of genuine change in the name of families. That third angle is the fundamental restructuring of the workplace, from the assumptions that underlie it to the manner in which it operates.

I am not by any means the first to propose that the solution to the work–family juggernaut lies in a radical restructuring of work itself. Here in the UK, Maeve Haran wrote about the need for balance in the workplace in her novel, *Having It All*. Patricia Hewitt advocated a change from the full-time, long-hours culture in *About Time*, and Penelope Leach made a plea for genuinely flexible workplace practices in *Children First*. The UK-based charity New Ways to Work has been preaching the message for nearly two decades. In America, Rhona Rapoport, Arlie Hochschild, Juliet Schor and Lotte Bailyn, to name but a few, have all reached the conclusion that changing the way we think about and organize work is the key to alleviating work–family conflict. The non-profit Families and Work Institute and the consultancy WFD concluded, after years of working with individuals and organizations, that the greatest potential lies in altering the norms, culture and rules of operation which characterize today's workplace.

This book aims to raise awareness of these individuals' and organizations' views and work, and in so doing to popularize the notion that there is a viable alternative solution to the work–family dilemma other than the Earthmother and Superwoman options which are consistently pressed upon mothers today. There are far too few within organizations who are aware of the work that has been done in the work–family and work–life fields, and of the exciting experiments that are currently under way; there are too few within the media who inject the work–life perspective into the debate about mothers and work, and too many who rely instead upon the instigation of formulaic confrontation between the Earth-mother and Superwoman camps; and there are far too many mothers, and fathers, who have resigned themselves to bearing the entire burden created by work–family conflict, and to working within organizations whose design and operation are based on a family structure that has not existed for decades, if it ever existed at all.

Ending the Mother War is primarily for and about mothers. It is their actions that are subject to such scrutiny; it is they who are trapped within a debate which offers them just two choices, one of which often involves sacrificing their own needs and ambitions, the other of which can lead to the sacrifice of their children's and families' well-being. But, although the starting-point for the book is mothers, the false choices they are presented with, and the lies they tell one another in the course of defending these choices, its conclusion is as much for fathers as for mothers. Many fathers feel trapped within lifelong roles as main breadwinners, living lives at a distance from their children. Increasing numbers would like to explore ways to combine successful careers with more involved parenting. Without their support and participation, the effort to transform the workplace will be doomed to remain an experiment taking place on the periphery of that workplace.

But men face even greater barriers than women if they wish to make major changes in their working lives. Many men have not yet even reached the point where they can articulate their suffering, let alone envision and craft changes that will relieve it. Those in the work–family field consistently assert that, though change must be made in the name of parents, it will be instigated and driven primarily by women. Women are willing and able to take greater risks in the work world, which in the end will be what generates change. And if women can influence workplace culture, there will eventually be no separating the women's culture from the men's. We will all benefit.

It is clear to me that without a change in the way we think and speak about the issue of mothers and work, and in the way we think about work itself, women will never fully embrace what Naomi Wolf calls the 'will to power', the numbers of women willing and able to shatter the glass ceiling will remain pitifully few, and we will never see a significant shift in the thinking about fathers and work. Yet many will think it naive to demand that the workplace absorb the lion's share of the changes needed to make working and parenting compatible. They will argue that organizations cannot afford to put in place the kind of flexibility that is needed, or that it is not possible to sufficiently alter the basic structure and culture of work to make a difference. But history should remind us that organizations have managed to accommodate a multitude of new requirements which technological, economic and social change have made of them, and my work as a management consultant has shown me that change of the most enormous proportions is regularly undertaken and success-fully made within organizations. A fellow consultant once com-mented that in our business we crack some of the most difficult problems with our clients, so she refuses to accept that we can't solve this one. I too refuse to accept it. We can and must crack this one. Our future happiness, as well as that of our families, depends on it.

INTRODUCTION: THE MOTHER WAR

✣

The polarization process that started in the 1980s has produced a sharp divide
between these home-centred women and the minority of career-oriented
women for whom employment is just as central to their lives as it is for men.
CATHERINE HAKIM, *Key Issues in Women's Work*, 1996

I felt I was being asked to choose between two extremes – meaningful work or
some 1950s home fantasy – neither of which suited me or was realistic.
ELIZABETH PERLE MCKENNA,
When Work Doesn't Work Anymore, 1997

✣ ✣

IN THE 1970S and 80s there was the Sex War. Then came the 90s,
and with those years the men's movement and much talk about a
new post-feminist era. Once this happened it was never going to be
long before the media began searching for a new war in which it
could take sides and apportion blame. It found this in the Mother
War.

The Mother War is a war between those who believe that mothers
should work and those who insist they shouldn't, between the
politically correct Superwoman and maternally correct Earthmother.
The most public manifestations of this war are the bitter media
debates engaged in by journalists and fuelled by politicians, academics and ordinary citizens eager to proffer their ideas as raw material.
But the war is not confined to the media. It rages beneath the polite
chat between mothers at school coffee mornings, and surfaces during
many a dinner conversation between women who have chosen
different ways of being mothers.

Scenes from a War

February 1997 was a time of heightened tension in the Mother War. On the evening of the 3rd, BBC1 aired a programme called 'Missing Mum' as part of its *Panorama* documentary series. The programme purported to show that the children of working mothers achieve poor exam results. The research upon which the programme based its conclusions was a study of six hundred two-parent families in Barking and Dagenham, a largely white community where mothers work mainly in lower-level clerical jobs. In this study, carried out between 1994 and 1996, the children of full-time working mothers had a higher failure rate at GCSE level than the children of part-time working mothers: 25 per cent versus 11 per cent. *Panorama* jumped from this result to the conclusion that working mothers damage their children's educational prospects, and that they may even be bad for their children – full stop.

During the days after the programme was shown the buzz in the air was palpable. Many a conversation began with, 'Did you see *Panorama*?' Many who had – and even some who hadn't – had strong opinions about it. Critics in the media were quick to point out the deficiencies in the research and the irresponsibility of the reporting. Articles and letters to the editors of every newspaper from the *Independent* to the *Yorkshire Post* poured forth in protest for a solid week. The programme was alternately branded a piece of 'witless propaganda'[1] and an 'outrageously sloppy piece of work'.[2] Its producer and presenter, Sarah Powell, was criticized for the way she had shamelessly force-fed her interviewees with the answers she wanted the audience to hear. ('Never have I felt under so much pressure to say what the interviewer wanted me to say,' claimed interviewee Ceridewen Roberts in the *Observer* of 9 February.) It was pointed out that there was a glaring inconsistency in the study featured in the programme: the children of stay-at-home mothers had an even higher failure rate that either of the other two groups. The statistical relevance of the study also came into question: Simon Hoggart wrote in the *Guardian* of 8 February: 'The spectacle of the British trying to come to a conclusion on the basis of a thousand duff figures is pitiful. You might as well try to work out the laws of mathematics from studying tonight's Lottery numbers'. Even the BBC itself seemed ashamed: *QED* editor Lorraine Heggessey accused the programme of 'scaremongering'[3] and Mark Thompson, the head of BBC2, questioned whether the programme had examined all the available research.[4] Sarah Powell made a lame attempt to defend herself in the *Independent* of 7 February, and insisted that her programme had merely aimed to 'inform the decisions that working parents have to make'. Few could be convinced by her arguments. Once it was revealed that Powell had had access to other research by the Economic and Social Research Council Centre on Microsocial Change at Essex University showing that having a mother in employment actually increases a child's educational attainment,[5] but had opted not to feature this in her programme, her credentials as an objective and responsible reporter became suspect.

Despite the reassuringly sane response from some quarters to this very shaky piece of television reporting, it was clear that the programme had done irreparable damage – to working mothers and to the quality of the debate about how our work affects our children. Because for all those who recognize the inadequacy of the research and the spuriousness of the programme's conclusions, there are others who will have seen the study as confirmation of everything they have ever believed to be true. The research is already out there, infecting the public view. As Polly Toynbee lamented in the *Independent*, 'It will remain in the popular imagination for a decade or more. People will quote it to one another for years to come, even if it were to be debunked at some later date.' This research could well have the same resilience as its equivalent of the 1980s, the 'statistic' showing that women over the age of thirty are more likely to be caught in a terrorist attack than to get married. This statistic is still quoted today despite the fact that American journalist Susan Faludi provided a mountain of evidence proving it to be false in her bestseller *Backlash*.

The airing of the *Panorama* programme, and the debate which followed it, were not isolated events in the Mother War. Just two months before the programme appeared, the country was snarled up in a debate about Britain's moral decrepitude instigated by the publication by Philip Lawrence's widow of her manifesto for a moral Britain. Journalist Lynette Burrows argued in the *Sunday Telegraph* that the 'chief cause of juvenile delinquency is the working woman'. Despite evidence provided by others that it is unemployment, poverty and absentee fathers, rather than working mothers, which generally lead to delinquency and crime, we were invited yet again to believe that the working mother was to blame for society's ills. Burrows's cry for mothers to return home was taken up by Bernard Dineen in the *Yorkshire Post* and supported by many letters to editors, such as the one suggesting that mothers 'should be doing part-time charity work and not putting the fathers of needy families out of work'.[6] In a superb piece of timing, Patricia Morgan of the Institute of Economic Affairs published her paper about the negative effects of day-care during the same week as Frances Lawrence revealed her manifesto, thus adding her voice to the fray. Journalists Rebecca Abrams and Yvonne Roberts rushed to even the score by delivering 'a few home truths in defence of working mothers',[7] but the moral high ground seemed to have been won by the anti-working-mother brigade.

As if that were not enough, the Nicola Horlick scandal had erupted in January of 1997, and proved to be a superb opportunity for people to question the morality of the working mother. Horlick, mother of five, was suspended from her high-paying job as fund manager for Morgan Grenfell when she was suspected of hatching plans to take her team to another bank. In much of the media coverage of the scandal, and indeed in much of the conversation about it, the staff-poaching incident and Horlick's subsequent public-relations stunts drew less attention than the intrigue surrounding her life as working mother to five children. She was quickly dubbed 'Superwoman', and people engaged in discussions about whether or not she was a good mother. Camps were distinctly divided: there were those who sympathized with Horlick, and felt it unfair that she should be suspected of being a bad mother simply because she had reached the top of her profession; others were condemning – 'How can she go on having all those children when she hasn't even got the time for one of them?' was a typical response.

For some Horlick was a heroine, but for many she was the epitome of the hardened and irresponsible working mother. The

BBC's *Modern Times* had already shown us what such mothers were like. For her programme *Quality Time*, about working mothers and their nannies, which was aired for the second time in January 1997, producer-director Lynn Alleway must have scoured the land for the three most frightening working mothers she could find. These women were the most selfish, neurotic, misguided creatures anyone could hope to meet, neglecting their children and exploiting their nannies at every opportunity. (Who could forget the sight of the daughter of one of them sobbing uncontrollably into her nanny's shoulder while, downstairs, her mother hosted a Sunday-afternoon cocktail party for business associates?) Glimpses of their lives made for shocking, and apparently award-winning television – *Quality Time* won the Press Guild's Documentary of the Year Award in 1996 – but did not present an accurate picture of what most working mothers are like. Still, like the *Panorama* research showing that children of full-time working mothers do poorly in exams, this programme will live on in the minds of many. I met one woman in Norway, a stay-at-home mother, who had seen the programme when it was shown there. She was, as a result, full of disgust for working mothers in Britain. As she knows so few British working mothers personally, and had only the show's word to go on, one could hardly blame her.

The view that mothers should not work is regularly aired in the press, usually followed by emotive reactions from the other side of the divide. Representing the Earthmother's perspective have been well-known names such as television presenter Paula Yates and journalist Kathy Gyngell, in addition to articles such as the *Tatler*'s 'Mother Courage', and the *Telegraph* magazine's feature about career women who give it all up, which was accompanied by a photograph of that paragon of Earthmother virtues, a mother in kaftan and bare feet. Standing in defence of working mothers have been the likes of ex-MP Edwina Currie and journalists Yvonne Roberts, Rebecca Abrams and Maggie Drummond. These vocal proponents of the working mother's cause have been bolstered by a continuous stream of magazine profiles of successful women managing to raise families *and* enjoy spectacular careers, seemingly without personal cost, and a veritable mountain of feminist literature emphasizing the mother's right to work and downplaying her responsibilities to her children.

The problem with this debate is not that there are too few people willing to engage in it. The problem lies in the attack/defend mode which the debate has taken on, in the truly warlike antagonism that characterizes it. Given an opportunity, such as that furnished by the controversial set of findings featured in the *Panorama* programme, everyone leaps to take up their extreme and entrenched positions, while waving at their enemies a set of worn-out clichés and the meaningless statistics used to support them.

Rarely does anyone ever give any ground in this war. According to the Earthmother and her supporters, any work is too much work for a mother, and children should be with their mothers twenty-four hours a day. Forget the last century of new freedoms and choices won. Ignore the fact that you might have spent years educating yourself for a career, that you have a talent for things creative, or an insatiable desire for knowledge and intellectual challenge. Dismiss your hankering after a role in public life. Forget, even, that you might need the money. You must not work if you are a mother. And if you do work, you will be damaging your child's self-esteem, confidence and brainpower, as well as undermining the family. You will perhaps even be a 'significant factor in the social disorder and rising juvenile crime we are facing today'.[8]

In turn, the defenders of the working mother, the Superwoman and her supporters, are loath to concede any aspect of the criticisms levelled against them. They respond with outrage to suggestions that there is any link between a mother's presence and a child's level of confidence or educational progress; they lambast the likes of Lynette Burrows for making working mothers feel guilty, and refuse to acknowledge that there is anything at all to feel guilty about; they talk smugly about the ability to 'have it all' if only you are organized and strong-minded enough – Edwina Currie wrote that having it all just requires 'bloody hard work and good organization, hard-nosed delegation and a sense of humour'.[9] They assert that most women are driven to work by economic need, and that there is no turning the clock back, as if that should put an end to the debate and make us all feel happier about the ghastly never-ending dilemma which is life with children and a full-time job; they insist, as Polly Toynbee did in the *Independent* after the *Panorama* report, that women 'have nothing to fear but fear itself', thus oversimplifying an issue which lies at the heart of almost every working mother's daily angst-ridden dialogue with herself.

While this depressingly narrow intellectual war is going on, another war is being fought on an entirely different battleground. In this one, mothers are fighting for a way of life that enables them to work but does not prevent them from being responsible and active parents. These mothers are working part-time, doing flexitime, sharing jobs, taking career breaks, forsaking promotions and forgoing sleep in their efforts to combine professional and personal lives. As Libby Purves has pointed out, mothering, indeed parenting, is one long compromise,[10] and most working mothers are making the compromises for the sake of their children. For these mothers life can be pretty gruelling. The struggle to maintain some sort of balance between work and family is difficult enough. Perhaps worse is the fact that they feel a member of neither camp and a traitor to both, enduring coffee-morning tirades against working mothers one day, and veiled inferences about lack of commitment at work the next.

There are a lot of these mothers about. They are represented by the 60 per cent of working mothers who work part-time,[11] those who wish they could work part-time but have been denied the opportunity, and those who make heroic efforts to carve out large chunks of time for their families within the constraints of full-time working weeks. My friend Penny is one: she's a single mother who walked out on a lucrative and high-powered job as a strategic planner within three weeks of starting when it became clear that she would be forced to travel for weeks at a time. Anne is another: she's a mother of four who works two days a week doing research for an investment bank, earning a quarter of what she is capable of, in order to be with her family. I could name dozens of women like these: women for whom the sterile debate about whether or not mothers should work, with all its images of wicked and heartless Superwomen who dominate the boardrooms without a thought for their children, is irrelevant. It does not reflect anything in their lives, and it does not help them.

Media Omissions

The public hears little about these women. They are ignored because they represent compromise. And in the Mother War acted out in the media there is no room for a middle ground. There is certainly no common ground. There's little hope, even, of a balanced discussion. Probably it does not make exciting enough journal copy. What does make good copy, it seems, is the sight of Superwomen and Earthmothers clinging fervently to their extreme points of view and slinging mud at one another.

Panorama could have featured the Barking and Dagenham research (p. 2) in the context of an entirely different sort of report. Rather than deploying the research to frighten working mothers into giving up their jobs, they could have used it as a platform to explore the question of how working parents can be enabled to spend more time with their children, or why the children of part-time working mothers appeared to fare better than those of either full-time working mothers or stay-at-home mothers. Either of these would have made a more interesting story. But *Panorama* was not discerning enough to tell it.

Nor was *Newsnight*, which followed *Panorama* and picked up on the issue. The obvious weaknesses in the *Panorama* research and reporting presented the *Newsnight* producers with a perfect opportunity to serve as informed critics and pursue an entirely different and more creative angle than that pursued by *Panorama*, perhaps steering the enquiry towards the question of how workplace norms might be changed to enable working parents to spend more time with their children. Instead, they elected to take the dramatic appeal of the research to new heights. The cast of characters was all too familiar: Jill Kirby, a stay-at-home mother and representative of Full Time Mothers, and working mother Alison North. Incited to heated argument by presenter Peter Snow, these women attacked the opposite position and defended their own, both forced by the pace of the questioning into proffering meaningless and predictable sound bites. While Kirby appeared to be enjoying herself, North looked distinctly uncomfortable. She probably knew herself to be falling back on half-baked platitudes, but felt powerless to engage her opponent in a more substantive and balanced debate.

Faced with the topic of mothers and work, most magazine editors and programme producers opt, as *Newsnight's* did, to explore it by deliberately instigating vituperative exchanges between parties with starkly conflicting viewpoints. Even those media not under pressure to create exciting bylines or draw large audiences seem enamoured of the heated quarrel. When *New Generation*, the National Child-birth Trust's monthly publication, featured an article on 'Work and Home' in its June 1997 issue, it framed the question in terms of 'a mother's place' and offered a series of interviews representing two opposing viewpoints: one characterized by the belief that a mother's working conflicts with the best interests of her children, and the other by the assertion that alternative forms of childcare can provide the same consistency of care as a parent.[12] Once again, the question of how to reconcile work with family life became a debate exclusively about mothers, and about day-care versus mother care. The reader was left stranded between two irreconcilable positions, struggling to make sense of a mass of contradicting studies and statistics. The article made no attempt to explore solutions to the work–home dilemma which might lie outside, between or beyond the two extremes represented by full-time mother care and full-time day-care. There was no mention of flexible working, family-friendly employment practices, or the benefits of alternative childcare on a purely part-time basis. Neither were there interviews with any of the many academics, charities and private consultancies who special-ize in the study of the effective reconciliation of work and family life.

The reasons for such glaring media omissions are complex. To a certain extent, that the media tend to feature the extreme points of view about mothers and work while ignoring those in the middle is merely an example of the media's general preference for polarized certainties over the equivocal middle ground. The *Guardian's* Bel Littlejohn ridiculed this 'For-or-against' approach to issue analysis in early 1998[13]. Linda Grant had earlier railed against Radio Four's *Moral Maze* for taking such a 'for or against' approach, and accused the programme of favouring 'bickering, barracking, interruption'[14] over the intelligent 'debate of complex social and political arguments'. The issues we now face, said Grant, 'are too complex to admit of simple solutions' like those proffered by the *Moral Maze*'s guests. Compromise is what is called for, and a middle ground, but people are afraid of the middle ground because it 'represents muddle and incoherence'.

These weaknesses in media coverage of complex issues are exacerbated by the fact that the owners often exert a strong influence over the type of coverage that a story can receive, and the particular angle of that coverage. Says Maureen Freely, 'The owner's agenda flows right through the organization, and freelance journalists soon learn that they will get more work when they fall in line with that agenda. They learn to edit out the subtleties in their arguments, or have them edited out for them.' On top of this, says Freely, journalists themselves often have a poor grasp of the subtleties of a particular issue. This is certainly true of the topic of work, how it is organized and how it could be made to change. 'Many journalists have no real language to talk convincingly about work.'

The intellectually destructive habit of either/or thinking is not unique to the media, and may be a natural reaction to a perception of scarcity and limited choice: 'When people feel they have no options, they cling to the assurances of polarized certainties. It is only when people feel rich in confidence and space that they dare to pursue the subtleties of what Gloria Steinem calls both/and thinking,' says Naomi Wolf in *Fire with Fire*. The media manipulate women into defending 'polarized certainties' within the Mother War, and many mothers allow themselves to be manipulated because they cannot imagine that there are any other options. They cannot believe in a world, or a workplace, that will not force women to choose between home and office. 'In their heads, they can hear the voices of their parents saying, "Just *who* do you think *you* are? Of course work is hard. That's why they call it work."'[15] 'We know no one will ever let us turn the work day upside down just for our own convenience or even for our family's mental health,' wrote one woman, exemplifying a level of resignation that is common.[16]

Personal choices are indeed limited, not just by the structural realities of a work world that won't let itself be turned upside-down, but by individuals' circumstances. And women who sense limitations in their particular choices may be more likely to lend their voices to support the extreme arguments in the Mother War. One woman noted:

> Very often you find that the women who are most vociferous about how mothers should stay home are the ones who had little real choice in their own lives – perhaps they had little education and few prospects for pursuing a challenging career, are married to men who want them to be home, or were forced out of their careers. Women like these whose decision to stay home was somehow forced upon them need to justify their lives, defending them with all that 'working mothers are evil' kind of stuff. On the other hand, women who genuinely have choices but decide to be full-time mothers are confident enough to say, 'I'm doing this because I want to', rather than resorting to defensive and self-righteous statements like, 'I'm doing this because it's best for children, and everyone else should do it too.'

So the media, and the voices that feed it are still hooked on an old and sterile debate 'which wonders whether mothers should work, when the debate should be about how parents – fathers and mothers – can reconcile employment with caring for their children,' wrote a frustrated Margaret Vaughan in the *Herald* of 6 February 1997. 'The media aren't interested in that broader question,' says Peter Moss of the Thomas Coram Research Unit, who is asked with 'depressing regularity' to comment on the problem of working mothers. 'They are forever enquiring about the effects of working mothers on their children. No one probes about the wider questions. Not a single journalist has called me to talk about the potential impact of the new parental leave directive, for instance. No one is interested.' Neither is anyone interested in speaking to experts working in the field of changing work practices. They are so rarely mentioned or interviewed in the articles of the Mother War that few would even be aware of their existence.

The either/or options are vociferously defended despite the fact that even their staunch supporters occasionally have doubts. Valerie

Stogdale, an executive headhunter and mother of two, was quoted in a *Tatler* article about warring mothers as saying: 'I am doing what makes me happy. I am not going to question it any more. I refuse to feel guilty.'¹⁷ A more enthusiastic and committed Superwoman you could hardly hope to meet. But it later transpired that she had downgraded her work responsibilities because her 'life wasn't ideal'. So was she in fact an unquestioning defender of the Superwoman faith – or yet another nail in its coffin?

Emma Bridgewater was the kaftan-robed Earthmother who graced the front cover of the *Telegraph* magazine issue highlighting the stories of 'career women who give it all up' (see p. 5). In fact, Bridgewater didn't give it all up at all; she continued to work for a few hours a day in her pottery business, retaining oversight of design.¹⁸ What she sought, and achieved, was balance, not Earth-motherdom. Neither Penny Hughes who resigned from her job as president of Coca Cola, nor Linda Kelsey who gave up her position as editor of *She* magazine, became full-time mothers, but instead began working in a way which better suited their lives.¹⁹ Even Brenda Barnes, the high-profile Pepsi chief who quit her job in October 1997 to spend more time with her children, may not be the vindication of the Earthmother's cause which its supporters would see her as. Chances are that she will be able to choose from a host of non-executive directorships to create a working life that she can fit around the needs of her family.

There are, it is true, some real Earthmothers – women who have willingly sacrificed their careers to devote every waking minute of every day to their children, and are so happy doing it that they don't think of it as a sacrifice. And there are some genuine Superwomen about – women whose passion for work overrides any desire for a life with more space for family and nurturing. But these women are rare. They are certainly rarer than we are led to believe by the media. Maeve Haran insists that 'the Superwomen we read about are so rare, and so different from the rest of us, that they almost don't count. So few of us can do, or would want to do what they do.' Haran was herself frustrated by the media's tendency to force women into one or other of the extreme role models. When she left her job as a television producer and began writing, the media were anxious to portray her as an advocate of the Earthmother's cause. 'I was nothing of the sort,' she exclaims. 'I was advocating balance all along.'

So long as the only points of view represented in the media are those of the Superwomen and Earthmothers, little real progress will be made. For Haran is right: Superwoman is the exception that challenges the rule. And 'so long as we continue to believe in her, the rules as we have seen them will stay exactly the same'.[20] During three recent forums on motherhood sponsored by *You* magazine, Superwoman was not much in evidence: 'Nearly all the mothers who spoke at the forums would prefer more flexible working hours. Most would like to be home earlier for their children.'[21] In a survey of 1,000 professional working mothers conducted in 1997 by London Business School MBA graduate Carole Savage as part of the research for her thesis, 89 per cent wanted more flexibility in their schedule. The true Earthmother is also a rarity, her lifestyle beyond the grasp or aspirations of many women. If the media continue to showcase these two role models as the only ones to which women can aspire, the valiant efforts of the women who are fighting for an alternative will be neither recognized nor rewarded.

It is difficult to see who gains from the current debate. Full-time mothers do not, for they are often made to feel inferior for their choice. Neither do working mothers benefit. The regular diet of criticism and blame that they are forced to digest makes it difficult for them to gain any sense of perspective on their lives, or any sense of their own genuine feelings about working and mothering. Neither the full-time mother nor the working mother can win in a debate that pits them openly against one another. Only a debate that seeks common ground and understanding between them can ever hope to leave either group with their self-assurance intact.

The Myths of War

The extreme, polarized viewpoints have such a strong hold over the public debate not simply because the media manipulate so success-fully and because women, perceiving a scarcity of viable options, allow themselves to be manipulated. The strength of these viewpoints also lies in the fact that they are rooted in some very powerful myths. These myths – which I call the Myths from the Superwoman's Briefcase, and the Myths from the Earthmother's Kitchen – have a lot to answer for, so thoroughly have they clouded the debate about women, work and children. They exist because some people fervently believe in them, while others are so desperate for theories that will help them make sense of their own lives that they will believe almost anything, and the rest are too busy or too afraid to question them. For the media, with their preference for fiery contest over considered exchange, the myths define the kind of sharp and uncompromising viewpoints that sell newspapers and attract large viewing audiences: the Myths from the Superwoman's Briefcase lend an irrefutability to the working mother's defence of her right to work; the Myths from the Earthmother's Kitchen constitute a fortress of moral correctness protecting the mother who has opted to raise her own children full-time.

What are these myths? There are four that the Superwomen and their supporters rely on to convince themselves and others that mothers can pursue fast-track careers without heartache or consequence. The first of these is the myth I call the Guilt Thing. According to this myth, the socially constructed role of motherhood imposes unrealistic demands which working mothers are unable to meet. The result is that they are consumed by guilt. Talk of guilt has overshadowed discussion of all other feelings that working mothers have, and has helped to make the word 'maternal' a dirty one – people dare not use it in any discussion about why women have difficulty reconciling the demands of work and family. So *human resources* magazine can attribute women's failure to break through the glass ceiling to their insecurity and their low expectations, and to their choice of the wrong functional areas in businesses, while failing even to mention the maternal experience and how that shapes women's willingness and ability to compete in the workplace as it is currently constructed.[22]

The second Superwoman's myth is the Myth of the New Father. This one pretends that if only men were prepared to take on more responsibility for childcare, mothers could stop feeling guilty about working and get on with the business of building successful careers.

It lies behind the flood of articles about new men, house-husbands, men of the 90s, and the new female breadwinners, all of which report that increasing numbers of men and women are happily swapping roles. The future is here, insists the myth, despite evidence that most women are not happy to work sixty hours a week while their partners care for the children, and regardless of the fact that most role reversals we have seen to date have been prompted by men being made redundant, not by women actively seeking to become sole breadwinners while their partners replace them in the home.

The third Superwoman's myth, the Myth of Managed Mothering, blends the concept of 'quality time' with the management concept of delegation: it insists that being a Superwoman with a brilliant career and a happy family is possible if only you are organized enough, delegate the less interesting jobs, and schedule the right kind of 'quality' interactions with your children. This myth lurks behind every sycophantic profile of a super-achiever with a successful career and six children. It underlies many a theory about why some women succeed while others don't, like the one offered by head-hunter Yvonne Sarch, who insisted in an interview in *human resources* magazine's November/December 1996 issue that 'women who have reached senior positions will be good enough at managing their time to have made provision for family commitments', as if family commitments were all tasks to organize and jobs to delegate rather than little people with unending and unpredictable needs for love, attention and time. This particular myth is also reflected in the misleading claim that today's working mothers spend more time – by which is meant 'quality time', not total time – with their children than did full-time housewives in the 1960s.

The Day-care Dream, myth number four, asserts that working mothers need full-time day-care for their children, and that a lack of it is what is holding them back. This myth is supported by a campaign for day-care that Patricia Morgan has called 'a juggernaut racing downhill' and carrying with it 'an unruly band of fellow travellers' including feminists, industrialists, left-wing academics and right-wing government spokespersons.[23] The power of this myth forced Paddy Holmes to resign from her position as chairperson of the Independent Schools Association after she dared to suggest that full-time day-care for under-twos might not be a great idea. The myth persists in its influence despite evidence from other European countries that more day-care does not necessarily mean more mothers who want to work full-time. And it remains steadfast regardless of British research that questions how many unemployed mothers would actually wish to work full-time if day-care were available to them, and raises concerns about full-time day-care's negative effects on children.

The Earthmother's position depends upon just three myths. But the first of these, the one that tells us full-time mothering is best for children, men and society – the Myth of the Earthmother, the Perfect Family and the End of Crime – is so morally compelling that no other myth is really needed to uphold the Earthmother's position. After all, if you can claim that working mothers are responsible for an increase in delinquency (as Kathy Gyngell did in March 1993, and several others have done since), and that stay-at-home mothers raise brighter children (as *Tatler* writer Helen Kirwan Taylor dared to suggest in 1995), then you really need no other argument. You can drive a nail into the Superwoman's coffin with just one blow of the hammer.

The immense allure of the first Earthmother myth notwithstanding, two others are often thrown into the debate for good measure. The first of these – Everyone's an Earthmother – pretends that most women would be happy to stay at home with their children if only society made it possible for them to do so. For the true believers of this myth, motherhood defines all women entirely, and they would be a good deal more content if they were to give in to it. Only society's failure to recognize the true value of mothering and reward mothers accordingly prevents them from doing so.

The third Earthmother myth is the Myth of the Few Short Years. This one maintains that children need their mothers for only a few short years, and that a mother is selfish if she denies them her full attention during this time. Curiously, there's another version of this one floating around in the workplace, and it goes like this: because children need their mothers for such a short time, a working mother only needs support in the form of a little workplace flexibility for a few months after giving birth. After that she's able to give her job her full attention, and behave at work like a man.

These myths enable the participants in the public debate about mothers and work to maintain adversarial positions, and prevent the establishment of any common ground between mothers who work and mothers who don't. And they let the workplace, with its traditional definitions of 'job' and 'career' and 'success', largely off the hook. Too few are pushing hard for the workplace to change. Feminists have traditionally told us that workplace change shouldn't be necessary and have resorted to talk of childcare whenever the topic of work and family has been raised. Companies seem to think that change in the workplace has already happened and is represented by improved maternity-leave policies and the trend towards teleworking. Vocal advocates of full-time mothering tell us that the change will never come about, or will never be enough to enable us to mother responsibly. By reinforcing extreme positions, and ensuring that the change agenda focuses on everything but the workplace, the myths prevent us from getting closer to the truth, and to the discovery of new solutions that offer greater prospects for happiness to greater numbers of women and their families.

But it *is* in the workplace that we need to look for change. There is no other panacea. Contrary to what we are told by the Earthmother's myths, not all women can find happiness for themselves and their children by staying home full-time, and a woman sacrifices more than just a few short years of her own career if she stays home with two or three children through to school age. And though the Superwoman's myths about Guilt, the New Father and the Day-care Dream aim to convince us otherwise, women do have a special and intense bond with their children, and many suffer immeasurably from denying the existence of that bond and pretending they are happy to work sixty hours a week so long as they have a place in the day-care centre or a partner who stays home with the children. Much as we would like to believe the line peddled by the Superwoman's Myth of Managed Mothering, no amount of delegation can help the mother and her children starved of time with each other.

The family-friendly workplace about which we often read is still a rarity, and is not yet the solution to the problem. In reality, the workplace has adjusted little – so little, in fact, that one working mother whom I interviewed was prompted to say that she felt 'the experiment of working mothers simply had not worked'. The vast majority of corporate cultures remain untouched by flexibility, and the normal working week for one in four people is in excess of fifty hours, and on the increase.

Would that it were otherwise. Would that there were some other solution to be conjured up out of the air. To the question of how we solve the modern mother's dilemma, talking about workplace change will seem to some an insufficient answer. Workplace change sounds dull, perhaps. People might think it has happened already, so there must be something else. But it hasn't and there isn't.

Despite the repeated calls for a revolution in the way work is organized, leading business journals have only recently recognized the creation of the family-oriented workplace as a significant challenge for business to take on. The topic of workplace flexibility has been relegated to the pages of human resource and personnel magazines, while mainstream business journals have cautiously danced around it. In the *Financial Times'* twenty-part Guide to Management, which included 125 articles, the issue of work–life balance was covered in a single short article. In 1996 and 1997 issues, international magazines *Business Week*, *Newsweek* and *Fortune* all featured articles about the challenge of juggling work and family life, and paid lip-service to companies who are implementing family-friendly policies. But those articles were a long time coming. Of some four hundred issues of *Fortune* published over three years, a mere handful focused on women in business. And there was little mention of children in any of them. Journals like these regularly concern themselves with the 'softer' issues in business, and feature articles on everything from managing people through technology to understanding what's going on inside Bill Gates's mind. But they rarely venture to ask how workplace norms and structures can be adjusted to accommodate the structural changes in the family and in society. The *Harvard Business Review* has featured hundreds of articles about how to re-engineer businesses to better utilize technology or serve customers. Where is the equivalent number about how to re-engineer businesses so as to enable employees to be more responsible parents?

Creating organizations where the needs of mothers, fathers and families are accommodated will not be easy. Becoming family-friendly is not simply a matter of allowing the odd employee to work part-time and expecting that person to be effective within a working culture in which nothing other than full-time will do. It is not just about flexi-hours, computer terminals at home and childcare advice helplines. All of these things are helpful, and they represent a beginning. But they can only go so far. They still leave the working parent, most often the working mother, pushing water uphill.

What is needed, in addition to these peripheral changes, is a rethink of how the work is done. Experts who have been working in the field for twenty years or more have concluded that the work, and along with it the roles, career paths and culture, need to be re-engineered. Only then will it be possible for work to be reconfigured on a reduced-hours basis, meeting parents' needs while also meeting organizational needs.

Re-engineering the business to meet parents' needs requires huge commitment from all the managers and employees within organizations, not just from the women who are asking for part-time jobs and improved maternity-leave policies. There are a few firms who are garnering the commitment, taking bold steps in the direction of a revolutionized workplace culture. We will meet them in the last part of this book. We will look at why and how they are doing it, and what they have learned.

Above all, change will require conviction and a steely-minded determination on the part of women – because no one will give us anything unless we ask for it. Women need to demand change, and then focus their energies on making it a reality, rather than on fighting each other and feeding the media with the ammunition they need to perpetuate the Mother War. Women must let go of the myths that support the uncompromising positions in this war, myths that aim to convince us that the solution to the problems faced by mothers who work lies somewhere other than at work. Some women are already doing this. They are fighting to create space for mothering within their own work lives. Some are even beginning the process of re-engineering the work within their organizations. We will meet some of them in Part Three.

There is a great deal to lose if we fail to envision and seek the right sort of change. Yet there is so much for all of us to gain if we can relinquish the notion that mothers have to compete in a male-defined workplace or not compete at all, and begin to remodel that workplace for everyone's benefit. This book is a plea for us to do just that. It asks us to examine with critical eyes the myths that are associated with the current debate about mothers and work. It suggests that there is an alternative role model to those of Earth-mother and Superwoman that have been offered to us thus far: namely, that of the parent working within a truly flexible environment which acknowledges and accommodates the parenting role. And it begins to define what that flexible environment should look like, what organizations have to gain from it, and how it can be created.

Workplace flexibility has suffered from being a fad, but it will not remain a fad for much longer. It is not something that we and the organizations we work for will be able to afford to treat as secondary to the 'real' objectives and agendas of business. For some, it is fast becoming a mainstream business issue. Organizations can tackle it now, and reap the benefits, or sweep it under the rug for another decade or so in the hope that it will go away. But it won't go away, and sooner or later we will have to come to grips with it. For all our sakes, let it be sooner.

PART ONE

MYTHS FROM THE
SUPERWOMAN'S BRIEFCASE

CHAPTER ONE

✜

THE GUILT THING

The myth of motherhood takes its toll. Employed mothers often feel guilty.
They feel inadequate, and they worry about whether they are doing the best
for their children. They have internalized the myth that there is something
their children need which only they can give them.
ANNIE OAKLEY, *Housewife*, 1974

There is no doubt that guilt, being such a culturally ingrained factor, is a
particularly destructive force in the life of women who choose both to work,
for whatever reason, and to bring up children.
EILEEN GILLIBRAND and JENNY MOSLEY,
When I Go to Work, I Feel Guilty, 1997

✜ ✜

GUILT: culpability, blame, sinfulness, wrongdoing, remorse self-condemnation. The word 'guilt' has become synonymous with the term 'working mother'. In its most acute form, this working mother's guilt is a deep-seated 'anxiety about depriving the children of maternal attention' and 'retarding their development'.[1] But the working mother's guilt has mundane sources too: working mothers reputedly feel guilty about missing events, forgetting dates, not having time for the things that matter in life; they are in its grip because their houses aren't clean enough, or because the time spent cleaning them is time stolen from their children; some feel it because their family have been living on the contents of Marks & Spencer's frozen-food cabinet for weeks, and home-baked cakes are a distant memory. You name it, working mothers apparently feel guilty about it.

There is no shortage of onlookers to attest to the guilt that working mothers feel. 'It is extraordinarily common for working mothers to feel guilty,' said Edward Melhuish, professor of educational psychology at the University of Wales to the *Daily Telegraph* of 31 July 1996. 'Women's guilt about leaving their children while they work is well documented,' writes Ros Coward in *Our Treacherous Hearts: Why Women Let Men Get Their Way* (1993). Kate Figes writes of the working mother that 'guilt can go with her everywhere, exacerbated by the notion that all women have a natural proclivity towards motherhood'.[2]

Observers are also keen to advise women that guilt is something to be dispensed with. 'This guilt is extraordinary because it runs contrary to all the studies,' said Dr Melhuish, as if a study should be all that is needed to resolve the complex set of anxieties that afflict a working mother when she doesn't see enough of her children. Adrienne Katz, author of *The Juggling Act*, offers a 'ten-point plan for dealing with guilt'.[3] 'Let's banish the guilt,'[4] writes Anita Roddick in the foreword to Eileen Gillibrand and Jenny Mosley's book, *When I Go to Work, I Feel Guilty*. Superwomen eagerly jump on to the guilt-banishment bandwagon. 'I refuse to feel guilty, there's no point,' said high-flyer Connie Duckworth to the *Wall Street Journal*. 'You have to try to learn how to ignore guilt when it rears its ugly head, otherwise you go mad,' insists a woman interviewed in *The Juggling Act*.

Professor Sheila Wolfendale, an educational psychologist at the University of East London, believes that if women feel guilt, the fault lies with society. 'Women still cannot free themselves from the feeling that they should be at home producing a baked cake every day when their child comes home from school,' she says.[5] The belief that women's guilt stems from the unreasonable standards of mothering imposed by the 'institution of motherhood' – the mothering role as 'socially constructed' – is fundamental to feminist analysis. The answer, say the feminists, lies in recognizing the influence of socially constructed roles, and erasing the ideals of motherhood that emanate from them. As they disappear, so, like magic, does the working mother's guilt.

It is mightily tempting to believe that guilt is at the heart of the working mother's malaise, and that it will in time be eradicated along with the institution of motherhood and old-fashioned ideas about the division of labour. And it is certainly true that guilt is something that working mothers, indeed all mothers, feel in great quantities. Guilt 'comes at the birth, is brought forth from us with the placenta, grows like the piles of laundry, and stays with us for ever,'[6] writes Abigail Stone. And guilt, it seems, can even be intensified by the weather. On seeing the bright sunshine outside the restaurant from which we had just emerged, one woman said, 'Oh, gosh, it's sunny. I always feel so guilty on sunny days, like I should be taking my boy out somewhere nice.' I would have thought her peculiar had I not entertained the very same thoughts myself on many a summer's day.

But to reduce all maternal yearnings to guilt, and assume that they can be eradicated along with societal constructs of motherhood, is to misrepresent them. For women speak not just of guilt, but of longing, yearning and sadness. They talk of missing their children, and of actively wanting to be with them. 'Guilt is empty and purposeless, whereas what I feel is wholly positive,' said advertising executive and Woman of the Year Lunch associate Carole Reay. The word 'guilt' does not adequately capture the complex feelings that mothers feel when they are absent from their children, or in some way falling short of what they perceive their children to need. Yet it has become shorthand for the working mother's condition.

When mothers do use the word, they imbue it with far more depth and complexity than do academics and feminist commentators. And they attribute it, not to the social construction of the mothering role, but to the intensity of feeling between them and their children. As one woman said to me, 'That's no institution of motherhood making me feel guilty, it's my child.'

Using the word 'guilt' to encapsulate the range of emotions experienced by a working mother is, in part, a strategy for containing those emotions. The containment strategy is reflected in articles like 'Twenty reasons not to feel guilty about being a working mother'. Indeed, some mothers might be reassured by such headlines, and by glib sound bites such as 'children of working mothers are more socially skilled, self-sufficient, emotionally mature and intellectually independent', 'it is not the first time a child achieves something ... that matters so much as showing it to you and witnessing your pleasure', and, the all-important one, 'it is guilt about working which can damage children, not work per se'.[7]

Gillibrand and Mosley's *When I Go to Work, I Feel Guilty* provides over two hundred pages' worth of such advice – advice that borders on the nonsensical in a section about how mothers can change their own negative behaviour to eliminate guilt from their interactions with their children. The authors describe a typical guilt-inducing situation. Mother has to go on a week's course to learn a new skill; she feels guilty and cannot stop worrying about the children; she rings several times a day and gets herself into 'a real state'; she ends up not getting much out of the course. The authors' solution? Mother talks through her week's absence with the children beforehand. They understand why she has to go and are happy with the arrangements she has made for them. She rings them every evening to talk to them. Being positive, she feels happy that the children are well cared for and accept her absence, and can fully enjoy the course. Such passages drew incredulous chortling from the women to whom I read them. All had tried the rational approach to guilt management recommended by Gillibrand and Mosley and *still* ended up with weeping children and pits in their own stomachs. All had discovered that the feelings that run so high when mothers and children are separated too often and for too long, or when work encroaches too much into family time, are deeper and more complex than the word 'guilt' could ever capture, or than could ever be banished by inane advice to 'talk it through with the children'.

Books like Gillibrand and Mosley's gloss over guilt, neither acknowledging its true source nor recognizing the other feelings that accompany it. And they offer glib 'coping' advice in place of the structural solutions, such as workplace change, that mothers need to be able to accommodate mothering within their working lives. They present a whitewashed version of the truth because it is less troublesome than an admission that valid and genuine emotions might enter into matters.

Psychoanalyst and feminist author Susie Orbach believes that 'emotional illiteracy exists because we have no shared language for emotional life. Words like love, hate, jealousy and competition reveal little more than the tip of an emotional experience whose depths we are unused to exploring.'[8] Language has become a way of 'hiding our feelings from ourselves, and a way of not disclosing them to others'. So it is with the word 'guilt'. But using the word 'guilt' to oversimplify the way mothers feel will not help us in the long run.

For however much we try to pretend that guilt is all we are feeling, and that by externalizing its source and attacking it we can somehow escape its grip, we will find that it retains a tenacious hold of us nonetheless. As Orbach warns, 'the feelings are there whether we acknowledge them or not'. What mothers feel for their children, and how they feel when they are separated from them for long periods or by great distances, is more profound, inscrutable and unswerving than guilt. Repeating, like a mantra, the 'twenty reasons not to feel guilty about being a working mother' will not cause it to evaporate. There is a tie that binds mothers to their children, and the denial of its existence ' – in private life and public policy – is contributing to a kind of madness in the lives of working mothers'.[9]

Greater than Guilt: The Tie that Binds

Mother love is greater than guilt. Yet, as Anne Roiphe remarks in *A Mother's Eye: Motherhood and Feminism*, mother love has been ridiculed again and again by feminists. To them, the tie between mothers and their children, and the maternal feelings that ensue, are mere lies: lies the patriarchy once told to keep women at home; inventions of the backlash used to persuade women back to the kitchen; fictions dreamed up by our own treacherous hearts to shield us from our fear of competing in the outside world.

So unconvinced of the existence of a unique mother–child bond was Germaine Greer that she considered it desirable for women to bear children and leave their care and nurture entirely to others. In *The Female Eunuch* she insisted that a brilliant woman should be able to 'contribute a child to a household which engages her attention for part of the time while leaving her free to frequent other spheres of influence'.[10] If she were to have a child, she said, she would send it to be raised in a commune in Italy, and visit it from time to time: 'If necessary, the child need not even know that I was his womb mother and I could have relationships with the other children as well.'

Like Greer, early feminists Kate Millet and Simone de Beauvoir gave little credence to the notion that the bond between mothers and children might be influenced by uniquely female mothering instincts. Millet asserted that 'while childbirth and breastfeeding are biological, child-care itself is *only* culturally [italics mine] assigned to women'.[11] She did not attempt to explore the strong links between the initial 'biological' acts of childbirth and breastfeeding and the subsequent development of the relationship between mother and child, or allow for the possibility that these biological events might exert a lasting influence over a woman and her children. For her part, de Beauvoir believed maternity to be 'a strange mixture of narcissism, altruism, idle daydreaming, sincerity, bad faith, devotion and cynicism'.[12] She claimed boldly: 'No maternal instinct exists: the word hardly applies, in any case, to the human species'; citing as evidence stories of women who felt miserable during the initial months of their babies' lives.

Greer's, Millet's and de Beauvoir's denial of the authenticity of maternal feelings lives on in the work of many modern-day popular feminists. In her 1991 bestseller *Backlash*, Susan Faludi set out to discredit everything to do with motherhood and women's apparent attachment to it. She deemed women's interest in motherhood to be part of the backlash and saw all media images of and enquiries into motherhood as 'a sign of a retrogressive force, drawing us back to the pre-liberated dark ages'.[13]

In Naomi Wolf's *Fire with Fire*, motherhood is not so much assaulted as ignored. Wolf encourages women to embrace the 'will to power' but she has little to say about how motherhood might affect women's attitude to power, or their ability to seize it. The index of *Fire with Fire* contains no references to the word 'mother'. It has only a few references to 'children', as in 'children – abuse of', 'children – aggressiveness', and 'children – care of', and there are only ten pages indicated. Wolf covers the subject of mothers and their children in just a handful of sentences scattered over eighteen chapters.

Motherhood and maternal sensibilities are further invalidated by British feminist Ros Coward. In *Our Treacherous Hearts: Why Women Let Men Get Their Way*, Coward argues that women are giving up on the feminist dream of equality and abandoning their careers not because of the genuine tug of maternal love but because of their complicity with traditional family structures and expectations, and their idealization of men. Women's 'treacherous hearts' are letting them down, causing them to take 'jobs that they can shape around their children', and to '*seem* to feel that their careers are unimportant compared with the overwhelmingly significant task of caring for and educating the future generation'.

For Coward, the pull of maternal love is a shield for women's guilt and ambivalence: crying 'maternal instinct' allows women to avoid the fact of their guilt, which is engendered by unrealistic standards of mothering, and prevents them from dealing with their own ambivalence towards power, success and responsibility. Guilt and ambivalence – not a longing to be with their children, or an innate desire to nurture – are seen to be entirely responsible for women's failure to progress in the world of work.

Feminists like Coward wish women to ignore or actively suppress whatever maternal feelings and desires they might believe themselves to harbour. Superwomen anxious to be regarded as indistinguishable from men have colluded in the suppression. The result has been the branding of 'maternal' as a dirty word. In some circles, even the word 'mother' is frowned upon, as Penelope Leach discovered when she dared to speak about 'mothers' and 'fathers' rather than 'parents' in a speech she gave in New York in 1993. She was taken to task by a journalist for being politically incorrect.[14] Rarely do those of any but the most conservative political persuasions talk about a maternal consciousness, or the dreaded 'maternal instinct', and since they invariably become inveigled by the 'all mothers should stay home' philosophy, they are heartily ridiculed by the alliance of Super-women, liberals and socialists who would see mothers and fathers become interchangeable and indistinguishable. Behind closed doors, many an ordinary mother will admit to a strong belief in the power of maternal emotions. But in public, more often than not, she remains silent.

Anne Roiphe is one of a handful of writers who are refusing to acquiesce in the silence. Roiphe speaks candidly about the authenticity of maternal sentiment and the maternal experience, which, for her, cannot be reduced to the guilt engendered by societal prescriptions about mothering. 'Motherhood,' she says, seems to be 'something more complicated, more essential, more primal than a capitalist scheme to sell baby clothes'.[15] Feminists have 'altered the climate for everyone' but 'they didn't stop most women from having children, raising children, enduring their children's childhood'. The pull towards children and mothering has proved too strong to be squashed by feminist theories, however compelling and sophisticated they might have been. 'If motherhood was prostitution and slavery, why did I persist in believing that it was my redemption, my core, my holy skywriting?' she asks.

Like Roiphe, journalist and author Maureen Freely criticizes feminists for having been too ignorant of mothers and how they feel. In the book *What About Us?*, she describes the feminist movement as having swung from being dominated by women fifteen years older than she was who were desperate to escape motherhood, to being dominated by women fifteen years younger than she was, who hardly seemed to realize it existed.[16] Freely describes how, encouraged by feminism, she tried to fight the feelings of selflessness that seemed to overtake her when her baby was born, feelings that she realized in retrospect had their roots somewhere within her, and in her experience of giving birth to her son:

> I remember thinking: it's happened. I've fallen off the edge of the earth. I've been expelled from the real world. I've become selfless.
>
> How had I allowed this to happen? Now that I had identified the horrible truth, what was I to do to fight it?
>
> I decided I had to find more ways of being selfish. But what exactly did this mean?
>
> I had no idea, so over the frantic weeks that followed I tried every feasible type of selfishness I could think of. I went to the mall by myself. I took a driving lesson. I bought myself a new bathing suit, an overpriced yoghurt, ran up a large phone bill. When nothing did the trick, I asked myself why. Another thing I couldn't understand was why I could not stop myself from continuing to perform the babycare tasks which I was now beginning to see as acts of self-sacrifice, and, it therefore followed, of moral cowardice. It was as if my mother had come to stay in my head, and was telling my arms and legs what to do. How did she come to have such control over my behaviour, I asked myself? Why am I so beholden to tradition? Where did I go wrong?
>
> The inevitable conclusion was that it was impossible to have a child without feeling this way.

Freely calls the institution of motherhood an 'overblown cartoon of a concept', a 'big, fat, idiotic myth', which has blinded us to what is really happening and 'mangled our understanding of mothers, fathers, children, families and just about any other association between two people'. The feminists' promotion of the concept constitutes a kind of intellectual bullying, ordering women to view their feelings about their children as inauthentic and entirely at odds with other aspirations. Academic Christina Hoff Sommers contends that intellectual bullying is characteristic of much of feminism. In her book *Who Stole Feminism?: How Women Have Betrayed Women* she reveals how many feminist writers have manipulated statistics to support feminism's extreme and exaggerated points of view – its 'noble lies' – about such trends and phenomena as the anorexia epidemic, male violence and rape, the wage gap, the threat to girls' self-esteem represented by schools, and the backlash.[17] Among the noble lies told by feminism are those which deem romantic love and maternal feelings to be inauthentic. Women are silencing each other about romantic and maternal desires, says one writer to Hoff Sommers, 'and we are doing it so effectively that we are even silencing ourselves'.

Writers like Roiphe, Freely and Hoff Summers demand of feminism that it now acknowledge the primal pull towards mothering, the intensity of the bond between mother and child, and the life-changing impact of motherhood. Where many old- and new-school feminists have seen the patriarchy prescribing role models, these authors see women choosing to become mothers because they cannot resist the pull; where feminists have seen guilt, they also see passion, love, adoration, and a 'real need to be near and with their children'. Where feminists have asked mothers to resist the guilt, they have seen that 'the tie to the infant, built into his or her survival, is also built into us and cannot be so easily waved aside'.[18]

Now even Naomi Wolf may have seen the light. Motherhood barely registered on the radar screens of her first two books, *The Beauty Myth* and *Fire with Fire*, but she later admitted to having been dramatically influenced by the physical experience of carrying a child. Behind closed doors, and out of the earshot of politically correct journalists, competitive colleagues and intolerant employers, many a mother will admit to having felt peculiarly maternal passions which have influenced their views of the world. Jane was a successful advertising account executive and is now studying for her PhD in Canadian history in Toronto, with a view to becoming a professor. She was also a fervent believer in feminism when we were at college together in the early 1980s, and all through her twenties. Then she had a son. Soon afterwards, she wrote:

> I see that for all these years I have been wrong . . . I have learned that contrary to the supermom literature of the 1980s, motherhood is not something you can fit into your 'to do' list between your career and your aerobics classes. It is a major life crisis, a turning point in our psychological development. For me, it was a big crisis. It also demonstrated to me that I have been quite wrong about some things for years, namely that we, as women, could follow the same pattern as, men – school, career, etc., with kids as just one element of our personal life. For me, mothering has changed how I do everything, what my priorities are, how I feel about myself, the whole shooting match. Motherhood, for me, does not fit into a compartment.

Every woman I spoke to during the writing of this book, from the most ambitious careerists to the most laid-back full-time mothers, confessed to a belief in the maternal bond. 'The experience of having and raising a child really is different for fathers than for mothers,' says Tracy Camilleri, managing director of the London PR firm WMC Communications. 'It's difficult to articulate precisely how it is different, but it is, practically and in almost every other way, and it probably always will be.' Lawyer Sally Bevan, asked why she felt so badly about leaving her children to go to work and why she had been so altered by motherhood, answered unequivocally, 'Because I'm a woman. You can't help it. It's inside you. You are programmed to burst into tears in front of newsreels of starving children in war-torn countries, as you are to feel tortured by leaving your small children'. Christine accuses anyone who denies the existence of maternal instinct of talking rubbish. Nancy, former owner of her own business and now a part-time management consultant, is equally adamant that there is something unique that distinguishes the mother–child bond from the link between father and child:

It's like this golden thread tying me to Emma. The first time I became aware of it was when she cried as a baby and I felt a physical knot in my stomach. I was the last person on earth you'd have expected to feel this way – I was a very committed career woman until I was thirty-four. And Glen is a great father, really involved, but there's no way that what he feels is exactly the same as what I feel. When he's out the door, he never looks back. When he's asleep, nothing will wake him. I wake to her at the merest whimper. And even if I had the equivalent of a wife, as Glen has in me, I don't think this link would disappear. I'd worry about her and yearn for her still.

Not once did any of these women mention guilt, societal expectations or the institution of motherhood, though they will all have been familiar with these as concepts. They spoke instead about the 'thread' that binds them to their children and lies at the heart of their inability to close themselves off from them – what writer Adrienne Rich once described as the 'invisible thread'[19] pulling taut between mother and child. Others have described this tie not as a thread but as a form of magnetism. Writer Constance Schraft talks of the 'power of the magnetic attraction' which develops with childbirth and which means that 'though a woman may look the same afterward, sound the same, laugh at the same jokes, she is not the same.' Elissa Schappell, formerly a sceptic about maternal instinct, writes of how, being on the street without her daughter, she feels 'a sharp pang of loss that makes me stop and catch my breath' and wonders if it 'isn't my maternal instinct stretching its wings a bit'.[20] My own pangs of loss, my 'invisible thread', has often felt to me like an enduring form of the let-down reflex, that involuntary response that causes a breastfeeding mother's breasts to leak milk when she hears her baby's cries.

Many of the women interviewed by Ros Coward spoke about invisible threads, magnetic attractions and pangs of loss, but she seemed not to hear them. She was, on the other hand, listening carefully for the word 'guilt', and claimed that at one point she thought she would never hear about anything else. So intent was Coward on exploring the guilt theme that she failed to explore women's other emotional responses, and chose to see them as rationalizations for career ambivalence, insecurity or neediness. One woman, Andrea, describes to Coward how the shock of being a mother really hit her when she was in Manhattan on a business trip, feeling miserable at the thought of her two-month-old baby being on the other side of the world. Though Coward acknowledges the power of the kinds of feelings Andrea describes, she strips them of any real validity by attributing them entirely to other factors, such as the 'ambivalence about work and career', which predated Andrea's 'conversion'.[21]

In alleging that women's ambivalence about success is central to their decision-making about careers, Coward is not entirely wrong. Indeed almost everyone is ambivalent about work to some extent, and if Elizabeth Perle McKenna, author of *When Work Doesn't Work Anymore*, is right, women feel even more ambivalent about work in its current form than do men.[22] Few of us are working to change the world, and so at some point or another most of us question why we are working. Work can seem trivial, and success empty, for many a man as well as for women.

So to say that Andrea, or any of the other women in Coward's book, feels ambivalent even before she has children, is not to reveal very much. The difference between men and women is not that women feel ambivalent, but that they experience such an increase in the ambivalence and a will to do something about it as a result of becoming mothers, that their ambivalence is for all intents and purposes caused by the pull of maternal love. Despite Perle McKenna's attempt to separate ambivalence about work from the experience of maternity, the link keeps asserting itself throughout her book. It is full of stories of women for whom the pain of infertility, the ticking of the biological clock, or the experience of giving birth have served as powerful instigators for the change in their working lives. Perle McKenna herself was influenced by the 'time bomb of dual identities' which had not ticked when she was childless. The experience of giving birth to a child and nurturing that child through the first few months of life changes many women inexorably. Meanwhile, most men happily roll along in their careers, brushing aside the career ambivalence they feel, because they have no equally compelling reason to do anything about it. For most men, a wife's pregnancy and a child's birth are not the same 'wake-up calls' that they are for most women. Other events – the death of a loved one, a health scare – sometimes serve as wake-up calls, causing men to re-evaluate their priorities and rethink the way they spend their time. There are exceptions, of course, but childbirth does not automatically, or even often, engender the same type of gut-wrenching transformation in most men as it does in most women.

Children Needing Mothers

Feminists such as Coward discredit the maternal love that draws a mother to her child. Feminism has also repudiated the authenticity of a child's need for its mother. Seventies feminist Annie Oakley wrote that there is no evidence either that mothers need children, or that children need mothers.[23] She claimed that children who experience 'mothering' but very little else cannot do without mothering, but that it is not necessarily paramount to the child, and she held the power of social construction responsible for all that passes for emotional bond between a child and its mother.

Oakley assumed, as have many others since, that if women went out to work and childcare practices were altered, children would cease to need their mothers. In theory, one might expect children deprived of their mother's care to cease to need her, and to look to others to provide what we call motherly love. In practice, things are very different. As Anne Roiphe remarked, unisex talk which white-washes the bond between mothers and children doesn't stick to real people.[24] In real people's lives, and despite the most heroic efforts to accustom children to other carers, whether they be nannies or fathers, mothers find that their children demonstrate a remarkably resilient need for them. True, they might also learn to need the other carers, expressing love and adoration for their fathers and nannies. But these other attachments do not seem to lessen children's need for their mothers. They most certainly do not weaken the need to such an extent that it is possible to go out to work without a backward glance. It was the most enormous shock to me that despite having freed myself from the position of sole carer – which Annie Oakley saw as the root of children's apparent need for their mothers – and regardless of the fact that my children were cared for from birth by a wonderful nanny whom they adored, it still mattered greatly to them that I was around. It still upset them when I worked too much and saw them too little. And they regularly expressed their preference that I stay home with them.

However much women seem to want to believe in the value of equal parenting and quality childcare, many are confronted with an inescapable truth: their children, uninfluenced by the institution of motherhood or the concept of guilt encapsulated within it, seem to need them. 'Let's be honest about this,' confesses journalist Allison Pearson, 'Mother Nature is a reactionary old bag',[25] and mother nature means that, however wonderful the substitute care, children would still rather have their mothers. When Paula Yates said the same thing, she was greeted with huge outcries from working mothers. 'No matter how we try to sugar-coat it', she said, 'the fact remains that, in the eyes of a baby or a small child, no one can replace the mother ... It is so obvious to say it that it sounds ludicrous, and yet this assertion will create a furore among many women.'[26] I was one of those who was outraged at the time, though I was not then a mother myself. Now I think she has a point. And although I don't share Yates's view that all mothers should stay home full-time, I think she was right to remind us that our special relationship with our children may be one worth preserving through careful balancing of work and family life.

In our house, my children seem to need my minute-by-minute presence and attention. They seek me out everywhere. I have not taken a bath or been to the lavatory by myself for five years. ('The insistence of some children on coming into the very lavatory with their mothers is something which recurs again and again in maternal confidences; it is somehow symbolic of the total taking over of your life,'[27] writes Libby Purves, assuring me that I am not the only one.) My eldest daughter Olivia once pointed out to her father that Joely, her sister, 'loves all the rest of us, but she's got a real *thing* about Mummy'.

This is not to say that fathers are not needed, that they are irrelevant. Fathers are vital. My children adore their father and we all need him. He is the rock within our family, the voice of reason when the children and I seem trapped within interactions of ridiculous emotional intensity, a calming and reassuring influence on the children where I am often an agitating one, an ever sought source of approval, and a strong source of comfort when things go wrong in the day or night. Our family would be in a sorry state indeed without him. But my children are content with a general, rather than a specific, minute-by-minute presence of their father in their lives. They can be near him without clinging to him, can sit in the same room without needing to touch him or be the sole focus of his attention, can say goodbye as he leaves for the office without shedding tears. Not so with me. And not so with most mothers.

Dr Philip Hwang, psychology professor at Gothenburg University and a writer on parenting issues, has studied families in which the children were cared for primarily by their fathers. He found that most of the children still expressed overwhelmingly strong needs for their mothers, and entered into the same kinds of interactions with them as did the children of stay-at-home mothers with theirs. Hwang acknowledged the possibility that the tie that seemed to link the children to their mothers may have been caused by the mothers' instinctive ways of responding and attending to them. Whatever it is that mothers are, however it is that they behave differently from fathers, and for whatever reasons, it seems to induce children to develop fierce attachments to them. These attachments are not easily dismissed in practice, in real-life families, where intentions to eradicate 'socially constructed' behaviour soon look astoundingly naive. 'I have changed my thinking on this somewhat,' concedes Professor Hwang. 'I used to believe that the mother–child relationship was driven completely by social influences, but now I'm not so sure.'

The Tie that Binds: Social Construction or a Biological Head Start?

The debate about whether and why mothers and children have a special bond with one another is older than feminism itself. Even women who are convinced that an unshakeable tie links them to their children can debate endlessly about whether that tie is biological or experiential in origin, whether it would disappear if we reinvented society from scratch, unlearned what we have learned, and gave all the boys baby dolls to play with from birth.

Predictably, those who see guilt as the heart and soul of

mother–child relationships also deny the existence of any biological roots to the feelings mothers have for their children. British academic and author of *Parents Who Teach*, Dr Pat Sykes, articulates a modern, mainstream academic version of the early feminists' views: 'My view of the world changed [when I had children] ... but I am sure that none of these changes were the result of instinctual prompting ... the only people who had anything to say about maternal instinct seemed to be those without children'.[28]

Adrienne Burgess, author of *Fatherhood Reclaimed*, insists that maternal instinct is illusory and that the drive to mother exists equally in men and women, and in the same form.[29] Burgess claims that demonstrating a 'biological imperative is desperately difficult and that although hundreds of experiments, surveys and other types of studies have been undertaken, almost nothing *definite* in terms of sex differences has shown up [italics mine]. When tapes of babies crying were played to both boys and girls aged fourteen years, their concealed responses, measured by such things as heart rates and blood pressure, were the same. And men's pupils, like women's, dilate when they look at their own babies. Burgess quotes social scientist Charles Lewis, who declares unequivocally that 'every parent knows that little boys under the age of three explore the feeding, bathing and nursing of babies with a vigour equal to that of girls'.

But some remain unconvinced by the theory that parenting is entirely biology- and gender-neutral. Penelope Leach insists that mother and father will always be different, and that 'biology is the rootstock of our species'.[30] Anne Roiphe's entire book reads like a testimony to the undeniable biological roots of the mother–child bond, and she insists that 'biology will not be banished by epigram'.[31] True, Roiphe wonders whether we might lessen the biological imperative by making childhood 'less of a war zone and more of a level playing field for both genders', and suggests that a fifty-fifty split of motherhood with fathers might make us feel better altogether, but her wish that men would feel 'this child necessity' too is a dream, not a statement of fact, and she does not sound wholly convinced that it will be realized.

Faced with Roiphe's depth of passion about motherhood, and the common-sense views of other women who are convinced of the influence of biology, it is difficult not to be persuaded that the mother–child bond has elements that are primal and deeply rooted. 'It's hard, when you look at how new baby girls and baby boys behave, not to believe that there's something in this biology thing,' says journalist Yvonne Roberts, despite her commitment to shared parenting. 'I trained as a biologist,' says Dr Juliet Hopkins of the Tavistock Institute, 'and I have to say that I don't believe we were made so differently for nothing.' Many other mothers to whom I spoke confessed to a belief in what they saw as politically incorrect notions about biology and maternal instinct.

Adrienne Burgess's attempt to prove the irrelevance of biology is far from airtight. Her case rests heavily upon the fact that the care of offspring falls to males in several animal species, though she herself admits that in all probability, the behaviour of non-human primates has no bearing on human primate behaviour.[32] Her example of a human society, the Aka tribe, in which men are intimately involved in the care of children reveals that fathers can indeed play a large role in child-raising, but fails to demonstrate that mothers feel no emotional pull towards their children, or can happily absent themselves from their children's lives to the extent that many full-time working mothers in Western society are forced to do. Burgess also fails to adequately explain the gender differences that parents in Western society witness every day. Most parents, for instance, do not know that boys like to explore the feeding and nursing of babies as much as girls do, as Charles Lewis insists. Most to whom I have spoken have witnessed that the opposite is in fact true. Almost every one of them has a dolls-and-trucks story to tell: no matter how many trucks you give to an eighteen-month-old girl, or how many dolls you give to a boy of the same age, you find the boys playing with the trucks and the girls playing with the dolls. You'll also find the boys building Lego towers, and the girls playing mummies and daddies.

The weakest aspect of Burgess's argument is her apparent belief that if a difference between male and female nurturing impulses is not evidenced in a pulse rate or a dilating eye, it cannot exist. Her claim that both men's and women's pupils dilate in the same way when they regard their own children will do little to persuade a new mother whose hormones are in full flood that her experience of parenting is identical to her husband's. One wonders what Burgess would make of the concept of 'talent', which is something that very obviously distinguishes those who have it from those who don't, but is not identifiable in any flutter of an eyelid, or even in the shape and size of a muscle. There are many things that we do not fully understand, and for which science has no foolproof explanation. This should not lead us to dismiss them as nonsense.

Burgess alienates by taking such an extreme stance. Her book would have been more persuasive had she acknowledged the power of biology while explaining how that biological imperative can be altered, shaped and even transformed by the environment. She would have been wiser to tell us that men and women have the power to shape the behaviours and attitudes that they start out with, rather than insisting that they start out with nothing different at all.

Careful reading of *Fatherhood Reclaimed* reveals that, despite her avowed scepticism about the validity of maternal instinct, Burgess has reluctantly conceded that biology cannot be ignored entirely. So, though differences between men and women in terms of perception, brain function and intellectual and nurturing capacity are 'shatteringly small', they are not non-existent. She introduces the theory that allows for the combined influence of biology and environmental factors (though she fails to clarify whether or not she supports it): 'The latest theory is interaction between environment and biologically based tendencies. The idea is that although gender behaviour is flexible and can be moulded by lots of things, boys and girls are predisposed to behave differently.'

The theory that biology and the environment interact, and that men and women have natural predispositions which are shaped by learning, is now more commonly voiced. 'New knowledge about the brain should end the "nature or nurture" debate once and for all ... Both are crucial,' writes the author of *Rethinking the Brain*.[33] After twenty years spent studying the brain, Professor Gerry Levy is sure there are some biologically based differences in our behaviour.[34] Though many gender differences are small and may be 'malleable and subject to change by experience', the differences do exist, and some have been detected as early as fifty-two hours after birth. Anne Moir and David Jessel, authors of *Brainsex*, reveal that virtually every professional scientist and researcher into the subject has concluded that the brains of men and women are different. Matt Ridley, author of *The Red Queen*, similarly asserts the incontrovertibility of the evidence that the average male brain differs from the average female brain.

In June 1997, Professor David Skuse of the Institute of Child Health and his colleagues at the Wessex Regional Genetics Laboratory announced the discovery of a gene that makes girls more sensitive, empathetic and socially aware than boys. While the scientists were careful to state that the absence of the gene did not mean that men were 'doomed', because they could learn social and empathy skills, they conceded that women will pick up social skills intuitively.[35] There was predictable outrage from some quarters – 'This is completely preposterous ... gender roles are culturally prescribed, they've nothing to do with genetics,' said one non-geneticist to the *Guardian* – but some scientists welcomed the evidence as a challenge to the 'prevailing belief that gender differences are largely culturally determined'.[36] 'It seems to me to make perfect common sense that the way we feel and behave is driven by a *combination* of biological differences, some of which are genetic, and social influences,' commented Professor Peter McGuffin of the department of psychological medicine at the University of Wales College of Medicine, when I interviewed him. In fact, the gene research merely confirms the results of brain research which, say Moir and Jessel, has revealed that women are equipped to receive a wider range of sensory information, to connect and relate that information with greater facility and to place primacy on personal relationships.

Even some scientists whose objective is to discredit unfounded claims of great biological differences between men and women affirm the existence of some important differences and argue for a mix of nature-and-nurture theories. In her book, *Myths of Gender*, feminist scientist Anne Fausto Sterling exposes the 'gross procedural errors'[37] sometimes contained in research about sex differences and overturns many of the claims frequently made about the differences between men and women. But she never contends that men and women are identical, or that influence of genes is inconsequential. Instead, she argues 'for a more complex analysis in which the individual's capacities emerge from a web of interactions between the biological being and the social environment', a web within which 'connecting threads move in both directions'.

It is telling that though Fausto Sterling dismantles many of the myths about male/female differences, she does not even raise the question of whether or not men and women are naturally predisposed to feel differently about nurturing. Presumably this is either because she found little work of any consequence that had been done on the subject, or because she was unable to find fault with the work that had been done. Either way, the absence of any chapter dismantling a 'myth of nurturing' speaks volumes.

The notion that biology and the environment interact in complex ways, with biology predisposing men and women to behave differently, and the environmental and cultural influences further shaping that behaviour, accounts for the differences in parenting behaviour that are commonly observed. The theory insists neither that biology is inconsequential, nor that it is our destiny. It merely contends that biology predisposes women to feel and behave in certain ways towards their children, giving them a head start in parenting.

That head start may well come partly from the 'sociability gene' discovered by Professor Skuse and his colleagues. It is almost certainly also born of women's experience of pregnancy and childbirth. Indeed, it is difficult to refute the head-start theory when confronted with the facts about the physical changes that a woman's body undergoes during pregnancy, childbirth and breastfeeding. The list of pregnancy aches and pains in Sheila Kitzinger's *Complete Book of Pregnancy and Childbirth* includes some twenty-five conditions ranging from low backache to sinusitis.[38] Personal experience confirms that pregnancy acts upon the female body in mysterious ways; doctors have held it responsible for my deteriorating eyesight, loss of dental bone density and darkening hair colour. Such symptoms say nothing of the dramatic hormonal changes experienced by all pregnant women, and the more serious conditions, such as eclampsia and hypertension, experienced by some.

To acknowledge the physical symptoms of pregnancy is not to make martyrs out of women, but to remind ourselves that *pregnancy is a big deal*, and that it is inconceivable that women should emerge from it unchanged, much less completely indistinguishable from men. It is now increasingly accepted that the physical experience of pregnancy may be nature's way of preparing women for parenthood, and shaping their early reactions to it. Doctors and antenatal advisers now acknowledge that even the mental and emotional symptoms of pregnancy serve a specific purpose in preparing women for their new role as mothers. Declining mental agility, increasing emotional sensitivity and 'primary maternal preoccupation' tell a woman to slow down, and allow her to create emotional space for the new baby, says Christine Hill, obstetric physiotherapist and co-author of *Your New Baby – How to Survive the First Months of Parenthood*:

> It is common for women in the later stages of pregnancy to find themselves less able to concentrate, more emotional, less decisive, more irritable, tiring more easily and less able to assert themselves. Do take terribly seriously the possibility that even you will experience this. Like PMT, it can apply to the strongest-willed and most capable people.
>
> At the same time as all this, broody thoughts about her forthcoming baby and babies in general will begin to intrude and preoccupy the mother-to-be during the last six weeks of pregnancy. The most unlikely women may find themselves peering into other people's prams and becoming riveted by the Mothercare catalogue. This is a well-recognized phenomenon known as primary maternal preoccupation. It helps the woman prepare psychologically for looking after a dependent baby and the forthcoming role transition into new motherhood.[39]

Research confirms that hormones do play a part in muddying mental clarity throughout pregnancy, and that some aspects of mental function are knocked sideways by the huge physical demands of birth itself. Such findings invite outrage from feminists, but they only confirm what many women have quietly suspected all along. 'Post-natal mental fuzziness', wrote Deborah Hutton in *Vogue*, is at best an altered state of consciousness, at worst a form of madness, and is one of the 'best-kept secrets of early motherhood'.[40]

Tony Buzan, the founder of the Brain Foundation interviewed by Hutton, claims not to be surprised to hear women describe how pregnancy and childbirth have affected their minds. 'If you consider what giving birth actually involves, it's a phenomenal requirement of the woman's entire being to focus on something other than herself. There are going to be changes by definition. You can't predict what the aftershocks will be, but they will be there. The focus will have changed.'

Breastfeeding may also have this mind-changing effect. One woman told Hutton she felt as if she was 'thinking through porridge' on returning to work shortly after giving birth and went to her GP for advice. The GP asked her if she was breastfeeding, and when the woman said yes, he just nodded sagely, indicating that the clue to the woman's mental state lay there. 'But I thought breast was best,' she said, astonished. 'Best for baby,' replied the doctor.

The view that biology – hormones, pregnancy, pre- and post-natal fuzziness – gives mothers a head start is shared by several well-known writers on mothering and childcare. 'Even a father who can stay close may still be aware that the biological mother has a unique head start into a relationship with their newborn,'[41] says Penelope Leach. Marni Jackson, the Canadian author of *The Mother Zone*, maintains that the head start makes the creation of gender-free parenting roles difficult, if not impossible. The two parents, she says, are starting from such different points, so it is not surprising that they forge different kinds of relationships with their children:

> A couple about to have a baby may agree beforehand to share the work equally. If the baby's nursing, the father, the breastless one, will get more sleep at first, naturally. The rest they'll split right down the middle. Great idea. But that's not how it works. The woman is already nine months ahead of the man in forging the bond with baby. The father's physical connection begins when the baby is finally in his arms. So he's at a handicap, or an advantage, depending on how you look at it. Regardless of the chore-division lists, the mother and father have different roles to play at first . . .
>
> The job of the mother is to separate herself from the baby. After birth, if she breastfeeds, that connection becomes an isthmus that keeps the bond from severing. Sooner or later, she has to extricate herself from the baby bubble. So she can take her choice: it's leave, or be left. It's a shift in distance, not a dilution of love.
>
> The task of the father is to create a relationship with the baby – to build it, like an engineer, day by day. It's a bridge that is constructed

out of imagination, drudgery, and the daily practice of caring for the baby, noticing him in all the detailed ways that children insist on being noticed. This doesn't mean that men can't mother. Many do, and the day-do-day, hands-on presence of men in the lives of their children strikes me as the best thing that could ever happen to the world, politically. But fathers can't hope to replicate a mother's experience.[42]

Libby Purves describes how the biological head start makes it difficult for mothers to disconnect from their children: 'The promptings of biology mean that in the first year, even the first three years, mothers move fast and urgently towards a child's distress, even if fathers happen to be moving that way too,'[43] she writes in *How Not to Be a Perfect Mother*. Even if the father makes heroic efforts to be involved, and forces himself to leap out of bed to respond to a child's midnight cries, the mother may still find that she can't tune out those cries: 'Couples in which the father gets up at night to the baby frequently report that the mother lies awake anyway until he gets back.'

The mother's biological head start renders the question about the enduring nature of the biological tie between women and their children somewhat academic, for even if the effects of biology can be proved to wear off after a period, as some feel they must, a mother's response to her children is unlikely to become less impulsive, less instinctive. As one woman put it, 'By the time all the hormones settle down, it's too late. You're hooked. You've learned whatever maternal instinct you weren't given in the first place. At that point, it's almost impossible to train yourself not to wake up in the night.'

Though theorists like Adrienne Burgess would persuade us that, all things being equal, mothers and fathers can parent in the same way and feel the same way about their children, biology means that all things are *never* equal. The casting aside of biology through the separation of reproduction and nurturing, long seen by feminists as the key to women's emancipation, is not easily done. Biology means that men and women start from different ends of the nurturing and attachment spectrum. And while it may indeed be possible for fathers to move towards the mother's end of the spectrum by being involved fathers, to learn to be more attached and more nurturing, it's infinitely more difficult for women to *unlearn* the feelings and behaviours that define their initial position in this spectrum. It is almost impossible for mothers to learn to become less attached, to disconnect themselves, to unpick the threads that bind them to their children. 'And why on earth would we want to unpick them?' exclaimed one woman I interviewed. 'What good would that do any of us?'

The Power of Emotional Honesty

Some argue that it matters little whether biology accounts for 90 per cent, 10 per cent or nothing at all of what mothers feel, and that what really matters is that women's experience and voice are recognized. Maureen Freely's greatest concern is that mothers' experience – what she calls the maternal tradition – will be lost to modern society unless we actively work to preserve it. Carole Gilligan, author of *In a Different Voice*, considers the question of whether gender differences are biologically determined or socially constructed to be 'deeply disturbing' and insists, instead, that women's voice, the 'wellsprings' of which are psychological, be recognized.[44]

Freely and Gilligan are right that, in the end, it is mothers' voice and experience that matter most. But there is a danger that the denial of any innate, biological roots to that voice will contribute to a blindness to the voice itself – what Freely refers to as 'gender blindness'. Women sense that their voice is connected to something within them, that their experience – not just of motherhood but of life – is anchored to something deeply rooted inside them. The disallowance of any innate roots to their experience seems to say to them that the experience itself is inauthentic. In the words of a woman who had lived in denial of her feelings about being a working mother for years, 'The language we use, and all our efforts to pretend that we are no different to men, end up stifling the feelings themselves. We literally bury them inside us.'

Women's experience of mothering – whether referred to as the maternal tradition, the mother's voice or the psychology of care –

must be accepted in its entirety. The tie that binds mothers to their children is genuine, urgent, powerful and complex, and what women are not born with they learn so well and so quickly that it becomes intrinsic to them. It will not disappear simply because someone labels it 'guilt' and provides all manner of research, logical argument and upbeat women's magazine jargon to persuade women that it is unnecessary. If we attempt to bury it, society will be bereft.

An acknowledgement of the strength and validity of the feelings mothers have for their children is no attempt to revive the Angel in the House, that nineteenth-century icon of feminine goodness immortalized by the poet Coventry Patmore. And it should not lead us to insist that mothers be exclusively responsible for childcare. But it should prompt us to seek the kind of change that will enable women to accommodate their feelings within rich and varied personal and professional lives. That change is not represented by full-time day-care, which enables women to be apart from their children, or by managed mothering which enables them to delegate mothering to others. Nor is it represented by the repeated unearthing of 'social constructs', or lists of helpful hints about how to banish guilt.

The type of change that is needed is, instead, the fundamental transformation of the structure, organization and operation of the workplace. Just as Carole Gilligan awakened psychology to women's experience and voice, and Sadie Plant author of *Zeros and Ones*, reclaimed much of the history of technology for women,[45] so women need to impress their experience of mothering and working on a work world that has for too long ignored it. When it is possible for parents to pursue fulfilling careers in less than a fifty- or sixty-hour week, to take short career breaks without being eternally penalized for it, and to stay home with sick children without inviting condescension and disapproval from colleagues and employers, then we shall see more women feeling increasingly comfortable mixing careers with mothering. We will no longer have to tut-tut about why women feel so guilty or ambivalent because fewer of them will feel that way.

We should not fear candidness about maternal sentiment. It need not invalidate the paternal experience. Indeed, it may well open the door to greater awareness of how men feel about fathering. For if women do not feel free to be honest about their own feelings, if they feel compelled to refer to them as socially constructed guilt trips, how can we expect men to take their own feelings seriously, much less openly discuss them? By allowing themselves the freedom to speak about maternal feelings, women will create greater possibilities for men to give voice to their own feelings and experiences.

Rather than living in fear of emotion, we need to recognize that honesty about it can liberate us, and might even enable us to be better parents. Orbach claims that 'we find children's emotional lives difficult to respond to because we are habituated to ignoring, suppressing and disregarding our own', and that 'instead of designating feelings and vulnerabilities as fearful' we need to integrate them and let them inform our experience.[46] This does not necessarily mean that 'people should go about emoting all over the workplace', warned Orbach when I interviewed her. It simply means allowing our emotions to be understood and digested so that they can strengthen our practices and policies.

Silencing our feelings is no route to freedom, or progress. But most feminists have seen silence as the only option, fearing that claims about women's special or distinct qualities reinforce the very ideology that justifies their subordination. But, as Maureen Freely points out, though the 'feminists' canon has it that we are the great beneficiaries if we can escape biological destiny', actually 'everyone else benefits even more. They get to continue business as usual. Run things just the way they did in the good old days when mothers and their children stayed quietly at home.' So instead of trying to escape our biological and emotional destinies, we need to leverage them in the name of change, 'rescuing the realm of mothers, children and families from its present obscurity and redefining it as a second sphere of action'.[47]

We are a long way from seeing parents able to be honest about their emotional and practical needs at work. And the simple presence of more women in positions of power isn't going to get us there. As we saw in the *Guardian*'s 1997 list of the fifty most powerful women in Britain, fewer than half of them have children, and those who do are as likely to be women who did not take maternity leave, who leave each morning before their children are awake and return after they are asleep, and who regard their family as their 'hobby',[48] as they are to be inclined to speak out in favour of emotional honesty, reduced working hours and increased flexibility at work. And having more female MPs in Parliament will not create the climate of honesty that is required so long as those women adopt male models of behaviour. The jury is still very much out on the question of how women in parliament will further the cause of working mothers outside it. 'I'm really not sure about this lot – what they will really do,' one female MP whispered to me confidentially.

Women need to stop lying to themselves, and resist being persuaded that guilt is all that they are feeling, guilt which should be belittled and banished. It isn't. What women feel is real and important, and we need to speak up about it. Then we stand a chance of seeing large numbers of involved parents in positions of power within organizations. Until then, all we will have is more clones of the many workaholic fathers who have lived in denial of their own emotions and squandered their relationships with their children en route to the top.

CHAPTER TWO

THE MYTH OF THE NEW FATHER

The key to being a successful working mother is choosing the right father.
Best Companies for Women, Barbra Brown, in Scarlett MccGwire, 1992

Instead of augmenting the anxiety of mothers who work by making them
bear the full burden of their children's well-being, we should be encouraging
men to be more involved.
Rebecca Abrams, *Guardian*, 1997

When new mother Ruth Kelly was elected to parliament as a
Labour MP in May 1997, she insisted that there would be no
impossible clash in her life between work and home because her
husband would take an equal role in family life.[1] With staggering
confidence, Kelly predicted that a participative father would, apparently singlehandedly, resolve the conflict between late-night sessions
in the Commons, endless rounds of constituency engagements and
the raising of a family.

Ruth Kelly will undoubtedly rely on a range of support systems
to survive her life as MP and mother – systems which may include
dedicated nannies, a highly supportive extended family and even,
eventually, some form of flexibility in her working hours. But an
unshakeable faith in the power of the modern New Father to smooth
out all the bumps in the Superwoman's road is what came through
in her early interviews, and it is far from unusual. There are many
others who see the New Father as the working woman's salvation,
sharing responsibility for the raising of children, sharing the blame
when child-raising goes awry – when children fail exams, suffer from
poor self-esteem, become delinquents. The story goes roughly as
follows: fathers can be every bit as nurturing as mothers – can
'mother', in fact; if they did more mothering, freeing mothers from

the double burden of the second shift and the guilt that accompanies it, mothers would soon secure the professional success and power that are both their desire and their due.

In the debate about British morality which followed the murder of Philip Lawrence, an affirmation of the importance of participative fathering emerged as a common response to allegations that working mothers are responsible for the decline in British moral standards. Rebecca Abrams wrote in the *Guardian* of 29 October, 'Instead of augmenting the anxiety of mothers who work ... we should be encouraging men to be more involved.'[2] After the airing of *Panorama*'s controversial 'Missing Mum' programme, several writers pointed out that the finger of blame for children's educational underachievement ought to be pointed at fathers as well as mothers: 'Where were the fathers? Working long hours, I should think,' wrote Margaret Vaughan in the *Herald*.[3]

Within the context of the polarized debate which is the Mother War, and set against the remorseless insistence by the Right that working mothers are to blame for all of society's ills, the view that the responsibility for children should be apportioned between both parents is understandable. And it is absolutely correct. It is most certainly welcome relief to the mother accustomed to being attacked at every turn.

But this dogged stance in favour of shared parenting and involved fathering might itself be muddying the waters of the debate about working mothers and their children, not because it is inherently wrong, but by virtue of the way it is framed and of the context within which it is articulated. For the emphasis on fathering is more than a harmless means of deflecting the heat from mothers or of inviting fathers to share in the responsibilities and joys of active parenthood. It gives life to a powerful myth – one that is the bedrock of the Superwoman's defence: the Myth of the New Father. Simply stated, it is the belief that the New Father who shares parenting equally with the working mother can at once resolve the problem of mothers with too little time for their children, and enable women to achieve equality within the workplace. Just as this notion serves to avert criticism of working mothers, it also discourages acknowledgement of the real difficulties that families face as a result of both parents working long hours, *even when* the father is involved in the management of domestic life. And it ensures that many important, complex and challenging questions never get raised, let alone answered. It allowed some critics of *Panorama*'s 'Missing Mum' to push fathers into the firing line, without forcing those critics to address important questions about the connection between the hours worked by both parents and the well-being of their children, and about the changes in the workplace that might be needed to enable mothers and fathers to adapt their work patterns to their children's needs.

The Myth of the New Father also prevents us from publicly acknowledging the pain many women feel as they struggle to reconcile their long hours at work with their desire to mother – pain that is alleviated little, if at all, by the presence of a New Father in the home. And it paints an excessively optimistic view of the extent to which shared parenting can, on its own, banish women's ambivalence about their careers.

It is easy to be taken in by the Myth of the New Father. Like Ruth Kelly, I was once a fervent believer that equality at home would mean equality at work. While pregnant and working my way up through the ranks within Gemini Consulting, I fully expected that having a husband who was prepared to share in parenting would enable me to successfully combine a traditional career with motherhood. In response to a *Sunday Express* survey about the barriers to women's progress, I wrote that women would only achieve equality at work when it became acceptable for men to spend time caring for children. It was not until I had been a mother for some time that I realized the naivety of what I had written. The core of my belief in the value of shared parenting remains, but it is now overlaid by a recognition of the complexities of family life, of how difficult is *any* kind of parenting when sandwiched between two careers, and of how my feelings for my children have created an unforeseen ambivalence about pursuing a career that would take me too far and too often away from them.

The Myth of the New Father has within it some important grains of truth. One of these is that truly shared parenting will be the best thing that can possibly happen to women, children and fathers. Another is that real commitment to childcare by fathers is a source of immense support to women pursuing demanding careers. But we are gravely mistaken if we think that the New Father can eradicate women's career ambivalence all on his own, and resolve in one fell swoop the logistical and emotional issues faced by working mothers. We are fooling ourselves if we think the New Father will enable women to march unfettered down the corridors of power – unless those corridors can be made to change too. And we will be sadly disappointed if we expect that the New Father can ever be synonymous with 'mother', replacing us within the home, and in our children's eyes, without anyone noticing the difference.

We are not wrong to want men to become New Fathers, not mistaken in thinking that New Fathers are good for children, mothers, even themselves. But the host of assumptions surrounding the belief in the New Father – assumptions about what he can and can't do, how he will change women's and families' lives, and how he will actually become a New Father in the first place – need to be re-examined. And having re-examined them, we are likely to conclude that some of the hopes for extrication from the knotty conflict between work and children that we have pinned on the New Father had better be pinned elsewhere.

The New Father, the Mother and the Mother's Career

Good fathers are enormously important. Anne Roiphe wrote that 'if you don't have a good father you mourn for him always'.[4] One only has to read the autobiographies of people who have not been fathered well to realize that she is right.

The benefits of fathers being more involved in parenting may be even greater and more profound than most of us imagine. There is evidence that fathers who are involved in caring for children are less likely to become sex abusers or commit violent crimes, and that children raised by involved fathers have higher IQs, better impulse control and more positive social adaptation.[5] Anne Roiphe supports psychoanalysts Dorothy Dinnerstein and Nancy Chodorow in their view that a radical change in our childcare assumptions would produce a very different world, one in which patriarchy, misogyny and all their attendant injustices to both male and female would fade away. When a mother is one hundred per cent involved in child-raising and the father is a bystander, the mother becomes the target of the anger that follows the child's fear of abandonment. This, and the child's resentment at the power of the mother, generate in men a psychology of male dominance and an anger that is first directed at the mother, then at women in general. Girls also feel an intense rivalry with their mothers, alongside their fear of being abandoned by them, and find themselves rebelling against their mothers. If children were to be raised more equally by both parents, the dramas ensuing from these complex feelings might be avoided says Roiphe in *A Mother's Eye*.

This analysis of the problems posed by traditional child-raising practices might be overly dramatic, and the proposed solution somewhat utopian. But there is something in the position adopted by Roiphe, Dinnerstein and Chodorow with which most mothers would agree: that the dramas and power struggles which form such a significant part of the relationship between mother and young child would be better shared more evenly between two parents. Just as mothers who have spent all day wrestling with the will of a toddler welcome the sound of father returning home from work as a signal that relief has arrived, so a mother might welcome more regular relief from the intense drama that can be day-in, day-out mothering.

Few women would argue for less involvement by fathers in parenting. Without exception, every woman I spoke to in researching this book wished for a future in which fathers did more of what we call mothering. Though acutely aware of just how different are boys and girls, mothers of sons hope to influence them to be more communicative, nurturing and cognizant of home responsibilities than the men of their fathers' generation. They subscribe to the view expressed by one writer that 'we've taught girls about ambition . . . now it's time to teach boys about laundry'.[6]

Parenting in the Nineties, a report published by the Family Policy Studies Centre in 1996, revealed that mothers' happiness and satisfaction with life are closely tied to their perception of how involved their partners are in childcare. More than one in five mothers (22 per cent) whose husbands did not contribute to the care and socialization of their children said they were unhappy in their relationship, compared with just 7 per cent of those in which these tasks were shared. Dissatisfaction with life in general was more than twice as high (28 per cent) among those with uninvolved husbands as among mothers whose partners contributed to all aspects of child-rearing (13 per cent). The number of women dissatisfied with life increased to 46 per cent among women who work thirty-five or more hours per week and get little support from their partners. Clearly, many women want their husbands to be involved in the care of their children, and feel unhappy when they are not.

But, despite being vehemently in favour of fathers being more involved, most women are wary of the fully fledged house-husband. Few say that having full-time support at home would enable them to devote all their energies to their careers, competing like a man in a male world. In a Gallup Poll sponsored by British Home Stores two-thirds of women said they would not be prepared to swap roles completely.[7] In researching her book, *Professional Progress – Why Women Still Don't Have Wives*, Terry Apter found that 'women did not expect to reverse roles with their husbands, but merely to share them'.[8] Scarlett MccGwire found likewise in researching her book about Britain's top employers for women. MccGwire concludes that few mothers want a job that entails being, at best, a weekend parent, and maintains that even the few women she interviewed who lived with 'house-husbands' expected to share the care and responsibility for their children.[9] My own interviews confirm that women are not looking to unload all their domestic responsibilities so that they can march unshackled along the corridors of power. The response of marketing executive Annabel Allott was typical. She spoke at length about how she wished her husband was more involved in the daily lives of their children, but she was adamant that she did not want to relinquish her own place at the centre of the family's social and emotional life.

Women who find themselves married to New Fathers often fail to find this a consolation for their own absence from the home. Kirstie Axtens, marketing and membership manager for the charity Parents at Work, previously worked full-time for a private-sector organization. She explained that having a husband who was willing and able to take on the bulk of the child-caring had not made her feel any better about working long hours in a full-time job. 'I was very lucky that he could do all the childcare stuff,' she says, 'but it didn't really make me feel better. The point is, I wanted to be doing it. I wanted to be there.'

Women who have assumed the breadwinner role are often ambivalent about the rewards that it has brought, and still more ambivalent about pursuing a career that threatens to take them away from their family. Clare is earning all of the family income while her husband stays home to care for their four-month-old baby. They have this arrangement because he can't get a job and she can. He's quite happy with the set-up, but she's miserable. She wishes she saw more of their baby. Another woman, Louise, is responsible for earning the lion's share of the family income while her husband gets a new business off the ground. Her husband isn't exactly playing house-husband – their daughter goes to a nursery – but he is taking on a large part of the responsibility for the child, and Louise is playing breadwinner. Rather than feeling liberated by this arrangement, Louise feels somewhat trapped by it. She misses her daughter, and were it not for the need to support the family through lean times, she would consider stopping work or reducing her work week from four days to two or three.

In an article in the August 1996 issue of *You* magazine by journalist Louette Harding, 'Wait till your mother gets home', Harding tells us that more and more women are their family's breadwinners. But Harding's interviews with house-husbands and their wives did little to persuade me that there are hordes of men anxious to take on the mother's traditional role, or of women desperate to let them so that they can pursue their careers unhindered. All three of the men she interviews came to be house-husbands because they were made redundant, or were experiencing financial difficulties in their own businesses. Harding's own husband took on the full-time carer's role for precisely that reason. And while the wives were quite prepared to be sole breadwinner during this time of crisis, for the sake of the family (and who wouldn't be?), none of them seemed happy about the prospect of doing it long-term. Neither were most of the couples in role-reversed marriages interviewed for a *Times* story on 21 May 1995. One woman who supports the family while her husband cares for the home said, 'I have to work because I'm the only one that can get a job'; her husband said, 'It's been terrible for the kids and frustrating for me.'

Stories like these are a testimony to how well families are coping with an increasingly insecure work world, not resounding proof of the fact that women and men happily choose to swap roles very often. The way women feel about becoming sole earners while their partners become primary carers belies the Myth of the New Father: Louise and Clare, like the breadwinners in the *Times* article, are free to work at their careers because their husbands have taken on most of the caring, yet they feel only regret. Career ambivalence has not magically disappeared, to be replaced with unfettered ambition. It remains steadfast despite the support of the New Father.

Telling mothers like these that they need not worry because their partners are at home with the children will not change their feelings on the issue. Having their partners learn to be more attached and involved will not lessen their attachment any. It will not make them any more comfortable working in jobs that demand they be away from home twelve hours a day, day in, day out.

Counting All New Fathers

There are some women who feel little ambivalence or regret (or who overcome what little they feel), dedicate themselves to their careers and depend on their husbands to take up most of the slack at home. But how many stories like this are there? How many successful and powerful women currently rely on their partners to care for their children and homes? And how many others can really hope to emulate them? How close are we to a world in which fathers are so involved, participative and caring – so 'new' – that women in great numbers can let loose their ambition?

Scanning the parenting section of bookstore shelves, one could easily be convinced that the New Father – involved, sensitive, nurturing, sharing in every aspect of parenting – is the norm today. So many books about fatherhood were published in 1997 – more than in any other year in the history of fatherhood, claims *You* – that both *You* magazine and the London *Evening Standard* declared 1997 to be the year of the father. The list of books published included both the sensitive and insightful, like Peter Howarth's *Fatherhood: An Anthology of New Writing*, and the glib and childish, such as John Crace's *Baby Alarm! A Neurotic's Guide to Fatherhood*. Adrienne Burgess's book *Fatherhood Reclaimed* is among the most important. In it, Burgess sets out to overturn the many myths associated with fatherhood, and to suggest how fathers can be brought back into the centre of families. She shows that they can be caring and loving, and that their involvement with their children leads to happier, healthier families.

In proclaiming her unerring faith in the ability of fathers to mother, Burgess is supported by an abundance of features and articles about New Men, house-husbands and stay-at-home dads. The aim of such journalism, it would appear, is to convince us that the new fatherhood is already so widespread that women's lives and careers are being dramatically transformed. Journalist Louette Harding claimed in *You* magazine to be able to count a dozen examples of role reversal among her neighbours and friends alone. The *Sunday Times* of 21 May 1995 shouted boldly: 'Women take over as breadwinners'. An earlier headline in *The Times* (25 March 1992) claimed that a British Home Stores sponsored poll had discovered that half of working mothers would happily swap roles with their husbands to be the main family breadwinner, though a much less dramatic conclusion was reached in the fine print. A *Daily Mail* article announced that men want to do a lot more than we are commonly led to believe.[10] And we are repeatedly informed that the number of women earning more than their partners has increased from one in fifteen in the 1980s to one in five today, though that fact says little about whether women and men are behaving any differently in the home.

Statistics and articles like these document an unmistakable trend: fathers are becoming more involved in home life than the generation of fathers before them, and women are steadily increasing their participation in the workplace. But bold newspaper headlines and confident assertions like those made by Burgess often exaggerate the magnitude and impact of the trend, and are controverted by the reality of life in most families today. Despite the wave of optimism driving contemporary accounts about the New Father, 'the evidence for the existence of such a man is much less convincing', says Melanie Henwood in *Inside the Family*.[11] Professor Cary Cooper at Manchester University maintains that, 'If you put new man in a zoo, you'd only need one cage.'[12]

Obtaining a completely accurate picture of family life, and men's place within it, from the news stories based on formal surveys is bafflingly difficult. The extent to which press reporting about the domestic efforts of men is misleading is reflected in the fact that, in January 1992, the *Sunday Express* declared that 'the new man really is a myth', while in February of the same year the *Daily Mail* announced that male and female roles were steadily converging.[13]

From formal surveys alone, it is virtually impossible to come to precise conclusions about how much men are doing. BSA (British Social Attitudes) studies throughout the 1980s showed equal sharing of domestic duties to be rare overall – in four out of five couples, the woman was mainly responsible for them. But, for dual-earner couples in which the wife worked full-time, the reported levels of sharing varied unpredictably from survey to survey. The 1980 BSA survey, for instance, found that 'where the wife worked full-time, nearly *half* the couples said they shared housework *equally*', but the 1987 survey found that 'over two-thirds of the women with full-time jobs were *solely* responsible for general domestic duties' [italics mine throughout].[14] Such results attest either to a disturbing trend away from equal partnering in the home, or to the difficulties associated with tracking the patterns of family life via self-reported surveys.

Other studies tracking the amount of time men and women spend on routine housework suggest that men did more housework in the 1980s than they did in the 60s. But progress is desperately slow, and has not resulted in anything like an equal sharing of domestic duties. Depending on which survey you read, women still spend between two and four times as long on housework as men, and women who work full-time spend almost three times the amount of time on housework as men who work full-time.[15]

There has been little progress, according to formal surveys, in getting men more involved in childcare. The 1980 BSA survey found that two-thirds of the couples where the woman worked part-time or full-time reported that she shared childcare half-and-half with her partner.[16] *Parenting in the Nineties*, published in 1997, seventeen years later, contained a similar statistic: in 66 per cent of families in which the wife works full-time, and in 48 per cent of those in which she works part-time, women report that they share responsibility for being with and looking after children equally with their husbands. Apparently, little has changed, and the dual-earner family in which the father takes most of the responsibility for childcare – perhaps the truest signal of the advance of the New Father – is still a rarity, representing just 2 per cent of full-time dual-earner couples.[17]

When surveys report such little change over a period during which most people perceive change to have been enormous, the alarm bells should ring, alerting us to the possibility that surveys relying on men and women to answer questions about the extent to which they share responsibility for children are not entirely reliable. A more reliable picture of the true state of affairs is likely to come from detailed observational studies. One such study conducted by Peter Moss and Julia Brannen of the Thomas Coram Research Unit during the same period that BSA surveys were reporting that childcare was shared equally in two-thirds of dual-earner households, found that full-time employed women spent an average of twenty-five hours a week in sole charge of their child, compared with only six hours for the fathers.[18]

Like Moss and Brannen, David Pichaud observed families in 1984 and concluded that 'by far the greater part (89 per cent) of the time spent on childcare tasks was spent by the mother', and that 'even a wide margin of underestimation of fathers' time use would not alter the overwhelming inequality between mothers and fathers in time spent on basic childcare tasks'.[19] More recent fly-on-the-wall journalistic exercises, such as that reported in *You* magazine of 28 May 1997, tend to confirm that, even today and in the year of the father, 'it is the mother with the part-time job whose life is characterized by complexity and connection, while fathers tend to focus their minds on one thing at a time'. Every morning, in homes all across the country, 'most dads get themselves up and out [to work], while mothers mobilize everyone else before they, too, get themselves off to work'. They gather school clothes, fill lunch boxes, supervise the daily brushing of teeth and hair, feed pets, sort school bags, load the dishwasher, tidy up, throw in some washing – and all before they take the kids to school. It is the mothers who plan and organize, who remember birthdays, and to whom children turn when they need to ask, 'Can I? Why not? Where is . . .? When are we . . .?'

Casual observation yields a similar picture. Advertising executive Carole Reay tells the story of a taxi driver who, for a time, regularly drove her from home to work. 'Gees I gotta hand it to you women, but I wouldn't want to come back as one of you,' he said to her one morning. 'I see you rushing out the front door, shouting last-minute instructions at the nanny, giving the kids extra hugs, wiping baby-food off your jacket and applying your make-up in the taxi while you catch up on last-minute preparations for a meeting. The blokes, they just walk calmly out the door, ties all neatly in place, and read the paper all the way to work.'

Even when we are invited to meet men who 'share the caring' out of choice, they rarely turn out to be quite the New Fathers they are advertised to be. In a *Times* feature on men of the nineties (14 October 1996) we were introduced to Jack Gordon, who had taken on more of the childcare since his wife's career took off. But Jack isn't the house-husband we expected to meet. He's simply a man who does the school run, teaches his son to swim and ride a bike, and works from home on Fridays. The story reminded me of the husband of a friend who for years claimed to be the primary carer in the house while his wife was the primary breadwinner. It wasn't until after they divorced that the wife revealed that, though she had indeed earned most of the family wage throughout their marriage, he had done very little in the way of organizing the house or taking sole charge of the children.

When New Fathers' stories are exaggerated, it is not always the fathers themselves who are to blame. In 1997 a friend of mine, David, found himself the central figure of two stories about fathers who combine careers with high levels of involvement with their families – one in the *Independent* and one in *You* magazine. Journalist David Cohen, whose interview served as the basis for both stories, was determined to make more of David's New Fathering than he himself was. David is genuinely concerned about being an absent father and makes considered efforts to spend less time at work and more at home. But he would be the first to admit that even during his 'breather' work weeks, which take up around forty hours, being available for both the school run and a bedtime story is next to impossible, particularly when two hours a day are taken up by the commute to work. During his peak weeks, when he can work seventy hours, he will hardly see his children at all. David's schedule may look New Father-like in the world of management consulting in which he works, but it still requires a wife at home to sustain family life: his wife Gill gave up her career to care for the children years ago. Yet Cohen was determined to see David as one of the fortunate few who 'could create room for their families'.[20]

My friend David is not one to exaggerate the time he spends fathering. (He insisted on not being labelled a New Man.) Others are more prone to embellishing their contribution to the home. That men exaggerate the degree to which they help with childcare, washing, cleaning, and anything else to do with running a home has been shown to be true in several studies. A 1993 survey of American fathers by the Families and Work Institute asked how working couples shared childcare. 'We share it 50/50' was the response of 43 per cent of the men – but of just 19 per cent of the women.[21] The British *Parenting in the Nineties* report similarly revealed that 'on every measure of parental involvement, fathers claimed more par- ticipation in terms of joint or sole responsibility than mothers reported in relation to their husbands'.[22] This finding would not come as a surprise to many women. We have all heard our husbands claim that they have cleaned the kitchen when they have stuck a few dishes in the dishwasher, or boast that they share the cooking when, in fact, they prepare scrambled eggs once a fortnight.

Claims about what fathers 'want' are as likely to be exaggerated as accounts of what they actually do. Adrienne Burgess insists that overwhelming numbers of men are anxious to be more involved in childcare, if women would only let them. But research by the Family Policy Studies Centre suggests that though some fathers would like to spend more time in the company of their children, they do not necessarily want or seek out more responsibility for childcare or domestic work.[23]

Far from being budding New Fathers, a surprising number of men *still* believe that they should be supported by a wife at home. A British Social Attitudes survey found that nearly half the husbands agreed with the view that 'a husband should be the breadwinner and the wife should look after the home and children'.[24] A survey of

British males conducted for *XL for Men* magazine resulted in a similar indictment of the New Father: 56 per cent of men 'would prefer a woman who is happy to look after them, the children and the home rather than continue her career'.[25]

Statistics like these lead to the inevitable conclusion that many homes are still inhabited by resolutely traditional fathers, not sharing, caring new ones. They suggest that if mothers want fathers to fill all the gaps they leave behind when they pursue challenging, time-consuming careers, they will have to look very hard for examples of families in which such arrangements actually work. There are indeed some very successful women who can depend on New Fathers to make up for their absence at home. Actress Julie Walters's husband cares for their daughter Maisi full-time. Pearson chief executive Marjorie Scardino has been reported as saying that her husband, a writer and lecturer, shares all domestic duties with her, thus enabling her to concentrate on her career. But one is hard-pressed to come up with many examples like these. Where was Superwoman Nicola Horlick's husband while she was earning over a million pounds a year at Morgan Grenfell and being mother to five children? Not at the school gates or making tea for the children, but out at another bank earning a six figure salary. And where was Anita Roddick's husband while she was launching and running the Body Shop? Certainly not packing the lunches and doing the school run.

As often as not, Superwomen are married to Supermen. About half of all mothers employed in professional or skilled manual occupations or as managers have partners in similar-status occupations.[26] Superwomen don't rely on their husbands to fill in the gaps at home – they just assume, or pretend, that those gaps don't exist. Or they hire help to fill them. Having studied the evolution of men's and women's careers in the United States, Arlie Hochschild has concluded that the part of the women's movement that pushed for shorter work hours, more flexible jobs and a restructuring of home life has somehow surrendered the initiative to feminists more concerned with helping women break the glass ceiling into long-hours careers.[27] And as women have worked longer hours, men are not compensating at home. 'Even during a decade when family-friendliness was on the agenda, mothers worked longer and longer hours and fathers did not cut back to compensate,' claims Peter Moss of the Thomas Coram Research Unit who contributed to the report entitled *Mothers, Fathers and Employment* published by the Department for Education and Employment in 1997. The result in many families is what Maeve Haran calls the dangerous phenomenon of the high-powered, dual-career couple, and a vacuum where parenting should be.

It is ironic that, though much that is written about how women can shatter the glass ceiling emphasizes the role that New Fathers need to play, it is in fact the high-powered career woman who is *least* likely to be supported by a partner who shares responsibility for childcare and housework. 'Working-class fathers are more likely to work shifts and operate "relay" parenting with their wives'[28] than middle- and upper-class fathers, writes Adrienne Burgess. They may hold more stereotypical views about mothers' and fathers' roles, but their behaviour is dictated more by income than by ideology.

Behind such generalizations, and the averages that emerge from formal surveys, of course, lie many variations. As Burgess points out, where one father will be home for just five hours in the week while his infant is awake, another will be present for forty-seven hours. So in any given family, a working mother may well be able to count on the presence of her partner to ease or remove the burdens of the double shift. But that family will not be typical. And the New Father within it will still be in the distinct minority among middle-class, careerist fathers.

Most women I interviewed acknowledged the great strides their own husbands had made to be more involved in family life, but reacted with scepticism when faced with Burgess's thesis that fathers can be as nurturing and involved in the daily lives of their children as mothers. 'She clearly isn't living in this house' was a commonly muttered refrain. The authors of *Parenting in the Nineties* found that some women who were adversely affected by a lack of support from their husbands did not see an amelioration of their situation in the future. Linda Kelsey, former editor of *She* magazine, confessed that 'we got quite hopeful about the idea of new men, then realized there weren't enough of them about'.[29] Like Kelsey, most women know that, today at least, co-parenting is a myth and there are some enormous obstacles on the road to the future state envisioned by the likes of Burgess, Dinnerstein and Chodorow. Not least of these is women's secret scepticism about whether or not men can really make the journey, the whole journey, every leg of it.

The Journey from Mars to Venus: Can they really do it?

Adrienne Burgess believes all fathers can mother if given the chance. Annie Oakley, writing in the 1970s, was equally positive about fathers' potential to mother. 'Fathers are not exempt on biological grounds from an engagement in mothering behaviour,'[30] she wrote in *Housewife*.

Others are less optimistic. 'We are not absolutely sure that men can do it,' said Anne Roiphe. 'Are they really capable of the day after day, two in the morning after two in the morning subjugation of their own egos and control of their own will that mothering requires?'[31] Just as Roiphe is not sure that men can do it, so many women are absolutely certain that they cannot do it *yet*. The overwhelming consensus among mothers I know is that most men cannot yet cope with the detail, repetition, and monumental amounts of patience and energy that go into day-in, day-out mothering.

Margaret Thatcher once said that men don't have the woman's ability to stick to the job in hand; she was referring to the job of public policy-making, but she might just as well have been talking about the job of running a home and raising a family. Other women elucidate Thatcher's point within the home context: 'Men don't do Easter bonnets for the school play after a day at the office,' said marketing executive Annabel Allott; 'Men don't seem to have the capacity to carry around in their heads the thousands of things which need to be done,' said lawyer Anne Marie Piper. 'It would never occur to my husband to stock up on the boys' swimming trunks in February when he happens to pass a shop which sells them, but I do that sort of thing all the time.'

'You will never find a man crying at the sight of four years' worth of unsorted family photos,'[32] writes Canadian magazine editor Paula Brook, putting into crystal-clear terms the differences that so many women see between themselves and men. Brook, like many women, knows that while mothering requires a scatter-gun approach, an ability to care about and juggle a hundred and one details including the unsorted family photos, 'men are from Mars, and on Mars it's OK to do just one thing at the expense of all others'. Women even juggle mentally when they are no longer able to do it in reality: women prisoners reportedly carry their families' needs and problems into prison with them, while men typically check them in at the prison gates.[33]

In her ground-breaking book first published in 1982, *In a Different Voice*, Carole Gilligan furthered our understanding of how women's experiences and perceptions of life beget a 'voice' that is markedly different from men's. Like Nancy Chodorow, she believes that girls have 'empathy built into their primary definition of self in a way that boys do not'. They have a stronger bias towards experiencing other people's feelings, and are more concerned with connection, intimacy and care than most men. These concerns are reflected in their approach to moral dilemmas: women's morality is one of responsibility, rather than one of rights, and is based on connection rather than separation.[34]

John Gray, author of *Men Are from Mars, Women Are from Venus*, articulated his own version of Gilligan's thesis about the differences between male and female psychology some fifteen years later. Men, or Martians as he calls them, 'value power, competency, efficiency, and achievement'.[35] Their sense of self is defined through their ability to achieve results, and they experience fulfilment primarily through success and accomplishment. Women, or Venusians, value love, communication, beauty, and relationships, and spend a lot of time nurturing one another. Their sense of self and experience of fulfilment are integrally connected to their experience of sharing and relating.

Martians' values determine their communication style, which is direct and oriented towards problem resolution. When Venusians communicate, says Gray, 'to share their personal feelings is much more important than achieving goals and success'. Extending his thesis, one could easily see how Martian and Venusian values lie at the heart of different behaviours within the family. While Martians focus effort to solve problems and manage situations, women are more prepared and perhaps even better equipped to cope with the ambiguity, changeability and multifacetedness of life at home with small children, and to take responsibility for the emotionally demanding aspects of family life.

Gray's thesis will strike some as sexist, but it need not be taken as such. He claims neither that men and women will for ever inhabit different planets, their emotional and communication styles uninfluenceable by experience and social expectations, nor that the differences between men and women should earmark them for entirely separate roles and status within society. He merely offers acute observations about the differences in the ways most men and most women emote and communicate. Straw polls around dinner-tables confirm his observations to be remarkably incisive. Asked whether Gray's theories accurately reflect what goes on in their own marriages, most people nod vehemently. And most women, asked to define the different roles men and women tend to play within family life, point to the man's need to focus, and the woman's ability to juggle – logistics, details and emotions.

Gray hardly mentions biology, but the differences between men and women that he describes may well have some of their roots in biology. The finding that girls have a 'sociability' gene that boys lack adds weight to the widely held view that women are naturally more verbally gifted, nurturing and empathetic than men.[36] Social skills, sensitivity to one's environment, and empathy are essentially what enable good 'jugglers' to juggle and multitask, picking up toys and wiping bottoms while also attending to toddlers' minor emotional crises. Without these skills, men often remain focused on the task in hand, oblivious to the fact that there is any juggling to be done. As Anne Moir and David Jessel confirm in *Brainsex*, their book about the differences between men's and women's brains, 'Women are simply better equipped to notice things to which men are comparatively blind and deaf.'

Men do have a concept of care, but today at least it tends to be very different from women's, claims Maureen Freely. 'It tends to diminish and compartmentalize emotions, in a way that women's concept of care does not. It can be insensitive to the emotional work of parenting.' Freely tells a story of an interview with a young father. When she asked him whether he would like to work less, he replied, 'Well, perhaps, but what would I do with all that spare time?' 'He was clearly insensitive to the relational and emotional aspects of parenting, and the amount of time it takes to bring them to life in a family,' observed Freely. Even 'experts' in child psychology and family relations can underestimate the emotional element in parent–child interactions. When I interviewed a male professor reputed to be a leader in the field of family relations, he dismissed women's feelings of responsibility for their children's happiness and well-being as 'irrational' and brushed aside children's need for more time with their parents as 'evidence of their extreme selfishness'. He had a concept of care and responsibility, but it was one that sought to minimize, categorize and trivialize the emotions involved.

In time, and with different experiences, men could learn to be effective jugglers, and to operate according to a more connected and emotional concept of care. For it is true, as Sarah Ruddick suggests, that actively caring for children gives rise to 'distinctive ways of conceptualizing, ordering and valuing', or what she calls 'maternal thinking'.[37] Adrienne Burgess shows that 'very high levels of involvement and responsibility change men's experience of parenting',[38] making them confident and more effective, and more attentive to their children's development. So, where today many a man will repeatedly step over a pile of dirty laundry even if it is strategically placed in his path, he could learn not only to do that laundry, but to care about how clean, soft and well sorted it is. Where a man might be horrified by the number of appointments, play dates and extra-curricular activities to which children are shepherded each week, he might learn to take a week filled with children's activities in his stride, even overcoming an acute sense of his own ridiculousness to the extent of joining in the hokey-kokey at a three-year-old's ballet class.

But no matter how good men become at juggling work and family life, they will not become mothers. Even as primary carers, they have their own 'male' style, as childcare experts and psychologists such as Penelope Leach and Philip Hwang attest. Dr Kyle Pruett, a professor of psychiatry at the Yale University Child Study Center, maintains that even when they are the primary caregivers, fathers do not mother, and 'the interactions between infant and father, as between infant and mother, follow a pattern that transcends social class and cultural expectations'.[39] Child psychiatrist Sebastian Kraemer has written that fathers, however diligent in performing physical tasks for an infant, do not have the baby in mind in the same way that mothers do, and warns against confusing the notion of fathers doing an equal share with an expectation that they should be the same as mothers.[40]

Most women want men not to become mothers, but to become more involved and capable fathers. And, encouraged by the knowledge that even innate traits can be altered by learning and experience, women hope that fathering will look different in fifty years' time. But most are not unaware of the enormity of the challenge that confronts us all if fathering in practice is to live up to its potential in theory. They will not be oblivious to the differences between men and women that need to be subdued in the process. Maureen Freely describes the prospect of women trying single-handedly to bring families into line with feminist ideas of equality, equity, freedom and justice as a tragic farce.[41]

Transforming a traditional father, or even a budding New Father, into someone whose level of involvement in home and family life matches that of most women, is indeed a monumental challenge. Most of us use any and all methods at our disposal – including gentle persuasion, perpetual nagging and the occasional staged strike. And many of us can claim both small and significant victories in the battle against Martian-like fathering habits, whether these be persuading the men in our lives to forsake weekly cricket with the boys for weekly swimming with the children, or to cook pancakes on Saturday morning while we sleep in.

Re-education on a grand scale would help. The Swedish government has played an active campaigning role in persuading Swedish men and women that equality and shared parenting are important goals. Swedish society would never have taken the ideals of shared parenting to heart without such a concerted public campaign, says Peter Moss. But the bigger victories, the ones that transform a father into a truly equal partner in childcare and housework, are not likely to be forthcoming so long as we rely mainly upon private persuasion and public re-education tactics. The New Father will never become a commonly observed phenomenon unless the old father's working habits change dramatically. According to the 1997 DFEE report *Mothers, Fathers and Employment*, almost two-thirds of fathers work over forty hours a week, and one in ten work over sixty hours. Not surprisingly, research also reveals that the proportion of fathers reporting that they share childcare responsibility with their wives declines as their weekly hours worked increase, as does the general quality of family life.[42] Given men's tendency to exaggerate the time they spend on childcare in the first place, it is evident that New Fathering is still more myth than fact.

Here we have a classic case of the chicken and the egg. Men can't change their behaviour at home unless they change their behaviour at work. But they are unlikely to change their behaviour at work unless they are forced to do so by the demands of their roles at home. So which comes first? Where is the greatest lever for change? Gloria Steinem believes that 'until men are raising babies and children as much as women are, until men cook what they eat, clean what gets dirty, work won't change'.[43] I believe the biggest lever for change lies, instead, in the workplace, and in women's willingness to challenge the way that workplace shapes behaviour within the family.

Those whose business it is to help companies develop and implement family-friendly policies have a fairly clear idea as to how change will be brought about. It will not be brought about by willing men to work less or relying on them alone to demand family-friendly policies. It will be brought about by women. Val Hammond, chief executive of the Roffey Park Management Institute and the author of several reports for Opportunity 2000, is adamant that family-friendly policies must apply to both men and women, but also believes that 'unless women demand them, sure as hell no one else will'. Liz Bargh, ex Opportunity 2000 campaign director and now chief executive of WFD, a consultancy and support service firm specializing in the work–life arena, agrees with Hammond. 'Women will be the ones who make change happen,' she says. Partridge Gardner, an independent consultant who works with senior managers to resolve organizational issues, likewise believes that men are suffering, and want change, but they are too afraid to ask for it, so women will have to take the lead.

No greater evidence that women are taking the lead in changing workplace culture could be provided than the fact that the over-

whelming majority of people working in the work–family reconciliation field are women. At a 'Striking the Balance' symposium
sponsored by the Royal Borough of Kingston in June 1997, 90 per
cent of the delegates were women. At a meeting of a Parents at
Work chapter convened to discuss ways of achieving a better balance
between work and family, every one of the attendees was female.

Women will lead the way because, on the whole, they are prepared
to take more risks with their careers, and it is socially more
acceptable for them to do so. As significantly, they are the ones who
are suffering the most acute daily pain resulting from the imbalance
between work and family: it is they who most often leave behind
small pleading faces and anguished cries when they go to work and
find themselves incapable of shaking that image from their minds.
Some men will support the demand for change, and a few may even
speak up about their own needs, but they will not fight in any great
numbers for the transformation of workplace culture and practices
unless women are fronting the battle.

The biggest element of myth in the Myth of the New Father is the
inference that fathering will change significantly enough to allow
women to devote more energy to their careers without women
enabling that change by spearheading the drive towards revolutionary workplace practices. It lies in the failure to see workplace change
as the precursor of a significant shift in roles within the family, and
to recognize women's central role in bringing that change about.
The myth is captured perfectly by Ruth Kelly's insisting that her
husband would enable her to combine a parliamentary career with
successful mothering, while failing to mention the need for an
overhaul of parliamentary practices and culture, which are antagonistic to family life. It is reiterated every time a journalist comments
on the need for men to change their habits, without mentioning that
some women, particularly powerful, successful women who have
made it to the top on the back of short maternity leaves, long hours
and long-suffering nannies, might need to change theirs too.

By all means, let's continue to talk about shared parenting and
new models of fathering. But that must not deflect us from considering women's need to work differently, and their obligation to fight
for workplace cultures and practices that make it possible for *everyone*
to work differently. Workplace change has hardly begun, as we shall

see in Chapter 8, and it will not be easily achieved. The revolutionary change in workplace practices and norms that will be required for organizations to be truly family-friendly will only come about if a structured, purposeful, committed approach is applied to its creation. It will only come about when enough women are prepared to stake their careers on seeking it. But it will never materialize if working mothers continue to hide behind the Superwoman's myth that their absence in the home goes unnoticed by their children because their father packs the school lunch boxes and attends sports days. It will never come true if we pretend that the only relevant question concerning work and family is that of how to get more men to take on their share of responsibility for the latter.

Workplace change, instigated by women, not wishful thinking and flippant rhetoric about New Fathers, is what will make balancing work and family a real possibility. That alone will enable men to become the fathers they have the potential to be. It is also the thing that will make the most significant difference to working mothers who struggle with the impossibility of meeting their children's needs and fulfilling their career ambitions within the straitjacket of traditional male models of work, career and success. Workplace change needs to be placed at the top of the agenda for change, not relegated to the position of afterthought where it now sits.

CHAPTER THREE

THE MYTH OF MANAGED MOTHERING

'It's bound to be incredibly tough. Won't having kids mean constant compromises? Aren't you afraid of spreading yourself too thinly?' 'Nonsense. It's all down to organization and delegation. I have a wonderful nanny.'
Working mother LIZ WARD talking to a journalist in
MAEVE HARAN, *Having It All* (1991)

A FRIEND RECENTLY attended a coffee morning for new mothers in London. At the gathering were half a dozen new mothers, all career women who planned to return to work after their maternity leaves. My friend is a mother of three who has worked part-time since her first child was born. In theory, she and these new mothers ought to have had much in common. Instead, she found herself feeling an outsider:

> These were really high-powered women – all merchant banker and McKinsey types in their late twenties and early thirties. And they were all talking with such optimism and certainty about how they were going to go back to work four days a week and hire a nanny, etc. etc. They seemed so convinced that they could control their situation, manage it like they'd managed everything else. And it just made me feel old, and cynical. I felt like saying, you have no idea how hard this is going to be. You have no idea how much those children are going to mean to you and how hard it's going to be when you're on a plane going to some meeting and the child falls and bumps its head, or gets sick. You have no idea how your children's lives are going to spill over into your work on a daily basis. But I didn't say it. You can't tell people what it's going to be like. They'd only resent you for it.

For women swamped by the daily reality of the working mother's life, cynicism and smugness are easily stirred by encounters such as these. Working mothers listening to childless women or new mothers talking boldly about plans for a highly organized, well-managed life, or reading interviews with young high-flyers who insist that motherhood will not affect their career, must make the greatest of efforts to resist muttering under their breath, 'Just you wait.'

But self-assured bullishness is more than just a characteristic of youth and inexperience. It is a by-product of a myth that pervades much discussion and writing about working mothers. This is the notion that all is possible if one is organized – that family life can be managed and family responsibilities delegated, and that children can be nurtured during carefully orchestrated slots of 'quality time'. This is the Myth of Managed Mothering.

The Myth of Managed Mothering comes in many guises. It is often seen in the cheerfully upbeat but misleading portraits of successful Superwomen that are regularly featured in women's magazines. I remember such a profile of a world-famous architect with six children whose home was said to run like a well-oiled machine. The secret of the mother's success, we were told, was her meticulously organized life and her ability to delegate to her two nannies, cook and cleaner. Because of her skill at managing, the architect's home was superbly organized and relaxed and welcoming, and all of her children received just the right amount of love and attention. Nowhere was there a hint that this woman and her husband might occasionally feel overwhelmed by the need to nurture, discipline and oversee the nightly homework of their six children while sustaining two fast-paced careers, or that the well-oiled machine might occasionally collapse into chaos when one of the nannies fell ill, or one of the children felt disinclined to cooperate with the routine set out at the beginning of the week.

Most profiles of successful Superwomen resemble this one. 'Chairwoman of ICI and mother of six, Dawn has a hectic life at home and at work ... Blah. Blah. Blah. It made you want to throw up,'[1] said Maeve Haran's fictitious journalist Steffi Wilson about biographies of Superwomen. They are full of marvel at the drive, discipline and superb organizational skills of 'have-it-all professionals who manage careers, homes, husbands and children with equal vigour'[2] and often include photographs of happy families smiling contentedly at the camera from within their immaculate and perfectly interior-designed sitting-rooms. They promote the idea that a spectacular career and a family life are easily combined if one is ruthlessly efficient and systematic – You can have it all provided you are very organized, insisted Edwina Currie in a 1992 issue of *Options*. They fail to question whether, in fact, something important might be missing in homes that are structured to accommodate two parents who are focused on work and away from the home for most of the week.

The Myth of Managed Mothering also colours much thinking and discussion about why some women are more successful than others. Headhunter Yvonne Sarch insists that only women who are not going to make it to the top seem to have difficulty juggling full-time work with mothering, and that the truly talented always find a way of managing the situation.[3] A letter to the editor of the *Daily Telegraph* in January 1997 echoed this view. Its author, Holly Bellingham, called the debate about the problems faced by Super-women 'unnecessary', and pointed to three high-profile women who seemed to combine careers and families effortlessly – the Queen, Lady Thatcher and Cherie Booth. Bellingham concluded that 'perhaps it's a case of those who can do, and those who can't … complain'.[4]

The dispassionate tone of such statements about the difference between highly successful women and the rest characterizes much of the academic discussion of women's career development. Barbara White, Charles Cox and Cary Cooper's book *Women's Career Development* contains much valuable analysis and insight. And the authors recognize that organizations need to 'rethink what constitutes a successful career' and 'reassess the logic that equates long hours with superior performance'[5] if more women are to succeed. But such suggestions are swamped by the use of detached phraseology that shields the emotional cost of juggling a fast-track career with mothering. The authors, and those whose work they review, refer to the angst that many women feel on being torn between love for their children and commitment to a career as 'role conflict' or 'role overload', terms that obscure the emotional aspect of the problem. Women are described as managing the conflicting demands of their roles by employing 'coping mechanisms'. These include the 'intermittent activation of roles', the 'delegation of tasks and roles' and the 'appeal to deadlines and organizational schedules to legitimize non-participation in family activities'. Through the use of such aloof, impersonal language, the problem of juggling career and family is reduced to that of selecting the most appropriate 'coping mechanism'. Expunged of any reference to emotion, or to real children, such an academic analysis reinforces the myth that mothering is something that responds to the 'mechanisms' of organization and delegation and can be 'managed' alongside a successful career.

Curiously, awards whose very purpose is to celebrate women's achievements may also reinforce the myth. The Woman of the Nineties Award is for women who 'successfully combine homemaking and creative abilities with financial management and the achievement of personal goals'.[6] The recipients of the award are women like the single mother to several children who managed to finance her way through medical school, and the mother of five who is also a botanical author, photographer and researcher. They are women deserving of our recognition. But the act of recognizing them is not without negative consequence. For these women then become what Joan Smith of the London *Evening Standard* has called 'the new incarnation of that mythical 1970s creation, Superwoman',[7] and they are competing in a contest whose underlying assumption is that women have to be good at everything: they need to excel on the domestic front and in their careers, plan their budgets with consummate skill and use their 'creative' abilities to the fullest extent. The side-effect of public celebration of their achievements is the reinforcement of the myth that it is possible for women to do it all provided they have enough determination and self-belief, and an abundance of finely honed organizational skills.

News stories about the rise of domestic services in Britain serve to shore up the myth even further. In January 1997, the *Times* reported that domestic service was sweeping back into two-salary homes, with spending on such services having quadrupled since the late 1980s.[8] 'As more females enter the workplace,' reported the *Times*, 'fewer are willing to mop the kitchen floor or clean the oven when they get home' and many have decided to pay someone else to do the work. Interviewed were a couple who work twelve- to fourteen-hour days, and so employ a live-in nanny, a housekeeper, a week-end nanny and a gardener to make their lives 'more bearable'. At first glance their arrangement sounds like a sensible, even enviable, solution to the problems faced by families in which both parents have high-powered, time-consuming careers. On deeper reflection, it looks more like a misplaced faith in the notion that children and families can be 'managed' and 'subcontracted' to others. Many a reader must have wondered how children fare when nannies are on call twenty-four hours a day, seven days a week, thereby relieving the parents of that obligation. More than a few must have questioned the desirability of subcontracting responsibility for family life to such an extent that family life effectively ceases to exist.

Stories about the increasing employment of domestic services and about the domestic arrangements of the very rich and busy would be harmless were it not for the fact that they create images of domestic organization that affect expectations about how most people should be able to run their lives. Someone once suggested to me that weekend work shouldn't be a problem for people like me, what with the weekend nanny services available these days. It never occurred to him that I might not want to hand my children over to a nanny at the weekends, or that I might not be able to afford it.

But, like other things Superwomen in the media tell us, and themselves, in order to deflect attention from the very real problem represented by parents who spend too much time at work and too little time parenting, the idea that mothers can manage, organize and delegate their way out of the work–parenting dilemma is a myth. The fact is, there is more to family life, and raising children, than those things that can be delegated. As author Maureen Freely has put it so succinctly in *What About Us?*, 'We are looking at a problem which is larger than laundry.'

Shirley Conran, the author of *Superwoman* who was famous for pointing out that life was too short to stuff a mushroom, was one of the first to claim that having it all was possible provided one didn't expect to adhere to the standards of housekeeping regarded as normal by the previous generation. Conran has since denounced her own creation, but the notion that being Superwoman is about how one manages housework – by minimizing it, delegating it, or being devoted to it – seems to have survived in some curious forms. That the primary challenge of combining working with mothering might *not* be represented by laundry or other domestic chores seemed to escape high-flyer Nicola Horlick, the mother of five and asset manager suspended from Morgan Grenfell. In a television interview given in the midst of the media frenzy surrounding her firing, she insisted that at the weekends she was a normal mother who did laundry and hoovering. What she seemed not to appreciate was that few of us watching actually cared about how she managed to keep house while working, whether or not she was a good housewife. All we were wondering was how she found time to spend with each of five children in two short days at the weekend, *particularly* if she was busy doing her own hoovering. The fact that Horlick felt compelled to defend her credentials as a housewife reflects the influence of the fiction which still equates a well-organized, well-managed home with effective parenting, and which places a premium on the ability to manage family life as if it were a series of tasks.

Horlick's autobiography, published in October 1997, did little to persuade the public that she saw motherhood as anything other than a series of tasks to be organized. Given the revelation that part of the Supermum strategy is to buy and wrap some seventy Christmas gifts in October, and that she made a presentation for Morgan Grenfell the morning after her sick daughter was brought back from the brink of death,[9] it is little wonder that many saw her as inhuman and 'terrifying'.

Unfortunately for her, and despite her protestations, Nicola Horlick's autobiography seemed to have the Myth of Managed Mothering written all over it. This particular myth exists in ever more subtle guises, but it is not new, and Horlick is most certainly not the first to personify it. It is simply a reincarnation of Quality Time – a concept that 'holds out the hope that scheduling intense periods of togetherness can compensate for an overall loss of time in such a way that a relationship will suffer no loss of quality'.[10] And, like the concept of Quality Time, it is belied by the realities of family life. It is controverted by the testimony of mothers who have found that there is an enormous price to pay for managing family life as if it were an assembly line and subcontracting the less convenient bits of it as a company subcontracts its non-core activities. It is discredited by the confessions of former Superwomen about the chaos that reigned beneath the smoothly managed surface of their old lives. Until we let go of this myth, we and the corporations we work for will continue to operate as if it were possible for mothers and fathers to be absent from the home for most of the week without anyone noticing, and both parents and children will continue to suffer for that pretence.

Quality Time Come Back to Haunt us

Quality time was an idea about which many people got very enthusiastic in the 1970s and 80s. Quality time was the half-hour of intense attention mothers devoted to their children when they arrived home from the office at 7pm. It was the trip to the adventure park on Saturday that made up for the fact that the mother hadn't seen the children for a week. It was the thing that was better for the children than the prospect of having a frustrated and unfulfilled mother around all day. And it was the thing that was supposed to assuage working mothers' guilt at being absent for most of their children's waking hours.

Not many people talk about quality time these days. They hardly dare, so widely discredited has the concept become. 'I think this idea of quality time is rubbish,' said Rosa Monckton, President of Tiffany and Co. and wife of *Sunday Telegraph* editor Dominic Lawson. Others I spoke to called it phoney, or 'a lie'. Penelope Leach calls quality time a 'snappy American term' for an absurd concept.[11] Sylvia Hewlett, author of *When the Bough Breaks: the Cost of Neglecting Our Children*, is equally condemning of the notion. Short bursts of quality time cannot in any way compensate for long absences, or for the fact that parents' work lives are often too stress-filled to allow them to be good parents.[12] Parents who arrive home exhausted and stressed out cannot give 'quality time', and this does not go unnoticed by the children. A recent survey of American children aged between six and eighteen found that they were resigned to the fact that their parents worked, but didn't like having to deal with the resulting bad moods. When asked, 'If you could do one thing to improve family life, what would it be?', most of the kids surveyed said they'd like their parents to come home 'less wired, less in a bad mood, less keyed up, less tired'.[13]

Newsweek announced that quality time was a myth in an article of May 1997. 'Kids don't do meetings. You can't raise them in short, scheduled bursts. They need lots of attention, and experts are warning that parents may be short-changing them,'[14] insisted the article's author Laura Shapiro. 'Quality time is just a way of deluding ourselves into short-changing our children,' claimed one of the experts she interviewed. 'To be able to have that high-quality time, you have to invest a certain amount of pure time,'[15] said Alison Clarke Stewart of the University of California, whose research showing that babies benefited from being actively talked to may have started us down the quality-time track in the first place. Here in the UK Louette Harding warned readers of *You* magazine not to fall for the quality-time trap.[16] (Unfortunately, her article offered little in the way of solutions to working mothers, and fell back upon the standard clichés about how to 'manage' one's way out of the work–family dilemma.)

Almost any mother who is being honest with herself will admit that the notion of quality time has little to do with what children seem to need from their parents. The time you set aside for it is rarely the time they want it. It isn't possible to *schedule* togetherness times. 'You cannot make a tired baby stay awake for a day's worth of cuddling [or] persuade a one-year-old who wanted you to play this morning to take his one and only chance to play right now,'[17] says Penelope Leach. And quality can be in desperately short supply during the slots of time typically set aside for 'quality' interactions. The after-work/pre-bedtime slot – what one man called the 'hulla-baloo of the kids falling over themselves and messing about with their tea',[18] is a case in point. Women I know regularly refer to it as the hell-hour. Lawyer Sally Bevan admits she used to drive around the block several times to summon up the composure necessary to face it. For me it most certainly represents the lowest-quality time I spend with my girls. As soon as I walk in from work they are transformed into hyperactive creatures tugging at my clothes, fight-ing for a place on my knee, and shouting at whomever else dares to steal even the merest sliver of my attention. If the phone rings in the middle of it all, things degenerate rapidly. It is the end of the day. They are tired. I am tired. They are desperate for my attention. We usually fall out as a result. There's nothing remotely 'quality' about any of it. The time my girls and I spend together is infinitely better when it comes in significant stretches, and isn't compressed into an hour at the end of the day or a morning at the end of the week.

Libby Purves, normally a voice of reason whose books have enabled me to look back upon many a minor domestic crisis with humour and perspective, comes dangerously close to advocating the value of quality time in her book *How Not to Be a Perfect Mother*. She says that 'if you keep covering key times in the child's day, you stay in close touch on fewer hours than a full-time mother'.[19] Purves believes the trick is not to 'lose touch with the daily life of a small child', and describes how this can be done: you can keep in touch by getting the children up and giving them breakfast every day, appearing at lunch-time, taking a child on a trip to do some photocopying or on a visit to the office – and, yes, by focusing on them during the 'sacrosanct half-hour or so before bed'. She adds that if you are 'happy and jokey at breakfast rather than snappish and preoccupied with loading your handbag and putting on your camouflage make-up', that time will be even more valuable to your children.

The key times in the child's day that Purves refers to are much greater in number than those originally envisioned by the quality-time concept, with its hour of stories before bed, and difficult to accommodate within the full-time working mother's diary. It can be hard enough being at home every breakfast time, let alone being 'jokey and happy', and being home every lunch-time and evening in addition. For many working mothers, abiding by Purves's version of the quality-time rules is a virtual impossibility.

Unattainable though Purves's vision of quality time may be, it will still not be good enough for many children, or many mothers. Whenever I try the popping-in-and-out method of staying in contact with my children, it meets with unmitigated failure. Each time I turn up it reminds them that I have not been around all day, and reinforces their desire that I should be. They become confused – am

I home or am I working? – and each departure becomes more fraught than the last. The children deal much more easily with my absence when it has a clearly defined and recognizable beginning and end. And our time together is far better when it stretches for a half or whole day, rather than being sandwiched in between meetings and phone calls.

Quality time may not be a term in frequent use today, but the concept is still with us. It lies beneath Purves's advice about staying in touch for the 'key times', beneath the notion of 'juggling', within books about how to be an organized working mother, and behind the sycophantic profiles of women who juggle a thousand domestic and professional balls without ever letting a single one drop because they are masters of prioritization and organization. The fact is that to be this organized, to juggle this well, you have to compartmentalize your life. You have to divide it up into pieces and allocate a precise amount of time to each piece, and never ever allow yourself to run over time. Time with the children thus becomes one of the pieces that needs to be scheduled. In other words, it becomes quality time.

The Price of Managing Too Much

All working mothers have to compartmentalize their lives and carve out time for their children. A certain amount of juggling is necessary to survive. But when the complexity of the juggling escalates to absurd levels, and time is so compartmentalized that no one child is ever getting very much of it, the quality goes out of family time, and out of family life. The point of it all gets lost, and it becomes what one woman called a sprint to nowhere. Good jugglers, those who have managed mothering down to a precise science, may look as if they're coping well, but many will simply have learned to keep their home lives invisible and under wraps. They are caught in what Steven Covey, author of *Seven Habits of Highly Effective People*, calls 'the activity trap', keeping up with the busy-ness of life, working harder and harder at climbing the ladder of success 'only to discover it's leaning against the wrong wall'.[20]

Most things that are beneficial in moderate amounts become

harmful when taken in excess. This is true of exercise, food, drink – almost anything one can think of. So while some good organizational and management skills can make family life easier, happier and richer, too much of them has the opposite effect. The over-crammed, over-organized family life is one lacking in spontaneity, intolerant of those things that don't fit into the plan, whether those things are the four-year-old who is so nervous about starting school that she clings to you and cries for twenty minutes every morning, or the ten-year-old who stops you for an unscheduled hour to ruminate about why he didn't make the school rugby team. Given that some of the most important times with children are unplanned times, this intolerance for the unplanned represents a lost opportunity to share experiences and build strong, enduring relationships with children.

The erroneous belief that we can structure and schedule everything in our lives is not held by working mothers alone. It is increasingly part of our culture. But 'You can't do everything with the time of your life,' warns Hugo Gurdon, writing in the *Daily Telegraph* in August 1995:

> The belief that life can be scheduled to the last nanosecond is, of course, an illusion, a sort of wishful thinking stimulated by the need to accommodate more and more hectic daily routines, to be committed simultaneously to families and social lives and jobs, and to have long leisurely holidays and enjoy brilliant careers ... Into twenty-four hours are crammed a morning jog, the delivery of children to school, eight hours or more of work, the commute home, a hug for the baby, a welcoming smile for friends who come round for dinner, the washing up, and finally the exhausted collapse into bed. We want to have it all. And when someone or something sticks a spoke into the works, the great roaring machine of our existence is revealed in all its precariousness.[21]

The time-management industry has neither helped us manage our hectic existence nor persuaded us to alter it. Steven Covey maintains that while three generations of time-management techniques have brought us some way towards increased effectiveness in our lives, for most people 'the gap remains between what's deeply important to them and the way they spend their time'.[22] Concerns about quality of life are just as likely to come from people with high levels of time-management training as from people without it. 'We're getting more done in less time,' Covey concludes. 'But where are the rich relationships, the inner peace, the balance, the confidence that we're doing what matters most and doing it well?'

In America, the philosophy of effective management may have infiltrated family life to an even more dangerous degree than in Britain. In her book *Time Bind*, Arlie Hochschild describes how a 'low-grade Tayloresque cult of efficiency has "jumped the fence" and come home'.[23] Where the 1920s engineering genius Frederick Taylor's principles of scientific management were once applied to improve the efficiency of production processes, *home* has now 'become the place where people carry out necessary tasks efficiently in the limited time allotted'. Saving time and squeezing more tasks into any given slot have become the sort of virtues at home that they have long been at work. The domestic time between tasks comes to seem like 'filler' between appointments. As the home becomes Taylorized, the simple pleasures and rewarding moments all but vanish from family life and relationships, and parents find themselves trapped 'in the management paradigm, thinking of control, efficiency, and rules instead of direction, purpose, and family feeling', comments Covey in *Daily Reflections for Highly Effective People*.

Homes that are forced to run according to Tayloresque principles are, more often than not, homes in which many of the caring tasks are delegated. Arlie Hochschild reports that more and more aspects of home life can now be subcontracted, particularly in America where it is possible to send children to summer camps, phone their dinner orders through to day-care centres, and even ask day-care centres to schedule children's extracurricular activities. Here in Britain, the delegation of many aspects of family life is becoming an increasingly popular strategy for coping with the seemingly intractable conflict between work and family in dual-earner households. Philippa Thorpe, head of Philippa Thorpe Designs and mother of three girls, declares 'my whole life is my job' and reveals that a nanny is responsible for everything to do with her children's lives.[24] Indeed, if you are wealthy enough, you can hire nannies who care for children for twenty-four hours a day, drive them to school and back again, take them to all of their activities, make and attend all appointments with dentists and doctors, and keep closets fully stocked with clothes and shoes. You can thus manage, organize and delegate your way free of most parenting commitments.

Delegation may appear to be a sensible way of relieving the stress of managing a household, but taken to extremes, it forces parents to play a peripheral role in their children's lives, and they soon get out of touch. Unless one of you, at least, is tuned in to your children's daily lives, then both of you are likely to be left floating around outside them. One of you has to be there to pick up enough of the signals, share in enough of the daily events, traumas and joys to keep the other parent connected as well. Mary Gibson, an ex-barrister turned stay-at-home mother, commented on the benefits of at least one parent being around for a substantial part of the time: 'Because I know everything about the children, I can plug him into them and enable him to be closer to them. They get far more from him as a consequence of getting more from me.'[25] Another woman, a working mother, echoes her view: 'I have changed my thinking on this a great deal – I really believe that children need at least one parent to be around for a substantial part of their day, most days of the week, to give the children the sense that they are the focus of someone's attention. Without that they feel marginalized.'

Taken to extremes, delegation amounts to the subcontraction of the parenting job. One woman told me a story of a couple she knew, both corporate lawyers who work fourteen-hour days and telephone home their goodnight kisses to their children every evening. 'It works, I suppose,' she said. 'They've set their life up so that someone else is always there. But you know, when you do that you more or less have to admit that the nanny is raising your children – that you've subcontracted your role as parent. And then you have to think, well what's the point in having children at all, then? Just to do your bit to populate the planet?'

The price of subcontracting the job is the lessening of your own influence over your children's development. In small measure this can be a positive thing, but in large measure it surely isn't. And neither is the sense of disconnection from children's lives that goes with both parents sneaking out of the house while their children are asleep, working sixty-hour weeks and blowing bedtime kisses down the phone. 'It is frightening how disconnected many parents are becoming from their children,' commented journalist Yvonne Roberts, who writes regularly about family issues. A recent survey of children by the charity Parents at Work bears out her view. It concluded that children whose parents are not at home much of the time *do* become more independent, but their independence leads to a lack of communication with parents about what is happening in their lives.[26] Former magazine editor Paula Brook recognized the distancing effect in her own family as she and her husband tried to sustain two fast-paced careers: 'While I always knew where my daughters were, I started to wonder who they were,'[27] she wrote.

Parents are often oblivious to the degree to which they have become disconnected from their children. This is probably because, as Yvonne Roberts points out, 'there is a natural tendency to ignore things which are profoundly wrong in family relationships, because in acknowledging them you open the floodgates to so much pain, and potentially the need to reassess one's life'. Granada chairman Gerry Robinson maintains that while children's need for time with their parents is real and important, it is often expressed in such subtle ways that 'if you choose to ignore it, you can'. And rather than face up to the truth, Arlie Hochschild believes some parents deploy a 'needs reduction' strategy – minimizing how much care a child really needs – to resolve the conflict between the structure of work and the demands of home.[28] Susie Orbach would see such parental blind spots as a symptom of the emotional illiteracy afflicting modern society causing people to actively ignore, suppress and disregard their own and others' emotions.

Close friends can often spot what parents cannot or choose not to. Most women I spoke to had stories of friends who seemed to be living lives distant from those of their children. One recounted her impressions of a family in which both parents work long hours in the City, in addition to having other interests which take up much of their Saturdays. Having watched the couple interact with their children on several occasions, this woman commented that the family seemed somehow uncomfortable together, almost unfamiliar to one another. 'Here is a couple who are totally out of touch with their children,' she said. 'They have almost no idea what's going on with them.' Another woman who is godmother to a child of parents who both work long hours was seriously concerned for the child's well-being:

> They never see that child during the week, and they even have a nanny on Saturday morning so they can have some time to themselves. And by Sunday afternoon, both parents are back in their studies again, preparing for the next week. Whenever I go round the child is so desperate for someone to talk to and play with that it makes your heart break. I love my friends dearly, but I think they are really screwing up.

Research shows that these couples are part of a trend: parents are giving much more time to earning a living and much less time to their children than they did a generation ago. One estimate puts the time American parents spend with their children at 60 per cent of what it was twenty-five years ago,[29] and 66 per cent of employed parents with children aged eighteen and under in America indicate that they don't have enough time with their children.[30] In Britain, where parents' working hours have increased during the past decade, a similar decrease in the time they spend with their children will have taken place. A recent survey by Parents at Work revealed that some 60 per cent of working parents feel they do not see enough of their children.[31] In families in which both parents work full-time (estimated to be almost one-fifth of all couples in the UK), and particularly, in which both parents are professionals working long hours (about 7 per cent of dual-income families),[32] the family 'time deficit' will be particularly acute.

It is routinely claimed by the Superwoman camp that mothers today spend *more* time with their children than mothers in the 1960s. But we should be wary of such claims. Many are based upon studies conducted by Jonathon Gershuny of the Economic and Social Research Council Research Centre on Microsocial Change at Essex University. These studies do indeed indicate that mothers spent more minutes per day on pure childcare in 1985 than they did in 1965. But Gershuny's methodology separates out childcare from other domestic duties in a way that completely distorts the reality of daily mothering. Despite the fact that 'childcare activities are enmeshed with other aspects of domestic labour where children are present', Gershuny's studies do not account for childcare that is done alongside other domestic activities like housework and cooking. And the aspect of childcare that is 'about dealing with and being responsive to the interpersonal relations among children and between children and adults' is missed out entirely from his analysis.[33] Which is why he ends up with nonsensical results showing that modern mothers spend forty-four minutes a day on childcare.[34] Equally spurious time categorization methods must underlie S. Horrell's conclusions, as reported in a book edited by Gershuny, that full-time housewives spent 19 hours a week caring for children in 1986.[35] Given that even school-age children require care for about 61 hours a week (excluding the hours when they are either asleep or at school) one wonders who made up the yawning gap between 19 and 61.

Using Gershuny-type analysis, it is possible to claim that mothers spend more time on childcare – that is, totally child-centred activities such as playing hide-and-seek with children or otherwise entertaining them. But the average mother in the 1960s would spend much more time in the presence of and interacting with her children, albeit often while she was peeling potatoes or hanging washing and they were playing outside, than the average mother in the 80s or 90s. To rely on the evidence, such as it is, that mothers today spend more time on pure childcare as some sort of proof that modern-day Superwomen have little to worry about, is to assume that this 'pure' time is somehow more valuable to a child than a more generalized presence. The growing body of experts who now reject the quality-time concept would maintain the opposite: that several hours of general presence go further than a single hour of focused quality time. Children will often tell us the same thing. My own would much rather have me around all day, even if I am cooking and doing loads of washing for much of it, than have me for just one 'quality' hour at the end of every day.

It is easy to get lured into a quality-time frame of mind, and to suppose that the children won't miss your presence while only routine activities are being carried out. But there is a price for subcontracting even the most apparently mundane of jobs, like that of taking the children to school. Any well-organized working mother would delegate the school run in a hurry, and within the normal work environment she would be seen to be 'taking advantage' if she didn't. But parents who never show up at the school gates miss out on valuable opportunities to understand their children's daily experience. They never pick up the gossip from other parents, gossip that can tell them what important changes are being made to the school curriculum, or how their own child is faring at school or even that the following week is 'mountain study week' and all children are required to turn up equipped with kit they think would help them survive a week at Everest base camp.

A certain amount of the trivial, the mundane – the eminently delegable – is necessary to bond your life to your children's. Without it, you may look like a well-organized parent, but you're unlikely to be a connected one. 'It's the banal – making packed lunches and doughnuts for tea and watching Blue Peter with them – that really counts, not the half-hour stories and treat trips to the zoo,' said Emma Bridgewater, interviewed by the *Telegraph* magazine in October 1997, having scaled down her own work commitments to spend more time with her children. 'If you stop wiping their bottoms for them, you're in real trouble,' said another woman, capturing in graphic terms the need for parents to partake in the hard slog of parenting if they are to share in its joys.

Children Paying the Price

On the whole, children are extremely resilient. With the exception of abuse – sexual, verbal or physical – they can stand almost all kinds of treatment, and all kinds of different ways of being raised by parents. So, of the children whose parents never see them during the week and organize life so that others do much of the caring, few are likely to grow up to be delinquents. Few will even turn out to be noticeably maladjusted. They will learn to love the substitute carers, and to tell them all of their stories when they come home from school. And they'll treasure like gems the hours they have with their parents at the weekends.

But parenting shouldn't be about minimizing the damage we do to children. It should be about doing the best by them, and getting the most out of our relationships with them. And long years of working habits and schedules that don't allow for this will leave weakened family relationships, and possibly anxious and insecure children, in their wake. A child will survive in a home in which both parents are gone most of the time, and wired and tired the rest of the time, but they will not be untouched by the experience.

Children have individual and varying needs for time and attention. And it is true, as Libby Purves has commented, that some can have 'two busy working parents and a patchwork of after-school arrangements and clubs and rather enjoy the social variety of it all', while other children 'genuinely need the peace and stability of a daily early tea at home for years' and cannot flourish without 'hours of soothing, supportive conversation'.[36] But however varied children's needs may be, there is a bare minimum of time and attention that all children need in order to thrive. And many today are not getting that bare minimum. Children 'are saying that they don't see enough of their parents', says Joanna Foster, director of the BT Forum for Better Communication. 'Their mums and dads talk logistics – who's going to collect so and so – and not the stuff that nourishes relationships.'[37]

That parental absence has a price is evidenced by the comments made by children of busy, high-profile working parents. In a *Sunday Times* magazine interview, Anita Roddick's daughter Justine described her mother as having been 'a big blur during childhood because she was always rushing from place to place'.[38] When she was twelve, Justine had to resort to faking appendicitis in order to get her parents' attention and communicate her unhappiness. And she felt inadequate when she realized that she wanted to be at home with her own baby rather than being the human dynamo that her mother was and is. Joely Richardson professes to have a strong relationship with her mother, Vanessa Redgrave, and has herself grown up to be a successful actress with a seemingly happy family life. But she still says that she resented the fact that her mother wasn't around much when they were growing up, and that even her mother wishes she had spent more time at home. Richardson says she wants her daughter to grow up a lot more secure than she felt.[39]

The saddest and most telling story I have yet heard is that of a high-powered, workaholic MP and her ten-year-old daughter. The MP was not accustomed to seeing her child during the week, and never had been, but decided to make an exception one Christmas and take her to visit Santa Claus. The two queued for over an hour and finally made it to Santa's grotto. Santa sat the little girl on his knee and asked her what she would like for Christmas. Her reply? 'A new mummy.'

Busy working parents may wish to pretend that their children do not suffer as a result of their work habits. But Yvonne Roberts contends that 'you'd have to be blind, deaf and dumb to your children's needs to insist that you can be absent all the time and not have your child suffer'. In her book, *When the Bough Breaks: the Cost of Neglecting Our Children*, American economist Sylvia Hewlett maintains that the 'time deficit' caused by long parental work days is associated with a series of alarming trends in child development, including higher levels of suicide, eating disorders, drug abuse and academic underperformance.[40] 'I see apathy, depression – a lack of the spunkiness I associate with being a kid,' says Ronald Levant, a psychologist at Harvard Medical School, confirming Hewlett's fears about many American children. 'These kids don't have the self-esteem which comes from knowing your parents are really interested in you, really behind you.'[41] Indications are that children in the UK are beginning to suffer in similar ways to American children. A 1997 Commons Select Committee report estimated that up to a quarter of all children in the UK are suffering behavioural and emotional difficulties.

Parents who work cannot be held solely responsible for trends such as these. The causes of children's distress are linked to those that are responsible for the higher levels of anxiety, depression and mental instability among adults. Poverty is most certainly a factor, as is the combined influence of capitalism, globalization and technology. According to psychologist Oliver James, author of *Britain on the Couch*, these factors contribute to a situation in which most people's expectations outstrip reality, leading to lower levels of serotonin in the brain, and higher levels of misery. To hold working parents responsible for children's psychological difficulties is to ignore this phenomenon. Nevertheless, as Peter Wilson of the charity Young Minds points out, parents whose working habits prevent them from spending enough time with their children are not available to help them cope with the increased pressures they face, and can even contribute to them.

One way in which harried working parents contribute to children's stress and unhappiness, according to Arlie Hochschild, is by attempting to maximize the efficiency with which they carry out domestic and childcaring tasks. In so doing, they 'may inadvertently trample on the emotion-laden symbols associated with particular times of day or particular days of the week', packing 'one activity closer to the next and disregarding the "framing" around each of them, those moments of looking forward to or looking back on an experience, which heighten its emotional impact'.[42] Rapid dinners, speedy baths and short stories are counted as 'worth the same' as slower versions of the same events, when in fact they are missing the rich emotional content and context.

Speeding up domestic life so as to fit it into an ever-shrinking time window leads to what Hochschild calls the 'third shift'. In this shift, says Hochschild, parents do the 'emotional dirty work of adjusting children to the Taylorized home'. This involves 'noticing, understanding and coping with the emotional consequences of the compressed second shift', making up emotionally for their children's unhappiness over a lack of family time. Tantrums, resistance to routines, withdrawal, refusing to leave places when it's time to go or insisting on leaving when it's time to stay – to some extent these are all part of the normal child's repertoire, but when they occur in extreme forms they may be pleas for more control over family time.

A shortage of time often leads parents to give priority to their children's important moments and significant events. Most parents, particularly very busy working fathers, set great store in being present for school plays and sports days – so much so that it is a commonly mentioned strategy for managing careers and family life. In Ruth Tait's book about successful corporate leaders, *Roads to the Top*, the older executives admitted to having some regrets about always having put work before family. The younger executives, on the other hand, claimed that their children always came first.[43] What this turns out to mean in practice is 'if there is a school play, you are there', or 'if they need me, I don't hesitate to cancel [meetings]'. Being present for the significant events and the big emergencies is equated with 'putting family first'.

But if the big events are all parents are present for, all that quality time will allow for, the effect on children could well be invidious. Children may experience childhood as a series of performances, and feel that they are not worthy of attention simply because of who they are, but must earn attention by performing, achieving, showing their parents something. And if parents are there only 'when their children really need them', that says to a child that the daily process of growing up isn't important enough, and only real emergencies will get them attention. It is not difficult to see why children might resort to faking attacks of appendicitis, like Justine Roddick, in order to gain attention. Nor is it difficult to see how they can grow up anxious, and with low self-esteem, as a result of having to 'perform' for the attention they get.

Mothers Paying the Price

If evidence of disturbing trends in child development, and interviews with the children of busy and successful career mothers, aren't enough to convince us of the fallacy represented by the notion that strong management skills and good organization can be a substitute for time with children, the confessions of former Superwomen should be. Read an interview with one of these women before she sees the light, and you'll hear her fervently defending her fast-paced life and outlining all of the mechanisms she uses to structure and survive it. (Barbara Cassani, the American appointed to head British Airways' cut-price airline in November 1997, claimed not to crave more time with her children or suffer from guilt. 'I feel comfortable with the choices I have made,'[44] she told her interviewer, obviously determined not to reveal any cracks in her Superwoman armour.) Read an interview with the same woman after she's decided to give it all up, or to do a less demanding job, and you get closer to the truth. Having given up her job as a designer for Laura Ashley, Antonia Kirwan Taylor looked back on her old life and described it as a 'living hell of domestic management'. She realized that she hadn't managed or 'juggled' at all, but had been 'egotistical, permanently exhausted, incredibly bad tempered' and had compromised every aspect of her life.[45] After resigning from her job as editor of a magazine, Canadian Paula Brook described herself as having been a 'sensationally efficient little machine, a one-woman military operation' who led what looked from the outside to be a rather 'impressive life'. But, on the inside

> I was a wreck, systematically short-changing myself and, as a result, many of the people around me for years, possibly even decades, though I can't be certain exactly when the charade began, because large chunks of time (between 1980 and 1993) seem to have slipped through the cracks in my memory ... By the last few years I had cultivated the appearance of a calm executive who'd happily reached her stride, while feeling more and more like a crazed carousel pony going up and down, round and round, faster and faster, about to become unpinned.[46]

When publisher Elizabeth Perle McKenna had a child at the age of thirty-eight she decided that she would just 'move some of my work life over to the side and let the kid in'. And she did it, for a while: 'I just left the office a little earlier. I didn't take the trips I didn't have to. I skimmed proposals faster. My house was no showpiece. I cooked less, I slept less, but I was doing it.'[47] But looking back, Perle McKenna realizes that she had failed to notice the stop signs and warning messages that flashed past her as she rushed through life and lost a good deal of herself along the way.

Author Ros Coward sees this type of recollection as disingenuous. She claims that women tend to look back and describe their situations as having been much worse than they actually were, because that provides them with a perfect excuse to escape the competitiveness of work without losing face. My conversations with working mothers convinced me that the reverse is more or as often true: many women go on for years denying how bad things really are, and can only fully appreciate the truth once they've stepped back from the fray. 'You can't fully appreciate what it is you have missed until you step back,' says Maeve Haran, 'and many women who are on the treadmill don't know what they are missing at all.'

Few women feel able to give the game away so long as they are deeply involved in it. Carole Gilligan's belief that women tacitly collude in not voicing women's experiences[48] is particularly true where today's working mothers are concerned. Lawyer Anne Marie Piper hates having to maintain the 'whole Superwoman front' but confesses she sometimes feels she has to. Carole Reay says she kept up the front for years, to the extent that she was 'like a schizophrenic', with her work persona living in complete denial of her mothering persona. Now, she believes it is wrong for women to collude in perpetuating the Superwoman image through denial of their 'mothering selves':

> I went to a conference and this woman was standing on the podium talking about having it all – you know, how you just have to prioritize, and organize, and manage the breastfeeding thing. She actually said she couldn't talk about this in the office because it would be unprofessional. I wanted to scream, 'Breastfeeding is neither professional or unprofessional. It just is!'
>
> What I heard that day was a lot of denial. I was hearing that we should put our Superwomen hats on and go to work and not talk about being mothers. One woman told me she never ever said she was going to her children's sports day, but always made some other excuse for her leaving. Well, I think men and women should be able to say they're going to sports day, or going home to see their children.

Journalists Sharon Maxwell Magnus and Yvonne Roberts agree that Superwoman is a mythical figure, belief in whom is perpetuated by women's failure to be honest about what life as a full-time working mother is really like. Referring to the finding that working mothers suffer from stress and exhaustion, and have a high risk of heart attack, Maxwell Magnus insists that 'until working mothers can own up to their family responsibilities, without being penalized, the heartache – and the heart attacks – are set to continue'.[49] 'There is so much silence about this. You hear women talking about juggling and managing, pretending life runs smoothly, when in fact it is chaos behind the scenes,' says Roberts, who is suspicious of the mantra of organization and efficiency chanted by the successful women who maintain that silence. 'The fact is that to be that efficient, you have to push yourself to the point of exhaustion. Exhaustion is usually followed by crisis, then a period of partial recovery, then renewed commitment to the treadmill, followed by more exhaustion. You never really recover. And eventually, it all gives way.'

Some women rethink their lives before the exhaustion reaches crisis point, and are incited to change their lives by what Steven Covey refers to as 'wake-up calls'. Maternity leave is commonly cited as a time during which women 'came to their senses' or 're-evaluated their lives'. Maeve Haran claims it was during her second maternity leave that she became aware of how much she was missing of her daughter's life. For others, long stretches of enforced rest or time away from work afford the same kind of opportunity to evaluate their lives. Rosa Monckton says she decided to change the structure of her working life after she spent several months at home with a broken leg and realized what it was like to have such long stretches of time with her children. For others, the wake-up call came in the form of a loved one's illness, or divorce.

For a few others, the wake-up call never comes, and they combine astonishingly successful and fast-paced careers with family lives without ever threatening to descend into the spiral of exhaustion that Yvonne Roberts describes. But the punishing routines by which they have to live would flatten most people. Tina Brown, the British editor of *New Yorker* magazine and mother of two, rises at 5:30am for her daily run, drops her daughter at school before a breakfast meeting at 8:15am, works until 5:45pm when she leaves to have supper with her children, then works at home until 12:30am.[50] She exists on five hours' sleep a night, and claims never to socialize with friends. Connie Duckworth, the co-chief of Goldman Sachs's Chicago office and mother of four who was interviewed for a *Wall Street Journal* feature in early 1997, spends just three hours with her children between Monday morning and Friday evening. She rises every day at 4:45am, is in bed by 9pm, spends three nights a week away from home, and rarely exercises or sees friends.[51] The writer interviewing Mrs Duckworth describes her life as being 'severely circumscribed'. Most mothers would describe it as horrifying. Portraits of women like Duckworth cannot serve as genuine role models for most of us because so few women are capable of doing it all – as she is purported to do – without cracking up under the strain.

Profiles of the likes of Brown and Duckworth are also, in all likelihood, unrealistic representations of these women's actual lives. For though they aim to astonish us with tales of near-heroic adherence to demanding schedules, they are ultimately designed to paint a picture of the good life, devoid of the chaos, stress, emotional turmoil and regret that overtake the lives of so many who try to juggle demanding full-time careers with motherhood. So in the same *Wall Street Journal* interview we are told that, despite her punishing schedule, Mrs Duckworth 'spends plenty of time sitting on the floor playing with trucks'. 'When, exactly?' we are tempted to ask. Few journalists probe into the price that successful prominent women have paid, or into the quality of their relationships with their children.

But, to steal a phrase from Maeve Haran's character Liz Ward, these images of 'women with the *Wall Street Journal* in one hand and a baby in the other, zapping the Board and still home for bathtime' are, for the most part, 'bullshit'. Superwoman is a fake. However successfully a career woman with children may appear to be managing her life, there is always another side to the story. The story may be one of daily domestic crises and the failure of carefully laid plans. Or it may be the tale of steadily mounting stress, unhappiness and exhaustion. A dear friend of mine, Laura, has long amazed those who know her on account of her apparent ability to withstand a near-tortuous routine. She is the human resources manager for a large multinational firm and lives in Geneva with her husband and three daughters. She leaves every Monday morning (or occasionally Sunday night) to fly to London, or elsewhere in Europe, works punishingly long hours while she is away, and does not return home until Friday. Often, she may have to be away for even longer stretches. Even through her husband's serious illness, she managed to keep up such a pace, and, with him, to raise three perfectly wonderful girls. No one understands how she does it. No one understands how she withstands the daily stress, the gruelling hours, the absences, the family crises. Her friends, men and women alike, constantly marvel at what an incredible person she is. Were someone to write a profile of her for a magazine, it might persuade people that women *can* have it all if they are made of the stuff of which Laura is made. But Laura's life is not as it seems. In private, she describes herself as living on the edge, being permanently over-whelmed by stress and increasingly pained by being separated from her husband and daughters. She has recognized that it cannot go on. She knows she needs time for herself and her family, so she recently took a short sabbatical from work, and is considering ways to reduce her work schedule.

Who knows when Tina Brown, Nicola Horlick, British Airways's Barbara Cassani or any number of other high-powered working mothers might decide, like Laura, that enough is enough, and write their own versions of the stories told by Paula Brook and Antonia Kirwan Taylor? Who knows when one of them might suffer a crisis of the kind experienced by *She* magazine editor Linda Kelsey, forced to quit her job and take up another less demanding one because she simply couldn't do it all? And, even if they are strong enough to avoid personal crisis and the temptation to give it all up for something else, how many of them will live to regret their choices, to claim later in life, as one prominent working mother did, that their generation has failed their children? Who knows when they will be forced to admit, as some of us have already, that managed mothering is a myth?

A Better Managed Workplace, not Managed Mothering

Something has to give. In a family in which both parents' careers are moving at the speed of light, and dragging the family along at the same speed, something will crack somewhere. It may not be the children who suffer most in the end. It may be the mother, or the marriage, instead.

Family life cannot be run like a factory. It isn't supposed to be entirely about fixed schedules, armies of back-up staff and books full of contingency plans. And all the schedules, plans and support staff in the world cannot be an effective insurance policy against the daily hiccups and periodic crises which make up family life. Hiccups and crises are difficult to cope with at any time, but they are infinitely harder to cope with if both parents' lives are stretched to the limit and there's not the tiniest bit of slack in the family timetable. If both parents are working sixty hours a week, if neither feels they have the right to go in late or leave early, and if they both always have briefcases full of work to do in the evening, there's precious little room for manoeuvre. Even with modern miracles like mobile phones, portable computers, modems, faxes and twenty-four-hour nanny services, it won't always be possible to prevent the unexpected in family life from spilling over into work life.

We need to unveil the pretence that it is possible, and admirable, to manage and organize one's family life so well that it can exist quietly and unobtrusively alongside a ten- or twelve-hour-a-day job. We need to call the bluff of those who pretend that no one and nothing suffers when children are raised almost entirely by parent substitutes and managed from a desk at the office. We need to replace our faith in the Myth of Managed Mothering with an honest and realistic appreciation of what children need from us, and what we need from the workplace, if we are to give it to them.

This means that we need a workplace in which it is possible to pursue a career without that career absorbing 90 per cent of our time and energy; where it is possible to work at challenging, interesting jobs that allow us to be at home by five, or where there are part-time jobs and job shares, not just in the lower ranks, but within all ranks of management, including the most senior. We need the flexibility to respond to special family needs and crises without feeling obligated to hide them, lie about them, or delegate them to others. This calls for a shift in working culture such that all of these things are incorporated within an overall commitment to balancing family life with work life. In Part Three we will see just how much the workplaces of today fall short of that vision. But we shall also look at how women, men and the organizations they work for can begin to effect the changes that are necessary to make the vision a reality.

Like all good visions, this one must be based on a commitment to change. And a commitment to change can only come from an honest appraisal of the existing situation, and the needs it creates. Without this honesty, change will never come. Organizations will continue to operate as if families could be raised in a few minutes a day, and individuals will continue to let them. The Myth of Managed Mothering will live on, and some women will appear to be living it, while those who refuse to or cannot will fall off the career ladder.

Surely things cannot go on like this.

CHAPTER FOUR

❖

THE DAY-CARE DREAM

All economic polls show that the principal stumbling block for women
furthering their careers is childcare.
CHRISTINE CRAWLEY, European Parliament's Committee
on Women's Rights, in the *Independent*, March 1992

The only evidence found in disfavour of day-care for young children
has yet to be proved.
KATE FIGES, *Because of Her Sex*, 1994

❖ ❖

IN 1991, PENELOPE Leach took part in an edition of Channel
Four's *Despatches*, which painted a bleak picture of a day at an
expensive private London nursery. In response, the National Children's Bureau took Leach off their mailing list, and the director of
the programme was hauled up in front of the Broadcasting Complaints Commission.[1]

In 1996, headteacher and chairperson of the Independent Schools
Association Paddy Holmes was forced to resign after she condemned
high-flying parents for abandoning their two-year-olds in private
nursery schools, saying that parents who gave up their children to
schools too early were endangering their mental health.[2] From the
'howls of pain from career women, and the yelps of indignation
from schools who provide the very best money can buy, you would
think she had uttered a heresy,' commented one *Telegraph* journalist.

In fact, Holmes's comments did constitute a heresy, as did
Despatches's suggestion that the day-care environment may not be
ideal for young children. The view that day-care might have some
shortcomings, might indeed be bad for children, flies in the face of
a belief that is supported by a host of groups from the Child Poverty
Action Group to the Labour Party to the Day-care Trust. This is

the belief that 'day-care is the source of every blessing', as Patricia Morgan says in her book *Who Needs Parents?*:

> If anything is incessantly and authoritatively acclaimed as the key to economic success, the solution to the demographic crisis, the basis for social justice and equality, the answer to every woman's dream, a great business opportunity, the remedy for poverty, welfare dependency, crime, educational failure and the basis for children's success, it is childcare. For the last ten years or more this has been hammered home as the catch-all miracle solution to a host of complex problems, which will transform the nation and open the gates to Utopia.[3]

Proclamations about the benefits of childcare in the form of group day-care centres are indeed so widespread that they threaten to drown out any assertions to the contrary. Day-care supporters claim that two-year-olds are unlikely to suffer harm from day-care and may even benefit from it,[4] that babies placed in childcare will have connections to their mother every bit as strong as those whose mothers stay at home[5] and that 'small children put into day-care have higher intelligence scores than pre-school infants who stay at home'.[6] The Labour Party's Welfare to Work strategy is based on the claim that good-quality childcare early on in life leads to better educational and employment prospects later on.[7]

Confronted by the din of so many voices all singing the praises of day-care, it is easy to be taken in. It is easy and tempting to see it as the solution to society's ills and to the daily problems faced by working parents. But we should not allow ourselves to be seduced by the miracle of day-care. We should, instead, open our ears and minds to the arguments of those who speak up against the cacophony, those who question the unquestioning faith that so many have placed in day-care. We should listen to parents who regularly weep as they leave their children at day-care centres, and to day-care workers who have witnessed the effects on children of being in large-group environments for ten hours a day. Unless we accommodate these perspectives, learn from them and incorporate them within our family support policies, we could all end up losing. For the Day-care Dream – a day-care place for ten hours a day, five days a week, for every child under five in Britain – could turn out to be a nightmare. And as we proceed towards it, we will be overlooking other forms of change that have far more potential for easing the burdens of working parents and enriching family life. The quest for flexible hours, reduced hours, family-friendly work cultures – all this will be sidelined and stripped of its urgency if the Day-care Dream becomes a reality. Who will be prepared to talk about the need for parents to spend less time at work when every employer can point to a day-care centre prepared to care for a child from breakfast to bedtime, and every working parent gets accustomed to relying on that support? Who will be prepared to speak up for children who miss their parents, when so many are shouting out in defence of the Day-care Dream?

Day-care has already assumed centre stage in the national debate about working mothers, depriving other measures of consideration. Discussions of the 'work/home dilemma', such as that featured in *New Generation*'s June 1997 issue, seem to turn immediately into debates about the merits of day-care versus mother care. Harriet Harman may want to encourage employers to be more family-friendly, but she is quoted most often about the need for childcare to help the '90 per cent' of lone parents who want to work. Anita Roddick has a 'rosy vision of the future' in which 'business acknowledges its responsibility towards protecting the family', but she appears to see that support only in terms of the provision of day-care facilities.[8]

The Day-care Dream, predicated as it is upon the provision of full-time group care for young children, could also lead us to overlook the opportunity to craft a child-centred, flexible childcare strategy – what Peter Moss of the Thomas Coram Research Unit calls a 'child services approach', supporting *all* parents in daily parenting rather than taking working parents' children off their hands so they are free to work long hours.

Britain desperately needs a childcare strategy, and day-care centres will necessarily be part of that strategy. And neither non-parent childcare, as a concept, nor day-care centres as one way of delivering it, are bad in themselves. What *is* wrong is the way the childcare debate is framed and conducted in this country, the way group childcare provision is posited as the answer to the work–family conflict, and the shortage of honest public enquiry into the conditions that render non-parent group care a positive rather than a negative experience for children.

The Conspiracy of Support for Day-care

The range of groups and individuals who express near-unconditional support for day-care is truly astonishing in its breadth and diversity. Feminist writers and journalists have long seen group day-care as the only way to enable women to escape the trap of motherhood and achieve equality. They cannot envisage mothers competing on an equal footing with childless women and men unless there is twenty-four-hour-a-day, fifty-two-week-a-year childcare available to all, and women are relieved of their primary responsibility for the care of children. And they point out, coincidentally, that day-care is good for children.

Politicians of all persuasions have pronounced day-care to be essential to Britain's economic health. Many believe that any expenditure which frees mothers to work promises to repay itself in the form of reduced benefits claims. They also see mothers as an enormous pool of untapped resources which must be recruited if 'we are not to slide into inflationary competition for the shrinking numbers of young in the workforce', and see childcare as the way to enable that recruitment. Many employers agree, and are calling for a national strategy for accessible, available, affordable, quality childcare to help companies be more competitive in world markets by increasing the labour supply, ensuring a flexible workforce, keeping down wage demands and reducing inflationary pressures. For some employers, workplace nurseries and childcare voucher schemes also represent a simple means of fulfilling their commitments to become more family-friendly without having to address the more fundamental barriers to family-friendliness that exist within their businesses.

Barnardo's sees childcare as a solution to child poverty, as 'children are the most at risk when mothers do not participate in the labour market'. There are those, like Dr Ian Roberts of the Child Health Monitoring Unit at the Institute of Child Health, who even see day-care as a means of reducing the rate of childhood accidents and deaths.

So day-care is seen as the panacea, not just for the dilemmas faced by working mothers, but for a whole array of societal problems ranging from Britain's competitiveness in the world economy to child death rates. But it is in the context of the debate about mothers, and whether or not they should work, that the general public most often hears the arguments in favour of day-care. In this public debate, and in response to frequently heard accusations that working mothers harm their children, defenders of the working mother are remarkably predictable in their insistence that day-care, not a return to hearth and home, is the answer. Only the claim that working fathers are the ones who really need to change their habits is heard as often as the assertion that day-care will resolve the working mother's conundrum and absolve her of any misgivings about leaving her children in order to go out to work all day.

When the proponents of day-care hold it up as the wondrous solution to the conflict between work and family, they mislead us time and time again. They misconstrue the link between a mother's ability and willingness to work full-time and the availability of day-care, thereby exaggerating the extent to which day-care can ever be a viable solution to the work–family dilemma. Even more shamefully, they almost invariably exaggerate the positive effects of day-care, while shielding us from its potential ill effects. It is on these two planks – the link between mothers' employment and day-care, and the supposedly overwhelming benefits of day-care for children – that day-care advocates have constructed their platform of unequivocal support for mothers' full-time working.

Day-care as the Working Mother's Salvation

It is frequently claimed that a lack of affordable day-care lies between thousands of mothers and the careers they wish to pursue. The authors of *Tomorrow's Women*, a Demos report on the trends affecting women in the UK, explain that 'partly because of inadequate opportunities at work, and partly because of anxieties about childcare, growing numbers of women will want to be at home',[9] implying that the lack of childcare is one of the primary barriers between women and careers. Among the studies regularly cited as evidence of such claims is one which shows that as many as four out of five non-working mothers would go out to work if they had appropriate childcare.[10] Another is the survey which purported to show that 90 per cent of lone parents (most of whom are women) are desperate to work but are prevented from doing so by a lack of childcare.[11] The experience of other European countries, where childcare provision is more extensive, is often held up as evidence that British mothers are being held back by the childcare problem alone. An article in the *Independent* in January 1992 stated: 'In France and Belgium there are [nursery] places available for 95 per cent of three- to five-year-olds; in Germany for 65–70 per cent; and in the UK for 35–40 per cent. The help that nursery schools give to working mothers is self-evident.' The Day-care Trust points to the fact that there is just one registered childcare place for every nine children under the age of eight as further evidence that working mothers in the UK are disadvantaged relative to other European mothers.[12]

In fact, the link between nursery provision or day-care and mothers' employment is not self-evident. And claims that four-fifths of non-working mothers and 90 per cent of lone parents would work if they had access to day-care are misleading, as are the studies upon which they are based. Moreover, the experience of other countries does not point overwhelmingly to the 'self-evident' help that nursery education gives to working mothers, or to the need for universal day-care to enable British mothers to work full-time.

Patricia Morgan, Senior Research Fellow at the Institute of Economic Affairs and author of *Who Needs Parents?*, exposes the spuriousness of claims that 90 per cent of lone parents are desperate to work. The magic number of 90 per cent is cited with alarming regularity – most often by Harriet Harman, who in late 1997 was managing to sneak a mention of it into every one of her speeches and press releases, but Morgan reminds us that the original survey found that just 28 per cent of lone parents wanted to work 'now' or 'soon', and another 63 per cent would like to work 'later'. 'The ninety per cent is all "in due course", often after the children have grown up, so it can hardly be a "lack of available and affordable childcare" which prevented them from returning to work.'[13]

The Day-care Trust's statement that a registered childcare place exists for only one in nine children under eight is similarly misleading. In the absence of any figures showing the actual level of demand for registered places, it is impossible to know whether 'one place for every nine children' is desperately inadequate, about right, or excessive. Given that most children over the age of five are in school, and that their after-school care needs are unlikely to be met entirely by registered childcare places, and recognizing that many mothers of children under eight are not working and have no desire or need for formal childcare, the figure almost certainly overstates the extent to which formal childcare provision fails to meet parents' needs.

Like the Day-care Trust, the authors of *Tomorrow's Women* oversimplify the link between the availability of childcare and mothers' employment status. Their claim that mothers will increasingly opt to stay home because of inadequate opportunities at work and anxieties about childcare fails to account for the fact that many women stay home full-time because they want to. Some full-time mothers might indeed wish to work if reliable childcare were available, and still others would no doubt work if they were able to find work sufficiently flexible to enable them to spend time with their children, but it is misleading to imply that better opportunities at work and quality childcare provision would dramatically shift the balance between working and home-based mothers.

More relevant than the figures regularly cited by Harriet Harman and the Day-care Trust and the misconstruction of mothers' wishes by the Demos authors is the finding that only 40 per cent of lone (non-working) mothers with children under five wish to be employed, and these have a preference for working part-time.[14] Also relevant is research conducted by Shirley Dex at Cambridge University, which showed that among the wider full-time-mother group, just one in twenty would go out to work if offered full-time childcare.[15] More full-time mothers might be inclined to work if they could obtain jobs limited to school hours or on some other flexible basis, but the availability of childcare alone won't persuade them back to employment.

The basic error in logic underlying forecasts of day-care demand – what Penelope Leach calls the 'blinkered bias of people in grey suits with computers for minds'[16] – leads day-care advocates to insist that huge investments in the expansion of day-care schemes are essential. And day-care expansion has become central to Labour policies, superceding most other initiatives to support working parents, as was highlighted during the debate about Welfare to Work during 1997. The Labour stance emphasized childcare as a solution to the problem of lone parents who are unable to work, and was virtually silent about the need to change workplace practices so as to enable parents to work and care for their own children. Labour's own policy document, *Getting Labour to Work*, highlighted the ways in which the Tories failed to break down the barriers that prevent lone parents from working. The barriers listed included inadequate childcare, an ineffective Child Support Agency, and an inflexible benefit system. Conspicuously absent from their list was any mention of the need to work with employers to improve workplace flexibility. Labour's one-dimensional approach did not go unnoticed. 'Nobody seems to be mentioning flexible hours,' wrote one woman in the *Guardian*. 'It is employers, not mothers, the government should haul in to explain why lone mothers find it so difficult to hold down a job,'[17] wrote another.

Integral to the Labour position is the claim that fewer lone mothers work in Britain than in any other European country because of a lack of childcare facilities. Penelope Leach points out the weaknesses in the assertion that the availability of day-care has necessarily led to vast increases in mothers' full-time employment in other countries: 'While it is clear in most countries that more mothers would go to work if they had access to acceptable and affordable day-care, it is equally clear that many still would not, especially while their children are infants.'[18] In several countries, 'substantial numbers of women who do have access to both day-care and to jobs are voluntarily forgoing the financial and other benefits of outside work during their children's first years,' says Leach. In the Netherlands, for example, fewer mothers are employed than in Britain, despite the fact that more day-care is available. In Denmark, where publicly funded day-care is universally available, fully 30 per cent of women with children younger than school age are not employed. And most Danish mothers who do work still express a preference for working part-time.[19]

So it is in Finland and Sweden. 'Despite the wealth of public day-care facilities for both pre-school children and school-age children, and despite the fact that these facilities, many of them run by local governments, are virtually costless to the parent, women still want part-time work, and they want it for family reasons,' reports Terry Apter in her book *Professional. Progress: Why women still don't have wives*. Patricia Hewitt concluded that the same was true of British mothers. In an article in the *Daily Telegraph* in February 1993, she commented that, though it is often assumed that part-time workers are only reluctantly part-time, none of the non-professional part-time working mothers she had interviewed wanted to work full-time until their children were older, even if childcare made them freely available, and that professional women, more of whom *do* work full-time, are much less satisfied with their lives than are lower-paid women.

Even those faced directly with the facts about women's preferences for fewer working hours find themselves upholding the tenuous logic linking mothers' working practices and preferences directly to the availability of childcare. In one article, *Guardian* writer Lynn Hanna wrote that over 40 per cent of working mothers want to reduce their working hours and that flexible work for both sexes could lead to more fulfilling family lives. Just two paragraphs later, all arguments in favour of fewer working hours, and all evidence that many working mothers want to work less, are cast aside. Hanna says, 'It is no accident that Britain already has the largest part-time workforce in Europe and is one of the poorest providers of nursery education.'[20] Once again, the link between work and childcare, which is complex and influenced by an enormous number of factors, is reduced to its simplest form. The very un-self-evident becomes self-evident in the hands of a journalist in thrall to the myth that day-care is the answer to the work–family dilemma.

The relatively enlightened, too, fall into the trap of seeing childcare as the most important answer to the work–family dilemma. Richard Exell, a TUC policy analyst concerned with family policy who reported to the hearings sponsored jointly by the All-parliamentary Group on the Family and the International Year of the Family UK in 1994, asserted that 'every parent knows that children need time, they need time from their parents. It is a bad lookout for the future of families in this country if work is demanding so much of parents that they cannot give children the attention they need.'[21] Within seconds, he seemed to have forgotten that the crucial issue was 'time' and had jumped on to the childcare bandwagon. 'There are certain important ways in which the government can help deal with this conflict. First of all, childcare,' he said.

Most tenuous of all is the link that is purported to exist between childcare and women's ability to shatter the glass ceiling. For, as Natasha Walter pointed out in the *Guardian* in May 1997, 'professional women are usually able to afford childcare even under the present piecemeal system, and their problems can't be answered by better nurseries and after-school clubs'. Even the theory that childcare will help get more women into the employment pipeline, thereby increasing the chances that any given woman will make it to the top, is ill-founded. There are already more than enough women 'in the pipeline' – women make up as much as 40 per cent of manufacturing workers, half of those in banking, insurance, finance, hotels, catering and shops, and two-thirds of the employees in schools, hospitals and public services.[22] Better childcare may be welcomed by them, but it is unlikely to be a decisive factor in their career progression.

The assertion of a direct link between childcare and work patterns is, to some extent, the inevitable result of the phrasing of the questions in the surveys that are regularly carried out to inform debate on the subject. These tend to ask whether childcare is a problem or a barrier for parents. Confronted with such questions, almost any mother, working or not, will say yes. Asked how important is reliable childcare in helping them return to work, most people, like three-quarters of lone parents who responded to a survey by the Department of Social Security, would say that it is 'essential' or 'very important'.[23] And the fact that 'mothers in professional and managerial jobs who have returned to work after a career break cite "the ability to organize satisfactory childcare" as the most important factor influencing their decision to return to work', or that three-quarters of such women claim that childcare has affected their job and career choices,[24] would not surprise anyone.

People *will* assert the importance of childcare and its influence over their career decisions because finding the right childcare is an enormous headache to parents, whether they are seeking it for five hours a week or forty. But the availability of a full-time day-care place would not necessarily alleviate that headache, because the 'importance of childcare' and the fact that it is a 'barrier' has only partly to do with the fact that day-care places are rare and expensive. It has as much to do with the fact that the task of finding a person (or people) worthy of trust and faith, who relates well to both parent and child, and deciding how much time is the right amount of time to leave a child in that person's care, is inherently difficult. It is a task that is rarely carried out without emotional anguish and torturous soul-searching. Losing a treasured nanny of five years and searching for a replacement who could match her in terms of competence, reliability and sheer love for my children proved to be one of the most stressful experiences I had ever undergone. My concern about childcare, my sense of it as a barrier, is simply integral to the childcare question. It would not have been alleviated in the least by the availability of state-subsidized places in a local day-care centre for my children. Neither would a child's anguish on the departure of a much-loved childcare worker from a day-care centre be eased by the knowledge that another would soon take her place. The *point* of childcare is relationships between carers and children, and it is the difficulty of creating and maintaining these relationships that causes most of the concern about childcare, not simply the unavailability, costliness and inconvenient opening hours of day-care centres. As the former Assistant Director for day and residential care in the London Borough of Camden, Trudy Marshall, pointed out, the '*qualitative* aspects of the relationship between the infant and his care-taker are vital for the infant's emotional development'[25]; most parents know this, and it is the reason why they take the childcare question so seriously and see childcare as such a barrier.

Childcare is undeniably a significant issue affecting women's choices about work, and for women who face the prospects of earning a below-average income the lack of affordable childcare is an enormous impediment to their searching for and finding employment. But there is no simple formula equating the availability of day-care places with willingness to work, or reduced anxiety about childcare choices, even for low-income, working-class mothers whose desire to work is based entirely on economic need. Says Maureen Freely of the 'New Deal' mothers she interviewed, 'They are no less picky about childcare than middle-class mothers. They would sooner starve than place their children in sub-standard care. Simply making places available, as the government hopes to do by training up unemployed youths, does not in any way meet these women's needs. And though almost all women would benefit from support in finding, selecting and paying for childcare, it is less certain that such help would significantly influence middle-class and professional women's long-term career decisions. Tax allowances for childcare costs were high on the wish lists of professional women I spoke to. Some also mentioned the need for more comprehensive regulation, in the form of a national register for nannies, and stricter monitoring of child-minders. But few saw day-care, or childcare of any sort, as a panacea. None mentioned the cost or availability of childcare as a key factor in their choice of whether or not to work and how much to work, or as a factor influencing their career aspirations.

Even fewer women saw workplace day-care as their ideal solution. Peter Moss claims that many people have come to realize that 'the concept of employee childcare is problematic', and that in the United States research has shown that many employees with access to on-site care were disillusioned. On-site day-care can involve dragging children on long journeys on public transport during the rush hour, and removing them from local communities and therefore causing dislocation once they start school. And it can place great strain on parents, binding them to work situations which they would otherwise choose to leave. 'Employee childcare is narrow in concep-tion, divisive in practice and starts from the needs of employers,' says Moss. Other options are preferable to workplace childcare, and 'the main area for employer initiative comes in tackling the culture and structure of the workplace'.[26]

Even employers who provide workplace nurseries are sceptical about their value. Fiona Cannon, head of equal opportunities at Lloyds TSB, which has subsidized nurseries at several sites, does not believe that workplace care is the answer. 'If you ask the parents who use it, they are grateful, but they don't view it as ideal,' she says. 'You can never provide it for enough people, and it is particularly difficult when decisions are made to close down particu-lar sites, and with them the nursery facilities. All of a sudden, wrapped up in a business decision is the care and welfare of fifty small children.'

Cannon, like Moss, has come to recognize that there is no straightforward, direct relationship between the availability of affordable childcare and parents' career choices. Many mothers, and an increasing number of fathers, want access to time with their children as much as or more than access to quality childcare. Assertions about the need for full-time day-care which fail to consider the childcare issue within the context of an understanding of parents' need for time with their children represent a corruption of the truth. They deflect our sights from the arena for change that is as important, if not more so, than that represented by childcare. That arena is the workplace itself.

Day-care 'for the Children's Sake'

Day-care advocates do not stop at oversimplifying the link between day-care and mothers' employment. They also misrepresent the facts about the effects of day-care on children's well-being. Almost every ploy imaginable is used to persuade us that day-care is not only not harmful to children, but is positively, and without qualification, good for them. History is called upon to demonstrate that mother care is unnecessary; expensive day-care 'show projects' are widely publicized and quoted whenever the case for normal day-care is put; studies of underprivileged children are called upon to demonstrate the benefits of day-care for all children; the subtle caveats and subtext of studies are omitted; evidence of the negative effects of day-care is regularly dismissed or ignored; and terminology is manipulated so that part-time nursery education becomes synonymous with full-time day-care, with all the benefits of the former being attributed to the latter.

Misinterpreting the lessons of history
The case for day-care is greatly enhanced if it can be shown that mother care is neither necessary, not necessarily good for children. So the denigration of mother care has long been a feature of writing about alternative forms of childcare, particularly in feminist literature. In *The Female Eunuch* Germaine Greer wrote that 'the intimacy between mother and child is not sustaining and healthy' because it

leads the child into 'badgering her with questions and demands which are not of any real consequence, embarrassing her in public, blackmailing her into buying sweets and carrying him'.[27] Twenty years later, Ros Coward denigrated the 'mother care is best' ethos that she saw as such a burden to women. As a remedy for the problem of mothers increasingly bearing 'the burdens of educating, disciplining, stimulating and comforting the child', she prescribed 'greater allocation of public funds to educational, health and child-care resources' and a publicly supervised and less 'haphazard' day-care system which would be less dependent on 'individuals finding other individuals'.[28]

For feminist writers, if mother care provides a poor model for childcare in the future, history provides a positive one. Feminists are quick to see historical childcare practices as proof positive of the benefits of communal care. Greer insists that 'stem' families from history, and from less developed parts of the world, represent a far superior model for raising children than the modern-day ideal of mother care. While children raised in the nuclear family 'wish their parents to be there all the time and scream when they go out,' she says, in homes where dozens of family members live, people come and go freely and children never scream or manipulate their parents. Feminists regularly hark back to the days of old in an effort to prove that communal care, and care by people other than the mother, is a far from outrageous notion, and many have uttered a version of 1970s feminist Annie Oakley's declaration that 'employed mothers are only, after all, doing what women have done throughout history and in all cultures, which is to participate in the economically productive life of society'.[29]

Though history does indeed provide alternative models of child-care, a simple translation of historic practices into current-day ideals is inapt. Most obviously some of the conditions which enabled women to be both economically active and certain of their children's care and well-being no longer exist to the extent that they once did. As society has become more mobile, parents often find themselves living at long distances, removed from their own extended families, and communities are not always made up of people willing and able to watch over each other's children. Where these changes have taken place, day-care centres cannot hope to fill the gaps they create. Day-care centres in which children are cared for in a ghetto-like environment by childcare workers who come and go do not in any way resemble the environment of a small, closely knit community, or a home inhabited by a large extended family.

Showcasing the underprivileged

Day-care supporters do not rely on history alone to make the case for day-care as a superior form of care. They hold up the results of a few well-publicized modern-day studies as proof that all children can thrive in group day-care. But, warns Patricia Morgan of the Institute of Economic Affairs in *Who Needs Parents?*, 'the public get fed partial or misleading findings from very unrepresentative early-intervention or other "showpiece" projects, usually for highly disadvantaged children', which are 'promulgated as if they were normal', when in fact they 'have little or no relevance to non-parental care as it is routinely experienced in the UK or the US.'

The showcase project most regularly highlighted by day-care advocates is the Perry Pre-school Project in Michigan, USA, often referred to as the Ypsilanti study. This study set out to determine 'whether high-quality, active learning programmes that supported children's cognitive and social skills with individualized teaching could provide both short- and long-term benefits to black children of low intelligence, living in poverty'.[30] The programme group contained fifty-eight children. Half of these were from families on welfare, homes in which the father was unemployed, or in families headed by single mothers, and the majority had IQs in the range of the borderline mentally retarded. The programme itself was as unrepresentative of normal day-care programmes as the children were of the general child population: it used consistent supervision by specialist consultants, involved a daily two-and-a-half-hour class-room session, and had a high level of outreach to parents, with weekly one-and-a-half-hours home visits to each mother and child. 'Twelve hours of teaching a week, with a highly intensive learning programme, cannot be equated with daycare, and neither are the results applicable to ordinary nursery-school provisions,' says Patricia Morgan.

Despite the fact that the Ypsilanti study is entirely unrepresentative in terms of both the programme itself and the children who took part in it, it is frequently quoted in support of arguments for universal day-care. Fran Abrams, writing in the *Independent* in April 1996, pointed to a US study which showed that 'after a good nursery education, young children were five times less likely to become delinquent and three times more likely to own their own houses when they grew up' – both of these facts were findings of the Ypsilanti study – to support an assertion that working mothers should not worry because 'there could be positive advantages to taking children out of the home'.[31] In *The Century Gap* Harriet Harman relies almost exclusively on the study to support her claim that day-care is beneficial for children. (Harman references just two other pieces of research, one of which involved children in nursery school rather than day-care.)[32] Kate Figes quotes the study as evidence of the benefits of day-care, saying that children with pre-school education were more likely to complete their schooling and go on to further education.[33] Like Harman, Figes's argument is heavily reliant on the Ypsilanti results. She cites just two additional studies, one of which involved children of impoverished families attending a high-quality nursery school.

That underprivileged children benefit from being placed in environments in which they receive more attention and stimulation and have access to greater numbers of books, games and toys than at home would not be news to many of us. But it hardly amounts to a ringing endorsement for day-care as the ideal childcare option for most children. Day-care advocates, consumed with enthusiasm for day-care and unwilling to accept the politically incorrect notion that the *relative* benefits of day-care depend, in part, upon children's income and social class, overlook this. For innocent parents, so often on the receiving end of these advocates' conclusions but rarely invited to dissect the studies on which those conclusions are based, making informed judgements about the merits of day-care becomes a virtual impossibility.

Ignorance is bliss

Using showcase studies involving underprivileged children to hood-wink the general public about the benefits of full-time day-care for all children is irresponsible. Failing to mention the caveats attached to studies is equally so, and neglecting to acknowledge those studies that have produced more negative assessments of the effects of day-care borders on the fraudulent.

Many studies that uncover positive effects of day-care on children have important caveats attached to their findings. These often concern the applicability of the findings beyond the sample group where that sample group is extremely unrepresentative, as in the Ypsilanti study. Other caveats have to do with the quality of the care received and the amount of time children spend in care. So, the fine print underlying many a report on day-care will warn that the positive results achieved in a particular study are relevant only where the care is of the highest quality, and where children are not in care full-time. Unfortunately, many day-care advocates neglect to draw attention to the fine print, and parents, unaware of the studies' caveats and the experts' ambivalence, are readily reassured by day-care professionals' jargon and their claims of great educational and social gains for children raised in groups: one survey in the United States showed that 'three out of four working mothers believe their child learns more in day-care than if he/she stayed home'.[34]

That day-care must be of the highest quality to benefit children is often added as an afterthought to reports of findings. It is uttered so automatically that a parent could be readily convinced that quality is easily achieved within the context of affordable group care. The word 'quality' is also used in the absence of any explanation of what, exactly, constitutes quality and how much it costs. So when the *Guardian* endorses researcher Kathy Sylva's conclusions that 'high-quality day-care produced positive results, low-quality adverse ones',[35] many parents may breathe a sigh of relief, being in near-complete ignorance of what quality means, and believing their own local day-care centre to be of the highest quality.

What is quality care? It is almost certainly not represented by the allocation of £300 million to training unemployed youths to be childcare workers, as recommended by Harriet Harman in 1997. In the words of educational psychologist Ed Melhuish in the *Daily Telegraph*, it is 'individual attention'.[36] For Penelope Leach too, quality means continuous one-to-one attention from a competent adult who cares deeply about the child and is in tune with his or her needs and moods (not necessarily the child's mother). Research into brain development has led experts to define quality care as that based on warm, caring relationships with carers, involving response to individual children's cues and clues and recognition that each child is unique, plus lots of one-to-one conversation with each child.[37] Quality care, as defined in this way, is not easily achieved in a group-care setting, particularly, as Leach points out, given current levels of tolerance for public funding. While the guidelines accompanying the 1989 Children Act recommend a ratio of carers to children aged under two of 1:3 (and a ratio for children aged between two and three of 1:4),[38] a survey of eighteen British nurseries produced an average ratio of 1:4.6, while data from an American study showed that the *recommended* ratios for infants ranged from 1:3 in three states to 1:8 in four others.[39]

A study of British nurseries by the Thomas Coram Research Unit found that most were very isolated and many had poor staff:child ratios, problems with accommodation, poor pay and conditions, and instability as regards care-givers.[40] A later study of 15 nurseries carried out by the National Children's Bureau in 1997 resulted in similarly damning conclusions. Researchers found that in the majority of nurseries, interactions between staff and children were fleeting, few one-to-one interactions took place, and the keyworker system (where one child is looked after by one or two members of staff) consistently failed to work.[41]

Achieving an ideal ratio of carers to children, paying the kinds of salaries that would be necessary to attract and retain high-calibre staff, and investing the kinds of sums necessary to train these staff, would raise the costs of day-care well beyond the levels seen today, and certainly beyond the budgets that most governments are pre-pared to allocate. One expert estimated in 1988 that American parents *ought* to be paying around $150 per child per week for quality care, when in fact they were paying just $55 per week.[42] Similar ratios apply in Britain. One excellent nursery showcased by a March 1998 *Panorama* programme costs £150 per week per child (this is subsidised by the local council), whereas others in the neighbourhood deemed substandard cost just £75 per week.

The cost of an early-childhood service of the type described by Peter Moss and Helen Penn in *Transforming Nursery Education* is even higher. Such a service would consist of not just day-care for under fives, but would be a 'comprehensive, integrated and coherent early-childhood service'[43]. Providing a range of facilities for all families, it would be overseen by a single government department, and reflect major reform in the training and employment conditions of the early-childhood teachers who ran it. The model for such a comprehensive system exists in Denmark, and parts of it are represented by services provided in Sweden, Spain and Italy. Moss and Penn estimate that the cost of running such a service in Britain would amount to about £8 billion, or 1.2 per cent of GDP per annum, excluding capital costs. That is the equivalent, says Moss, of about a quarter of the current education budget.

Moss is a fervent believer in the potential benefits of providing such early-childhood services, having witnessed them in operation in Scandinavia and Italy. But he is acutely aware of their cost, and of the difficulty of persuading a government and its electorate to foot the bill. He and others are working to change perceptions about what 'quality' care for children means, and to lobby for the funds to be allocated. Unlike so many others who participate in the day-care debate, he does not pretend that full-time day-care, as we know it, is the answer to the work–family dilemma, or bandy around the term 'quality' as if it were easily achievable within existing frameworks and funding limits. He doesn't try to pretend that parents need not be concerned about the possible risks to children of day-care as it is currently construed.

The facts about time in care, like those about quality and what it costs, are often omitted from reports that sing the praises of day-care, or hidden within the small print and footnotes. An American magazine, *Self*, announced in August 1996 that working mothers could 'rest a little easier' because research shows that fifteen-month-old infants in childcare didn't have trouble bonding with their mothers. The fine print revealed, however, that the conclusion only holds true when the care is of extremely high quality and provided the child isn't in care for lengthy periods. 'Lengthy', according to that study, means more than ten hours a week. The upbeat message of the piece, intended to reassure working mothers, would have been more accurate had it read: 'Very young children fare best when they spend less than two days a week in childcare.'

That time in care is an enormously important factor is borne out by many other studies. The Thomas Coram Research Unit found that children who went to nurseries before the age of nine months for more than twenty hours a week showed distress and negativism at eighteen months. A study in Texas carried out by Deborah Lowe Vandell and Mary Ann Corasaniti found that 'children who received the most extensive and earliest childcare received the poorest teacher and parental ratings for peer relationships, compliance, work habits and emotional health, as well as the most negative peer reports'. A large-scale synthesis of eighty-eight studies conducted by C. Violato and C. Russell concluded that 'regular non-parental care *for more than 20 hours per week* had an unmistakably negative effect on social–emotional development, behaviour, and attachment' [italics mine]. American childcare expert Jay Belsky's work also suggests that the risks associated with day-care are much higher when children are in care for more than twenty hours per week.

Even those who work in day-care centres are wary of advocating full-time day-care for young children. An experienced workplace day-care worker interviewed by Arlie Hochschild for her book *Time Bind* thought that most children did well under her care but was convinced that nine hours a day in care was too long, and that most three- and four-year-olds should have a maximum of six or seven hours a day of centre-based care.[44] The day-care workers who took part in British researcher Trudy Marshall's study felt that the nursery hours for the children were too long and thought that a period from 9am to 3:30pm or, alternatively, part-time places, were long enough.[45]

Time of entry into day-care has also been proved to be a critical factor influencing its effects on children. Belsky's work suggests that the risks are greater when children enter day-care in the first year of life. This belief is reflected in Swedish parental-leave policies, which allow for eighteen months' leave on almost full pay, and in the fact that few Swedish parents put their infants into day-care.[46]

With findings like these, why is it that time is almost never mentioned in the popular media debate about the merits of day-care? Why is it that day-care advocates tend to insist that day-care is good for children, full stop, without disclosing that time in care is an important factor determining its effectiveness? Why is it that, in the media Mother War and the debate about day-care that is part of it, we are being conned into thinking that the only relevant question is whether or not day-care is good for children, when the real question is actually, 'How much non-parent care should children have, and how can parents' working patterns be structured to accommodate that?'

Just as the caveats about time in care are so often omitted from the discussion, so is evidence that paints a negative picture of the effects of day-care. Its advocates are inclined to make grandiose claims about the extent to which research supports a positive view of day-care. Susan Faludi claimed that 'research over the last two decades has *consistently* found that if childcare has any long-term effect on children, it seems to make them slightly more gregarious and independent [italics mine]'.[47] British author Kate Figes claimed: '*All* research into the effects of day-care has shown that children with nursery education have better developed language and better cognitive and social skills [italics mine]'.[48] Fran Abrams proclaimed in the *Independent* of 26 April 1996 that in the academic world there is *little disagreement* about whether or not day-care harms children [italics mine]. And in February 1997, Dr Ian Roberts, Director of the Child Health Monitoring Unit, was quoted in the *Daily Telegraph* as having said: 'There *isn't a scrap of evidence* that putting children in day-care while their mothers go to work is bad for their health or education [italics mine]'.

In an effort to promote the merits of group care over those of care by mothers, Adrienne Burgess cites evidence that 'almost one in three children raised by stay-at-home mums exhibit, in psychological testing, an anxious attachment, which means that they do not feel sufficiently secure to be able to freely explore the outside world'.[49] What Burgess neglects to mention is that several studies have shown an even higher rate of anxious attachment in children in non-parental care for over twenty hours a week.[50] Some children *are* anxious, and their anxiety is not necessarily engendered by their spending long periods in a mother's care; rather, it can be intensified by extended periods of non-parental care. That more subtle interpretation of the facts found no sounding in Burgess's book.

As Patricia Morgan showed in *Who Needs Parents?* her comprehensive review of work on childcare, there is more than a scrap of evidence that putting children in day-care can be bad for them in some circumstances. Studies by the Thomas Coram Research Unit in Britain, and by Anne Robertson, Deborah Lowe Vandell and Mary Ann Corasaniti in the United States, all concluded that day-care could adversely affect children's emotional health and social competence. A study by P. Schwartz found more avoidant behaviour in eighteen-month-olds who had been in full-time day-care, and another study in Chicago found a higher rate of anxious attachments in children who had been in non-parental care for more than twenty hours a week. Four studies by Jay Belsky produced 'an overall rate of insecure attachment' of 41 per cent among children in out-of-home care, compared to 26 per cent in home care. And, as mentioned previously, a large-scale meta-analysis of eighty-eight studies found that excessive amounts of non-parental care have an unmistakably negative effect.[51]

Apart from the large-scale studies and meta-analyses, some short-term studies of individual day-care centres suggest that the day-care environment as we know it is often inadequate and potentially harmful to children. These include the studies of British nurseries conducted by the Thomas Coram Research Unit and the National Children's Bureau in the 1990s, and earlier studies of single nurseries such as those conducted by Trudy Marshall, then assistant director for day and residential care in the London borough of Camden, and Dr Juliet Hopkins, child psychotherapist with London's Tavistock Clinic. Having observed the care of nine under-twos in a local day-care centre for a total of just over forty-eight hours, Marshall concluded that the care provided was entirely inadequate and potentially harmful to the children. In the nursery she observed in 1980, she noted that the attention of adults flitted from child to child and rarely lasted more than thirty seconds with any single one; that nurses frequently missed signals about children's needs and levels of distress and tiredness; and that 'to comfort a distressed child did not appear to play any part in the repertoire of adults in their daily care of the children'. Her appreciation of the difficulty of improving such institutional practice under the prevailing conditions of resource constraint and staff inexperience led her to suggest that 'sensitivity cannot be found and sustained in group care of infants under two',[52] and that policy and practice ought to be changed to facilitate the provision of individualized care. Having studied the practices in a group of day-care centres for children from disadvantaged backgrounds in 1987, Dr Juliet Hopkins reached similar conclusions. And the recent study of 15 nurseries carried out by the National Children's Bureau in 1997 suggests that practice is sub-standard even in some privately funded nurseries.

Some mothers have reached the conclusion that day-care is potentially harmful, basing this on the observation of their own children and without the benefit of objective observational studies like those conducted by the Thomas Coram Research Unit, Marshall and Hopkins. One friend of mine removed her daughter from a day-care facility catering for children between the ages of three months and five years because it was frenetic and noisy and her child was clearly not happy there. Another mother witnessed the way children were being cared for at a local, privately funded crèche: a group of young, uninterested girls chatted and ate their lunch while fifteen two-year-olds wandered around the room aimlessly, talking and interacting with no one. She vowed never to leave her children there. Another mother, Lucy, reduced the time that her two children spent in day-care from three days per week to just two mornings. For her, day-care did not in reality in any way match up to the Day-care Dream, and she believed her children were suffering as a result:

> The worst thing is that it tires them out. They have to be in an environment with lots of other children all day, sharing their toys and sharing the attention they get from their carers all day. That's exhausting, and not fair on them. My two used to come home utterly shattered from the whole experience, whereas now they love it. They go to the centre just two mornings a week, and they love spending the rest of the time at home. The other thing about day-care is that it institutionalizes children from such an early age. They learn how to behave in an institutional environment. They don't learn how to go to Sainsbury's, or play with children in their own home, or do any of the normal family things.

Day-care workers themselves often have the worst horror stories to tell. A nanny I spoke to began nannying after having become disillusioned with group care. She described the privately funded day-care centre where she worked as having been overcrowded, noisy, stressful, and staffed by carers who were completely uninterested in the children: 'The children were treated like animals, even to the point where their plates of food were thrown on the table in front of them.' Another former day-care worker confirmed that such uncaring, noisy and stressful conditions existed in several day-care centres in which she had worked. Two former operators of a quality day-care centre quoted in Morgan's book closed their centre after 'three years of watching how children in day-care suffer from separation anxiety and depression despite competent staff'.[53]

Observations such as these are rarely accounted for by day-care supporters. But in discounting them, we tempt parents into believing that long days in group care are associated with no risks for children. It is important to listen to people like the mother who wrote that her twenty-two-month-old son would throw his hands over his eyes and scream as he approached the nursery gates; and the parents who found that their son 'would clutch our knees and cry harrowing sobs of despair' when dropped off at the nursery, and would be found 'sitting in a row of high chairs, like an orphan, waiting to be fed, or lying in his cot, awake but silent, dazed, and almost catatonic'[54] when they returned at the end of the day. The way the childcare propaganda conflicts with the experience of many parents should alert us to the possibility that all is not what the day-care advocates make it out to be.

Set against the multitude of formal studies, observational exercises and anecdotal horror stories that have raised questions about group day-care as a satisfactory form of care for young children, claims that no evidence exists to suggest that day-care is harmful or that all research points to its benefits are grossly misleading. Much is yet to be proved. Some studies have resulted in positive assessments of day-care, and a great many others have produced negative assessments, but no study has produced unequivocal conclusions. Day-care advocates themselves might admit to this when not embroiled in the heated debate about whether or not mothers should work at all, a debate which invariably forces people to adopt extreme positions. Dr Roberts, for instance, qualified his statement to the media in a private interview with me. He claimed *not* that research showing day-care to be harmful does not exist, but rather that no research based on randomized trials exists. Randomized trials are, according to Dr Roberts, the best and most reliable way to assess results, while other forms of enquiry can mean misleading conclusions. Roberts and his team spoke to childcare experts and scanned electronic databases and literature worldwide in search of randomized trials. They found eight, none of which produced any evidence that day-care was harmful to children.

Careful reading of the paper that Dr Roberts and his colleagues produced to support his claims reveals, however, that he is as guilty of making sweeping generalizations based on inappropriate or loosely interpreted data as are the likes of Harman, Figes and Faludi. One of the eight studies used by Roberts to substantiate his claim that day-care has only beneficial effects is the famous Ypsilanti project, the study of severely underprivileged children with IQs in the range of the borderline mentally retarded (see p. 115). In fact, of the eight studies footnoted in Roberts's paper, six were very obviously conducted with underprivileged or mentally retarded children: they examined the effects of day-care on 'teenage mothers and their children', on 'preventing mental retardation in children at risk' and on 'the prevention of intellectual impairment in children of impoverished families'. It would be abundantly clear to any lay person that studies of the mentally retarded, children of teenage mothers, and children at risk should not be used as the basis of generalizations about how care affects the behaviour and prospects of the average child.

Roberts would be justified in saying that the eight randomized trials he looked at indicate that day-care is not harmful, and that other forms of enquiry are less reliable than random trials. He would be correct to suggest that day-care which takes disadvantaged children out of impoverished environments in which they receive little stimulation or supervision renders them more likely to stay on at school, hold down a job, and avoid conviction for criminal offences than their even more disadvantaged peers who do not receive day-care. But he is wrong to claim that not a scrap of evidence exists to suggest that day-care can have negative effects.

When I spoke to Roberts, it became clear just why he had delivered such a crisp, unequivocal statement in favour of day-care. 'I just felt that the *Panorama* programme ['Missing Mum', see p. 2] was so outrageous that something had to be said to refute it,' he said. There could surely be no clearer example of how the Mother

War, in which the wrong questions are posed and only extreme and unequivocal responses are sought, forces even those with the best of intentions into corners and eclipses the truth.

Strong pro-day-care statements, like those made by Dr Roberts, directly contradict observations of individual nurseries as well as a vast body of research which suggests that any advocation of day-care's benefits should be matched by concern for its potentially negative effects. Such an assured public stance implies that judgements about day-care can be made independent of knowledge about its quality, or that quality in day-care is easily assured and afforded. Such a stance dissuades people from investigating the nuances of the available research, nuances which confirm the importance of care that provides individual attention to each child, the need to limit any individual child's hours in care, and the importance of the children's home environment in determining whether they will thrive or suffer, relative to others like them, in a day-care environment.

The Ultimate Ploy: Day-care as Nursery Education

In case the suppression and manipulation of evidence should prove insufficient in the quest to persuade us that day-care is the answer to the work–family dilemma, and is beneficial for children, the day-care advocates keep one more ploy up their sleeve. The ultimate ploy, the one with the greatest smoke-and-mirror effect, is that which rests on semantics: it is the use of the two terms, 'day-care' and 'nursery school', interchangeably, as if they were one and the same thing.

Kate Figes is so anxious to affirm the merits of day-care that she presents evidence about nursery education to defend it, even confusing the terms 'day-care' and 'nursery education' within a single sentence: 'All research into the effects of day-care has shown that children with nursery education have better developed language and better cognitive and social skills.'[55] Figes regularly flip-flops between the terms 'pre-school education', 'nurseries' and 'day-care' as if they were the same. Harriet Harman falls into the same trap in her book *The Century Gap*. She cites the finding that those children who attend *nursery schools* on average adapt better to primary school, as well as the US Ypsilanti study, as evidence that *day-care* is good for children. Journalists regularly use the term 'nursery school' when they mean 'day-care', and vice versa. Colette Kelleher, director of the Day-care Trust, does not help to clarify matters when she says that what working parents need is 'early-years care and education for their children' because research shows that 'this is good for children',[56] thereby reinforcing the misconception that 'early-years care' is the same as 'education', and that the same research applies to both.

But day-care and nursery education are very different things. Nursery education is most often for children aged over two and a half years, and typically consists of between six and twenty hours a week of care, depending on the ages of the children. Day-care, on the other hand, can be for children as young as three months old, and can mean ten hours a day, five days a week, in a group-care environment, separated from parents. To confuse the two through terminological inexactitude and to use evidence in support of one to demonstrate the value of the other is irresponsible.

Penelope Leach writes of the dangers of confusing the two in *Children First*. She claims that popular and positive images of day-care are formed on the basis of pictures of groups of three- and four-year-olds happily playing together in an educational, nursery-school-like environment. But infants are not children, and neither are toddlers. And neither infants nor toddlers are in need of groups to join in, but benefit most from calm, one-on-one interaction with adults, interspersed with some time around other children. Citing the educational and independence-inducing benefits of day-care betrays a lack of understanding of what children want and need at different stages of their development. Educational and challenging experiences might be what parents want for their babies, she says, but it 'is not right to assume that the experience is, or can be, equally valuable for babies'.[57]

The tendency for day-care advocates to confuse day-care with nursery school is a symptom of the mess that the day-care debate is in. As well as terminology being regularly confused, it is day-care, as opposed to honesty about parents' and childrens' needs, that dominates the debate about work–family issues and childcare. This, in Peter Moss's view, is partly because the field is so fragmented.

'There is a whole group of people who are interested in education, there's another group of social workers who deal with day-care for children in need, and a third group of people who are interested in childcare for working parents. In my experience, they have very little contact with one another. So the whole debate becomes incredibly compartmentalized.' This compartmentalization leads not just to poor-quality debate, but to an emphasis on day-care at the expense of a wider, more child-centred strategy, one which acknowledges children's need for time with their parents, and parents' need for flexibility at work as well as in childcare choices.

Time is the Answer

Staunch supporters of day-care in the medical profession, politics and the media emphasize only the good in day-care. On the other side of the argument those who seek to enlighten the public about the potentially harmful effects of day-care often do so in an attempt to persuade mothers that they should stay home. Though Patricia Morgan's *Who Needs Parents?* provides some much-needed clarity about day-care, her conclusions hurl the reader straight into the centre of the tired, polarized debate that is the Mother War. For Morgan believes that the only response to the day-care research is for mothers to exit the workforce to care for their own children full-time.

But there is another response. We need not be trapped by a choice between blind endorsement of day-care's value and righteous insistence that no child should ever, under any circumstances, be left in day-care, or even be removed from his or her mother's side. Day-care is neither as good for all children as the day-care advocates would have us believe, nor as potentially harmful to all children as its detractors claim.

It is important to remember that the research about the effects of day-care cannot predict how any *individual* child will fare, but merely suggests the likelihood that children will respond to day-care in a given manner. Studies purporting to demonstrate that it is beneficial, such as the Ypsilanti or Perry Pre-school Project (see p. 115), indicate that children are *likely* to prosper in day-care, but there are plenty of children who do not prosper, even from well-funded, intensive programmes like the Perry Project. Similarly, studies which emphasize the adverse effects of day-care suggest a risk of these effects materializing, not a certainty that they will. Tavistock Clinic child psychotherapist Dr Juliet Hopkins, who has witnessed the effects of poor-quality day-care, does not condemn day-care outright. She insists that 'it is impossible to say how any particular child will react. Children are all so different, and so are the families of which they are part. And one child might thrive in a perfectly miserable day-care environment, against all the odds, while another will suffer terribly in what we might consider to be an adequate environment.'

So research which concludes that day-care children are at risk of developing weak infant–parent attachments, aggressive behaviour, or poor communication skills, should not lead us to insist that *no* child should ever be placed in day-care. It should, first and foremost, indicate to parents that day-care *can* have negative effects and that their own vigilance in selecting quality day-care and in watching their own child's reactions to it is critical. Hopkins says that while she almost never advises parents to withdraw troubled children from day-care, she does try to help them to be more attuned to their children's needs and experiences, and to make judgements based on that sensitivity. In some instances, this may well lead to their withdrawing their children from day-care.

The body of negative findings about day-care should lead parents to be more sensitive to the needs of their own children, and to a more widespread appreciation of the importance of maximizing the quality of day-care provision and minimizing the time in care for any individual child. Those two words – time and quality – which are included in the caveats and subtext of almost every study and yet are studiously ignored or misused by so many protagonists in the Mother War, hold the key to an informed, responsible stance in the debate about working mothers and the use of day-care.

What is the right amount of time for children to spend in day-care, or any non-parental care? The magic number of twenty hours is thrown up time and time again by research. The fact that twenty hours is so often posited as the dividing line between children who are at risk and those who aren't, may have much to do with arbitrary divisions between samples made by researchers. Had they chosen to study children who spent more or less than fifteen hours, or twenty-five hours, in non-parental care, one of those numbers might have emerged as the vital determinant of the level of risk faced by a child. Thirty hours may indeed be the magic number: day-care workers asked to comment on the question of how much time children should spend in group care often volunteer that six hours a day, or thirty hours a week or less, would be ideal. And Peter Moss maintains that Swedish policy is based upon a widely held belief that around six hours a day, and a maximum of thirty hours a week, is about right. Whatever the precise number of hours is believed to constitute the point at which risk increases significantly, one thing is clear: the longer she or he spends in non-parental care, the greater the risk that a child will suffer long-term adverse effects. Some might suffer from fifteen hours a week in day-care, while others will be perfectly happy to spend as many as thirty. It is unlikely that many would thrive on the fifty hours a week that a full-time place implies. Day-care from 8am to 6pm, five days a week, week in, week out, will be too much for most.

The amount of time children spend in non-parental care is consequential even when that care is high-quality individualized care such as that provided by a nanny. Belsky's conclusions about the risks of poor infant–parent attachment hold true for all non-parental care, not just group day-care. Patricia Morgan reports on a study by Jacobson and Whille which found that children in non-parental (mainly childminder) care for over twenty hours a week had a higher rate of anxious attachments (61.5 per cent) than those with little or no day-care (31.4 per cent).[58] Professional nannies themselves know how much non-parental care is too much: 'I may be employed to take on a long day, which includes getting a child up and giving him breakfast, and perhaps bathtime and bedtime. I don't think that's ideal for the child because they do need time with a parent to feel valued,' said one nanny interviewed by Angela Neustatter for a feature on day-care in *You* magazine in November 1996.

The recognition that children should not spend excessively long periods in non-parental care is reflected in Swedish parents' use of day-care. Most choose not to use it in the first year of a baby's life, and many do not use it at all. Moreover, it is rare for anyone to place their child in care for a full day. Day-care in Sweden is provided in the context of a culture that believes time with family to be important. It is unlikely that a Swedish child would ever have to spend ten hours every day in day-care because the normal working day is shorter than that in the UK. There are generous provisions for parental leave after a child is born (eighteen months for each child), and for career breaks and reduced working hours; and it is almost unheard of, says Penelope Leach, for a parent not to stay home when a child is ill, needs a medical or dental appointment or has a birthday or some event at school.[59] The Swedes' most precious commodity is the right to time with their families, not full-time day-care.

Even the best of non-parental care should aim to support and enrich what parents have to offer, not replace it. 'Parents need to spend enough time with their children to make them feel valued,' says Carolyn Douglas of Exploring Parenthood. 'Research has shown that children can only survive a certain amount of time away from the person they look to for absolute security before becoming very distressed.' Most parents do not need research to tell them this. Their children will tell them clearly enough, if only they will listen.

A New Direction for Public Policy

Public policy on day-care, and how it should be used to support working parents, needs to reflect an understanding of the full body of formal research, including that which raises concerns about the effects of full-time group care. That policy should aim to attain the maximum standards in childcare. But, just as importantly, it should embody the objective of minimizing the time children spend in day-care, or in any other non-parental care.

The vision for public policy contained in Peter Moss and Helen Penn's *Transforming Nursery Education* represents the best way to ensure that care is of the highest quality and truly meets children's needs. It does so by ensuring that early-childhood services are uniformly managed, adequately funded, and provided by qualified, well-paid staff. It also ensures that all children benefit from the same high level of care, rather than catering differently for the children of stay-at-home mothers, those of working parents, and children in need.

But Moss and Penn's vision is costly, and may be politically unacceptable for some time to come. Meanwhile, the government's decision to fund up to 70 per cent of childcare costs for low income families, announced in March 1998, represents a very positive step in the right direction. But, unless additional steps are taken, these initial fragments of a childcare strategy could backfire. Government regulation, and community and employer involvement is needed to ensure that the government funding creates a healthy boom in the provision of quality childcare rather than a sudden burgeoning of the type of substandard care witnessed by the Thomas Coram Research Unit and *Panorama*'s research team, among others.

The Government must step up its efforts to more effectively oversee and regulate the quality of all care, including those forms currently excluded from Government schemes. Given that there will always be parents who opt for individualized care (such as that provided by nannies) and carers who prefer to care for one or two children in parents' homes, a national carers' or nannies' register is essential.

But as essential as a national childcare strategy, and support for private childcare initiatives, is the encouragement of workplace change that enables parents themselves to provide most of the care for their own children. Top of the government's priority list should be a public campaign for flexibility in the workplace, and incentives to firms to move in this direction. Just as a war has been waged on smoking, so a war needs to be waged on long working hours. Legislation, advertising, funding – all manner of means are available to a government that wishes to encourage some behaviours at the expense of others. All of them should be used to encourage the nation to adopt a different way of thinking about the care of its children.

Childcare advocates can do their part to encourage the right sort of change. They can support day-care in principle, but be more honest about what constitutes quality care and how much it costs, and about the need to encourage parents to minimize the time their children spend in day-care. They can resist the temptation to provide us with a clear-cut case in favour of day-care, to insist that not a scrap of evidence exists suggesting that it might, in some circumstances, be harmful. And they can speak as often and as vehemently about the need for workplace change as they do about the need for universal day-care.

Childcare is only one of the complicated set of issues faced by working parents. And day-care is only one answer to the childcare problem. It has been portrayed as the key to utopia, but in fact the key to utopia lies elsewhere. It lies in establishing a different balance between work and family in the workplace itself, and in supporting that with quality care options which meet the needs of both parents and children.

PART TWO

MYTHS FROM THE EARTHMOTHER'S KITCHEN

CHAPTER FIVE

✥

THE MYTH OF THE EARTHMOTHER, THE PERFECT FAMILY AND THE END OF CRIME

The mother is the heart of the home . . . if you remove the heart,
you have a corpse.
NORA BENNIS of the Irish Mothers Working at Home Association,
in *Irish Times*, February 1993

Are working mothers bad for their children?
Opening question in *Panorama*'s 'Missing Mum', February 1997

✥ ✥

I REMEMBER A conversation with a friend, Cynthia, about another mutual friend, Janice. Janice had returned to work part-time after being at home with her three young children for almost six years, and was feeling miserable about it. She hated leaving her two pre-schoolers with a babysitter, and was convinced that her children hated it too. Her second child had started to behave badly, throwing tantrums at the slightest instigation, refusing to go to bed at night. Janice worried that her return to work was the cause of this misbehaviour, and Cynthia, a full-time mother, felt certain that it was. 'There has to be something in it, don't you think?' she asked me. 'Hmm, perhaps,' I muttered in as non-committal a tone as I could muster, attempting to distance myself from what could easily have become a heated debate between two highly defensive mothers about the merits of working or not working.

Janice's child's temper tantrums and pre-bedtime naughtiness might well have been a reaction against her working. On the other hand, both could have been associated with the staggeringly tenacious assertion of will that is often seen in children aged between two and three years. Small children are unfathomable beings, and the roots of their behaviour can mystify parents and psychologists alike. But, faced with new and undesirable behaviour, the cause of which they have difficulty understanding, and desiring some explanation that can help them make sense of it, many resort quickly and easily to an interpretation that rests on a direct link between children's behaviour and mothers' work. The uncertainty felt by so many working mothers makes them vulnerable to the criticism implied by that interpretation.

Being a full-time mother, Cynthia has never had to deal with accusations that the way she chooses to spend some of her days is having an adverse effect upon her children. Yet her children have misbehaved, and refused to sleep, sometimes for quite long periods. As a three-year-old, her eldest was prone to throwing the sort of tantrums that stopped passers-by dead in their tracks; her second woke up crying several times a night until he was almost six. But no one rolled their eyes and whispered behind Cynthia's back, 'It's because she's a full-time mother, you know.' Because she is at home full-time, she is invulnerable to accusations linking her working status to every one of her children's behavioural peculiarities.

The belief that a mother should be there for her children and exclusively concerned with their well-being at all times is ubiquitous. It was implied by Cynthia's comments about Janice, and is suggested by every story praising a mother who sacrifices everything for her children. It is also within us, shored up by the images of good mothering that we have created in our minds, as well as by our children's pleas for time and attention, which at times we attribute to some deep and genuine suffering on their part. From all around us, and somewhere inside of us, is broadcast the message that the selfless, full-time mother is the best mother. She raises brighter and more contented children, has a happier husband – and, incidentally, is responsible for stemming the tide of crime and delinquency that threatens to overwhelm our society. The working mother, by both implication and direct accusation, raises insecure low-achievers, threatens her husband's self-esteem, takes a job that by rights should go to a man, and sends children out into the world to cause trouble and commit crimes. This is the Myth of the Earthmother, the Perfect Family and the End of Crime.

Full-Time Mothers is unabashed in its support for this myth, particularly the aspect that is concerned with children's security and happiness. Its promotional leaflet is entitled *Full-Time Mothers – a Child's Need, a Mother's Right*. The organization states that its primary aim is to promote understanding of the child's need for a full-time mother. And though it also talks about 'choice' for mothers, it is difficult to see how choice is promoted by the suggestion that only full-time mothers can meet children's needs.

Kathy Gyngell became leader of Full-Time Mothers when she abandoned her career in television to care for her own children full-time. Though her efforts on behalf of this voluntary organization, and her journalistic endeavours look suspiciously like 'work', she continued to advocate that other mothers should not do any. In 1996 she wrote in the *Mail on Sunday* about the danger of becoming a career woman at any cost.[1] When she gave up her career to raise her children full-time, she said, her colleagues were concerned about how and when she might return to work, rather than how her child might grow up. The inference: if she worked, her children would *not* grow up all right.

Gyngell claims that Full-Time Mothers is 'not reactionary', but shares a certain amount of common ground with the Working Mothers' Association – now Parents at Work – such as demands for flexible working hours.[2] This may be true. But the message that mothers who work need to be supported by a workplace that acknowledges their parenting responsibilities is rarely seen or heard amid the organization's pro-full-time-mother rhetoric. It was certainly not in evidence when full-time mother Jill Kirby represented Full-Time Mothers on *Newsnight's* debate about the research findings showcased in the now famous *Panorama* programme, 'Missing Mum'. And Full-Time Mothers chairman Ruth Liley's article for the spring 1997 newsletter conveyed pride in the fact that 'FTM is now widely recognized in the media and regarded as the organization that offers *the other view* on the "working mother debate" [italics mine]'[3]

The *Panorama* programme, which, as mentioned earlier, manipulated research findings to imply that working mothers damage their children's academic performance and prospects, is itself a perfect example of this particular myth in action. The *Tatler's* 'Mother Courage' feature, written some three years earlier, is another: it could have been written by a Full-Time Mothers representative, so perfectly did it serve as a mouthpiece for the trumpeting of their beliefs. Its author Helen Kirwan Taylor pointed to the 'hot new theory of attachment' – in fact, attachment theory has been around since the 1950s – and to new research about how the brain develops during the first eighteen months of a child's life, in order to support the assertion that working mothers who stop work once their children are born have 'probably got it right'.[4] 'The efforts of every mother whose instinct was to stay home as long as she could, sacrificing income and status, have finally been validated,' concluded Kirwan Taylor.

Countless letters to newspaper editors have, over the years, given voice to opinions similar to Kirwan Taylor's. One in *The Times*, from D. Goodman, the chairman of the organization What About the Children?, was particularly heavy-hitting, and in the space of two sentences made the leap from mothers who work to children who fail to become mature adults: 'We all need to recognize that the bond between mother and child is unique and there is a risk of psychological damage when mothers return to work before their babies are emotionally ready ... if we deny children's emotional, moral and intellectual potential for the sake of adult priorities we must not be surprised if they fail to become mature adults fit to parent the next generation.'[5]

Alarming stories about children's mental health and educational development add further fuel to the fire. 'Four out of ten children are mentally ill,' declared the *Sunday Telegraph* in December 1996,[6] and the breakdown of the family and 'latchkey children' are the chief causes of the problem, according to an MP interviewed. Though working mothers were not blamed directly for the rise in children's mental illness, the inference that they were at fault was there for anyone who cared to pick it up, the terms 'family breakdown' and 'latchkey children' having been linked so regularly with the term 'working mother'. Working mothers have been blamed directly, along with the rise in the number of single-parent families and high unemployment levels, for a fall in reading standards.[7]

Children are not the only ones to suffer at the hands of the working mother, according to the Myth of the Earthmother, the Perfect Family and the End of Crime. Working mothers undermine men's position in society by taking jobs that should go to them. 'Ninety per cent of new jobs in the economy have gone to women, often displacing men in the process,' lamented Lynette Burrows in the *Sunday Telegraph* in October 1996 in her plea for mothers to 'spare the job' and 'save the child'.[8] 'How I agree with Lynette Burrows,' wrote a *Telegraph* reader from Aberdeen, lambasting working mothers for 'putting the fathers of needy families out of work'.[9] A similar theme ran through Melanie Phillips's paper *The Sex-Change State*, published by the Social Market Foundation in October 1997. Assisting lone mothers into the workforce 'may well push hundreds of thousands of young men out of that market,' she wrote.

That men lose jobs to women is not the worst of it, according to Phillips. She holds that policies which encourage or support women who work, and by implication, the working women themselves, are responsible for making men feel disrespected and marginalized. Though proffering the self-protecting disclaimer that she doesn't believe all women should be forced to stay home, she nevertheless urges policy-makers to construct policy that encourages them to do so, insisting that giving men a role as the family's principal provider 'makes them feel not just valuable, but invaluable'.[10]

Phillips references the work of Patricia Morgan, who used her otherwise excellent review of the evidence about day-care, *Who Needs Parents?* as a platform for espousing her socially conservative beliefs about men and women. Morgan blames working mothers for high stress levels among fathers: 'While fathers experience more stress than men who are not parents, fathers in dual-earner families are most stressed of all.' Dual-earner fathers seem also to be less satisfied with their work, their marital relationships and their personal lives than are single-earner fathers, she claims, though a footnote referencing research to back up her claim is conspicuously absent. Morgan rounds off her attack by proclaiming that fathers whose wives work full-time behave less sensitively towards their children, are more aggravated by them, and generally make poorer fathers.[11]

The Promise Movement, which has swept across America and threatens to cross the Atlantic,[12] blames men, not women, for America's social ills and broken marriages. But its ultimate aim is essentially the same as Morgan and Phillips's: to convince women to take a back seat and a traditional role within the family. The movement, which claims to have over two million male followers in the US, stresses the importance of 'men returning to the family unit with zeal, and taking both the material and spiritual lead in the household'.[13] Underlying their seemingly innocent and admirable promises to honour Christ, form relationships with other men, lead pure ethical and sexual lives, serve the family, support the Church, fight racial prejudice and love God, their neighbours and themselves is a belief in men's 'God-given right to lead', and women's duty to submit. Despite the denials of movement leaders anxious to place the movement in a positive light, this belief often translates into a desire to keep women down, and out of the workplace. Like Morgan and Phillips, 'Promise Keepers' seem convinced that men can feel valued only when they are leading families and making decisions on their behalf: one Promise Keeper, as reported in the *Sunday Times*, suggests that men wrest the family leadership from their wives by saying, 'Honey, I've made a terrible mistake. I've given you my role. I gave up leading this family and I forced you to take my place. Now, I must reclaim that role.'[14]

Like the Promise Keepers, right-wing academic Francis Fukuyama is quick to criticize men for their failure to take their obligations to families seriously, but in his book, *The End of Order*, he nevertheless insists that the way to restore social order is to implement policies which recreate men's financial power. The advent of the working woman was partly responsible for men's loss of status and sense of social obligation, so, as Fukuyama's logic would have it, the working woman's influence must be curbed.

In case the accusation that working mothers cause mental illness in their children, wreck men's self-esteem and undermine the institution of marriage should prove to be insufficient ammunition in the fight against them, the myth-makers keep one final weapon in reserve: the assertion that working mothers are responsible for the breakdown of society and the rise in crime levels that has accompanied that breakdown.

For a clear articulation of this aspect of the myth of the Earthmother, the Perfect Family and the End of Crime one need look no further than the words of Nora Bennis of the Irish Mothers Working at Home Association (MWAH). Bennis blames 'the breakdown of society' – teenage suicide, unemployment, marriage break-up – on the absence of mothering and says, 'I think a woman shouldn't separate herself from her children'[15] – for which read: should not work under any circumstances. Lynette Burrows, author of *Good Children*, similarly holds working mothers responsible for juvenile delinquency,[16] as does Kathy Gyngell. At a Cambridge Union debate in 1993 Gyngell proposed the motion, 'A woman's place is in the home', and supported it with her proposition that feminism, and the selfish working women it had spawned, was 'a significant factor in the social disorder and rising juvenile crime we are witnessing today'.[17]

Such stinging accusations as those fired by Bennis, Burrows and Gynell temporarily knock the wind out of the average working mother. But, subjected to just a few moments' scrutiny, the notion that mothers, by virtue of their wish to use their brains, test their talents or support their families economically, have caused the collapse of society, collapses, itself, in a heap. Most working mothers are worried by the suggestion that their children are unhappy when they work, and shaken further by claims that their academic per-formance suffers. But by the time the argument has been enlarged, making working mothers culpable for every societal weakness imaginable, many of us have begun to shake our heads in bemused disbelief. It is such a preposterous idea, that perhaps the rest of the myth doesn't stand up to close examination either, we think.

And we are right. The Myth of the Earthmother, the Perfect Family and the End of Crime is more full of holes than the rest of the erroneous notions attached to the Mother War put together. Full-time motherhood is no magic wand conjuring up happy, intelligent children, satisfied husbands, and cities free of theft and violence. And working mothers are not the villains – vis-à-vis children, men or society – that they are so often made out to be. There are many roots to problems such as childhood anxiety and mental illness, marriage breakdown and crime, and both the roots and problems themselves are hard to disentangle. We cannot yet, as a society, disentangle them completely, but there is enough infor-mation available to tell us one thing: persuading the working mother not to work will not move us very far towards the re-creation of the post-war home fantasy – that future utopia – that this pernicious myth dangles enticingly in front of our eyes.

The Myth's Children: Poorly Attached, Mentally Ill and Academically Underachieving

There is no doubt that children want and need time with their parents, and many need more than they are currently getting. That assertion constitutes the very premise of this book. But an insistence that many children need more time than they are getting, particularly in dual-income families in which parents work long hours, is not tantamount to exhorting mothers to stay home full-time. Neither does an acknowledgement of the barriers to effective parenting that are created by existing work cultures and practices lead to the conclusion that mothers should not work. Both time with children *and* work are important. The key questions are how much of each, and how to create the conditions under which a healthy balance can be maintained.

In the children's story 'Guess How Much I Love You', a mother hare and her baby play a game in which they try to outdo each other in demonstrating the size of their love for each other. On every page, the baby hare stretches his arms wider and wider apart in an attempt to demonstrate the boundlessness of his love. Every time I read that story I am reminded, not just of the boundlessness of children's love for their parents, but of their seemingly limitless need to be with them. Ask children, 'How much would you like mummy to be at home?' and they will stretch their small arms as far apart as they possibly can. 'Every day, all day' more or less sums up a typical response. Even when they are not at home, they would like their mothers to be!

Some children express the need for parental time more than others. My eldest daughter, Olivia, hates separating herself from me, and misses me terribly if ever I have to go away for a few days. Joely, on the other hand, only rarely subjects me to the tearful clinging-to-the-leg treatment when I leave, and often greets my arrival home with distinct nonchalance. When I went away for a few days and she was asked whether or not she missed me, she responded with a categorical 'No'. She is always warm and loving when we are together, but her need for time with me is in no way comparable to Olivia's.

Differences between them aside, most children want more time than we can ever give them. Even full-time mothers cannot give them all they demand. One friend of mine who was contemplating reducing her working hours was warned by her sister, a full-time mother, that this would not necessarily make her children more content with what she had to offer. 'Children are like sponges,' she said. 'The more you give, the more they want. And even if you only go out once a week to an art class, they will not want you to go.'

Full-time mothers with more than one child have to separate themselves from one or other of them quite regularly. To attend one son's soccer game, a friend has to miss the rugby game of another; in order to take her daughters to school, another mother of four has to send her young son to school with a neighbour. He's not overly keen on the idea, but there is no other way, logistically, for his mother to handle the school runs. Yet the myth-makers persist in pretending that full-time mothers can be everywhere and do everything for their child, while working mothers cannot. Kathy Gyngell told a story of a high-flying barrister who cried whenever she dropped her son at school. Here was 'a mother torn between her maternal instincts and a demanding profession. No one with an ounce of humanity would want to force this kind of daily agony on any woman,'[18] sobbed Gyngell. Yet some separation from our children is a fact we must all face, working mothers, full-time mothers and children alike.

Children, particularly young ones, dislike separation from their parents intensely. They will beg for and absorb all the parental time they can. But if they don't get all that they beg for, if they are not with their parents for every waking minute of every day, they will not necessarily end up insecure and poorly attached to them, mentally ill, or underachieving at school, as we are so often warned they will. Most research shows that the key to raising happy, healthy children, and keeping insecurity, stress, mental illness and even delinquency at bay, is the quality of parenting – not 'quality time', but quality parenting over time, as represented by love and affection, good communication, clear and consistent discipline, and effective supervision. What parents need to consider is whether they are able to provide that quality of parenting in the time they have left over once their work week has finished. If they can't, then one of them needs to scale back, work more flexibly, provide the cover. This suggestion is a far cry from the insistence that every family needs a full-time mother if its children are not to go off the rails.

The attachment question

The question of how mothers' employment affects their children's attachment to them is an important one, because the extent to which children are securely attached influences their subsequent development. 'Infants with secure attachments to their mothers are found to be better able to solve problems, to explore, and to be independent in the toddler years. In the pre-school years, securely attached children tend to be more constructively involved at school, to play better with other children, and to be cooperative and compliant with adults.'

Alison Sidle Fuligni, Ellen Galinsky and Michelle Poris of the Families and Work Institute in New York analysed the available research on attachment in the course of their review of over 150 studies of the impact of parental employment on children. They concluded that 'the preponderance of studies of infants with employed and non-employed mothers did not find differences in the security of attachment relationships for the children of employed and non-employed mothers'. Some studies concluded that infants separated from their mothers for more than twenty hours a week are at greater risk of forming insecure attachments, and that mothers employed full-time are 'less invested in parenthood' and, therefore, potentially less sensitive and responsive. What these studies show is that it is not the mother's working or not working that determines whether or not she will be invested in parenthood and whether or not her children will be securely attached, but the questions of how much she works, how long are the separations, and whether these separations prevent her from being sensitive to her children's needs. As I argued in Part One of this book, the amount of time parents work, rather than the fact of a mother being employed or not, is a critical determinant of how well or badly children adapt to their absence.

'Attachment' is the catchphrase in studies involving young children. Where older ones are concerned, researchers are more interested in how parents' working habits affect the overall quality of the relationship between them and their children. Quality relationships are indicated by such things as parental warmth, sensitivity and verbalization; children's perception of family relationships; degrees of conflict and cohesion; and the reciprocity of children and parents in their interactions. As with early attachment, quality relationships between parents and children are important, for they affect children's social, cognitive and emotional development.

Some of the studies surveyed by the Families and Work Institute paint a positive picture, and others lead to more negative conclusions. One study found that maternal employment is associated with parents engaging in more activities with their school-age children, while another found that the more time mothers spend working, the fewer free-time hours children spend with parents. Overall, however, the Insitute's researchers concluded that studies comparing the quality of parent–child interactions in families with employed mothers and non-employed mothers found few differences. Those differences that did exist were related to factors such as family income and mother's working hours: for low-income families, maternal employment provides economic and social stability which positively affects parent–child relationships, and boys whose mothers work long hours tend to have more insecure relationships and negative emotional expression than those whose mothers work shorter hours, for instance.

The researchers were also unable to find any evidence that children with working mothers were socially undeveloped in any way. In fact, 'the research on the social development of children with employed and non-employed mothers generally supports the conclusion that maternal employment doesn't harm – and may even benefit – children's development of self-esteem, independence, peer relations, and egalitarian views'. The quality of childcare arrangements, the nature of fathers' involvement and mothers' satisfaction with their roles are all factors that 'play an intermediary role in the linkage between maternal employment and children's social and emotional development'.[19] To the extent that parents' work demands allow for fathers to be involved and mothers to feel happy, in control and relatively stress-free, mothers' working will enhance children's social development. If, however, both parents' work is so demanding and time-consuming that they feel overstretched, out of control and unable to give enough to their children, there is a problem. Again, it is the time and energy consumed by work that is the key, not the fact of work itself.

Children's mental health: what creates 'time bomb' children?

The children comprising the quarter of all children in the UK who are suffering behavioural and emotional difficulties, according to the *Mail on Sunday* of 16 March 1997, are not necessarily mentally ill. At the same time, they do not enjoy perfect mental health. Peter Wilson of the charity Young Minds explains the difference:

> When we talk about figures like 25 and 40 per cent we are talking about children who don't feel entirely well in themselves, who have some difficulty functioning, concentrating, studying and enjoying life, or who might be somewhat withdrawn and in need of extra help and support. We are not talking about this many children being mentally ill in the clinical sense. A more generally accepted fact is that around 10 per cent of children have fairly serious problems, while another 20 per cent have some difficulties.

While it is important to distinguish imperfect mental health from clinical mental illness, and to avoid being overly alarmist about the former, it is equally vital not to ignore the signs of imperfect mental health, or its causes. Children *are* experiencing more difficulties and higher levels of stress, something that has been documented by Michael Rutter and David J. Smith in their book *Psychosocial Disorders in Young People*.[20] There has been an increase in criminal activity among the young, and depression, drug-taking and eating disorders are also on the rise. 'From my work with teachers I know that children are more agitated, complex, anxious and fretful, and less contained,' says Peter Wilson. But the cause of these things is not, as the Earthmother myth-makers would tell us, the working mother.

Rutter and Smith attribute the decline in children's mental health to a range of factors, including increasing levels of family discord, the rise of a 'youth culture' and the climate of dissatisfaction and envy engendered by people's awareness of their 'relative' poverty. Wilson also points to the influence of technology:

> Technological advancement has influenced everything about our and our children's lives. For example, it has enabled us to travel, thereby leading to family separations and multiculturalism, both of which complicate life. It has created an urgency within business, and intensified the pace at which business is carried out. And, through television, videos and computers, it has brought an entirely new level of stimulation into children's minds and lives. All this produces a morass of complexity which we and our children have to cope with and which makes us uncertain. At the same time, values and traditional support systems are shifting, leaving us less able to cope.

Work, and particularly working mothers, cannot be held directly responsible for the phenomenon Wilson describes. But work can affect parents' ability to cope with stress and complexity, and to help their children cope. 'Work can make parents edgy, and sometimes they take it out on their children, which then exacerbates the anxiety the children already feel,' explains Wilson. 'Some dual-income families are in a particularly desperate state. They are charging around like mad flies, working long hours, feeling shattered when they come home. That means there is less space and receptivity for children, and it must matter. It leaves children feeling abandoned, unsure and resentful. Of course, most adapt, but at what cost? What does it take out of them in the process? How will that come out later in life?'

Like Wilson, the Families and Work Institute conclude that 'difficult job conditions exacerbate psychological distress in parents, which in turn affects their parenting and thus their children's development'. Studies have found that 'employed mothers and fathers with more demanding and hectic jobs have higher levels of work–family conflict, more stress and poorer coping skills than their counterparts in less demanding jobs'; that heavy workloads can cause parents to withdraw, and feel depressed; and that 'unbounded work demands' are related to working mothers' decreased satisfaction with sex, increased depression and 'increased psychiatric symptomatology'. The adverse effects of overly demanding jobs on parents themselves are linked to parenting behaviour: for example, those who experience great time pressure at work often exhibit harsh discipline, and on days when mothers are very stressed they are less emotionally and behaviourally available to their children than on days when their workload is lighter; and mothers who worked long hours in demanding jobs were more likely to have children 'with lower personal maturity and poorer adaptive and receptive language'.

Neither Young Minds nor the Families and Work Institute would advocate that all mothers should stay home. A large-scale retreat to the home would do little to alleviate the wider societal causes of stress and declining mental health, and would almost certainly exacerbate some, such as poverty and depression among mothers. Instead, experts like these stress the importance of understanding and improving the broader context of parental employment, such as job conditions, economic needs and resources.[21] Clearly, if parents are to parent effectively and children's mental health is to improve, a work culture that encourages people to work increasingly long hours in stressful full-time jobs needs to be challenged.

Parents also have to remain vigilant to the signals their own children are sending them, distinguishing run-of-the-mill complaints from serious cries for help and attention. This isn't easy. It is difficult to know when a child's complaints are serious enough to merit action, and whether that action needs to include more time spent with a parent. My eldest daughter cried every morning of her first term at school. I was quietly fearful that this was a sign of insecurity caused by my working and not having been available to her all the time. Then I learned that my daughter's friend, whose mother had always stayed home full-time, also cried every morning. Clearly, there was no simple equation between my work and my daughter's reaction to her first six months at school, and no easy answer as to what to do about it. 'I think you have to look at the situation very objectively,' says Lucy Daniels, former head of the charity Parents at Work and a mother herself. 'Clearly, you can't just slavishly do everything they want you to. But you have to listen to individual children's needs at different phases in their lives and try to balance when they have the greatest need with your other needs as well.'[22] Objectivity and honesty are all you have to enable you to get the balance right. As Libby Purves advised working mothers in the wake of the working-mother-bashing that was rife in the spring of 1997, 'Do what you judge best. As long as you are honest in the judging, things will probably be all right.'[23]

Academic underachievers: another working-mother product?

The latest brain research reveals that the brain's development is affected by environmental conditions, and that the most crucial time for brain development is between birth and three years. The myth-makers' conclusion? That it is essential for mothers to stay home with their children to ensure that their mental capabilities are developed to their fullest. *Panorama*'s 'Missing Mum' programme claimed that the children of working mothers do poorly at their exams. The myth-makers' conclusion? That mothers who want their children to succeed academically should not work.

It would be easy to conclude that working mothers are bad for their children's brains. But matters are not so simple. There is not the direct link between mothers' working and children's brain development and academic performance that some would make. And full-time mothers are not the only mothers who can produce intelligent, achieving children. Research does indeed show that parents' behaviour can affect their children's mental development and academic achievement, but there is no simple equation between mothers who stay home and children who succeed, or, indeed, between mothers who work and children who fail.

The vast body of brain research that has led many to conclude that full-time care by mothers is essential to children in the first three years of their lives is summarized in simple layperson's terms in a report entitled *Rethinking the Brain*, which was published by the Families and Work Institute following a conference on brain development attended by 150 of America's leading brain scientists, experts in child development and early education, business leaders and policy-makers. The report draws the following conclusions. First, human development hinges on the interplay between nature and nurture. Second, early care has a decisive and long-term impact on how people develop, their ability to learn, and their capacity to regulate their emotions. Third, the human brain has a remarkable capacity to change, but timing is crucial – the brain is most adaptable in the first decade of life, and particularly within the first few years. And fourth, there are times in a child's life – such as between birth and three years of age – when negative experiences or the absence of appropriate stimulation are more likely to have serious and sustained effects. During these times, stress and trauma, whether physical or emotional, can adversely affect the brain's development.

Mothers hearing these conclusions might be tempted to pack in their jobs and devote their lives to raising and educating their children, as they are so often urged to do. But the experts reach no such conclusion. They recommend, instead, that parents practise quality parenting. This means providing consistent, stable and responsive care to cushion children from the adverse effects of the 'bumps and bruises which are inevitable in everyday life'.[24] It also means being warm, responsive and communicative. The experts also recommend that public policy be developed to support parents: the quality of childcare and early-years education needs to be improved, more parent education/family support programmes provided, and community services enhanced for the benefit of families.

A full-time mother might well be able to provide the kind of quality care these experts are talking about. Then again, she might not. If she is rendered poor or depressed by staying home, she will almost certainly not. By the same token, there is little reason to suppose that parents in dual-career families cannot provide the kind of quality care that develops children's brains. (Most researchers cannot document poorer cognitive outcomes in the children of employed mothers.)[25] For the guidelines for the care of young children encourage parents to be warm and caring, to respond to children's cues, to talk, read and sing to them, to establish routines, and to minimize exposure to television.[26] (Conspicuously absent are suggestions that they need to spend every available minute of the day reviewing number and letter flash-cards with their children.) Working parents who manage to create space within their lives to follow these guidelines, and who can ensure that the people who care for their children in their absence follow them too, need not worry about harming their children's brains.

Parents' working is only bad for children if it prevents them from practising good parenting according to guidelines such as those contained in *Rethinking the Brain*. In that light, forty-, fifty- and sixty-hour-a-week jobs that absorb most of parents' time and energy, and substitute care that does not meet the children's needs will almost certainly be detrimental. The key to maximizing children's early mental development, then, is to seek the kind of change which creates jobs that leave space for parenting, and that provides high-quality support for all parents, particularly those whose economic circumstances actively prevent them from providing their children with an enriching environment themselves.

These changes rather than a mass exodus of mothers from the workplace, are also required if children are to be helped to reach their long-term academic potential. Though Professor Margaret O'Brien's study of Barking and Dagenham children was held up by *Panorama* as evidence that working mothers harm their children's academic performance, it actually showed that the children of part-time working mothers achieved better exam results than *even* the children of non-working mothers. And there is plenty of other evidence to suggest that the children of working mothers perform as well academically as the children of full-time mothers.

Research results contradicting the assertions of the *Panorama* team are plentiful. Studies conducted in the 1960s and 70s suggest a positive relationship between mothers' working and their daughters' academic performance. For example, one study found that career-oriented women were more likely to be the daughters of employed women. And in studies of highly educated professional women, several researchers found maternal employment to be a significant background factor.[27] Professor John Ermisch of Essex University, who has himself conducted a study of 1,565 pupils over five years, claims that recent statistics indicate that children with two working parents do better at school.[28] A 1993 survey by the Department of Education and Science gauged parental involvement in their children's school life – a strong predictor of student behaviour and in turn, student achievement – and found that mothers in the workplace were, overall, more likely to be involved in their children's school life than mothers who were not employed.[29] Research involving low-income families in the USA shows that school-age children with employed mothers perform better on measures of IQ and standardized achievement tests than children of non-employed mothers.[30]

In the final analysis, however, children's educational attainment is a more complicated matter than a mere equation between parents' working status and children's exam results would suggest. Peter Lee, director of the Early Years and Family Network, insisted in a letter to the *Guardian* that a mother's working status is not the most important influence on a child's educational attainment and that there are many other factors involved – all of which are likely to have been relevant to the Barking and Dagenham study. These include: the nature of childcare used by working parents, the amount of social interaction with peers and friends, the socio-economic nature of a community, the amount of parent/child interaction, the nature and type of sibling interaction, the employment patterns of parents, poverty levels, crime levels, mortality rates, and grandparents' involvement. Whether a mother affects her children's academic performance for the better or for the worse will depend, not on whether or not she works, but on factors such as these, all of which need to be fully understood before firm conclusions can be drawn. The term 'parent/child interaction', for instance, suggests a whole range of relevant questions: do the parents provide a stable environment in which children can learn and study? do they have the time and energy to supervise, support and encourage their children in learning? are they available to discuss problems that may be affecting their children's abilities to learn? do the children see their parents as positive role models for work and achievement?

Any strategy for enhancing children's academic performance that rests solely on a mother forsaking her own career clearly rests on fairly shaky ground. Such a strategy may in any case be self-defeating when applied to daughters, as Tracy Camilleri, the part-time managing director of the London public relations firm WMC Communications, pointed out when I interviewed her.

It has always struck me as crazy that we should sacrifice our own education and careers in order to create the conditions under which our daughters can excel. We will educate them and nurture their ambition, only to leave them confronting the very same false choice between work and family that we now face. Unless we can free ourselves from this false choice by showing that work can be done in such a way as to accommodate family life, many of them will end up having to give up the very careers we sacrificed our own to educate them for! And if many of them do that, it will not be long before people start asking the question, 'Why educate girls in the first place?' That could lead us right back to where we started thirty years ago.

Rather than lead our daughters and sons down a path towards the dead end that Camilleri describes, we would do far better to support role models of a new way of working, or to become such role models ourselves. Our children's future happiness will depend far more on their ability to balance their professional achievements with rich personal and family lives than on startling academic success attained through the constant attention of a stay-at-home parent.

The Myth, Men and Marriage

Working mothers put men out of work. They usurp men's role within the family and damage their self-esteem. They make men and marriages unhappy. All these things are uttered today with a surprising regularity and lack of self-consciousness. When we read and hear such statements, working mothers like me turn and look curiously at our husbands, searching for signs of the supposedly crumpled, downtrodden, depressed creatures to whom we are *reputedly* married. Rarely do we find any.

Some fathers undoubtedly suffer if their children's mothers work, particularly if they grew up expecting to be supported by wives at home full-time. Some will resent their wives' pay cheques, even if they are the only ones coming into the home. Research conducted in the 1970s and 80s, such as that summarized by Ronald Kessler and James McRae in 1982, concluded that, among husbands, a wife's employment was associated with higher levels of depression and low self-esteem.[31] But, as Kessler and McRae point out, this distress might well have been 'associated more with attitudes about the appropriateness of women working than with structural sources of role strain' such as actual work overload. Men with more flexible sex-role orientations, who also get involved in childcare – what we call New Men today – were much more comfortable with and happy in a dual-earner situation.[32] The more traditional a man's outlook and values, the greater the likelihood that he will be distressed by his wife's employment.[33]

How happy men are, both in themselves and within their marriages, has also been linked to income and education. One review of the relevant literature in 1989 found that a positive relationship between marital satisfaction and maternal employment is more likely for better-educated, middle-class parents. The age of children is also a factor: parents of pre-school-age children studied in the 1980s reported more satisfaction with their marriages when the wife wasn't employed.[34]

According to the report *Parenting in the Nineties* published by the Family Policy Studies Centre in conjunction with the Joseph Rowntree Foundation, men in single-earner families with only themselves in employment continue to be slightly happier with their marriages, and with life overall, than men in dual-earner households.[35] But the operative word here is 'slightly'. Fifty-one per cent of fathers whose wives stay home veiw their marriages as happy, as against 47 per cent of fathers whose wives work full-time, and 44 per cent of those whose wives work part-time; 26 per cent of fathers who are sole earners report being satisfied with life so far, as against 23 per cent of fathers whose wives work full- or part-time.

Though the likes of Patricia Morgan and Melanie Phillips insist that the loss of the breadwinner role leaves men feeling devalued and marginalized, and that encouraging men to be more involved in the daily tasks of child-rearing reduces the status of father to 'drone',[36] statistics such as those in *Parenting in the Nineties* do not tell an overwhelmingly convincing story of men made miserable by their wives' working status. Phillips trips up on her own logic in arguing as much. For though she believes that some differences between mothers and fathers are biologically determined and immutable, and lead to different behaviours within the family – something that I also argue, in Chapters 1 and 2 – she also seems to fear that fathers' unique influence within the family is so precarious as to be put at risk by their being deprived of their breadwinner role and asked to fry a few fish fingers for their children's tea. Parenting is about more than working or not working, and different parenting styles are rooted in things far more complex than the tasks of food preparation or nappy-changing, yet Phillips wants to draw a direct link between fathers' alienation and the loss of their roles as breadwinners.

The small statistical differences in contentment that have been found to exist between men whose wives stay home and those whose wives work are very likely attributable to the stress experienced by dual-earner couples who work excessively long hours or under poor conditions over which they have little control. There *is* evidence that very long working hours and high levels of involvement with family life – whether voluntary or demanded by the wife – in both single- and dual-earner families, leads to more unhappiness among men: 21 per cent of fathers who worked very long hours (sixty-plus) and were also relatively involved in both the care and raising of their children reported feeling dissatisfied with life so far, compared to 11 per cent of fathers who worked very long hours but were uninvolved in the care and raising of their children.[37] Clearly, many men find the balancing of work and family demands within a long-hours work culture exceedingly difficult.

At one level, life is most certainly more comfortable when a working father is supported by a wife who stays home. On hearing a few years ago that I was vaguely contemplating giving up work for a while, a friend of my husband's whose wife stays home responded: 'How wonderful. You're going to love it. The house will be warm when you get home, there will be this wonderful dinner on the table, your life will be so much better.' Fortunately for my husband, and for me – for I did not give up work – his satisfaction with life is not dependent on things like freshly laundered shirts and hot dinners. Like anyone else, he wouldn't turn his nose up at them and is delighted when he occasionally receives them, but on balance he's happy to trade them off for what we have. If I were to stop work to spend more time with the children, as I would if their needs became such that we could not meet them while both working, he would support me wholeheartedly. But it would be mine and the children's happiness he would be thinking of, not life's creature comforts.

My husband is undoubtedly one of the 23 per cent of men whose wives work and who are 'satisfied with life so far'. There are another 62 per cent with working wives who are not too dissimilar to him, for their are 'moderately satisfied' with life.[38] Then there are those with working wives who are dissatisfied, but they are almost equalled in number by dissatisfied men whose wives are full-time mothers. The point is that there is no *startling* statistic pointing in any particular direction. Beneath the general trends are individual couples and partnerships, each one unique. What makes one work beautifully would cause another to crumble. There are happy – and unhappy – women, men and marriages to be found amid all sorts of earning arrangements: dual-earner, single-male-earner, and single-female-earner. The myth-makers will have to work a little harder if they hope to convince us that sending mothers back to the home full-time will relieve all male angst and lower the divorce rate.

In light of the myth's tendency to keep stubbornly reasserting itself, it is worth calling to mind how working mothers can, and often do, positively affect their husbands' lives. They do so by giving them freedom: freedom from the burden of sole breadwinning, freedom to make career changes and choices, freedom to be deeply involved in their children's daily lives. Through that freedom, men can discover aspects of themselves they never knew existed, even become people they never thought they could or wanted to be.

Men can lose out in a world in which they are expected to support their families economically but play only a marginal role in their children's daily lives, as Adrienne Burgess contends in *Fatherhood Reclaimed: The Making of the Modern Father*. She turns on its head ex-Employment Secretary Norman Fowler's declaration that men should play a bigger role at home in order to free their wives to go out to work, insisting instead that 'women should play a bigger role in the workforce to *free their husbands to spend more time with their families*' [italics mine].[39]

Burgess believes that men are trapped by the breadwinner role. Some certainly are. Single-earner fathers were found most likely to work long hours by the *Parenting in the Nineties* researchers,[40] and this inevitably leads them to be less involved in family life. At its most extreme, it can mean that they are 'effectively exiled' from their children.[41] Their confidence and comfort in the work environment can be matched by a distinct lack of confidence and discomfort in the home, and they may become more accustomed to playing 'dad' to their employees than to their children. Some become almost afraid of the tasks and routines of daily life with children. The childcare process looks difficult to them, and if their initial attempts at it result in minor domestic disaster, this does not help to alter that view. Neither do stories like the one featured in the *Daily Telegraph* of 21 March 1992 that asked, 'What happens to the intelligent, professional, hard-working adult that leaves him unable to cope with beans on toast for two at tea-time, get the Hero Turtle costume assembled by bed-time and review his notes for tomorrow's meeting?'[42]

Not all fathers who are sole earners fall into this trap. Some manage to succeed at work *and* to be competent and involved fathers at home. Mark, whom we will meet in Chapter 11, runs a small business and cooks half the family meals, frequently drives his children the fifteen miles to school, regularly oversees their homework and music practice, and is a fully hands-on father every weekend. My own father was a competent nappy-changer who got up to us most nights when we were young and was intensely involved in our lives as we grew up, despite being a sole breadwinner, and in an era when these things would have singled him out as an anomaly rather than a fashionable New Man. But many men who provide the sole income for their families are forced, or tempted, by that role into sidelining themselves from family life, even when they can see the damage it is doing. Three out of four men believe that their family relationships are in some way damaged by their working life,[43] but few of these feel able or inclined to do anything about it. Demos research shows that many young fathers, in particular, want to be more involved in parenting but feel incapacitated by the pressure of long hours or the lack of father-friendliness in companies.[44]

'There is a lifetime of good things which flow from having a father actively involved in childcare,' wrote Jerry Adler in *Your Child*, a 1997 special issue of *Newsweek*. Aside from the more obvious of these 'good things', there are some of which many of us are probably unaware. For instance, children whose fathers help care for them are less likely to become violent, have higher IQs and better social adaptation; men who have been involved in the physical care of young children are less likely to become involved in the sexual abuse of children; and controlled studies with inner-city men show that those who take care of their children are less likely to join gangs and commit violent crimes. 'Few forces are as powerful, and as underused in our culture, as this sacred bond between father and child,' concludes Adler.

If having a wife who works creates opportunities for men to get more involved in family life – doing the school run on the days when she can't, staying home with a sick child when she has a meeting – it can only be a good thing. The rewards to the man are tangible, and quick to materialize. When I went away for a week one autumn, leaving the children in the care of their grandparents and my husband, he was forced to step up his involvement in the children's lives significantly. When their grandparents were, in the end, unable to care for the children because of illness, he found himself managing the early-morning breakfast routine, doing school runs and trips to ballet class, telephoning round to other mothers to ask if they could help out for an hour or two, and coming home to put the girls to bed at night, all during a week when work was no less demanding than usual. He says it was hard, but he wouldn't have missed it for anything. We both learned that not only could he do it, but he could do it well, and further, his doing it delivered immediate dividends in terms of his relationship with the girls. They were already close to him, but they moved one step closer that week.

Working wives may also provide their husbands with the freedom to change their own working lives as they want and need to. A second income, even if it is not one that can, on its own, sustain the family for long periods, can be an invaluable backstop for someone who needs to take a drop in income in order to change direction, or who loses his or her income through redundancy. My income gave Patrick the freedom to change the direction of his working life when our first daughter was born. His income gave me the same opportunity five years later. The fact of our both working has provided us with enormous latitude to alter the structure of our working lives to better suit our needs and aspirations.

As a group, working women provide that latitude to working men within the workplace at large. Gender segregation, which is famously bad for women, is bad for men too, warns Adrienne Burgess. 'Males working in men-only workplaces find it well-nigh impossible to negotiate family-friendly working, or challenge the long-hours culture, or the ageism that insists they've failed if they haven't made it to the top by forty.'[45] Only if women are present in the workplace, working alongside men, pushing for the recognition of family life within work structures and practices, will men in any large numbers ever be able to combine successful careers with deep involvement in their families' lives.

The Working Mother and the Delinquent Society

Late 1996 was a time of great public soul-searching in Britain. Frances Lawrence, widow of the murdered head teacher Philip Lawrence, published her manifesto for a moral Britain, stimulating debate about just what a 'moral' Britain would look like, and how it could be created. One message that was broadcast loud and clear was that a decent, remoralized society would emerge if we returned to the golden era of the 1950s when father worked, mother stayed home, and everyone was ashamed of divorce and illegitimacy. Never mind that the 50s family model – to the extent that it ever represented reality – was driven by the needs of a 50s marketplace that no longer exists.[46] We were asked to see it as the solution to every societal ill.

The suggestion that a moral society, free of young thugs who vandalize and murder, of drug-pushers and drug-takers, could be brought about by a retreat of mothers to their homes is, as journalist Yvonne Roberts has politely pointed out, crude to say the least. It betrays a certain naivety, a blindness to the complexity and causes of the problems besetting British society, and a tendency to seek scapegoats for those problems. Nor are the British alone in having made scapegoats of working mothers, as American author Diane Eyer documents in *Mother Guilt: How Our Culture Blames Mothers*

for What's Wrong with Society.[47] While scapegoating panders to
people's need for an immediate and easily grasped explanation, it
furthers genuine understanding of our problems not at all. Crime,
including juvenile delinquency, is caused not by mothers who work,
but by factors such as poor education, poverty, and the poor-quality
parenting that they so often engender.

A report entitled *Crime and the Family*, authored by David Utting,
Jon Bright and Clem Henricson for the Family Policy Studies
Centre, is unequivocal in its endorsement of this explanation. In an
attempt to understand, not simply the social and economic pressures
that make it more or less likely that individuals will commit crime,
but the specific question of 'Why do they do it?', Utting, Bright and
Henricson reviewed existing research about juvenile crime, or
delinquency. (Juvenile offenders constitute almost half of all known
offenders.) They found that most of the available research, and
particularly the three best-constructed and most informative longi-
tudinal surveys – the 1946 Cohort Study, the Newcastle 1,000 Family
Study, and the Cambridge Study in Delinquent Development – tell
much the same story.

That story is that the roots of delinquency lie in a range of factors
associated with deprivation: it is more common among the children
of unskilled manual workers, in large families – particularly those
living in run-down and overcrowded conditions, in very poor
families, in broken homes, in homes where a parent is a criminal
offender and where children have suffered physical abuse or neglect
at the hands of their parents. Having a working mother consistently
failed to distinguish delinquents from non-delinquents, once factors
like these were taken into account. What *did* distinguish delinquents
from non-delinquents, however, even when evidence of deprivation
was present, was the quality of parenting. 'Parents whose child-
rearing practices included harsh or erratic discipline, a cruel, passive
or neglecting attitude, and poor overall supervision were more likely
to produce delinquent teenagers.' By contrast, parents whose child-
rearing practices were positive were often able to overcome other
risk factors, raising non-delinquent children despite perhaps living
in overcrowded conditions and extreme poverty.

The report's authors concluded that 'the tangled roots of delinquency lie, to a considerable extent, inside the family' and that

children whose families suffer financial and environmental poverty are at greater risk than those whose parents have sufficient income to provide them with a comfortable, uncrowded home.[48] Yet the authors also conclude that social deprivation does not appear sufficient on its own for delinquency to develop. Factors within the care-giving environment, in particular high-quality parental supervision, could modify the influence of poverty and disadvantage. Economic deprivation is a cause of delinquency in as much as it brings with it powerful stress factors which conspire to make effective parenting more difficult. Economic and social pressures affect the way parents behave, and that, in turn, affects the behaviour of their children.

The working mother, then, can be seen as causing delinquency only in as much as her working causes her to parent badly – to dish out harsh or spasmodic discipline, to be cruel or neglectful, to fail to involve her children in shared family activities, to fail to supervise them. The average working mother will not be driven, by the simple fact of her working, to parent in this way. She is not the problem. The problem is largely in families like this one described in the *Sunday Telegraph* in October 1996 by inner-city doctor Theodore Dalrymple:

> Last week I visited the home of a woman in her mid-thirties with six children between six months and twenty years. She had never worked, and neither had two of the fathers of her children. The first was violent and jealous; the second came to see her only when he needed sex, a meal or money for the horses.
>
> She lived in a decent but run-down council house in which two vast televisions competed for attention. Every imaginable electronic provider of entertainment was present. A child aged four, still in nappies, ran otherwise naked through the rooms. The back garden was liberally strewn with the usual headless dolls, wheel-less prams and empty shampoo bottles ('I've asked the council to clear it up').
>
> One child was attending a school for the behaviourally disturbed, another was stealing cars, and a third was pregnant. The father of her child had left her. A warrant was already out for the arrest of the woman's younger brother, because he had broken the jaw of his common-law wife in one of his jealous rages, though she was trying to get the police to drop the charges (as usual).

Dalrymple describes this family's life as 'the most miserable form of human existence I have encountered anywhere', but 'only a dramatic instance of the life millions are leading'.[49] His description brings into sharp relief the true meaning of the term 'social and economic deprivation' used so often by Utting, Bright and Henricson in their report.

In November 1997 ITV's *The Big Story* provided the British television-viewing public with a glimpse of how social and economic deprivation can lead to ineffective parenting, and to children who run wild and loose. The programme filmed a week in the life of a 'Supergran' who moved in to help a single mother and her five children living on a council estate.[50] What Supergran found was a mother who had so little authority over her children that she was unable to make them get out of bed each morning, consume anything other than crisps and pop for breakfast, sit down for a family meal in the evening, or desist from roaming the streets until the wee hours. The teenage boy walked out of the door whenever he was chastised, and regularly stayed out until three, four or five in the morning. Even the five-year-old could not be made to go to bed before 11 o'clock at night. Worst of all, the mother seemed not to comprehend how her behaviour was contributing to the mess the family was in. She knew the household was running more smoothly after Gran had been there for a week, but could not put her finger on the reasons why. And asked whether she thought the changes would stick, she merely said, 'Hopefully . . . we'll have to see.' That she would have to work hard to set boundaries for her children, provide more structure to their days, offer them guidance and assist them with their homework, had completely escaped her. Without the continuing presence and efforts of Supergran or someone like her, this mother was destined to slip back into her old ineffectual parenting ways, and some of her children were most certainly destined to become young offenders.

Preventing the juvenile crime that sets the pattern for lifetime antisocial and criminal behaviour requires more than policies that simply get tough on disadvantaged families, such as the fines and parental-control orders which Conservative Home Office minister Michael Howard proposed in early 1997 to impose on parents whose children have been in trouble. It demands more than the chanting of the simplistic refrain, 'Working mothers, go home!' Utting, Bright and Henricson maintain that 'since the risks of delinquency are often greatest in families where clusters of adverse social factors occur, it is evident that an effective prevention strategy will need to target several factors at once'.[51] The starting-point for prevention should be the targeting of three important predictors of offending: poor parental child-rearing, failure at school and economic deprivation. Utting, Bright and Henricson provide many examples of social policies that would target these three areas – including the extension and improvement of programmes that promote maternal and infant health, educate parents and improve their skills, provide care for children whose parents are at work, help families become self-sufficient, and improve children's educational attainment. A programme to provide parents like the one featured in *The Big Story* with the ongoing advice and support of an experienced parent or grandparent would be one such programme. The Labour government's summer literacy programme, launched in 1997, was also conceived in the spirit of the Utting recommendations. By tackling illiteracy, found by many studies to be a major cause of delinquency,[52] the Labour government will have done more to prevent crime than all those who insist that parents of offenders should be fined, or that mothers should concentrate on providing the moral fibre within the home rather than selfishly pursuing careers.

Celebrations of Full-time Motherhood in Place of Myth-making

There are many good reasons for a mother to stay home with her children. Because she wants to and can. Because she enjoys spending time with them more than anything else she could be doing. Because, as one mother put it, 'it is the biggest privilege imaginable'. Because one or more of her children are particularly in need of special care and attention or because the complex logistics of running a home with three or four children in it go far more smoothly when one parent focuses on attending to them.

All of these are positive reasons for being a full-time mother – far more positive than the myth that pretends that a mother *must* stay home or risk wrecking her marriage and her husband's self-esteem, damaging her children's educational prospects, and turning juvenile delinquents loose upon the world. Far more positive, also, than having to stay home because the only alternative is to work long hours within an inflexible work culture which fails to recognize that children need parents to spend time raising them.

It is time for us to celebrate the joys of those who care for children full-time, instead of throwing stones at all mothers who work. Time to demand genuine choices – choices which enable those who want to work *and* parent to do so without going crazy in the process; choices which also mean that a full-time mother can create a work life for herself if and when she wants to. Time to reject the Myth of the Earthmother, the Perfect Family and the End of Crime, and start marching in the name of the workplace revolution.

CHAPTER SIX

✤

EVERYONE'S AN EARTHMOTHER AT HEART

> If you ask women, 'If you continued to be paid a decent wage to stay
> home and look after your own baby, would you?' the vast majority of
> mothers would say yes.
> Letter to the *Guardian*, September 1996

> She is the archetypal nineties woman. A single twenty-nine-year-old
> who is driven by her high-powered career . . . yet Nicola Foulson, who was
> today named Veuve Clicquot Businesswoman of the Year, dreams of
> giving it all up to raise a family.
> *Evening Standard*, April 1997

FULL-TIME MOTHERS exists to promote the interests of children,
who they believe need full-time mothers. But it also exists to 'help
all mothers who would like the choice to look after their own
children' and aims to 'enhance the status and self-esteem of mothers
at home', whose contribution to society is little recognized.[1] Mothers
who make the choice to stay home should be rewarded and
respected, says the association.

It is difficult to disagree with this stance. But, like so many other
points of view in the Mother War, this plea for support for full-time
mothers metamorphoses into something altogether more extreme
and dogmatic in the hands of journalists and association spokespersons. The Full-Time Mothers' aim of helping mothers who *choose* to
stay home became an insistence that mothers make that choice when
Jill Kirby represented the Full-Time Mothers' position on BBC's
Newsnight, and the appeal for rewards and respect for full-time
mothers often evolves into an assertion that we should encourage
them to stay home because that is where most of them really want
to be. Thus is born the myth which pretends that all women are

Earthmothers at heart. Were it only economically feasible and socially acceptable, says the myth, most women would opt for the full-time mother's life. Only economic need, antagonistic taxation policies and societal devaluation of the mother's role stand in the way of women becoming full-time mothers.

In *Who Needs Parents?*, published in the autumn of 1996, Patricia Morgan made a case for mothers staying home for the sake of their children. In that book, Morgan provided a valuable and much needed review of the evidence about the effects of day-care, but deployed it to exhort mothers to stop working. She insisted, not only that children need full-time mothers, but that full-time mothering would be better for mothers themselves. 'For better-off mothers going out to work, especially full-time, may increase the risk of depression,'[2] she warned.

Others support Morgan's view that mothers would be better off at home. One informed us, in a letter to the *Yorkshire Post* in November 1996, that most mothers 'go out to work not because they are keen on working but because they need or want the money to pay for the standard of living they aspire to', so the obvious solution had to be to make it more attractive for mothers to stay home with their children.[3] In a letter to the *Guardian* another wrote that, if paid a decent wage to stay at home, the vast majority of mothers[4] would do so. Ex-television executive and one-time president of Full-Time Mothers Kathy Gyngell wants to make it financially viable for mothers to stay home, and claims that most mothers would like to.[5]

The view that most mothers work *only* for money, and would be happier if society enabled them to stop, is continuously drip-fed into the veins of the ongoing debate about mothers and work. In her impassioned plea for women to realize that they would be better off staying home,[6] Paula Yates wrote in *Options* magazine in 1992 that most jobs are essentially boring and certainly not 'more glamorous than raising your child'. Dillie Keane wrote in the *Mail on Sunday* in December 1995 that a successful career means 'single-minded slog from dawn till bedtime for forty-five years' and that some women have sensibly realized that they neither want nor have to pursue one, but would be happier at home.[7] Minette Marrin wrote that 'the price of women working – as opposed to being housewives – is very high'[8] for women themselves as much as for other family members. But women work because, otherwise, they would have no status, money or security. The solution, she insists, is to subsidize the housewife in order to enable more women to stay at home.

Working mothers are vulnerable to the suggestion that the complications and stresses of mothering dissolve with decisions to forsake careers and stay home. A colleague of mine once told me that his wife had experimented with working full-time, then three days a week, then two, and had finally opted to stay home full-time. 'It's not perfect, but it is the cleanest option,' he said. I often hanker after that clean, neat choice. And like many women, I can readily conjure up an idealized picture of what it involves. I fantasize about spending long, lazy days baking and playing with my children, gardening while they play happily around me, passing my time at peace instead of in a state of frenetic tension. I long to create my own version of the domestic paradise reflected in the portraits of serene mothers and joyful children that are regularly splashed over the pages of women's magazines. When, at a children's birthday party, I sit in a circle of mothers and children, feebly mouthing the words to songs I have never heard, while the other mothers sing every line of every song without missing a beat, I am temporarily overwhelmed by the wish to become immersed in the life these mothers represent, to feel less of an outsider. And when I read that yet another high-flying career woman – like Maeve Haran, Linda Kelsey or Penny Hughes – has abandoned her career, I am fleetingly seduced by the subtle implication of their stories that being at home leads to greater happiness.

But, at the same time, I know that staying home with children isn't all dreamy days in the garden. I know that for every jolly moment spent singing songs there are hours of energy-sapping, soul-destroying effort spent ferrying children around, setting boundaries they wish to overstep, dealing with moods you don't understand and wish they didn't have. I also know that the Harans, Kelseys and Hugheses of this world have *not* traded work for full-time motherhood: Linda Kelsey returned to a different, less pressurized job; Maeve Haran achieved a better balance in her life by writing novels; Penny Hughes took on a host of non-executive directorships.

Not only am I aware of the realities of daily life at home with children, but I am cognizant of my own need to work, and of the pleasure I derive from it. Certainly, I see the attractions of taking brief periods of time off work, and can foresee circumstances that might lead me to take a break from it, or change the nature of what I do. But, over the long term, and barring unfortunate circumstances that might demand significantly more of me at home, I would work even if our family had no need whatsoever of the money. I know that while full-time motherhood is the best choice for some, it is not the best for me. It would not make me happier, more relaxed about life, more certain of my own capabilities as a mother, or any of the other things that the Myth suggests it would.

Natural Born Mothers

That there are contented full-time mothers for whom the lure of the world of work is so weak as to be almost non-existent, is incontrovertible. There may be more today than several years ago: national statistics reveal that the proportion of women aged nineteen to fifty-nine who work or are looking for work fell from 73 per cent in 1992/93 to 69 per cent in 1997.[9] Feminist theory and a kind of pre-motherhood arrogance once persuaded me that mothers who didn't work were secretly bored, and boring. But I have looked for signs of boredom and dullness among the full-time mothers I know well and found none. Most that I know are as active, interesting and happy as their working counterparts. They seem not only to have escaped the grip of Betty Friedan's 'problem with no name', but to be unaware of its existence.

London School of Economics academic Dr Catherine Hakim caused something of an uproar when she insisted that there are 'home-centred' women who have no desire to interact with or compete in the world of work, and whose primary focus and source of enjoyment is the home.[10] (One of the studies Hakim called upon to support her claim was Bonny and Reinach's survey of 500 housewives showing that most enjoyed being at home, and that as many as 37 per cent intended never to return to work.) Those who were outraged by Hakim's assertions could not have been paying attention to the women among their friends and neighbours who were not raging against their lot as full-time mothers, but positively revelling in it.

Of the contented full-time mothers I know, a few have always known that they wanted nothing more intensely than to have and raise children, and have waited impatiently through their years as career women for the opportunity to do so. Others were converted to full-time mothering later in life for a variety of reasons. Lilly, a former advertising production assistant, spent her early twenties longing to have children. She always knew she wanted them, and she always knew she would stay home with them. She and her husband now have four, and she is as content with her life as it is possible to be. She gave up work when she was pregnant with her first child, and has not uttered a single word of regret since. She never says, with any seriousness, that she misses the colleagues, the challenge, the pace, the glamour or the money. Certainly, she'd like more money. But she wouldn't trade anything in her life to get it.

Not only is Lilly happy as a stay-at-home mother, but she's eminently suited to it. Almost everything about her is in sync with what it takes to be at home. She has an easy way of being with her children, and is not easily distracted by thoughts of things she ought to do, or would rather be doing. Where many women struggle with breastfeeding, she managed it effortlessly, even when faced with the challenge of twins. She is a confident, competent mother, and a lively, interesting person. Her children are charming, happy and very unsmothered.

Like Lilly, Helen is happy at home, though she hasn't always been possessed of Lilly's certainty that she would stay home with her children full-time. She trained as a lawyer and had planned a long legal career. Six months into it she had her first child. Though she managed to secure a part-time arrangement with her firm, that still meant working forty-five hours a week. On top of this, finding good childcare proved to be a struggle. As the months passed, she felt increasingly uncomfortable with the situation.

What translated Helen's discomfort into a decision to stop working was the re-emergence of an illness from which she had suffered in her early twenties, a neurological condition which left her incapable of getting out of bed for more than a few hours a day for several months. The condition had been diagnosed as a severe reaction to exhaustion and stress. When signs of the illness began to reappear while Helen was in the midst of her heroic new-mother–new-lawyer juggling act, it frightened her. 'I thought, why am I doing this? This is clearly not right for me or my health,' she recalls.

Helen left the law and became a full-time mother. She now has four children, and describes her life of the past ten years as having been immeasurably happy. She insists that she is no 'finger-painting all day' Earthmother, and is frequently driven to frustration by her children. She also misses the intellectual stimulation of work and has occasional worries about what she will do when the children are older. But she has never regretted her decision to be a full-time mother.

'I've had a couple of bouts with my illness since my twenties, and once had to stay in bed for several months. And, you know, if you've lain in bed wondering if you will ever be able to take care of your children, when you get the chance to care for them you see it as the most enormous privilege. That sense of this being a privilege has never left me.'

Helen acknowledges her good fortune in having a husband who can support the family and pay for childcare help. Because of her good fortune, and her recognition of the complex set of factors that influenced her decision to stay home, she is wary of advocating full-time mothering for everyone:

> My decision was not a simple matter of 'My children need me' or even 'I really want to stay home.' At one point I could have gone either way – stayed a lawyer or become a full-time mother. But a lot of factors, particularly my health, pushed me towards staying home. It was the right decision for me. But I wouldn't propose for a minute that it would be right for everyone. Most women probably have an equally complex set of reasons for staying home, just as working mothers work for reasons which are unique to their family situation. You just can't know what those are as an outsider looking on.

There is much to envy in Lilly's and Helen's lives: their ease with the pace and routines that make up everyday life with children; their self-possession and self-confidence, the preservation of which does not rely on the praise of bosses and colleagues, or on an ever-increasing salary; the luxury of being able to focus on family. But such contentment as theirs will escape any woman who is unsuited – in terms of character, temperament or aspirations – to being at home all the time. No dictionary definition of suitability for life at home exists, but most full-time mothers are willing to venture opinions about it. In Helen's case, a sense of being privileged to care for her children after many months of illness has contributed to her happiness and sureness of purpose. Others proffer that their lack of ambition makes them ideal stay-at-home mothers – 'I haven't an ambitious bone in my body,' said one. Yet others point to a love of freedom and the outdoors – 'It's such a great life, physically active and outdoors all day with the boys,' said another. Almost all seem to agree that patience and unflappability are great assets for anyone spending long days with children.

Unfortunately, 'calm in a storm', 'goes with the flow' and 'has the patience of Job' are not phrases anyone has ever applied to me. I'm not alone in knowing that, given my somewhat hyper, task-oriented and impatient character, my household is better off when I'm not in it all the time. When I am at home with my children, I am conscious of making the most enormous efforts to keep under check that side of myself that is impatient and eager to accomplish. I would find it difficult if I had to do so all the time, if that side of me had no outlet. One woman who felt equally unsuited to the home life responded to the suggestion that she should be at home with her children with the retort: 'Would you sic me on a child twenty-four hours a day?'[11]

Not so long ago, many women in Lilly's and Helen's position felt depressed, unhappy and trapped. 'People have very short memories – they forget what it used to be like,' says Roz Morris, managing director of TV News London who herself worked from home as a freelance journalist while her children were growing up. 'But believe me, the women who are now in their forties grew up very close to all of that. Our mothers were the ones who had neuroses and warped lives – the ones who were brilliant at school, did well, got married, then couldn't work. *Were not allowed to.* We should be eternally grateful to all those women who kicked in the doors.'

It is, indeed, frighteningly easy to forget what life used to be like for women who were thrust unwillingly into lives as homemakers.

This is not surprising, for the homemaker's life today bears little resemblance to that against which Annie Oakley and Betty Friedan railed in the 1960s. Household technology, changing standards of household care, and different attitudes to men's and women's roles within the home have all altered the homemaker's role irrevocably. But, more important even than labour-saving washing machines, less exacting dusting standards and men who do the cooking, is the fact that women are freer than ever to choose whether or not they wish to be homemakers. Much of the happiness of homemakers like Lilly and Helen depends upon their having freely chosen to be at home. It is tempting to take their happiness for granted, as if its replication called merely for the waving of the magic wand of public policy and moral persuasion.

But not all women are like Lilly and Helen. Not even all full-time mothers are like them. Many women are more conflicted, more conscious of competing needs and desires within themselves. Maeve Haran says, 'I think the extremes are very rare. Most Superwomen have a little Earthmother in them, and most Earthmothers want to be Superwomen sometimes.' Penelope Leach, once accused of antagonism towards working mothers, maintains that few people can embrace the full-time mothering role without *some* sense of internal conflict.

> Bringing up a child is a uniquely creative activity with satisfaction to be derived from both the process and the product, but that does not mean that many people can build a satisfactory lifestyle entirely around a baby. Some women do make a personally satisfying way of life out of mothering ... there are some women for whom the good life of the moment is filled with the minutiae of childish lives; whose hackles do not rise at the thought of being financially supported by a partner in parenthood, and who can do the chores and get the evening meal because they are at home, without feeling typecast in a retrograde role ... But those women, and especially those men, are a minority ... most mothers feel that unbroken parenting would drive them crazy.[12]

For full-time mothers who are conflicted about their choice to stay home, the joys of walking at a snail's pace with a two-year-old or passing an afternoon submerged in poster-paint may well be overridden by a sense of frustration at missing out on something else that is important to them. For them, the only way to keep any sense of well-being is to make time for work outside the family.

Mothers Who Work and the Question of Money

Mothers work for all kinds of reasons. Money is usually one of them, though it is top of the list for some and bottom for others. Six out of ten British women in a general survey said they needed to work for financial reasons.[13] However, another survey, of professional women, found that only 8 per cent cited money as a motivation.[14] Clearly, the economic imperative for women to work varies according to overall family income, social class and personal motivation.

Among working-class women in particular, there will be many who need to work in order to sustain even the most frugal of lifestyles. But the extent to which women, and particularly mothers, work *purely* for economic reasons is often overstated. Many of those who comprise the six out of ten women who claim to work for financial reasons may in fact be driven as much by other factors. In their study of 250 households conducted in the late 1980s, Peter Moss and Julia Brannen found that 63 per cent of women in high-status jobs and 72 per cent in low-status jobs mentioned housing costs and other financial pressures as reasons for returning to work after the birth of their child.[15] But, warn the authors, 'the significance of money is a complicated matter', and financial reasons for working take on several meanings. For some, the financial reason was not represented by the need for money to pay the mortgage or household bills, but was a way of avoiding marital conflicts over money, having to budget as tightly as they would or had done on only one income, or having to be financially dependent on their husbands. Moreover, for those whose decision to work was driven primarily by financial reasons, other factors were also important. Fifty-four per cent of Moss and Brannen's sample of high-status returners and 27 per cent of those in low-status jobs also cited job satisfaction as a reason for working.[16] The decision to work is driven by a complex set of factors of which money is only one, and the meaning of money, as well as how it influences and is influenced by other motives for working, is far from straightforward.

The think tank Demos found that no more than 13 per cent of working women would rather be at home.[17] Yvonne Roberts, writing in the *Guardian* of 4 November 1996, and Natasha Walter in *The New Feminism* (1997) highlighted that 76 per cent of women would work even if there were no financial need. And one survey of Australian working mothers who put their infants into childcare centres found that just one-third would prefer not to work if they had a choice, implying that their working was driven exclusively by financial need.[18] How many of these women actually do work for financial need is unclear. What *is* clear is that it is wrong to attribute women's – and, among them, mothers' – participation in the work-force exclusively to financial necessity. All of the above figures suggest that the percentage of working mothers who are driven to work for that reason alone, and who would be tempted – by taxation provisions or wages for housewives – to stay home, is very likely closer to 10, 20 or 30 per cent than it is to the 60 per cent or more suggested by the myth-makers' claim that most mothers would stay home if society enabled them to do so.

Smaller-scale surveys and interviews bear out the assertion that women have a range of reasons for working. One survey of 107 managerial and professional women revealed that 67 per cent consider work to be the major motivating force in their lives. And their motivation to work stemmed from a desire for recognition (25 per cent), a desire for influence (16 per cent), for self-fulfilment (12 per cent), for enjoyment/fun (9 per cent), for money and duty (8 per cent), and for power (3 per cent).[19] Statistics like these make a mockery of claims that 'if you paid women to stay home, most would'.

My own interviews confirm that many women work for the independence and power that money brings, as well as reasons that have nothing to do with money. Laura, the human resources manager introduced in Chapter 1, said everything in her background had made her wary of being economically dependent. Advertising executive Carole Reay is driven to work partly by her conviction that fair and equal relationships are impossible when one person is totally dependent upon the other. Lawyer Sally, also introduced in Chapter 1, experienced the powerlessness that accompanied her economic dependence on her husband, and wished never to experience it again: 'I became a non-person in the marriage once I stopped working,' she said. 'All of a sudden, every decision was his and I was expected to follow along.' Elaine, a financial analyst, says she can't talk about 'children and schools and the National Health Service all the time without going crazy', and needs the outlet of work to be able to talk and think about other things. Stephanie, also a financial analyst, claims to be driven by the fear that she would be swallowed up by her life with three small children, whereas working three days a week gives her something of herself to hang on to. Others mention that the tedium and isolation of life at home would drive them crazy. A few simply say that they love their work so passionately that being without it would be like being without food.

The point is not that women don't work for money – most do. Single mothers and those in families living on below average incomes certainly do. But there is a big difference between needing the money and working exclusively for the money, and most working women do not fall into this latter category.

Yet the myth-makers remain attached to the 'financial need' explanation, as do many individual mothers attempting to justify their own working to critics. 'Going back for the money' is a socially acceptable response[20] which working mothers feel comfortable articulating, and others feel comfortable hearing. What women are often *not* comfortable with is facing the truth about their relationship with the money, status and lifestyle that their work makes possible. Elizabeth Perle McKenna recalls that she used to link working with money because she didn't want to confront her spending habits and wasn't ready for economic powerlessness after so many years of being independent. She had become so used to her lifestyle that she defined it as 'need'. But in reality, like many of us, she was living in 'that gap between absolute need and perceived need'.[21] In his book *The Hungry Spirit*, Charles Handy echoes Perle McKenna's view that we often overestimate the role of money in determining our choices about life and work: 'Except to a minority, and to those who haven't got any – [money] doesn't matter most.'[22]

Each woman will have her own combination of reasons for

wanting to work, ordered and weighted differently in her mind from the next woman's. But there are two overwhelmingly important motives that consistently crop up in discussion: the need to retain a strong personal identity, and the yearning for intellectual stimulation. These represent what a great many women seek from work, and what they fear losing by giving it up. Formal surveys do not always pick up these motives specifically, but they are there, buried within other categories. For a desire for recognition and self-fulfilment is in part a need for a distinct, recognizable identity. And a desire for 'job satisfaction' is often a desire for the satisfaction of an intellectual challenge, the desire for the fun that comes from using one's brain to solve a problem. In interview after interview, women told me that the fear of losing their identities and their minds was what kept them working.

The Identity of a Mother

To the non-homemaker, homemaking looks like 'falling off the face of the earth',[23] wrote Paula Brook, who left her demanding job as an editor to work freelance and spend more time at home. Falling into an abyss, becoming invisible, losing a sense of who you are – these are other terms that women use to describe what is most feared about giving up work to be a homemaker. The will to stay clear of the abyss, to retain a strong sense of self, is what keeps many women working even when the juggling of work and family seems overwhelmingly taxing. 'I work to keep a sense of Rosa Monckton alive,' said Rosa Monckton, president of London jewellers Tiffany & Co. 'Much as I love my husband and children, I don't want to be known as Dominic Lawson's wife, or Savannah and Domenica's mother, which is what I would rapidly become.' Maeve Haran agrees that the will to preserve a strong identity provides an important impetus for working. 'A person's identity is key, and being a mother is only part of it. How do you keep the rest of that identity alive if you don't have anything outside your life as a mother? It's not impossible, but much more difficult.'

Carole Gilligan, author of *In a Different Voice*, has found that women's sense of identity is much more closely bound up with relationships of intimacy and care than is that of men.[24] Women are less likely than men to experience and articulate their identity as one of pure individual achievement, and are more likely to see their 'professional activities as jeopardizing their sense of themselves' when those activities leave them torn between achievement and caring. But women's sense of identity is not exclusively about relationships or unconnected to achievement. And this is increasingly true now that women are better educated and more active in the world outside the home.

Women fear that their nurturing, caring self will be overtaken by the demands of work, but many are also wary of allowing their achievement-oriented selves to be overwhelmed by the demands of nurturing. They speak and write often about 'the annihilation of the very self'[25] which comes from the constant, unbroken alliance of oneself with a baby. 'Loving an infant,' writes author and mother of six Louise Erdrich, 'is uncomfortably close to self-erasure.'[26]

For a time the sensation of losing oneself in the love for a baby can be blissful. I remember thinking, during the first few weeks with my first daughter, that I never wanted to be apart from her, never wanted any other life other than holding her, staring at her, breathing her in. Losing my sense of who I was and what I had done was a heavenly experience. But it passed. Within months I felt the need to rediscover some of what I had been before, and what I was independent of Olivia. The prospect of losing my identity to her, and to other children, for a decade or two, became something I feared rather than relished.

Were the loss of independent identity to last for just a short time it might not be so frightening. But full-time motherhood can mean many years of putting the self on the back burner, if not out of sight completely. The author Penny Vincenzi coined the term 'invisible-mother syndrome' to describe the tendency of families to deny the mother her own life and her own strong identity. The invisible mother, says Vincenzi, is supposed to 'lurk invisibly, speak only when spoken to, modestly dressed, neatly coiffed, but poised with chequebook in one hand, car keys in the other, ready to move into action at any time of the day or (more likely) the night'.[27] She is supposed to be available to talk to her offspring whenever they want to even if she's 'crawling up to bed, dropping from exhaustion, or the one programme [she watches] all week is just beginning'. She's everybody's secretary and chauffeur. And ideally, she is all of these things without being intrusive, obvious or embarrassing.

The invisible-mother syndrome will not necessarily be kept at bay if the mother has a job. Without a job, though, she will find it much harder to prevent its onset. The singularity of her role makes it easy for the rest of the family to take her for granted, to treat her like the invisible doormat. ('I became a doormat at home, went into depression and lost my self-confidence,' recalled forty-eight-year-old mother Bridgit Williams at the 1997 *You* magazine forum on motherhood.[28]) In any family with school-age children and a full-time mum at the helm, the mother will be the only one without more than one role, or identity. The father is father, as well as accountant, lawyer, engineer or factory worker. The children are children, plus students. The mother is mother. And while the rest of the family leave the home to do other things and return at the end of the day to talk about them, she stays home and waits for them. Of course, the mother does untold numbers of things – things that sustain and nourish family life and without which it might collapse – while the rest of the family are out. But these things don't make up a role and identity that are distinct from that of 'mother'. And however much the rest of the family appreciate all that mother does, because she only has the one role, which is essentially to support them, they can easily take her for granted.

The fact that mother has no other role to which she can run for shelter might explain why her role as homemaker becomes so elastic, eventually comprising every task that no one else has time for or can be bothered to take on. It's the reason, as one exasperated full-time mother pointed out, the mother becomes everyone's dogsbody and errand-runner. When a working mother decides to stay home full-time, suddenly, and with astonishing predictability, everyone else in the family becomes incapable of collecting their own dry-cleaning, returning their own videos, or stopping at the chemist to pick up their urgently needed toiletries. And that's to name just a few of the thousands of little tasks that the full-time mother finds dumped on her to-do list.

There are mothers who are secure and strong enough to success-fully withstand the pressure to become invisible dogsbodies, permanently at the beck and call of their families. To these women, the rest of us should take off our hats. That their sense of self stands up to the daily onslaught of family life is a credit to them and their characters. But for many other women, the fear of losing the self within the family is very real, and is likely to be realized unless they fight hard to hold on to some outside role. Even women who are adamant that mothers should not work can recognize this. Rosalind Miles, who responded 'No' to the *Mail on Sunday*'s question, in August 1997, 'Should mothers work?', nevertheless admitted that 'work gives significance to our lives'.[29]

Identity is integral to self-actualization, which sits at the top of American psychologist Abraham Maslow's famous hierarchy of human needs. A strong personal identity is essential to human life in all its phases, from childhood through to adolescence, from the pre-parenting years through to old age, but it is perhaps never so important as when the family ceases to be so needy. When the nest empties, a crystal-clear sense of the self, independent of the family, and the confidence that accompanies it, are critical if a mother's feelings of loss and abandonment are to be minimized. Anne Roiphe describes the 'awful empty-nest syndrome' experienced by women who spent their twenties and thirties in child-rearing and then found themselves 'vacant, limp, lacking training, and way behind in all the skills in dealing with the workplace' as a disaster. Even for the working woman the passage from being needed most of the time to being needed very little is difficult, she says. What one is left with once the children have left – 'one's work, one's mind, one's enjoyment of one's own life for its own sake' – is perhaps not enough. She writes, 'I do know that it is better not to have the sum of one's worth in the bank of motherhood.'[30]

But while work helps people to form a strong sense of personal identity, an identity that rests exclusively on work is neither robust nor sustaining. In the future world described by the renowned consultant on work transitions and author William Bridges, in which jobs as we know them today become rare, work is packaged differently and people become responsible for defining and obtaining it themselves, the exclusively job-associated identity will be 'much too fragile a peg on which to hang a healthy life'. Even work itself, as opposed to jobs, cannot serve as the sole source of identity. The jigsaw puzzle of most people's identity is incomplete without pieces that come from the many aspects of personal life as well as from work. In the words of sociologist and author Barbara Ehrenreich, 'Meaningful work *and* a balanced life are deep-rooted and genuine needs. Like any needs they can be repressed or ignored for years at a time, but sooner or later they're going to assert themselves.'[31]

Preserving the Life of the Mind

A childless working woman in her mid-twenties once told me that she thought mothers should continue working once their children were born. 'I think women who stay at home lose the plot,' she said, unaware that two extremely bright and clued-in full-time mothers were within earshot. I was embarrassed, both for her and lest the other women thought that I shared her condescending perspective. I was also angry that someone with so little understanding of what it takes to have and raise a child should feel so confident in pronouncing women who do it all the time to be somehow incapable.

My conversation with that young woman was interrupted, and I never did have the chance to tell her how wrong or how presumptuous I thought she was. With hindsight I have come to think that she probably did not mean exactly what she said, but was merely repeating some short-hand version of the self-deprecating remarks many mothers make among themselves – 'I haven't read more than two sentences at a stretch for years', 'Who would have guessed my Masters degree would come to this?' In her carelessness and ignorance she confused a lack of opportunity to use the mind with mindlessness.

Of course, women (and men) who raise children full-time have not 'lost the plot'. One is no more or less likely to find a mindless drone in their midst than to find such a person in a group of employed persons. But it is equally true that the job of caring for children all day offers little in the way of intellectual stimulation. Full-time mothering engages the heart, tests reserves of patience, exhausts the body, and matures the character in a way that no other job can. And it is undoubtedly one of the most valuable things a person can spend his or her time doing. But, as Kate Figes writes, it can also be the most boring.[32] So much so that, in one survey of fifty mothers, two-thirds said that motherhood had given them a sense of purpose, but half said that *childcare* itself was a predominantly frustrating and irritating experience. And many found their own interests and identities disappearing when they focused on children's play.[33]

The best way to survive long days at home with small children is, in fact, to actively forget about one's own interests, and switch off the mind. It is by immersing oneself in a childlike mindset that one can most happily spend long periods with small children. Not doing so makes it difficult to meet their needs, and even more difficult to adapt to their pace.

How else, other than by switching the mind off, by turning it to daydreams, by ignoring one's rational sense of what could and should be accomplished in any given hour by a competent adult, can one happily take half an hour to walk a hundred yards with a two-year-old, or sit patiently while a stubborn toddler spends twenty minutes trying to dress a doll in clothes that any adult can see are too small? How else to enjoy living in what writer Alisa Kwitney describes as the 'eternal now' that is life with babies and small children – 'caring intensely about the stage you're going through, while forgetting everything that happened more than a week ago'? How else to avoid being driven nearly mad by the fact that, though your days are long, 'it is almost impossible to get anything done'?[34]

The degree to which the rhythms and rules of life at home with small children differ from those that characterize adult and work life cannot be exaggerated. They are expressed in crystal-clear terms in an anonymous article listing the 'twelve simple tests for expectant parents to take to prepare themselves for the real-life experience of being a mother or father' which was sent by a friend of mine to all the new parents she knew. Reading it, I was led to wonder how any parent, let alone a full-time one, emerges from a day with children with their sense of humour even vaguely intact. 'Dressing small children,' wrote the article's author 'is not as easy as it seems.' To get an idea of what it is like, 'buy an octopus and a string bag. Attempt to put the octopus into the string bag so that none of the arms hang out. Time allowed for this – all morning.' If you want to know what it is like to talk to small children all day, she continues, try 'repeating everything you say at least five times'. To prepare yourself for going out with small children . . .

> Get ready to go out. Wait outside the toilet for half an hour. Go out the front door. Come in again. Go out. Come back in. Go out again. Walk down the front path. Walk back up it. Walk down it again. Walk very slowly down the road for five minutes. Stop to inspect minutely every cigarette end, piece of used chewing gum, dirty tissue and dead insect along the way. Retrace your steps. Scream that you've had about as much as you can stand, until the neighbours come out and stare at you. Give up and go back to the house. You are just about ready to start walking with a small child.

There is no way of carrying on like this, day after day, without adjusting one's horizons, rethinking one's goals. The satisfaction of tasks accomplished is in extremely short supply during whole days spent caring for children – and that deriving from engagement in an intellectual or creative task is all but non-existent. Lilly, whom I described above, has consciously scaled down her expectations as to what she should achieve, and what a 'good day' looks like. 'Aside from keeping the children fed and happy, if I manage to do a load of washing and iron it, that's all I can do. That's a good day,' she says, without a hint of irony.

Those with little appreciation of what it takes to care for children all day and every day can mistakenly assume that the modern homemaker's life provides ample opportunity for the pursuit of intellectually satisfying endeavours. Dillie Keane of the *Mail on Sunday* hinted as much when she wrote that 'staying home doesn't mean one has to busy one's brains with trifles like how to make one'.[35] The chairman of the Association of Catholic Women, Josephine Robinson, spoke out against day-care and in favour of full-time mothers in *The Times* in June 1997, claiming that full-time mothers of young children need not let their brains languish, but have time to write novels or study for qualifications.[36] One *Times* reader responded that Ms Robinson must be out of touch, for 'genuine full-time mothers are a good deal more constrained'.[37] Indeed, the only mothers who can write novels or study are the few who are wealthy enough to afford both not to work *and* to hire childcare help – or those who can make the novels pay. (In which case, the novel-writing becomes work, like anything else.) For most, stopping work means caring for their children all the time, splashing out on a babysitter once a week if they're lucky. There is precious little time for reading the newspaper, let alone writing novels.

Women who are happy at home are not unaware of the impossibility of stretching their mental and creative faculties within the confines of their days. They are not unaware of the frustrations of living life at a snail's pace, of learning to regard the simplest and most mundane of tasks as significant accomplishments. As ex-lawyer Helen explained, 'You have to face the fact you're not going to get that pat on the back from your boss for a job well done. You're only going to see your real rewards when your children have grown up to be happy, well-rounded people.' But such women are able to accept the frustrations and live with the sacrifice of the life of the mind because they are certain that home is where they most want and need to be.

In the absence of that certainty, resentment at having to go through day after day starved of intellectual and creative stimulation brews dangerously. Turning off the mind, ignoring its needs as one tends to the all-engulfing needs of small children, may even be an impossibility for some. For women who have spent years in education and working within a dynamic environment, the drive to create some space for the vital life of the mind will not magically disappear once children arrive, no matter how strong the desire to mother, no matter how strenuously the moral and political stance in favour of full-time mothering is asserted.

Square Pegs in Round Holes

The stunningly obvious yet easily overlooked fact is that each mother is different from the next, and expecting them all to be happy doing the same job for years on end is like attempting to fit mostly square pegs into mostly round holes. All the subsidies and tax incentives for housewives, deserved and welcomed though they would be, would not change that fact. They could not render every mother well suited for a life at home, any more than they could equip them all to spend their days working as airline pilots, dentists or teachers.

The key is to know yourself. Each woman must understand what makes herself tick, what she needs to be happy and fulfilled, what will keep her sane. May do have that understanding and are using it to craft a life that suits them, whether it be working outside the home or entirely within it. In the *Parenting in the Nineties* survey, around a third of working mothers and 38 per cent of stay-at-home mothers report being satisfied with life.[38] And, according to Bonney and Reinach's study of housewives, most don't regret the lack of a job and some 37 per cent intend never to return to work. But what about the rest? Some may be trying to conform to someone else's idea of what's good for them and their family, or are prevented by a range of constraints from acting upon their self-knowledge. Some in the *Parenting in the Nineties* survey may indeed be working mothers who would like to stay home, and who would do so if they could afford to. Others may be full-time mothers who would love to work. In a *Guardian* article of November 1997, Maureen Freely asked, 'If the constraints were different – if it were possible for women to limit their work time to school time – would they be balancing their lives differently? When women choose to stay home ... how often is it out of resentment at employers who are blind to their needs? And just what is the long-term price they pay?'

In some cases, the price of suppressing a need to be active outside the home can be severe depression. Gay Haines, the mother of three boys and managing director of the executive search, freelance placement and film production firm hat pin, spent years feeling dispirited, energyless and depressed. After several consultations with her doctor he advised her to return to work. 'You are a very creative, high-energy person, and you are stifled at home. You need to get a job,' he told her. She did, her depression soon lifted, and her energy returned. She went on to found the firm and has never looked back.

Another woman I know has not been so fortunate. She became seriously depressed and anorexic partly as a result of her unhappiness at having given up her career to stay home full-time. Yet she found herself in a trap she could not escape: unhappy as she was at home, and much as she craved her former life, she could not convince herself that it was possible to work while raising children. For her, a career is all or nothing, and she remains trapped in the nothing.

When a woman denies her need to work she may do more than invite severe depression and lethargy. Research shows that mothers who aren't satisfied with their employment status have more negative interactions with their children.[39] Journalist Deborah Hutton cautions that a woman who leaves a brilliant career for the sake of her children may find that she can't leave the competition of work behind.[40] She may find herself turning parenting into a profession. Instead of seeking self-fulfilment through a career of her own, her 'job satisfaction comes through the reflected glory of the child's achievements – from first faltering steps to PhD and beyond'. If this leads to 'competitiveness and ambition dressed up as selflessness' it does the child no favours, claims Hutton. Hutton caught herself becoming a 'professional parent' when she stopped working for a while. She now recognizes that when she is not using the switched-on, competitive-business part of her character, it emerges in her dealings with the children. Like Rosa Monckton, Maeve Haran and other women I spoke to, Hutton sees self-knowledge as crucial.

What's *Really* Best for Mothers?

It is one of life's cruel jokes that motherhood transforms women but does not at the same time equip them all to spend every waking minute caring for their children. Motherhood makes it impossible to take up one's old life with the same commitment, energy and glee, while one's old life, and the non-mother self that grew from it, prevent one from becoming completely absorbed by motherhood. As my friend Jane wrote, 'Motherhood is this transformational experience, but at the same time it isn't what I want to spend all my time doing. That makes me crazy!' How is one to escape the craziness of needing to be with one's children, and yet needing to be away from them?

To escape it completely is an impossibility. 'You will never eliminate that dilemma between needing to work – for yourself – and needing to be with your children,' said Rosa Monckton. To a large extent, the dilemma is intrinsic to mothering. It cannot be eradicated. But the burdens and pressures that the dilemma brings, even the dilemma itself, can be alleviated. Not by giving in to the wishful and idealistic view that women would be happy at home if they were financially enabled to stay there; not by suppressing the self and the need to work to such an extent that they re-emerge as depression or anorexia. The only way to avoid being torn in half by the tug-of-war between the mother and the other inside is to acknowledge and accommodate both.

'That child-rearing may be the centre of the soul does not mean that there isn't room for other things,' writes Anne Roiphe. 'It has done us no service to have work opposed to our child-rearing.' The difficulty, in much of today's work world, is that work is something that can be nothing other than antipathetic to child-rearing. When work means five or more days a week, ten to twelve hours a day, and one hundred and fifty per cent of one's heart and soul, there is precious little left to give to child-rearing. Motherhood and work life, which need to be like glove and hand, are more like dog and cat.[41] Seeing this, it is little wonder that so many women give up trying to reconcile the two, and become convinced of the need to choose home over work.

But the creation of space for parenting within thriving work lives is something we can accomplish if we devote sufficient will and energy to it. It requires a change in the way we do our work and the way we structure it. It means altering the prevailing view that long hours spent sitting at a desk or in meetings are synonymous with productivity, achievement and success. These are not changes that are easily made, but neither are they beyond our capability. There are some who have succeeded in making them already. From them we can learn about the true possibilities for making work and parenting fit together like glove and hand.

The greatest thing we can do for mothers is to support, encourage and enable them in their efforts to craft working lives that leave room for parenting. Therein lies the path to giving those who need and want to work the same kind of peace of mind and contentedness as those whose true calling and every desire are represented by being at home full-time. Therein lie genuine choices for women.

CHAPTER SEVEN

THE MYTH OF THE FEW SHORT YEARS

Brenda Barnes . . . chief executive of Pepsi Cola, North America, says she's
resigned from her powerful job because, after working for twenty-two years,
she wants more time to spend with her family. Ms Barnes is forty-three. A few
years ago her little ones, who are now ten, eight and seven, needed her far
more than they do today. Ms Barnes, I suspect, is using a sudden apparent
emotional yearning to be a full-time mummy as a shrewd smoke screen.
LYNDA LEE-POTTER, *Daily Mail*, 1 October 1997

WHEN I WAS five months pregnant with my first child I made a
routine visit to my obstetrician. Being early, I was ushered towards
a comfortable sofa in the waiting-room of the hospital, where I
proceeded to flip absent-mindedly through back issues of *Country
Living* magazine. As it happened, the waiting-room opened directly
on to the hospital pharmacy, where a woman was in the process of
paying for whatever had been prescribed her. Although I could not
see her, I could hear her voice very clearly. I could also hear the
officious but kind voice of the female pharmacist, and the faint
gurgles of a baby.

The pharmacist made generally polite and admiring noises about
the baby, then asked the mother whether she would be staying home
with the baby or returning to work. 'Oh, staying home. Absolutely,'
said the mother. 'You know I really can't understand mothers who
want to rush back to work. After all, children are only little for such
a short time. Before you know it, they're grown up and gone. A job
can be picked up at any time, but you can never have back those
years with a young child.' The pharmacist agreed so vigorously that
I could almost see her head nodding up and down despite the brick
wall between us.

I was not so engrossed in the 'how tos' of creating the simple country-kitchen look that I didn't stop to consider what I had heard. I wondered, just for a few moments, whether I ought to reconsider my commitment to returning to work after the birth of my own baby. Then my mind got going on the maths involved: three children separated by, say, two and a half years each; four years at home with each one. That makes nine years in total just to see them through to school age, I thought. How trivial is that? And how easy is any job to pick up after a complete absence from the workforce for nine years? How likely is anyone to hire a forty-one-year-old who left the workforce at age thirty-two when IBM mainframes were the ticket, and returns to a world of Windows and Netscape? Or a forty-one-year-old whose only written words for nine years have been to her children's teachers?

The maths won me over in the end. After a couple of minutes' consideration, I decided that however sympathetic I might be to the emotion underlying that woman's point of view, I couldn't accept her argument. Children are not young for just a short time. They are young for a good many years. And if you have more than one, and stay home with them, you'll spend many years out of the workforce, and a not insignificant number struggling to get back in.

I left the waiting-room with renewed confidence in my decision to work, in some capacity or other, after the birth of my baby. What I did not then realize was how often I would hear that same conversation during the next few years, and how often I would find myself going through the mental arithmetic of children multiplied by years at home and coming up with the same large number. What I also failed to realize was that I had come face to face, albeit via a brick wall, with one of the Earthmother's favourite lines of reasoning – the Myth of the Few Short Years. I was unaware that I would encounter this myth, in another guise, at work, where some would be expecting me to return to full-time work before my child was six months old.

If I did not recognize the myth then, I do now. It comes in many forms. It is most frequently seen in the guise of the righteous public stance of the stay-at-home mother and those in the media who amplify her voice. It is also represented by most workplace policies that provide for flexibility in the first months after a woman gives birth. It is embodied in public policy initiatives which focus on early-years childcare while offering little to support families with school-age children beyond a few after-school clubs and holiday camps. Whatever form it takes, the myth can be boiled down to the following few simple statements. Children are little for a short time. They need you only when they are little. You are selfish, as a mother, if you deny your children your full attention during these early years. You are uncommitted, as an employee, if you deny your employer your full attention beyond these early years.

Two Sides of the Same Fiction

Vocal, high-profile Earthmothers insist that a mother is selfish if she denies her children her undivided attention and round-the-clock presence during the short time when they are young. You need to realize, says the media Earthmother, that if you stay home during your children's early years you are sacrificing very little, and that once they are at school you will be able to pick up that job you left.

Paula Yates spelled out the Myth of the Few Short Years in early 1992. 'Once your desire for children overrides your desire for work,' she advised, 'quit your job and perhaps pick it up again later; or have children when you're young, stay with them until they have grown up and then embark on a career.'[1] Yates was as conveniently vague about the exact age after which children are deemed to be 'grown up' as she was seemingly incognizant of how difficult it is to relaunch a career after a lengthy period of time out of the workforce.

The myth was given a new lease of life in 1995 when, in the light of 'a wave of evidence' suggesting that a child's intellectual and psychological well-being is determined during the first eighteen months of its life, *Tatler* writer Helen Kirwan Taylor suggested that mothers ought to stay home full-time during their children's early years. She interviewed full-time mother Belinda Scott, who asked, 'Out of a whole lifetime, what's seven years?',[2] even though with children aged seven, five and two she was still facing another two years before all were in nursery school, let alone 'grown up' enough not to need their mother.

In early 1997, in the midst of the public wrangling that followed *Panorama*'s 'Missing Mum' programme, research about babies' intellectual and psychological development was again cited as a reason for mothers to stay home for those early years. The research, which revealed that children's brains develop physically in response to the stimulation they receive, particularly during the first three years of life, is fascinating and valuable, but has proved lethal in the hands of the Earthmother myth-makers. At about the same time as *Missing Mum* was aired, a journalist for the *Scotsman* denounced the trend towards depriving children of 'the maternal presence during their first three vital years,'[3] and advocated paying mothers to stay home with their children at least until nursery school. Also about the same time, Patricia Morgan, researcher at the Institute of Economic Affairs and a champion of the Earthmother role model, was quoted as saying, 'You can always go back to work, but the damage done in the early years can never be rectified.'[4] Another woman, explaining her own mothering choices in her commentary on the Nicola Horlick episode, wrote that she felt it to be important for a mother to be at home, 'at least for the first two years'.[5]

The 'few short years' notion according to Superwoman and her boss differs from the Earthmother's version only in its definition of the term 'young'. For while the maternally correct would appear to believe that a child is 'young' for three to four years – that is, until he or she goes to nursery school – organizations, and the flexible policy documents they produce, would seem to have decided that a child is 'young' – in other words, needy of its mother – for anything from three months to about two years: workplace flexibility, in the form of part-time jobs and phased returns to full-time work, is often temporarily granted to new mothers in the expectation that they will be back on the full-time track before long.

After my initial encounter with the Myth of the Few Short Years outside my obstetrician's office, I came up against its workplace version when I returned to work after my first pregnancy. I was discussing assignment options with one of the firm's vice-presidents that would allow me to work a three-and-a-half-day week. As we went through them, he asked me how long I thought I would like to work part-time. 'Oh, about the next fifteen years,' I replied. His expression made it abundantly clear that six months was more like the answer he had expected to hear.

I remember a similar conversation when my children were three and a half and eighteen months old. A male colleague broached the possibility that I might return full-time in the near future. 'After all,' he said, 'your children must be in school now, so they won't need you as much.' Only his secretary's timely plea that he take an urgent call saved me the embarrassment of having to repeat my line about the fifteen years, and him the discomfort of having to hear it.

To their great credit, both these men overcame their initial shock on hearing that my part-time status might endure beyond the first six months after maternity leave, and they proved to be great supporters of mine and of other women's efforts to combine careers as management consultants with mothering. They are now light years ahead of most male managers in terms of their understanding of work–family issues, and in their ability to deal with them. Their initial astonishment at the idea that the need for part-time work might span years rather than weeks or months, may perhaps have been due to the fact that their wives stayed home, thereby shielding them from the daily reality of raising children while they worked long hours. Or perhaps it was because they have known only Superwomen – or ordinary women doing a sterling job of pretending – who returned to work two months after giving birth and never mentioned their children at the office again.

In not fully appreciating that children's need for mothering – by one parent, if not necessarily by the mother – endures beyond a three-month maternity leave and a brief period of short hours on return from it, these two men were not alone. The fact is that many senior managers within organizations still fail to appreciate this, and family-friendly policy in those firms reflects this lack of appreciation. It is written as if mothers with children had no special need to be accommodated beyond day ninety of the breastfeeding marathon. Scarlett MccGwire reports in her book, *Best Companies for Women*, that many of even the best firms provide flexible opportunities for mothers only during the early months or years of their children's lives. Some 25 per cent of the 120 organizations covered by an industrial relations survey conducted in 1989 allowed women to work part-time or to job-share when they returned from maternity leave, but for almost a quarter of these the arrangement was purely temporary.[6] Though a later survey of 240 large UK companies revealed that most would allow permanent part-time work,[7] Isabel Boyer, a consultant to employers on work–family issues and author of *Viable Working for Managers*, reveals that most employers *expect* part-time arrangements to last between two and five years.

If senior managers often fail to understand that a mother's need for flexibility might persist beyond the initial few months or years of her child's life, Superwomen in the office and in the media do nothing to enlighten them. Women who return to work having taken only a third of their maternity leave, read bedtime stories to their children over the telephone and are unflinching about spending three weeks at a time attending conferences in foreign countries, might be very happy and able to cope with their own situation, but they do little for the average working mother, who is desperately unhappy and very often unable to live this way. Their attitude forces her to stifle her unhappiness, and makes her feel she's letting the side down if she dares to voice it. In the constrained and emotionally barren work environments that result, women become fearful of articulating their needs as mothers to others; men become incapable of articulating their needs as fathers even to themselves.

Even academics specializing in the study of women's career development can unwittingly perpetuate the myth that mothering is demanding for only a few short years. One whom I interviewed was adamant that factors to do with mothering should not be overestimated in explaining women's failure to progress within organizations. 'I don't accept that it's the most significant factor,' she said. 'After all, those child-bearing, child-raising years are for *such a short time*.'

Unveiling the Myth

Both the Earthmother and the Superwoman versions of the Myth of the Few Short Years rest upon the assumption that children's need for mothering can be confined to some conveniently short period. The myth according to the Earthmother also rests upon a second assumption: that it is easy for women to pick up their careers once that short period has passed. The woman I overheard in the obstetrician's waiting-room believed it to be true. So did another, who said to me: 'You can never have those first few years with your children back, but you can *always pick up the job.*'

In fact, both halves of this woman's statement fail to stand up to scrutiny. As already indicated, the 'first few years' – that is, when your children need you – aren't 'few', and you can't always pick up the job. Mothers with children in their teens know all too well that those children continue to make demands on them that are not easily accommodated within fast-paced careers. And the experience of women returners, women who have been absent from the workforce for eight to ten years and have struggled to re-enter it, suggests that picking up a career once all the children are in school is an enormous challenge.

It's important that we confront these types of falsehoods. Unless we recognize, collectively, that children's needs change rather than diminish as they get older, becoming more rather than less discordant with traditional long-hours careers, and unless we acknowledge the difficulties faced by women who attempt to re-enter the job market after protracted absences, we will fail to embrace a new way of thinking about the work–family dilemma. And we do need that new way of thinking. For if children's need for mothering does indeed go on and on, well past the age of four, it means that neither the Earthmother nor the Superwoman options can serve many of us well. The former can involve the enduring sacrifice of the self, and of selfish ambitions, rather than sacrifice for a convenient three- or four-year period; the latter can mean sacrificing our children's longterm well-being, as well as our relationships with them.

Just How Long is a Child a Child, and What Does a Child Need?

Women who are no longer under the sway of the Myth of the Few Short Years, as well as the honest journalists who reflect their views, recognize that, as Sunday Telegraph writer Minette Marrin pointed out in March 1992, 'family life is not just looking after a couple of babies for five years'.[8] It is also seeing four-year-olds through their first exciting and traumatic year at school, nurturing the development and learning of five-, six- and seven-year-olds, guiding ten-year-olds through the awkwardness of pre-puberty, spending time with teenagers who are worried about their GCSEs, and supporting local school projects. In other words, if you're raising a family, you need to be prepared for a long haul. As television executive Roz Morris put it, 'A baby is for life.' You can't expect that staying home for a couple of 'short years' will do the trick, and that sixty-hour weeks will suddenly become possible once the children are settled in school. There's nothing 'few' or 'short' about the needs of children as they are growing up.

In striking contrast to Lynda Lee-Potter's view that children need their mothers most when they are tiny, expressed in her commentary on Brenda Barnes's resignation from PepsiCo, most women discover that children's needs actually increase as they get older, and are irritated by suggestions that only the first few years are the demanding ones. Of all the myths of the Mother War, the Myth of the Few Short Years is the one that seemed, to the women I spoke to, most at odds with reality. Almost without exception, every woman with a child over three whom I interviewed volunteered her belief that mothering is more demanding, more complicated and more time-consuming as children get older. 'If there's one thing which really irritates me, it's this glib assumption that you're home free once the children are in school,' said investment banking analyst Karen. 'It really annoys me when I hear young working mothers with babies and toddlers who think they've got this stuff all worked out, when, in fact, it only gets harder as the children grow up,' said obstetric physiotherapist and mother of three Christine Hill. Psychotherapist Susie Orbach described the school years as a 'logistical nightmare'. BBC Radio journalist Sheila Cook spoke for many others when she said, 'Actually, I think things get much more difficult once you're past the toddler stage.'

Mary, a tax accountant, managed to stick with full-time work while her daughter was young, but ended up resigning from her firm to work fewer hours, from home, when she turned fourteen. 'I just felt I needed to be there for her a lot more,' she said. 'She's going through all kinds of difficult things at the moment, like preparing for her GCSEs. And she was resenting the fact that I couldn't spend any time with her. Since quitting, I've been able to spend more time just talking, or taking her shopping after school, which she just loves.

You wouldn't believe the change in her and in our relationship. We are both so much happier.'

Like Mary, several prominent mothers working in the media cut down their working hours in response to their children's ever-escalating needs. Carole Barnes switched to part-time newsreading when her children were nine and twelve, explaining in an article in the *Daily Mail* in January 1992 that 'as they develop into little adults, they need more love and support rather than less'. Linda Kelsey resigned as editor of *She* magazine to spend more time with her son when he was past the toddler stage. Cherie Blair told the *Guardian* that the difficulties involved in being a working mother 'don't end when children go to school'.[9] Jenny Abramsky recalls thinking it extraordinary when a friend gave up work when her children were twelve and sixteen, but admits, 'Now that my children are virtually the same age, I understand her.'[10]

These women realize that family life gets more complex over time, and that children require continuous nurturing. Creating a sense of fun and order – or a pulse, as one woman called it – in a family whose children are becoming more active and independent is a challenge that is not easily slotted into the evening hours of eight to ten and frazzled and frantic weekends. Neither is it a challenge that is easily delegated to others: film-maker Angela Holdsworth discovered that 'what seemed to work if you had a marvellous nanny or childminder to make life fun for the under-fives can fall apart when the children are in their early teens and need a sympathetic ear to a new set of problems'.[11] She believes that 'breaks of one kind or another, changes of direction and family commitments, should be accepted as normal', and has found herself working less, and in a more flexible way, as her children have grown older.

Child development expert Penelope Leach believes that we often ignore the years between seven and thirteen, erroneously believing them to represent an 'easy phase: a rest between the exigencies of babyhood and early childcare, and the upheavals of puberty and early adult-care'. In fact, this span of years is enormously important to the child's development. 'If only one period were important in a child's development, it would be the first. But if those years of infancy and early childhood shape the individual, this next span of middle childhood meshes that individual into his society. Seven – or six, or maybe eight – is acknowledged as some kind of watershed by almost every school of thought in Western culture,' writes Leach in *Children First*.

During the critical middle years children become more aware of a wider society, and are keen to acquire its new knowledge and skills, learn its history and 'understand its concerns and aspirations'. They begin to think about 'the internal workings of people and the world', ask difficult value-laden questions, and form value systems of their own.[12] Parents cannot shrug off such 'moral stuff', nor can they expect schools to serve as the primary source of guidance through the child's learning about society, values and morals. Leach warns that we may be in danger of overvaluing the influence of the peer group relative to individual relationships with adults.

Like Leach, American social worker Alice White believes that 'many of today's kids don't understand how the world works because they haven't spent enough time with their parents to understand how decisions are made, careers are pursued, personal relationships are formed'.[13] White exhorts parents to accept responsibility for the critical role they continue to play in helping their children develop. They can't do this if they are away from the home for sixty hours a week and preoccupied by stress and endless lists of chores when they are home. Kevin Dwyer of the National Association of School Psychologists in America is concerned that many parents are drained at the end of the day, which leads them to devote too little attention to their children and to discipline them inconsistently. As a result, the children of very busy parents tend to be 'more aggressive, more deviant and more oppositional'.[14]

According to child development specialist Barbara Coloroso there are three points of rebellion in a child's life: at age two, age five, and the onset of the teens.[15] At each of these points, the child's need for parental guidance, understanding and time is enormous. Yet the provision of moral guidance and emotional support is difficult when both parents work long hours. Even the basic logistical challenges of family life are difficult to accommodate within long-hours careers – school runs, sports, music and ballet lessons, homework sessions, dentist and doctor appointments, family dinners and celebrations, birthday parties, outings and invitations to play with friends who live ten miles away and nowhere near the bus route – but the emotional elements of family life are by far the greatest factors at risk when parental time with children is limited. MP Margaret Hodge found it quite easy to compartmentalize her life when her children were very young. She could switch off from work and on to them when she came home, and her children could do the same. But as they get older, she remarks, 'they just don't switch on and off to you in the same way'.

Public policy is often unrecognizing of children's continuing need for moral and emotional support, and of parents' difficulties in providing it when they are both working full-time. A key aspect of the Labour government's answer to the problems faced by working parents with school-age children is after-school clubs. Second to a 'national childcare strategy', this is Harriet Harman's most frequently proffered answer to the question of how Labour will help women juggle work and home duties. After-school clubs may be a way of keeping children off the streets and out of harm's way, and they may even provide ideal play situations for some children. (One boy who regularly attended an after-school club claimed that he would be cross if he was no longer able to attend his club, where he liked to 'play games' and 'make lots of friends'.)[16] But they are not a solution, in themselves, to the more acute problem of parents with too little time to give to their children. Quite apart from the fact that after-school clubs cannot hope to provide individual moral guidance and emotional support if a parent fails to, they will not suit all children. Many are tired after a day at school, and would react badly to the school day being extended through organized games and supervised homework sessions. Magazine editor Paula Brook discovered, after a period during which she had kept her children busy with one after-school activity after another, that they 'didn't appreciate all those productive and expensive hours skating, singing in choirs, tap-dancing and learning to build with clay'. Instead, they asked, 'Why can't I just come home after school today?'[17]

Children need time to reflect, to emote, and to generally hang about. They need to do this, some of the time, with a parent around to notice what it is they are reflecting on or emoting about, even if that parent is simply hovering in the background. Fifty- or sixty-hour-a-week careers for parents and after-school clubs for children won't allow for this, whatever Superwomen say to the contrary. And those who would advocate the Earthmother route, believing that a few short years at home buy complete freedom to resume a career later on, will find, instead, that they become increasingly embroiled in the sustenance of their children's emotional lives, and that the possibilities for resuming a fast-paced career become ever more remote.

Picking up the Job After the Few Short Years are Over

Journalist Maggie Drummond wrote in the *Daily Telegraph* in February 1992 that her research into the experience of women trying to return to work in middle age had turned up 'stories of misery and humiliation' that made her weep. Scarlett MccGwire, also, found that it is tough getting a good job if you are over the age of forty, particularly if you are female,[18] and that instead of being welcomed back into employment, women returners are often treated as if they are over the hill. Other researchers note that women suffer as much from a lack of confidence as from actual discrimination against them.[19]

This reality is often hidden from view by publicity and research that aim to convince us that career breaks are working for women. A 1992 study by the Institute of Manpower Studies Cooperative Research Programme, entitled *Beyond the Career Break*, stated that the women in their survey felt positive about most aspects of the way their break had been handled, that many of them had been promoted since the break, and that there is indeed career progression beyond the break.[20] But the career breaks they refer to are short – 80 per cent of the sample had taken nine months or less off work. Only 10 per cent had taken breaks longer than a year, and 90 per cent of the women who had taken more than one career break were still off for less than two years in total. This is a far cry from the kind of career break advocated by the maternally correct – the kind that sees two or three children through to school age and lasts for six or more years.

Women contemplating a return to work after several years at home frequently express pessimism and trepidation. Liz, a former

PR consultant, is very doubtful about being able to rekindle her career. Apart from the fact that she sees few jobs in her industry with hours flexible enough to meet the needs of mothers with school-age children, she questions her ability to find a job at all. 'I've lost all my networks and contacts, and the business has changed so much. I would have to start from scratch and retrain,' she says. Another woman who has spent eight years at home complains that any job she could now find would pay her almost nothing. She also believes that she would have to retrain completely if she wished to work again. Other women comment on their loss of skills and networks, and on a decline in their confidence. They see the hurdles associated with returning to work as enormous, and even insurmountable.

One woman who took just a few months off to be with her children, sees her return to work as something of an insurance policy against being unable to re-enter the workforce once her children are in school full-time. 'I could be happy staying home for a few years while my children are young. I've loved every minute of these past months,' she says. 'But when they're both in school all day in a couple of years, I'll want something to do. I see mothers whose children have all gone to school full-time and they're just walking around wondering what to do with themselves. But re-entering the workforce when you've been away from it completely for several years looks like an impossible challenge to me. It seems easier to keep hanging in there.'

An appreciation of the barriers to restarting a career after a protracted absence from the workplace leads many women to favour working part-time over taking career breaks while their children are young. IBM offers a generous maternity leave policy allowing for three years' leave for each child, but has found that relatively few women actually take the full amount of time. They prefer to continue working, though on a reduced-hours basis. Several women I spoke to saw provisions for lengthy career breaks as undesirable. BBC journalist Sheila Cook, who works part-time, doesn't think career breaks are a good idea. 'The BBC enables people to take career breaks of five years, but I never felt I wanted to do that because I would lose touch. And in an industry where technology is changing very fast, if you went away for five years you would come back and find the equipment you used to work on had literally gone ... Plus you would be divorced from all the changes in management and the power structure. It would be very hard to start again.'

Tracy Camilleri, the managing director of WMC Communications who works part-time, echoes Cook's views about career breaks. 'The timing of an extended break is bound to be terrible,' she said. 'Most people don't figure out what they want to do and what they are good at, or gain the confidence to do it until they're in their late twenties or early thirties. To stop work at that point, just when you're getting into your stride, is a terrible waste. And regaining the confidence to start again must be almost impossible.' Carolyn, a veterinary surgeon who has just set up her own practice at the age of thirty, similarly believes the likely timing of a career break for child-raising would make it almost impossible to consider. She is contemplating having children at the very same time that she is launching her new practice. Were she to take a break while her children were young, she would have to give the practice up. 'That is unthinkable to me,' she says. 'I've just worked and studied for ten years to get to where I am. I'm not ready to stop working yet!'

Some plead for mothers who take career breaks to be provided with the retraining necessary to help them re-enter the workplace, whether that be training in computer skills, new radio recording technology, or new marketing techniques. Full-Time Mothers asks that 'employers be encouraged to perceive mothering as valid work experience, and provide further training, should a woman wish to return to paid employment once her children are older'.[21] Mothers who stay home full-time *do* amass valuable experience and useful skills. Many develop communication, interpersonal, financial and supervisory skills that would stand them in good stead in the workforce. But however worthwhile the experience of full-time mothering as a training ground for communication and supervision skills, nothing will persuade employers that mothering provides the grounding in computer technology, factory management models or market research techniques that would enable a woman to launch a career with just a little 'further training'. The skills required for most careers are not easily learned on short training courses. They are garnered over years of training and experience. No amount of wishful thinking on the part of organizations like Full-Time Mothers can alter that. Nor can it serve as a remedy for the loss of confidence that many experience when they remain out of the workforce for long periods – confidence not easily restored by a three-week retraining course.

The barriers to re-entry represented by the loss of skills, confidence and contact with former colleagues will matter little to women who are happy with and fulfilled by life at home with their children, and who have no need or desire to return to work even once the children are grown (some 37 per cent of homemakers, according to the Bonney and Reinach study, noted in Chapter 6). These women will find ways to fill the hours when their children are in school, and will be welcomed with open arms by charities and voluntary organizations. But for other women who eventually want or need to work, the difficulties associated with re-entry are daunting and serious indeed. Their 'few short years' at home may lead to many longer years re-educating themselves and struggling back into a game they have forgotten how to play.

Moving from the Myth to the Future

Whether uttered by a stay-at-home mother or a mother with a career, the Myth of the Few Short Years obfuscates the truth and muddles the public debate about whether or not mothers should work. The truth is that children are developing all the time, and they have enormous needs for love, time and attention when they are five, seven, ten and fifteen. So there is no easy way to confine our intense parental involvement with them to a few years. It won't work for the mother who hopes to stay home for a short while and then return to a fast-paced career. And it won't work for the Superwoman anxious to resume full-time work, sixty hours a week, within a few months of giving birth.

What we need is widespread acceptance of the continuing requirements, in time and in physical and emotional energy, that parenting makes of parents, and mothering makes of mothers. We need to weave that acceptance into our view of work and careers. We need to create an environment in which mothers, and fathers, can acknowledge their long-term commitment to their children *and* their commitment to a satisfying career.

Such an environment is one in which the long-hours mentality has loosened its grip on working culture and practices, and many people, parents and non-parents alike, have the opportunity to work less than full-time. It is one in which considerable effort is devoted to constructing part-time roles and to making them function effectively, one in which 'part-time' is not synonymous with 'sidelined', and successful long-term careers can be made out of part-time jobs.

A pipe dream? Many will say so. But there are a few risk-taking women and men, and a few inspired organizations, who are bravely choosing the path towards this future. They are encountering many stumbling-blocks and much resistance from the entrenched work culture, but they are fighting the fight. And they *will* win. The question is, how many others will follow them now, and how many will wait until it is too late for their own families to benefit?

PART THREE

NO MORE MYTHS

CHAPTER EIGHT

✣

THE FAMILY-FRIENDLY WORKPLACE:
HOW FAR HAVE WE GOT?

Seven out of ten blue-chip companies now employ part-time managers and
over 80 per cent believe that part-time working for managers will become
increasingly popular.
Demos, *Tomorrow's Women*, 1996

More managers are striking deals for flexible working schedules. They have
more time for their kids and – surprise – their careers are prospering.
Fortune magazine, 20 May 1991

✣ ✣

ONCE THE MYTHS in the Mother War are exposed, so is the
inadequacy of the role models they support. All work or no work are
not good enough options for many women. So it is to the workplace
itself that we must turn. Most mothers, and increasing numbers of
fathers, need a radically different sort of workplace if they are not to
be broken by the dual demands of work and family.

Guided by the advertisements in women's magazines, one might
easily conclude that such a workplace is already in existence. We've
all seen that well-groomed executive mother sitting at the desk in
her kitchen, tapping into a computer with one hand, holding a
telephone in the other, cradling a two-year-old on her knee. Both
the two-year-old and the mother are all smiles, the atmosphere
sunny and untroubled. It is obvious that the woman is both a devoted
mother and an achiever, and that, above all, she represents what can
be achieved in the much vaunted 'family-friendly workplace', the
workplace in which it is possible to pursue a challenging career and
spend time with one's child by working often from home, staying in
touch with the office by fax, phone and modem. A truly inspiring
picture, not dissimilar to that painted by the publicity shots for the

successful film, *Baby Boom*, in which Diane Keaton is seen seated at a desk, pen in hand, smiling warmly at the eighteen-month-old baby whose bottom is firmly planted upon the papers Keaton is about to sign.

Such is the picture regularly painted by advertisements, women's magazines and the 'family-life' features in the Sunday newspapers. I challenge any woman to recreate it in real life. In real life, if you watch a mother working from home, it is more likely to look like this: telephone conversations punctuated by the persistent attempts of the two-year-old to grab hold of the receiver and participate, or by his alarmed cries from another room as he attempts to launch himself from some piece of furniture or other; complex computer spreadsheets annihilated by small sticky fingers eager to experiment; files upturned, papers scribbled upon, and computer discs hidden irretrievably in the depths of saucepan cupboards; concentration interrupted by sweet young things bearing biscuits, toys, or snails from the garden – almost anything that can serve as an excuse to visit mummy; thoughts and sentences unfinished; mother frustrated and harassed, child sulking, mother feeling guilty.

The plain truth is that, for many people and certainly most women, working at home when there are small children around is extraordinarily difficult. Like so many aspects of the much heralded 'family-friendly workplace' or the 'new flexibility', it doesn't yet work very well. But the media often pretend that it does. Most of the images of people working from home that the media choose to portray conveniently omit the complications that are part of the package.

So it is with media coverage of other types of workplace family-friendliness. A family-life feature in a Saturday *Telegraph* of April 1995 tells us that more and more parents are adapting their working lives to better suit their children. It introduces Simon and his wife, who job-share with each other, and Rachel, who works three days a week as a solicitor for a major corporation and still managed to get offered a promotion. And we are told that in Britain generally, employers are adopting family-friendly policies – largely as a result of initiatives such as Opportunity 2000, the business campaign launched in 1991 by Business in the Community to improve the quality and quantity of women's employment. Another article, in the *Sunday Telegraph*, one year on, features an interview with Heather

Knox, who has just won the 1996 Hanson Management Award and has a 'healthy focus that family comes first'. Heather has just had twins and plans to go back to work as manager of an NHS trust four days a week. She has always had a 'setting boundaries' approach to business, which means that she avoids taking meetings at 8am, but now she'll be even tougher about that because of her family.

We often hear managers and business leaders like Knox claiming to put family first. Many of the leaders interviewed by Ruth Tait for her book, *Roads to the Top*, subscribed to a 'family first' philosophy, with one even putting family details first on his curriculum vitae. According to a survey by the *Harvard Business Review* in 1991, family life was among the most important concerns of senior international managers.[1]

Such stories are encouraging, but they tell less than half the story. While there is undoubtedly a trend towards people trying to shape their work lives around their families' needs, we are still only at the front end of that trend. Even the business leaders who are famed for their efforts to achieve balance in their lives often turn out to be doing little that is truly remarkable – they might try to get home by 6.15pm to put the children to bed or refuse to work at weekends, but few are placing family first in any dramatic way within their work lives. As one American middle manager noted, 'Higher-level managers all tell you that family is number one ... but you look at how they live and you have to wonder.'[2] And for every story of a pioneer of the new balance, ten could be written about women still struggling to leave work by six o'clock twice a week so that they can read the bedtime story. For every account of a part-time job that works, there will be ten examples of part-time jobs that involve spending all of Friday on the phone, doing a one hundred per cent job for a 60 per cent salary. The fact is that we are still a long way from seeing the family-friendly workplace become anything other than an interesting experiment, a novelty-shop trinket. We do not even have in place the basic structures for family-friendliness in most of the working world, let alone the shift in culture and mindset that would allow it to become woven into the fabric of organizations and society as it needs to be. Today, family-friendliness is, in the words of two researchers from the Institute for Employment Studies, merely 'old wine in new bottles'.[3]

This reality was neatly summed up for me at a conference sponsored by Parents at Work. The conference was designed to explore parents' concerns about long hours and workplace inflexibility. As we all walked in, we were handed a 'Long Hours Campaign Take Action Pack' full of booklets and brochures. The working mother next to me thumbed through the pack with some interest, then shook her head and sighed. She leaned over to me and said: 'This is all interesting stuff, and it sounds great. But it doesn't really work like that, does it?'

Having Babies at the Office

At first glance, British working women who wish to have children do not seem to fare badly. They are entitled to fourteen weeks' maternity leave, regardless of their years of service, and to be paid 90 per cent of their salary for the first six weeks of that leave, plus £54.55 for each of the remaining weeks. A 1995 survey of 240 organizations employing one in ten British employees revealed that 80 per cent give more than the statutory minimum period of leave, and 78 per cent offer pay in excess of the statutory minimum.[4] British maternity benefits come nowhere near those provided in Scandinavia, but they are far superior to those available to American women. So the British do not look like front runners in the maternity-provision stakes, but neither do they appear embarrassingly antiquated.

But behind the statutory provisions and company policies lies another story. Workplace prejudice against pregnancy and childbirth still exists, as was revealed by two news stories that appeared in 1996. In one, a woman who worked for Virgin Airlines tells of how she was fired, having been told that 'there was no room for pregnant women in the company'.[5] In the other, a delivery driver won a victory over an employer who fired him when he insisted on being with his wife during the birth of their baby. The employer maintains that his employee was 'the author of his own misfortune'.[6]

Stories about workplace insensitivity this extreme might be rare. But we should not kid ourselves into believing that insensitivity to the rights and needs of new parents has disappeared altogether, even in the most family-friendly of workplaces. Having babies at the office may be easier than it used to be, but it's still not the uncomplicated affair it should be. Says psychotherapist Susie Orbach, 'We live in a culture where instead of being proud of having a baby, it's treated like it was never supposed to happen.'[7]

Men face workplace insensitivity immediately after the birth of their child. Few have the right to paternity leave, and even fewer are actively encouraged to take it. ('We granted three days' paternity leave against my better judgement – personally I think it's a real con,' said the personnel manager of an award-winning family-friendly company.) For a woman, the trouble starts almost as soon as she becomes pregnant. About three weeks into her pregnancy, she may begin to experience increasing amounts of physical discomfort – nausea, throbbing legs, perhaps headaches, almost certainly tired-ness. As pregnancy's aches and pains hit her in quick succession it might cross her mind that it would be sensible to arrange her life differently in order to cope with them. She might wish to travel into work at a later time so that she does not have to stand in crowded train carriages gasping for air, resisting the urge to vomit; or she might think about taking a short break in the middle of the work day, or ending the day early, so that she can put her feet up as her doctor has advised her to do. But in all likelihood she won't be able to do these things. The chances are that she won't even dare to suggest them to her boss or her colleagues.

Most women slog on relentlessly, ignoring what their bodies tell them, maintaining the front, and only allowing themselves to collapse late at night once they are at home. But most I have spoken to believe that even minimal recognition of their pregnant state in their place of work – the granting of flexible hours to prevent rush-hour commuting, or the provision of a rest-room for hour-long afternoon naps – would be welcomed with enthusiasm and relief. Most welcome of all would be the simple recognition that pregnant women have legitimately different needs. Said one human resource professional, Sally, 'We all work in a culture where it's accepted that you often work right through lunch without a break. And most of the time I guess that's OK. But when you're pregnant, someone needs to say to you, look, have your lunch, have a rest. Otherwise you feel ashamed of acting in a way that's counter-cultural.'

Human Resources manager Laura described how she suffered as a result of her colleagues' insensitivity to the effects of a miscarriage, and later to her needs throughout pregnancy. 'I hate to say this,' she said, 'but I really feel that you are almost disabled when you are pregnant, yet you are supposed to carry on as if everything were completely normal.' Yet she, like many others, had colluded in perpetuating these perceptions, partly out of fear of losing her position within the company. She worked until just days before her second and third babies were born, and returned to work before she was contractually obliged to. Despite her collusion, she could recognize that the needs of pregnant women should be acknowledged. She recalled the experience of a pregnant colleague who had attempted to carry on as usual at work, skipping lunch and working through twelve-hour team sessions like her colleagues: 'There she was, looking like she was about to faint, and everyone was asking, "What's wrong?" And I just said, "She's pregnant. She can't just not eat like everybody else. She has to eat, and she has to get some rest."'

Another woman found herself pregnant with her second child, accidentally, when her first was only ten months old. Her second pregnancy was complicated by high blood pressure and debilitating nausea during the first few months. The effects of this were compounded by the exhaustion she felt as a consequence of her first baby not sleeping through the night. Both the woman and the firm tried to pretend that despite all of this, she could take on the management of a difficult project requiring her to spend significant amounts of time away from home. Not surprisingly, the woman reached a state of near-collapse, and ended up having to be pulled off the project. 'That was crazy,' she said afterwards. 'I'd have been better off to come clean, and to ask for some lower-key assignment during that brief period. The firm would have been better off too. It was ridiculous to think that I could perform at the usual pace.'

I shall never forget being six months pregnant with my first child and sitting alongside one of our document production staff putting the final touches to a client presentation at two o'clock in the morning. (One of the reasons I'll never forget it is that I am frequently reminded of it by a female colleague who saw it as the height of insanity.) The whole team was there, everyone from the twenty-three-year-old analyst to the senior vice-president on the assignment. But not one of them said, 'You probably shouldn't be doing this in your condition. Perhaps you should go and get some rest and I'll take over.' Not even the senior partner said it, despite the fact that his own wife was heavily pregnant and you'd have thought he'd have known better. Far worse, not even I said it. What kind of dreadful fate did I think would befall me if I gave in to common sense and my body and suggested that I go home at midnight, or eleven o'clock? Removal from the assignment? A halving of my bonus? Termination from the company? Or just the indignity of having my colleagues think that I was not up to the job, not committed?

It is difficult to admit to feeling feeble and in need of special support. It is even difficult to take advantage of those legal and policy provisions which *do* exist to protect women in the latter weeks of their pregnancies. 'The pressure to "do pregnancy well" is intense – that means not talking too much about your baby or the experience, and basically carrying on much as you did before,' said one woman who works in publishing. The reluctance to reveal any physical weakness during pregnancy, or to ask for any special concessions, has its roots in the long battle to minimize perceptions of women's differences, which has been integral to the effort to achieve equality of opportunity. Even now, thirty years on in this battle, one feels a terrible sense of betrayal in speaking out about the possibility of the physical demands of pregnancy requiring that women be treated differently at work from men.

Women, their colleagues and their employers may be reluctant to concede that the physical demands of pregnancy necessitate some special treatment at work or, at the very least, require women to be sensible about when they stop work. But even if women's own bodies can't convince them to make concessions, the experts can provide plenty of reasons to do so. My own doctor repeatedly reminded me that plenty of rest was important to ensure that the placenta received an adequate blood supply and the baby enough nourishment. During an ante-natal visit late in my first pregnancy, she took one look at my face, took out a pen, and wrote a note to my firm insisting that I be able to leave work every day at five o'clock. Obstetric physiotherapist and ante-natal adviser Christine Hill also stresses the importance of rest throughout pregnancy, and particularly during the last few weeks. In her book *Your New Baby – How to Survive the First Months of Parenthood* she advises women to give up work at thirty-four weeks, and to avoid being taken in by macho values:

> Many pregnant women fall into an understandable trap. They think that the right thing to do is to work up to the very last moment so they can then have the maximum amount of time off after the birth to spend with their baby. While that is perfectly true in terms of time allowed for maternity leave, it is not usually the best plan for you or your baby's health. Even worse, it can be justified by inappropriately tough-minded values ('I'm going to work up to the last possible minute, I can cope with having it under a hedge, if necessary') or mistaken psychology.[8]

Hill provides four very sound reasons for stopping work early. First, the baby is totally dependent upon you and you owe it to him. Second, giving up work is one major and potentially traumatic life event and having a baby is another one. Women shouldn't have to cope with both at the same time. Third, it pays to get into some good habits, like taking an afternoon rest, before the baby is born. And last but definitely not least, things happen to your mood and thought processes after about thirty-four weeks, sometimes earlier. Drowsiness, irritability, emotionalism and 'primary maternal pre-occupation' set in (see p. 43). When they do, says Hill, you don't really want to be at work having to feign mental agility, high energy and total commitment.

Though I felt wretched by the end of my pregnancies, and was armed with all Hill's good advice, I was reluctant to tell people that I was giving up work a full five weeks before my second baby was due. I discerned muted disapproval beneath the superficial expressions of support. 'Yes, why not?' people said. But comments such as this were invariably closely followed by stories about how they, their wives or some admired colleague had only managed to stop a day before going into labour, told in tones of such obvious pride that one could not mistake the implication that the last-minute dash to the labour ward is still the most appropriate approach for the serious working woman.

Corporate disregard for the demands of pregnancy is equalled by its underestimation of the impact of childbirth. Many employers still treat birth and post-birth experiences as if they were mere blips in a woman's experience curve, to be handled with professionalism and minimal fuss, and cast aside as quickly as possible so that 'normal' work life can begin again. 'Women are duped into thinking that having a baby is like getting a dog, and that somehow it will be possible to pick up the pace within days,' says Roz Morris. Though maternity leave legislation in Britain now entitles women to fourteen weeks' paid leave and a further twenty-eight weeks of unpaid maternity absence, many female managers do not take the leave to which they are entitled. They are subjected to the subtle but powerful pleas of those for whom they work, who want them to return to work early, take faxes at home, or breastfeed in the corner of the office so as to minimize the disruption caused by their leave.

The American economist and writer Sylvia Hewlett, who suffered the miscarriage of twins and a difficult third pregnancy and birth while she was a professor at Barnard College, was scathing about the lack of support she received from the college through these experiences, being expected to resume work at full pace within two weeks of their occurring. For Hewlett, the prevailing view in the 1970s that 'women were supposed to jog through pregnancy and give birth to their children with joy and ease' contrasted sharply with her own experiences and with what she knew to be generally true. 'The miracles of conception and birth can still be fraught for women. It is true that modern women don't die while giving birth to a child, and babies generally survive the ordeal of being born ... But real problems of infertility, miscarriage and of birth itself continue to haunt women.'[9]

Hewlett was writing in 1986, about experiences she had been through and observed in the late 1970s and early 80s. She was also writing about America, where provision for maternity leave was disgracefully inadequate. At that time, fully 48 per cent of children under one year old had mothers in the workforce, yet the majority of these mothers had no right to time off for pregnancy or childbirth.[10] Maternity provision is better in the America of the 1990s, though still abysmal. One survey of 188 manufacturing companies drawn from the largest 500 industrial and 500 service companies revealed that only 23 per cent formally offered family leaves of absence (including maternity leave), and only 28 per cent offered leave to mothers informally.[11]

Leave provisions are far superior in Europe and the UK. Yet Hewlett's observations about corporate insensitivity to the demands of childbirth still apply in many places. Women may have access to longer maternity leave, but their right to it isn't always respected. Many are asked to do work during their time off, or to return to work early. Others have returned to work of their own accord, driven perhaps by their fear of falling behind within intensely competitive environments. Publisher Helen Fraser, who was featured in the *Guardian*'s 1997 list of the fifty most powerful women in Britain, refused maternity leave following the birth of her two daughters;[12] Philippa Rose, head of a City of London headhunting firm, boasted about having been to a meeting within hours of giving birth to her son,[13] and Philippa Thorpe, head of Philippa Thorpe Designs, claimed she was still working on the days she had her girls, and working in bed afterwards.[14] One woman adopted a particularly macho stance in speaking about her own experience of maternity leave. Calling the Health and Safety regulations protecting expectant and new mothers evidence of the 'nanny state', she claimed proudly that she had worked until the day each of her children was born and expressed breast milk for each of them while at work.[15]

If the *Harvard Business Review* is an accurate barometer, the corporate world's appreciation of how childbirth impacts upon a woman's life is pitifully limited. A 1991 issue features an article entitled 'The expectant executive and the endangered promotion', a case study of an American woman, Diane Bryant, who is a candidate for promotion to the directorship of a high-technology firm. Diane is a strong candidate for the job of division director, but will be away on maternity leave for two months immediately prior to a critical product launch by the division. The question posed at the end of the story is 'Should the firm promote her or not?'[16]

Six 'experts' are invited to give their views on the case, and they expend much text deliberating about whether or not Diane deserves the promotion, and whether she will be able to meet the product launch deadlines if she gets it. The comments made by those experts who support Diane's promotion despite her impending maternity leave, and who undoubtedly believe themselves to be progressives, are indicative of the degree to which corporate leaders and managers are out of touch with the reality of new motherhood and how it needs to be catered for. They expose a complete lack of understanding about the state that a woman's body and mind are in when she has a baby. One says Diane should be promoted and then supported by policies like those in his own firm, where new mothers can 'bring in their infants to allow for nursing and other essential care', and where parents who have to work late at night at the office can arrange for a company babysitter 'and work whatever hours are necessary'. Another offers: 'Perhaps the company can set up a private area for her to bring her new-born and sitter to work so that she can be on the scene if that becomes necessary during the last stages of the project.' A third asks, 'If Diane is promoted, could she communicate with her staff by telephone and fax during her maternity leave?' Another male expert echoes her suggestion: 'With e-mail, voicemail, faxes, etc. readily available, there's no reason why she shouldn't be able to keep up with the major decisions before the product launch while caring for her new baby at home.'

What none of these experts seems to realize is that if Diane is like most first-time mothers, during the first few months after her baby is born she will be living as if shrouded by a dense fog. She'll be wandering about in her dressing-gown all day because she won't have time to get dressed, and she'll have left half a dozen cups of coffee around the house because she won't have had time to drink them. She'll consider posting a letter to be a great accomplishment, because most of her days will be consumed by the demands of her baby to be breastfed, changed, cuddled or pushed around in the pram to stop him crying. There will be no time for faxes and voicemails, and even if there were she wouldn't feel inclined to receive or send them. And breastfeeding may well be difficult enough[17] – without her having to do it in a corner of the office, amid the din of telephones and frantic colleagues, while she oversees the project.

If Diane knew what she was getting into, and if other working mothers had been honest with her instead of singing the praises of juggling, or boasting about having attended key meetings or clinched critical deals within days of giving birth themselves, she wouldn't even want the promotion. She'd wait a while for it, or ask that it not be made commensurate with her taking on the particular project under consideration. She might ask that the experts reconsider some of their 'progressive' attitudes and the expectations that go with them. For if a progressive workplace is one that places the burden for coping with the conflict between work and motherhood entirely on to the woman herself, asking her to minimize disruption, breastfeed in the corner of an office and continue to send faxes and voicemails while she is going through an experience that will have left her body, her emotions – indeed, her life – in a state of turmoil, then we don't need progressiveness. We need realism, understanding and accommodation.

The kinds of ideas represented in this *Harvard Business Review* article are being regularly passed off as 'family-friendliness' across America. The American *Working Mother* magazine compiles an annual list of the best companies for working mothers (now available to UK mothers on the Internet). One of the most commonly mentioned benefits provided by the firms on this list is a 'lactation room', where new mothers can breastfeed or express breast milk. This may be considered a great step forward by the firms, and might be welcomed by some of their female employees, but it is a poor substitute for a policy that recognizes the nature of the demands that a newborn places on a mother, and the needs of the mother herself. Such a policy would not require the woman to be at work expressing milk in the first place. Lactation rooms, like workplace day-care facilities for sick children, are, as Susie Orbach pointed out, so far removed from what parents really need that they are 'obviously policies dreamed up by non-parents'.

But we shouldn't point the finger at corporations and their bosses alone. For their failure to acknowledge the demands that childbirth and the first months of a baby's life make of a woman is nearly matched by women's own naivety. Anxious to appear committed, first-time mothers will often agree to 'stay in touch with the office', to perform special projects while on maternity leave, or to rush back to work after just three or four weeks. A male friend recently told me that an interior designer friend of his was planning to supervise the redecoration of his newly purchased home while she was on maternity leave. I could not resist the urge to set him straight, telling him: 'You're going to be living in a half-decorated construction site for months. Because there's no way that woman will be able to redecorate your house in the first month after she's had that baby.' I felt great sympathy for her, and wondered how she would feel when, after just two hours' sleep and eight hours with a baby on her breast, she faced the prospect of a visit to the Designers' Guild to choose curtain fabric.

Even second- and third-time mothers can suffer from what Marnie Jackson, author of *The Mother Zone*, calls the 'mother's amnesia' that allows them to think that they will accomplish all sorts of things while on maternity leave. The fact is that little gets done on maternity leave, except the constant care and nurturing of a tiny baby. Even a calm, quiet newborn spends relatively so little time asleep as to render unachievable the completion of any task more demanding than the tidying-out of a kitchen drawer. A mother who finds herself caring for a colicky baby will have to work hard at emerging from the first few months of motherhood with her sanity intact, even without faxes, e-mails and 'occasional' meetings to add to her distress. (One mother kept a log of her colicky baby's sleeping patterns and found that he slept for just five and a half hours out of twenty-four, mostly in twenty-minute snatches. 'The rest of the time,' she wrote, 'he was either writhe-nursing or shrieking, unless I was pogoing with him.'[18] Until we and the corporations for which we work accept that newborns make enormous demands of their mothers, and even of their fathers (the father of the colicky baby above also spent many hours 'pogoing' with his son and got precious little sleep for three months), there will be little real impetus for workplace change that enables parents to satisfy those demands. We will go on pretending, like the personnel manager referred to earlier, that paternity leave is really a con, a ruse to enable fathers to take an extra three days' holiday, and that a fax machine, laptop and modem are all that is required for a new mother to sail through maternity leave causing minimal disruption to the business.

It is easier to be a pregnant woman or a new parent in today's workplace than it was in yesterday's. But, as we have seen, we still have some way to go before the needs of expectant and new mothers are fully recognized and catered for. Widespread recognition of new fathers' needs, and of the role that they can and should play in supporting their partners through the first few months of a baby's life, is even more remote. And what about the other aspects of the family-friendly workplace, the ones that make it easier for parents to work once their children have progressed beyond the infant stage? To what extent do homeworking and part-time working arrangements currently ease the juggling burden?

Raising Babies at the Office: Is there a Home–Office Heaven?

The trend towards homeworking is undeniable. A recent study showed that an increasing number of people see working from home as an attractive option, and would like to have the opportunity to try it. Some estimates predict that by the year 2000, some 40 per cent of workers will be self-employed, and that many of these will be working from home. Companies are attracted to homeworking because of the £3,000 to £5,000 per person it can save them in annual direct costs[19] and because some studies have shown homeworking to lead to increased productivity.

Homeworking may represent a cost-saving opportunity to employers, but for homeworkers themselves it does not always work as well as advertised. Isolation and difficulty with self-discipline are two of the much cited drawbacks. For mothers of young children, a little isolation would be heaven-sent, for the problems of working at home are the constant interruption and the difficulties children have in understanding where mummy time stops and work time begins. One survey revealed the reality of homeworking to be characterized by overwork and the constant intrusion of work into home life: 20 per cent of teleworkers put in upwards of fifty hours a week, and women working at home claim to be at the mercy of both employers' deadlines and constant interruptions by children.[20]

Many employers continue to resist homeworking because they fear losing control over their employees' time. But even among those employers who have embraced homeworking, many fail to fully understand how it works in reality. They suffer from the illusion that allowing an employee to work at home makes up for a multitude of other sins, such as the setting of unreasonable deadlines or the allocation of excessively heavy workloads, and according to the authors of *The Family Friendly Employer: Examples from Europe*, erroneously believe that homeworking solves the childcare problem.[21]

Celebrity interviews and media images do little to disabuse them of such misconceptions. A *Vanity Fair* interviewer wrote that scriptwriter Nora Ephron 'has always been able to churn out copy with a baby or two crawling around at her feet banging on pots and pans'.[22] And according to advertising images, most women are capable of this. But despite the fact that many advertisements and profiles of Superwomen depict women working and caring for their children at the same time, most women who've tried this have found it impossible. 'You can't work and look after children at the same time,' says Gill Weiser of ICL Human Resources. 'Working at home is not a substitute for childcare,'[23] says Val Tyler who runs courses on new ways of working for the Industrial Society. 'To make a success of working at home a mother requires as much childcare support as she might if she went to an office every day. And even then it can be difficult.' Linda Hass, an American sociologist and work–life expert, believes many female entrepreneurs initially thought that they would have less need for childcare if they set up their own businesses, but soon discovered that this was not the case.

Libby Purves writes about the reality of working at home, with or without a nanny, in her bestseller *How Not to Be a Perfect Mother*. On the face of it, says Purves, working from home is 'a wonderful compromise' and some 'heroic' women manage to do it even without childcare help. They tell us they do so by playing song cassettes to their infants, by taking advantage of afternoon sleeps, and by climbing into the playpen with or instead of their children. Purves maintains that even with a full-time nanny in the house, though, there are many problems associated with working from home. Among these are the toddlers who refuse to let you go to your study, and who shout 'Poo-poos to your boss' down the phone, the minor domestic crises which erupt every day, and the Norland-trained nannies who prove to be incapable of resolving such crises independently.[24]

Quite simply, small children and working in the same place don't mix easily. 'It is hard,' wrote American academic Sylvia Hewlett, 'to exaggerate how wrenching it is to try to carry out work responsibilities with a baby in attendance. Simple tasks like dictating a letter or meeting with students become impossible.'[25] Even when there is a nanny or other child-carer present, it is not easy to shut yourself in a room, away from a small child, ignoring his questions and pleas for attention. 'This working at home business is dreadful,' concluded one woman I spoke to. 'Children never understand it. It always results in tears.' Another echoed her view: 'Working from home is constant agony. There is always that little face, waiting for you to play.'

Despite having been warned by the likes of Hewlett and Purves, we all fall for it at some stage. We fall for the images of women gesticulating into the phone enthusiastically while tapping their foot against a baby-bouncer containing a smiling six-month-old. We fall for the pleading tones of colleagues and bosses who persuade us to do a little bit of extra work, or to take that three-hour conference call on a day off, because, after all, we can do it from home, it won't intrude too much. I have fallen for it so often, and suffered the consequences, that I now literally kick myself to prevent myself agreeing to do extra work at home during the days when I am supposed to be caring for my children.

Not only does work not belong at home when there are children about, but children don't belong at work. I discovered this when I decided to take my two-year-old, Olivia, to the office on a Sunday, because she pleaded with me to go, and because I, naively, thought the outing would serve as some sort of happy bonding exercise. I sat her down in a corner of the conference room with her books and some paper and coloured pens, and attempted to get on with the business of proofing the poster presentation that had been carefully arranged on the conference room floor. Within minutes we were both in tears. I failed to respond to her repeated requests for me to 'please draw a fish or a cow' on her paper, to which she reacted by scribbling her two-year-old's signature, in bright-green marker pen, on one corner of the immaculate poster I had just reviewed. I screeched with horror and raced over to where she sat, first stunning the poor child, then inciting her to tears which were soon flowing unremittingly over a quivering bottom lip. My embarrassed (male) colleague ducked hurriedly out into the hallway.

Within minutes of the mishap I realized that I should never have expected a two-year-old to be able to sit quietly in a corner for an hour when more interesting things were going on at the other side of the room, or to know the difference between the piece of white paper I had given her and the one that I was working on. But because I did expect these things of her, and because I harboured some ridiculous notion that perhaps the radiant-working-mother-and-child advertising images were right, I placed both her and myself in an awful situation that forced me to become impatient and angry with her. Not fair on her, or on me. Either she should have stayed at home or we both should have.

Homeworking does work for some people, and it can provide more opportunities than does office working to see children during the day, even if fleetingly. It works best when they are of school age and out of the house for much of the day. For mothers of pre-school children, it is impossible in the absence of childcare, and will not solve the childcare problem. Neither is it a real solution, on its own, to the problem of a mother with far too little time to give to her children. A mother who needs and wants to spend more time child-raising does not need a computer at home so that she can meet impossible deadlines by working through the day and night, or the flexibility to bring mountains of work home in her briefcase so that she can spend fifteen hours doing the work in her dining-room over the weekend. She needs less work, and a restructured job which allows her to be really at home, in her children's definition of the term, when she is at home.

Mrs Steve Shirley, life president of the computer services firm, FI Group, founded the company with the explicit intention of enabling mothers of young children to work from home, but discovered that homeworking does not, on its own, provide the flexibility that mothers need. Real flexibility has to be broader in context and offer a range of genuine options – of which homeworking is only one as to how, when and where to get the work done.

Raising Babies at the Office: Is there a Part-time Paradise?

Looked at from one perspective, part-time working has already become a significant feature of the modern work world. Almost one in four employed people in Britain works part-time. Part-time working among women is even more common. Of 10.3 million employed women in the UK in 1991, four and a half million, or 45 per cent, worked part-time.[26] In 1994, part-time employment among women remained high, at 44 per cent for employed women overall, and 59 per cent for employed mothers.[27]

A 1995 survey of 243 organizations employing one in ten British employees found that women who went on maternity leave had the opportunity to return to work on a reduced-hours basis in nine out of ten of those organizations, and that in just over 80 per cent of them the arrangement could be permanent.[28] A 1997 survey of Britain's largest blue-chip employers revealed that almost all were happy to offer part-time working.[29] Both surveys show that corporate acceptance of part-time working has increased since the late 1980s, when a survey of 120 large organizations showed that just 40 per cent allowed women to work part-time after their return from maternity leave, and for almost a quarter of these the arrangement was purely temporary.[30]

But, although part-time work is prevalent and the corporate willingness to offer reduced-hours working has increased, part-time working currently represents more purgatory than paradise for many. A third of Britain's part-time workers have no holiday entitlement, and a quarter earn less than £3.12 an hour compared to an average of £7.40 an hour for full-timers.[31] Part-timers generally have less job security than their full-time colleagues. Employment-law protection for part-timers has declined since the 1980s, with just 40–45 per cent of female part-timers being protected by the law in

1989 as against 60 per cent in 1980, and compared with 60 per cent of female full-timers in 1989.[32]

More telling still is the fact that career progress is still contingent on the ability to work full-time. One estimate puts the proportion of management jobs that are part-time at only 10 per cent, and many of these will be part-time on paper only. Another estimate reveals that managers represent some 14 per cent of the total workforce, but only 2.3 per cent of part-timers.[33] Patricia Hewitt's study of part-time work, *About Time*, is full of stories of how imagination has been applied to enable factory, shift and clerical workers to work part-time, but examples of part-time working among managers and professionals are scarce indeed. (Eighty per cent of organizations responding to a survey conducted by IRS Employment Trends listed clerical work as one of the main occupational categories of part-time workers.[34] Career progress eludes most part-timers[35] and is likely to continue to, so long as the so-called 'normal' working culture within which part-timers operate is one in which employed fathers work an average of forty-seven hours a week, and 10 per cent of fathers work sixty hours a week or more.[36]

Despite the fact that most companies now say they offer part-time working, throughout much of the working world the idea that only full-time work is real work continues to dominate people's thinking.[37] In some industries, and at senior levels, anything less than sixty hours a week is considered to be less than full-time. Nicola Horlick, the Morgan Grenfell fund manager who reportedly worked a nine-to-five day in order to spend time with her family in the evenings, was reputedly frowned upon by many in her industry for pushing the boundaries too far. When forty-five hours a week is considered to be 'pushing the boundaries', real part-timers have little hope of parlaying their jobs into successful careers.

Even in organizations which formally allow part-time work, there are significant barriers to part-time options being taken up, particularly for those in supervisory and management positions. The take-up of part-time policies, particularly by men, remains low across Europe.[38] In organizations without formal part-time policies, few women feel confident enough to suggest that they be allowed to experiment with flexible work options. And some are penalized for suggestions bravely made. When Carolyn Robinson asked to return to her job as a manager with Oddbins on a part-time basis she was, instead, offered a job as a sales assistant, on a salary of £9,000 – this despite the fact that she had worked for the chain for six years and put in fifty-hour weeks. Sarah Rolls, an advertising manager for *Woman and Home* magazine, was told she was no longer required when she asked IPC Magazines to adjust her job after she returned from maternity leave.[39] Both of these women took their cases to employment appeal tribunals and won compensation. But it will be some time before the impact of such claims seeps deep into corporate culture and norms, or even into corporate policy. And many women will avoid confronting in court the corporations for which they work because of a desire and need to keep their jobs.

Those who dare to ask for part-time status, and receive it, often find that it is the silver lining to a very big cloud. Liz worked for years as a banker and then as a consultant before she had her two boys. After her second son was born, she requested a part-time working arrangement with her consulting firm. After experimenting with various ways of making her part-time arrangement work, she settled on a role as expert adviser to project teams doing work in a particular industry. This was to mean that she would not have to work more than three days a week or be away from home overnight. Perfect. Or so it should have been. But it didn't work out that way. In her resignation letter, which she wrote more in frustration than in anger, she explained that she could no longer cope with the unpredictable schedule which came with her part-time arrangement. Her days at home, she said, were perpetually interrupted by urgent calls from colleagues, few of whom seemed to understand her role or her working arrangement. The requirement that managers at her level devote time to non-client focused activities made a three-day week impossible, and the unpredictability of her schedule made keeping part-time childcare difficult.

Stories like Liz's are commonplace. They are stories of part-time jobs that turn into full-time ones because the role has not been properly structured; days with children constantly interrupted because no one in the firm has been told about the part-time arrangement – or, if they have, they don't know how to respect it; flexible arrangements which become so flexible that they equate to chaos, and make finding and keeping decent childcare impossible. Elaine, describing her four-day week, said, 'In theory I have Fridays off, but they are a nightmare. Tense from the minute we wake up. I spend the whole day driving the children around and screaming instructions to the office into the car phone.' Another woman, Jane, has tried several types of flexible working arrangement in the media world and has found none entirely satisfactory: 'It's like trying to get to sleep when you have really bad sunburn,' she says. 'I've tried working full-time, working part-time, freelancing, job-sharing and not working at all. And I still can't find a position which feels comfortable.' Judy, who works for a television production company, could see the downside of part-time work without actually experiencing it herself: 'We have this great policy which says you can work four days a week. But it's all hot air. I know it would mean me working ridiculous hours on my four days, and probably on the fifth as well. That's not for me.' Anne Marie sums up the scepticism that many feel, having tried part-time working: 'Hah, we've all fallen for that one at some point,' she scoffs.

Writing to the *Guardian* in response to its May 1997 feature on the fifty most powerful women in Britain, E. Stannard, a banker who has enjoyed generous maternity leave, career breaks, and now a switch to a permanent part-time contract in management, wrote that career breaks and flexible working patterns as currently implemented are not 'a solution in themselves ... They provide robust entry and exit criteria for the working mother, but not long-term sustenance. They are not supported by job designs, performance criteria and reward mechanisms which recognize the unique demands of part-time working. Instead, the approach depends on structures which were designed to support full-time work.'[40]

Stannard's conclusions are similar to those reached by Carole Savage, the London Business School MBA graduate who conducted a survey of 1,000 professional women with MBAs as part of the research for her thesis. She concluded that women can make it to the top, but only if they work full-time and are totally committed. Flexibility means less pay and few promotion opportunities. Of Savage's 1,000-woman sample, fully 89 per cent who work either full-time or part-time wanted more flexibility in their schedules, and many are leaving corporate life to get it. She estimates that corporations lose 63 per cent of those who want to work in non-traditional ways.

Stannard's and Savage's conclusions are borne out by interviews. Promotion from part-time positions, and part-time arrangements at senior levels, are rare in even the most family-friendly of firms. The human resources manager at a large consulting firm maintains that although the firm does have six female consultants who work part-time, it 'has yet to be proven that a part-timer can be promoted to partner, or even continue to work on mainstream client work'. A shortage of opportunities for promotion may not bother women when they initially opt to work part-time.[41] They are often grateful for the chance to work while also regaining some sanity in their lives. But eventually, the absence of the recognition and rewards that accompany promotion can dampen morale and motivation.

Most of the onus for making the part-time role work continues to rest squarely on the part-timer's shoulders, say Rhona Rapoport and Lotte Bailyn in *Relinking Life and Work*.[42] It is up to her to work out how to compress five days' worth of responsibility, demands and expectations into three or four, preferably without anyone noticing, and most certainly without anyone else having to change. Mary Anne, a personnel manager responsible for implementing flexible working policies in a female-dominated publishing company, acknowledged that, for the most part, women who take up the part-time option are responsible for making it work. This usually means that the jobs are not changed in any way to suit a part-time schedule, but that the women 'just somehow commit to making it work. They don't want to forgo the opportunity to get promoted, so they just do it.'

Lawyer Sally's experience corroborates the reality explained by Mary Anne: that the burden of proof and effort still lies almost entirely with the part-timers, who are mostly women, themselves. Firms may agree to let them work part-time, but will make no effort to ensure that part-time work is feasible. After several years at home with her children, Sally interviewed with several law firms, and found herself being pursued by a large and reputable firm who were so keen to recruit her that they promised her a part-time job, from ten until four every day. Sally accepted. For the first few weeks things seemed to work well. Then the firm took her assistant away and refused to replace her. And they began to send more cases and responsibility Sally's way. Before long she was working twelve-hour days and seldom leaving the office by five o'clock, let alone four. Sally decided to take up the matter with her boss. She told him that things were not working out well since she had been given the extra cases and denied the support of an assistant. 'You did say that I could work part-time,' she reminded him. 'Oh, Sally,' he replied, 'we meant you could work part-time if you could get all the work done in that time.' Sally resigned.

In her book *Best Companies for Women*, Scarlett MccGwire describes in detail the range of equal-opportunity and flexible-working policies offered by the 'best companies' in Britain, and introduces women who work for these companies. What comes through from their stories is that while these companies may well be ahead of the pack in terms of putting in place policies supportive of working mothers, they are still a long way from having made these policies work as they should. And individual women who work for the companies are still paying a high price for flexibility.

MccGwire's book is full of women who benefit from flexible arrangements, but still take work home at night and at the weekends, find themselves ineligible for promotion, and end up starting at the bottom again after each maternity leave and period of part-time work. And many of the women working at these 'best companies' are still pursuing a career in the traditional fashion – working long hours and pretending to the firm that they don't have a family. Rosemary Leigh says she has made 'a conscious effort not to let motherhood impinge on her work', but that she is finding the juggling increasingly difficult and is worried that she will have to choose between work and family. Marcia Cotton, a marketing manager at Bull HN Information Systems in Middlesex, says, 'I always work late, so my child suffers.' Her colleague Sue McClaren-Thompson, a senior sales manager, sings the praises of ICL's enlightened managers, but she has had little reason, as of the time of her interview, to require their enlightenment or their support: she works sixty-hour weeks, travels two days a week and has no children.

MccGwire notes that flexible options like job-shares and part-time weeks are prevalent only in the lower job grades in most companies, even in these 'best companies'. In some of those featured, not even part-time policies or job-shares are available. At British Aerospace Dynamics, there is 'only the offer of minimum maternity leave and pay, and any arrangement above that would have to be personal between [a woman] and her manager, and consequently her chances of promotion would be limited.'[43]

Most of the companies featured in MccGwire's book have made significant advances in the effort to provide equal opportunities for women and to put in place policies that allow women to capture those opportunities. And there are some real success stories, such as the job-shares at Rank Xerox and the head of London Weekend Television's commitment to making flexible work hours the norm. But in many of these 'best companies' change is only skin-deep, and very much in its infant stages. There are large pockets of even the most enlightened organizations which remain untouched by flexibility, or even hostile to it. So, though Boots is reputedly among the companies most serious about implementing flexible policies, it is still possible to meet, as one friend did, a Boots director who believes that the employment of women between the ages of twenty-five and thirty-five is 'basically uneconomic'; while Coopers & Lybrand is an Opportunity 2000 firm, there are those who whisper that their support for flexible working is 'really just lip-service'; and though Morgan Grenfell was included in *Working Mother* magazine's list of family-friendly employers, a Morgan Grenfell manager was heard to say that he believed all mothers should really be at home with their children.

Even in firms renowned for their sense of social responsibility, such as the Body Shop, family-friendliness appears to be more in evidence in public relations releases than in the organization and operation of the firm. The Body Shop's founder and Chief Executive Anita Roddick has written about the need for businesses to take their responsibilities to families seriously,[44] and the company has experimented with part-time working arrangements. But when I asked a manager in their personnel department about how many successful part-time arrangements there were in the management grades she laughed and said, 'You won't find many of those.' My requests to talk to the Body Shop in detail about their efforts to implement flexibility were discouraged: personnel agreed to a first meeting, but insisted that anything I wrote about the firm would have to be vetted by the publicity department; the meeting was eventually cancelled, and my subsequent calls to reschedule it were never returned. Anita Roddick also declined to speak with me.

Even at Midland Bank, which has an energetic and widely respected Equal Opportunities Director in Anne Watts, and which is undoubtedly at the forefront of change, providing parents with access to flexible working arrangements and subsidized childcare facilities, flexibility has yet to genuinely penetrate the workplace culture. Equal-opportunities manager Christine Camp claims that though there are a hundred part-time managers in the bank, most of these are at very junior levels, and none have been promoted since they started to work part-time. Even job-shares, of which there are around a thousand at Midland, do not always work well at senior management levels. The most senior manager in a job-share had just resigned when I spoke to Camp, having concluded that 'she just couldn't face the struggle any more'.

Gemini Consulting, where I have worked for ten years, is among the best employers in the consulting industry. Senior vice-presidents in the firm have bent over backwards to enable women with children to pursue careers part-time. Friends and family marvel at the flexibility demonstrated by the firm, which provides for three months' maternity leave on full pay, part-time arrangements on request, sabbaticals and term-time-only working for all, parents and non-parents alike. Yet, as Gemini's leaders are the first to acknowledge, flexibility has not penetrated the firm to any great depth. People still work extraordinarily long hours, and part-time roles have not yet been made to work well on mainstream client assignments. Gemini's leaders know that ad hoc flexible policies aren't fully delivering the goods. They are now exploring ways to take a more fundamental and structured approach to redressing the work–life imbalance from which consultants suffer.

Then there are the firms which, in contrast to the likes of the Midland Bank and Gemini Consulting, have made no attempt whatsoever to introduce family-friendly policies and practices. Many of these are in the law and in the City of London. Among working mothers and organizations like Parents at Work there is an unofficial ranking which places the large retail banks, large consumer and pharmaceutical firms and public sector organizations at the top of the 'family-friendly' list, professional service firms somewhere in the middle, and merchant banks and law firms well down at the bottom. One woman worked as compliance director for a major merchant bank which actually had a policy *forbidding* part-time work. The bank's leaders have been forced to make exceptions to the rule on very rare occasions, but have done so only by obliging the part-timers to change the nature of their employment contract, becoming associates rather than employees, so that the bank could continue to state that it had no part-time employees. The woman I spoke to once attempted to persuade the bank's personnel manager to consider the merits of family-friendliness, but found that he refused to shift his thinking, and even became hostile. 'When he stuck his tongue out at me, I knew I wasn't going to get very far,' she said. She has since left the firm to work for another which allows her to work four days a week.

That aspiring family-friendly organizations like the Midland Bank and Gemini Consulting have not yet seen flexibility make a dent in the long-hours culture, and that examples of recalcitrant firms like this merchant bank can still be found, attest to the fact that the effort to reshape workplace practices and cultures is only just beginning. Yet popular magazine features, company publicity and family-friendly awards can give the impression that family-friendliness is a widespread reality. *Guardian* writer David Rowan's recent survey of fifteen of the UK's largest employers led him to conclude that employer support for childcare was patchy compared to the across-the-board support for flexitime and job-shares.[45] Deeper probing by him would have revealed a big difference between employers who say they are 'happy to offer job-shares or flexitime' and those who actually do offer them and make efforts to integrate them into corporate operations. A *Newsweek* feature which criticized the work–family balance achieved by many Americans claimed that 'Europeans place a high value on quality of life not quality time', and held up British art director Rachel Hudson, who works part-time, as an example of how European employers tend to be more flexible.[46] Anyone reading the feature, which failed to distinguish between European countries, would have thought Britain was a virtual haven of family-friendliness, on a par with Norway and Sweden.

'All the publicity surrounding a few family-friendly companies has resulted in a kind of glib optimism which is not very helpful,' says Peter Moss of the Thomas Coram Research Unit. 'People tend to think family-friendly is common, when in fact, change has hardly begun.' The authors of *Family-Friendly Working: New Hope or Old Hype?* also conclude that 'family-friendly' is a long way from becoming the widespread, let alone normal, term applicable to conditions of employment.[47] Professor Cary Cooper and Dr Susan Lewis concur, believing that family-friendly initiatives currently have limited accessibility and fail to challenge traditional work structures, definitions of time, or career rules.[48] Joanna Foster, head of the BT forum for Better Communication and former head of the Equal Opportunities Commission, is hopeful about change, but equally convinced that there is a long way to go. 'We just can't let up, not for a moment, in the battle to change the workplace,' she insists.

Val Hammond, chief executive of the Roffey Park Management Institute and the author of several Opportunity 2000 reports, admits that even among Opportunity 2000 member firms (of which there are some three hundred), there are those who still only pay lip-service to family-friendliness. Liz Bargh, former Campaign Director for Opportunity 2000 and now chief executive of the work–life consultancy and support services firm WFD, tells a story to illustrate just how far we still have to go in the campaign against traditional work practices and assumptions. The chief executive of a major company had declared himself strongly in favour of flexible working practices because 'you always get five days' work out of four days' pay with part-timers'. 'That said it all,' said Bargh. 'At present, people do work five days for four days' pay, and that is wrong.' She believes that much more change lies ahead, and that only an approach that restructures the work itself will result in genuine flexible working arrangements.

While glib optimism is the order of the day in some quarters, and measured scepticism prevalent in others, some appear downright confused. The authors of the Demos report *Tomorrow's Women* claim at one point that Britain's main institutions have failed to adapt to the revolution in women's work, and that only a small minority of employers offer flexible working. Later they adopt an altogether more positive tone and point out, in an attempt to demonstrate that flexible working patterns are gaining acceptance, that seven out of ten blue-chip companies now employ part-time managers.[49] The apparent contradiction between these two asser- tions captures more truth about the state of family-friendliness in corporate Britain than either statement on its own. Flexibility *is* gaining acceptance, particularly among blue-chip employers, but we are a long way from seeing it become embedded within normal workplace practices and cultures.

Family-friendliness, American Style

Much has been written about family-friendliness in the United States, but the reality is less impressive than the headlines, just as it is in Britain and the rest of Europe. While significant numbers of companies offer flexible working arrangements, take-up of these arrangements is still low. A survey of 1,034 US businesses found that 60 per cent offer some kind of flexible scheduling. But a survey of employees at eighty major companies found that fewer than 2 per cent of eligible employees take advantage of flexible options. Policies may be in place, said one journalist, but you need 'good luck [to find] companies where the use of these programs is widespread or wholeheartedly embraced by management'. Employees often pay a price for taking what's offered to them, and they know it. 'Face time still counts. Putting in long hours, even if you're twiddling your thumbs, is still viewed by many bosses as a sign of loyalty.'[50] Deborah Swiss, author of *Women Breaking Through*, also concluded that the number of people who take advantage of existing work–life benefits remains exceedingly low in many organizations because 'there is too much work and too many penalties, perhaps even job loss, if they do'.[51]

In her book *Time Bind*, Arlie Hochschild confirms the low take-up of flexible policies in American firms. She spent three years analysing a large family-friendly corporation she calls Amerco. She concluded that few employees were taking advantage of flexible options like job-sharing and part-time working, and that family-friendliness had not significantly transformed the firm's practices and culture. Amerco is not atypical, according to Hochschild. She cites a 1990 study of 188 Fortune 500 manufacturing firms (the 500 largest industrial firms as listed annually in *Fortune* magazine) which revealed that while 88 per cent formally offered part-time work, only 3–5 per cent of their employees made use of it. Just 1 per cent took advantage of job-sharing options.[52] Hochschild maintains that, not only is family-friendliness not overtaking American corporate life, but American working parents seem to be putting in longer and longer hours.

Because family-friendly policies have not been wholeheartedly embraced, and take-up is low, one encounters the same kinds of anomalies seen in Britain: even companies highly regarded for their family-friendliness can appear distinctly family-unfriendly to many who work for them. American telecommunications provider Sprint appeared on the 1992 *Working Mother* magazine's list of flexible employers, prompting one single mother who works in Sprint's customer service centre in Dallas to comment: 'When we saw that Sprint made the list, we said, "Do we work for a different company, or what?"'[53]

Why has Family-friendliness Not Taken Root?

Arlie Hochschild's thesis is that many American workers are not taking advantage of family-friendly policies because, for many families (between 20 and 50 per cent of those she observed at Amerco), work has become home, and home has become work. 'In this model of family and work life, a tired parent flees a world of unresolved quarrels and unwashed laundry for the reliable orderliness, harmony, and managed cheer of work. The emotional magnets beneath home and workplace are in the process of being reversed.'[54] Hochschild acknowledges that there are many versions of this reversal going on, and that some are more far-reaching than others, but maintains that significant numbers of people find in work a respite from the emotional tangles at home.

Experts in the field such as Ellen Galinsky at the Families and Work Institute, and Rhona Rapoport, codirector of the Institute of Family and Environmental Research in the UK and co-author of the Ford Foundation sponsored report, *Relinking Life and Work*, believe that Hochschild raises an important point but that not all the data support her thesis. The reasons family-friendliness has made little real impact on American working life are probably more complex than Hochschild's thesis about the home–work reversal makes out. Even Hochschild sees her theory as relevant to only a subset of the working parent population; in her book she covers many other reasons for negligible low impact that family-friendly policies have had on American corporate life.

To a large extent, the fact that family-friendliness is only superficial in most corporations, layered on top of existing workplace practices and culture rather than deeply rooted within them, is a reflection of the fact that most firms are in the early stages of change. The Families and Work Institute in New York describes four stages in the evolution of the corporate work–family agenda. These stages both chronicle the evolution of the work–family agenda as a whole, and represent the current state of the family-friendly agenda within particular firms. Stage one in America is about childcare, and stage-one firms continue to be focused on childcare provision. A stage-one company also tends to define family concerns as women's issues. There remains considerable resistance to work–family policies within such a firm, and champions spend considerable time justifying these policies.

In stage two of the movement chief executives become more supportive of the work–family agenda and adopt an expanded, more integrated array of policies and programmes. In stage three, companies recognize that policies and programmes can only be effective within a supportive culture. Companies that reach stage three begin to look for ways to affect that culture, by articulating different but equally valued career paths, for instance. The business rationale at stage three becomes less focused on recruitment and retention and more about supporting employees' well-being and thereby enhancing creativity and commitment.

Stage four of the work–family agenda, which is emerging in the current work of work–life experts at the Families and Work Institute and elsewhere, as well as through the experiments at a few leading-edge stage-four firms, is focused on the work processes themselves. It is recognized that both the source of and the solution to work–family problems are linked to how the customer is served, how projects are planned and staffed, how work is scheduled, and how day-to-day problems are handled.[55] Companies at stage four are focusing on how to bring a work–family perspective to daily operations and task management.

'We now understand that work is the key variable in the work–family challenge, that it's the nature of people's jobs which are key,' says Ellen Galinsky of the Families and Work Institute. But while thinking by experts and some enlightened corporate leaders has progressed, there are individual firms at both ends of the change spectrum, and 'most firms are still stuck at the level of policy and programmes'. Galinsky's colleague Arlene Johnson agrees. 'I think it's fair to say that though the re-engineering of the work itself is recognized as the direction to go in, hardly any firms are, at this point, going in that direction.'

Others agree with the diagnosis put forward by Galinsky and Johnson. Rhona Rapoport, who conducted research with several companies for the Ford Foundation, believes most firms are still stuck at the policies and programmes stage. Felice Schwartz, writing in the *Harvard Business Review*, March/April 1992 issue, says that American corporations are spread across a wide spectrum in terms of the change they have undergone, but that most are stuck in the early stages of the change process: they track numbers of women in their ranks, fill out equal-opportunity forms, and might have implemented some equal-opportunity policies, but they have not come to terms with the deeply rooted preconceptions within their organizations. A few can genuinely say they are doing well by women. But the organizations that are truly egalitarian, and where 'the whole management structure is not a power-oriented hierarchy of ascending status at all but a jungle gym with lateral sidebars and many-levelled challenges, with help and rewards available to employees at every step', are mythical.[56]

Leslie Chin of WFD's Boston office agrees that the focus of the work–family movement has shifted since the early 1980s and is now about 'committing employees to the work and the firm'.[57] She believes that more attention is now being paid to how to make policies work by changing the structure and culture of work, but acknowledges that many firms remain stuck in change efforts that were more common among the front runners in the 8os, and that few have yet fully embraced the new, broader thinking.

In Europe the identifiable stages in the family-friendly movement are similar. Because statutory social policies, state childcare provision, the legal and trade union context, and attitudes towards male–female equality vary so widely between European nations, a common work–family agenda is more difficult to discern in Europe than in America.[58] The issues faced by working parents in Sweden, where childcare provision is abundant and an ethos of equality is widespread, are worlds apart from those faced by working parents in Spain, where mothers are still fighting against entrenched attitudes which question their right to work at all.[59] But broadly speaking, the movement in Northern Europe has progressed from a focus on designing and implementing policies to an emphasis on changing culture and restructuring the work itself. And, as in the USA, there are firms at all stages of the change process, with a very few considering cultural change and work-restructuring after years of having experimented with flexible policies, and others having only just begun to consider things like maternity leave and the occasional job-share. The authors of *The Family Friendly Employer: Examples from Europe* believe that most European firms remain at stage two on the Family and Work Institute's scale.[60] An emphasis on flexible work cultures is certainly lacking among the twenty-six firms featured in their book. The vast majority boast progress on childcare and other referral services, not on restructuring work processes to be more family-friendly.

With many firms in America and Europe stuck at stages one and two of the change agenda, it is not surprising that we cannot feel the impact of family-friendliness as much as we would like. Neither is it an astounding revelation that change efforts have been piecemeal and focused on the easiest, least disruptive forms of change. Workplace nurseries, lactation rooms for nursing mothers, and on-site parenting seminars, have all been offered by American companies to a much larger extent than have flexible and reduced-hours working options.[61] And in family-friendly firms like Hochschild's Amerco, programmes which allowed parents to work undistracted by family concerns (such as childcare) were endlessly in demand, while policies offering shorter hours that allowed workers more free time or family time languished.[62] In Europe, too, firms have generally made more progress on childcare and maternity-leave provision, whereas arrangements which allow flexible working on an ongoing basis, and are therefore perceived to be more disruptive to daily patterns of work, are still rare, particularly at senior levels.[63]

European Union and British government efforts to further the reconciliation of work and family life reflect the tendency to tackle the least daunting and complex aspects of change first. Most EU policy papers and initiatives to date have aimed to increase provision of childcare services and provide more generous maternal and parental leave.[64] The current Labour government is vociferous about the provision of childcare for single mothers, but much less so on the topic of workplace change that might allow single parents to work.[65]

The Families and Work Institute points out that fear and scepticism are common among the managers and employees in stage-one and -two firms. This discourages employees and employers alike from moving beyond the initial stages of change, progressing from the provision of childcare support and parenting classes to considering the fundamental transformation of working practices. Hochschild discounts the fear factor in the low take-up of family-friendly options in America, but Deborah Swiss (author of *Women Breaking Through*), Ellen Galinsky (of the FWI) and others believe fear is a genuine driver of behaviour. Kirstie Axtens of the British charity Parents at Work maintains that people are still greatly inhibited from seeking flexible working arrangements, even within the best companies. 'Even when we launched the "go home on time campaign" which required people to go home on time on one particular day, it was amazingly difficult to get people to sign up for it. And people didn't want to be quoted, or singled out as having participated,' she says. A newsletter published by the City of London chapter of Parents at Work confirmed that women are failing to take advantage of family-friendly working arrangements because they fear they will be seen to be lacking career commitment.[66]

When people fear change they tend to cling to traditional sources of security. And security, for many, is represented by traditional notions of work, commitment, reliability and success. When Carole Reay, a partner in an advertising firm, broached the subject of her working part-time, she was surprised at the strength of her colleagues' emotional attachment to 'the way things were'. 'The practical problems associated with my working part-time are the least of it,' she said. 'The biggest barrier is an emotional one – they cannot cope with the fact that I want to do something different, because it seems to call into question what they are doing, and all kinds of emotions, like jealousy, resentment and fear come into play.'

Scepticism ranks almost as highly as fear among individuals contemplating the available options for enabling work–family balance. Sally, the lawyer mentioned earlier who has attempted to work part-time, is convinced that the corporate world will not change, and that it is up to women to find their own solution within it. Patricia Hewitt found that many people were 'conservative about the possibility for flexibility in their own firms or industries'.[67] For many, the pressures at work were already so great that there seemed little hope of reorganizing their working time. Ignorance is in part responsible for this scepticism. Hewitt notes that older men in particular tended to see flexible working practices such as term-time-only working as 'preposterous' ideas, despite the fact that reputable firms like Boots and IBM have begun to experiment with them.

Senior management is often more incredulous about the potential benefits of flexible working practices than are employees. The fact that many of the benefits of family-friendly and flexible arrangements – such as the reduced costs of stress-related absenteeism and family breakdown, and lower recruitment and training costs – are hidden, and accrued over the long term, makes it difficult to shake their scepticism. Were there line items in every income statement highlighting the costs of stress-related illness, divorce and low morale, more executives might sit up and pay attention to the potential benefits of family-friendly programmes.

Dubiousness about the benefits of family-friendly working, and the corporate inertia that is engendered by it, are lived out in the working habits of senior managers. Fearful of making risky changes in their own working lives, most work according to the traditional, full-time, long-hours model. Many senior male managers reached the top on the back of long working hours and were supported by stay-at-home wives. They are what Paula Brook calls VSMs – virtually single males – who keep framed photos of their spouses and children on their desks but are not interested in them, or in yours, between the hours of 8am and 6pm, and do not see these framed and smiling faces as any serious obstacle to after-hours bar visits or impromptu business trips.[68] Many VSMs are happy with their work arrangements – and, as Hochschild points out, their work does a lot to make itself lovable. Travel, however burdensome, often calls for 'staying at hotels in which one might find a chocolate carefully placed on the pillow of one's bed, hear the morning "sssh" as the newspaper is slid under the door, sip coffee brought by room service, and savour that rarest of commodities, time free of responsibilities'.[69] Accustomed as they are to the pleasurable routines of corporate life, and to the unqualified support of their wives, VSMs have 'concerns so different from those of many of their employees that they may as well be living on another planet'. They could hardly be expected to understand the need for family-friendly policies, much less seek to be role models by applying them in their own working lives.

Even those senior male executives who profess to support family-friendly initiatives and work–life balance rarely live out their beliefs in their own working lives. Gerry Robinson, the Chairman of Granada, is famed for his balancing of home and family life. He has gone on record as saying that it is very important to him that he doesn't work really long hours,[70] and by all accounts he does not: he arrives at work between nine and ten, usually leaves before six o'clock, and frequently takes Fridays off. But Robinson's genuine commitment to balance is rare among senior executives. One woman recounted how she had listened to a high-profile chief executive of a blue-chip firm wax lyrical about the virtues of balanced living at a conference. Faced with a question about how he put these beliefs into practice, the chief executive was revealed as a leader with good intentions but not much genuine commitment to work–family balance: he admitted that the only time he spent with his own family was on Sunday mornings.

Women who have reached the top to date have, by and large, and by necessity, done so by replicating male behaviour. 'Women still tend to try to fit themselves into this boy's culture rather than create their own,' said one respondent to a survey of working women in the City.[71] Many successful women are childless, and of the ones who aren't, many have been forced to become female versions of the VSM, keeping pictures of their children on their desks but rarely seeing them. 'My whole life is my job. I have three girls ... the sacrifice I make is not seeing much of them,' said designer and entrepreneur Philippa Thorpe in an interview in the *Sunday Times* in November 1997.[72] Of the fifty most powerful women in Britain interviewed by the *Guardian* in 1997, half had no children. Of those who had, several admitted that they had made enormous trade-offs in their family lives. One even described her family as one of her hobbies – a VSM comment if ever there was one.

Such women are problematic role models. On the one hand, their talent, determination and ability to 'hack it' according to male rules are inspiring, and we recognize that without their dedication to make it to the top at all costs, many of us would not now be in a position to question the rules that determined how they got there. But for women who are not prepared to sacrifice all for their career, role models like these can also serve to demotivate. 'If that's what I have to do, forget it,' I hear many women saying. Fiona Cannon, equal opportunities manager at Lloyds TSB, experienced a backlash of sorts when she brought in a prominent childless career woman to talk to young female managers about career management. Far from being inspired and motivated by the speaker's presentation, many in the audience left dispirited. For them, the career woman whose success has been achieved through long hours and a sacrifice of family life was less a galvanizing influence than a depressing one.

The Culture of Work: the Last Hurdle

To move from stage two to stages three and four of the work–life agenda, companies need to confront the issue of culture. Workplace culture – the set of norms and rules, both written and unwritten, that govern work processes and behaviour – is the single greatest barrier to parents' ability to achieve genuine balance between work and family life.

The most obvious manifestation of existing work culture is long working hours, which continue to be a prerequisite for career success. Equal opportunity for women will come, it seems, but at a great price. Between 1984 and 1994, overall employment rates in Britain doubled for working mothers with degrees, and trebled among graduate mothers working in 'longer-hours full-time employment', suggesting that women who are headed for the top are working long hours in their efforts to get there.[73] Even those organizations that have made significant progress in implementing family-friendly work practices comment that the long-hours culture remains steadfast.[74]

Several factors are responsible for the intensification of the long-hours culture and the tenacity of its grip on the corporate world. Not least among these are the globalization of competition and the technological revolution, which have led corporations to embark upon downsizing, 'Total Quality' and re-engineering programmes. As Hochschild points out, the Total Quality movement empowered employees, invited them to take responsibility for problem solving, and encouraged them to feel relaxed and at home while on the job.[75] The quid pro quo for empowerment and a relaxed, friendly work environment was total commitment to the goals of the firm, which very often translated into a commitment of long hours. Re-engineering efforts aim to achieve similar objectives: employees are empowered to redesign their own work processes in order to solve their own problems. They are empowered, recognized and rewarded for taking responsibility for their own work and their own customers. In return they are expected to commit themselves unwaveringly to the re-engineering effort.

As a consultant I have witnessed many a Total Quality and re-engineering programme in operation, and have been part of several. I have seen employees get drawn deeper and deeper into the world of work as a consequence of their role within change programmes and the seemingly limitless demands on their time made by them. Where these programmes are relatively short-lived, being a necessary part of a business turnaround or a one-off effort to address the way customers are managed, for example, the increased effort and hours demanded are tolerable. But when efforts go on for years, as many do, and where they become part of everyday corporate life, they can prove overwhelmingly stressful for the employees involved. Certainly, they override any well-intentioned family-friendly initiatives that may be in place: an individual who has been selected to be part of a Total Quality effort will not be looked upon favourably if he or she wishes to work part-time, or leave at 5pm, when all around them are up to their necks in analysis, meetings, debriefs, and the ever important socializing that is deemed essential to bond team members together.

It was the prospect of two years in the leadership team of a major re-engineering effort with a big client that made me stop and rethink my own work life and career. As I sat in a large hall with two hundred of the client's 'best and brightest' managers, all brimming with enthusiasm for the massive change effort that lay ahead, all I felt was horror. In the first two months of setting up the effort I had already found myself working five fourteen-hour days per week, rather than the prearranged four, and had spent two solid weeks in a hotel with team members, working on plans, running training sessions, and building up team spirit. I knew instinctively that if I stayed with the assignment I would be so absorbed by it that I would become a virtual stranger to my family. Two months pregnant with my second child, virtually incapacitated by nausea, and fighting a daily battle with my longing to spend more time with my daughter, I resigned.

In the end I was persuaded not to resign, and I returned to work after a short absence. But the image of all those people – almost every one of them parents – in that hall, committing themselves to endless fourteen-hour days in a great public display of enthusiasm and commitment, sticks with me. It remains a symbol of a whole set of cultural barriers that prevent family-friendly initiatives from making anything other than slow and superficial progress.

For long working hours, whether driven by a firm's day-to-day operations or by the demands of a re-engineering programme, are but a symbol of a work culture that is fundamentally antithetical to work–family balance. This is a culture that eclipses women's experience as mothers, and indeed the reality of family life, a culture founded on the principle of work–family separation. As the authors of *Relinking Life and Work* point out, that principle rests on the assumption that individuals can devote most of their time and energy to work, that work can be their number one priority, because someone else is taking care of the rest of life. Even though most working people today don't have anyone at home taking care of life, the work world still operates as if they do.

All other aspects of workplace culture, what Elizabeth Perle McKenna calls 'the rules', spring from this one basic assumption. These rules aren't found in any employee handbook, says Perle McKenna, but you have to follow them to the letter if you wish to suceed.[76] They include the rule that work comes first – above all personal and family concerns – the rule that 'face time' is a requirement, and the rule that there is only one career in your life and only one path, and 'if you step off it, you're out of luck'. In addition to McKenna's rules, there are the definitions of a 'good employee' (one who works long hours) and commitment (long hours, again) which spring from the assumption that work and family life are separate concerns for separate people. Even the corporate bias against hiring older employees has its roots in this assumption about work–life separation. Anyone who is looking for a job at the age of forty, perhaps because she has taken a break to raise a family, or who is not a resounding success before that age – because she has not made work her number one priority during her thirties – is written off by the traditional workplace culture.

Cultures are extremely resistant to change, and workplace culture is no exception. At Gemini Consulting, we long ago discovered that the only way to change individual workplace cultures was to change the work processes that were intimately linked to those cultures. By changing the way work is done, and beginning to challenge the work culture at the level of individual work processes and jobs, culture begins to shift. Such is the conclusion that has been reached by a handful of family-friendly employers. Companies like Xerox and IBM are beginning to fundamentally challenge the way certain jobs are done. After years of implementing family-friendliness in a piecemeal fashion, Lloyds TSB is embarking on a fundamental change effort. Says Fiona Cannon, equal opportunities head, 'I finally reached the point of thinking that if I had to arrange one more one-off job-share roster I would scream. Ad hoc flexibility isn't working fully for employees, and it isn't working effectively for the bank either. We need a more fundamental approach which redesigns the work.'

Cannon and her team will be working with the work–life consultancy and support services firm WFD to analyse jobs and roles within the bank, with a view to restructuring them in order to make truly flexible working a possibility. The 're-engineering for flexibility' will be integrated with other ongoing re-engineering efforts. Cannon believes that there is almost no job that can't be restructured to be part-time or shared, even the top jobs. When she pushed a senior executive about why his own job would not be eligible for part-time working or job-sharing, he was unable to come up with a strong reason. His instincts told him it wouldn't work, but Cannon and her team will be working hard to overcome those instincts.

Getting the Rhythm

Because most family-friendly flexible working options are forced to operate within corporate cultures that are inherently hostile to them, and because they are not based on the fundamental restructuring of work, they can only marginally improve parents' abilities to reconcile work and family life. They cannot and do not facilitate genuine reconciliation of the two. Part-time job-holders who are truly able to devote two days a week to their children usually find themselves in peripheral roles, their careers forever stalled; those who manage to translate part-time jobs into promotions and viable careers will usually do so by forgoing any genuine part-time element – they will be working evenings, weekends and days off, giving five or six days' value for three or four days' pay.

Most flexible work options, as they are currently conceived and implemented, respect neither the rhythm of children's days nor the rhythm you need to adopt when caring for children. Children demand patience, endless bucketfuls of it. They demand that you move at their slow pace, not your own frantic one. It is not possible to give them what they need if you are putting the finishing touches to a document while making playdough shapes, or if your conversations with them are constantly interrupted by urgent calls from colleagues. If flexibility only means doing more work at home, in the midst of trying to be a mother, then it is no flexibility at all. The integration of working and parenting roles that many, including the Ford Foundation, now talk about needs to signify an integrated awareness of those roles, and easier integration of them within the same person. It should not mean making work an ever-present feature within home life.

The pressure to devote more time to work, and to allow work to dominate our home lives, will become greater. A colleague of mine made a presentation about the impact of technology and the telecommunications revolution. He said:

> It will change the way we live and work. We now think of work time and private time as coming in chunks, with a large chunk of work time wedged between two chunks of private time at the beginning and end of each day. In the future, technology and telecommunications will allow us to see work time and private time as coming in thin strips, not chunks. Our day will not be divided up into chunks of private and work time, but will instead be composed of strips of private and work time intermingled during the day and night.

'Work, play, work, play, work, play. That's how our days will look,' he added triumphantly, to an audience whose intakes of breath and hushed conversations seemed to convey awe at the possibilities.

I wondered if he or anyone else in the audience was privately thinking what I was thinking, which was what a nightmare that future scenario would be, and how little it seemed to recognize the needs of children and the rhythm of their lives. I knew my children would be miserable in circumstances where I was working on and off throughout the day, and if they had to adjust to an endless series of work demands that intruded at half-hourly intervals upon whatever we were doing. And I knew that such a scenario would render me a nervous wreck. Surely I was not the only one?

We need to resist being driven by technology to do things that make us and our families miserable. And we need to demand more of the 'new flexibility' than that it allow us to squeeze the same work into fewer hours, or move that work from the office to the home. We need to demand instead that technology and flexibility help us to fall into the rhythm of our children's lives rather than disrupting it. But we are a long way from this now. The truth is that all the family-friendly policies in the Western world added together do not yet amount to much more than a pinprick on the surface of that immovable, sluggish giant – the family-ignorant workplace culture. And the surfeit of glossy family-friendly policy papers and magazine profiles of 'pioneers of flexibility' should not persuade us otherwise. The sociologists Deborah Swiss and Judy Walker said it best in 1991:

> For twenty years now working mothers have done all the accommodating in terms of time, energy, and personal sacrifice that is humanly possible, and still they have not reached true integration in the workplace. [They still] find themselves in an intense battle with a society that cannot let go of a narrowly defined work ethic that is supported by a family structure that has not existed for decades.[77]

It's time the family-friendly workplace stepped up to the challenge and helped them.

CHAPTER NINE

❖

BEYOND FAMILY-FRIENDLY POLICIES: THE CASE FOR A WORKPLACE REVOLUTION

It's time we found a new way to think and talk about work, for until we do,
we'll see no hope for ourselves and our children. It's a complete doable task.
The clues and signs are everywhere – in how people are actually finding
wonderful work situations and in how innovative organizations are already
getting work done. The bad news is that, like all large societal changes,
it is requiring us to abandon the vehicle that got us this far and strike out
on foot for a while. And that is a frightening prospect.
WILLIAM BRIDGES, *Creating You and Co.*, 1997

❖ ❖

THE FAMILY-FRIENDLY workplace in its existing state will not resolve the clash between work and family, making them fit together like a hand in a glove. As the Families and Work Institute in America and European work–life experts such as Peter Moss point out, too few firms have embraced the family-friendly agenda, and at too superficial a level. Many firms are stuck at stages one and two of that agenda; others have yet even to recognize it as legitimate.

Asked to envision a work world in which individuals can achieve genuine balance between work and the rest of their lives, most people's imaginations venture far beyond the boundaries represented by today's typical family-friendly firm. Their images of stage-four firms, in which the culture and work processes are fully aligned with individuals' needs to balance work and life, have little to do with lactation rooms for breastfeeding mothers, or helplines providing childcare advice to parents. The basis of most people's visions is time: radically different ways of thinking about it, using it and organizing it.

Psychotherapist and feminist author Susie Orbach's vision is 'something radical, like an imposed thirty-hour work week'. MP Patricia Hewitt sees the reorganization of working time as a 'vital element in the creation of a new balance between employment and family'.[1] The parents surveyed by Adrienne Katz for her book *The Juggling Act* provided twenty-one suggestions for supporting parents, of which nine pertain to changes in the organization and rewarding of working time. They include maternity-leave improvements, paternity leave, parental leave, career-break schemes, the synchronization of school and work hours, less separation of work and home time, full-time rights for part-timers and job-sharing. (The other eleven are concerned with childcare provision and taxation.[2])

Arlie Hochschild's vision is *all* about time. Having witnessed the ineffectual family-friendly policies in operation at Amerco, where parents struggle unsuccessfully to free up time for their families within a traditional, long-hours job culture, she makes the case for a 'time movement' based on a clear vision of how much better life could be for the parents she has met and the community in which they live:

> Any successful movement for social change begins with a vision of life as it could be, with the notion that something potential could become real. So let's imagine Gwen Bell picking up her daughter Cassie at childcare twice a week at 3 pm instead of 6 pm and saving those fudge bars for late afternoon treats. Picture John Bell working a half-day Fridays and volunteering at Cassie's center. And what if Vicky King arranged with the eight male executives in her office for coverage and took Wednesdays off? Let's imagine PTA meetings to which a large majority of the parents come, libraries where working parents can afford to devote their spare time to reading or literacy programmes, and community gardens in which they and their children have the leisure to grow fresh vegetables. Picture voting booths in which parents choose candidates who make flexible work possible.[3]

The women I interviewed for this book came from a wide range of professions and industries. Most had a vision of how time could be used differently in their workplace. Some suggested a series of minimal changes which, added together, would make a big difference to individuals; others could see how time could be turned upside-down for the benefit of both individuals and organizational creativity and productivity. Carole Reay insists that there isn't a job in advertising that couldn't be made flexible if the will was there and people could drop the emotional baggage preventing them from accepting different ways of working. Fiona Cannon at Lloyds TSB is equally convinced that there are few jobs that would prove to be impossible to restructure according to non-traditional schedules. Yvonne Roberts and Maureen Freely argue that journalism could be made infinitely more family friendly. Bridgit, senior finance executive with a multi-national holding company, can see dozens of ways in which time could be reorganized in her line of work, and across the firm. Margaret Hodge is able to describe in detail how job-sharing for MPs could work, right down to how committee responsibilities would be divided up and who would do the voting. Even the top jobs should not be immutable, according to executive search consultant Ruth Tait. 'I don't see why a chief executive or managing director role could not be done part-time or as a job-share if it was structured correctly and the right people were doing the sharing.'

But the optimism of women like these is, today, all but submerged within a sea of doubt. Among the sceptics are those who feel a mild sense of disquiet when confronted with the possibility of workplace change, as well as the more ardent challengers who see the radical restructuring of working time and workplace culture as a hare-brained scheme dreamt up by a crackpot socialist/feminist pressure group. The 'time movement' will never make more than halting progress unless these cynics' concerns are understood and addressed.

Critics of flexible working oppose it on the grounds that it poses threats to both the economy as a whole and individual firms operating within it. The government is unlikely to express outright opposition to a time movement, but signals indicate that it will offer only hesitating support to it, justifying its caution in terms of the need to protect the competitiveness of the British economy. Corporate leaders, those whose interests are primarily in the prosperity of their own businesses will raise two main objections to flexibility: first, that it could undermine the health and competitiveness of businesses, and second, that it will result in a complex array of working practices that will be all but impossible to manage.

These apprehensions about the impact of change upon the health of the economy and individual businesses are not trivial or easily allayed. But neither need they stop a time movement in its tracks. There is historical evidence to suggest that altering the parameters of the working day and the working week need not have an adverse effect on economic competitiveness. And there are powerful arguments to support the view that more flexible working practices will solve more societal problems than they will create. Business leaders' fears for their organizations' competitiveness should also be assuaged by the evidence that flexibility actually reduces many of the hidden costs of existing working practices, thus enhancing competitiveness. And though flexible practices are in some ways challenging to manage, they are no more so than are the dozens of other working practices that have been introduced within organizations over the past two decades; and, like these other practices, they bring with them sufficient benefits to compensate for the challenges.

Looking Out for the British Economy: are Flexible Working Practices a Threat to British Competitiveness?

The present Labour government, like the Conservative one that preceded it, is a big fan of flexibility. It attributes Britain's comparatively low unemployment and inflation rates and strong growth rate to the flexibility built into the British economy. But the term 'flexibility' as used by this government means something quite different from 'flexibility' as I am using it here. The government's favourite brand of flexibility is the labour-market sort, which enables firms to adjust the size of their workforces in response to market signals and to pay their employees rates determined by market forces as opposed to collective bargaining, while enabling employees to move around freely in their search for work. In this book, 'flexibility' means flexibility of working practices: the creation of alternative models for the use of time, for the allocation of work and for the management of careers within organizations. And to the extent that this flexibility appears to have been dreamed up to meet the needs of employees rather than employers, it looks like a threat to the latter.

But should we, and the government that represents our interests, be afraid of working practices that enable workers to balance work and family life? Do shorter working hours, part-time jobs, job-shares and annual term-time breaks necessarily lead to lower levels of the other, government-favoured form of flexibility, and thus to lower business productivity?

A glance at the history books suggests that the answer is no. History provides several examples of proposals that were once resisted on the grounds that they would create works patterns which deviated from the then current practice, but which were subsequently adopted without any serious adverse consequences. Arlie Hochschild notes that the transition to the eight-hour day was resisted in the United States in the late nineteenth century because people felt that a ten-hour day was most efficient in most employments, and feared that the introduction of an eight hour limit on working time would result in lower productivity and competitiveness: 'With the eight-hour day there would be fewer things provided by labour and therefore fewer things to divide as rewards of labour ... So there would be fewer houses built and fewer chairs and tables and fewer carpets and fewer tools ... It comes to this, then, that in order to work fewer hours we must all be content with one fifth the results of labour, less food, clothing, tools, traveling, cigars or beer.' Other fears were that limiting work hours would open up new jobs to 'idlers', and render the United States a magnet for cheaper immigrant labour. There was also concern that employers would pass on the cost of offering ten hours' pay for eight hours' work by raising prices, and that workers would, in any case, be incapable of doing anything with their extra free time.

In the end, of course, the eight-hour day was implemented and none of the doomsters' fears were realized.[4] It was proved that there was nothing inevitable or natural about the ten-hour day, and that no great hardship would result from altering the way work had been done for as long as people could remember. Sobering thoughts indeed for those who would insist, today, that nothing short of five twelve-hour days a week could ever be enough for the effective discharging of senior management responsibilities, or that organizations could not possibly survive if large numbers of employees worked thirty hours a week or less and there were no such thing as a standard working week.

Patricia Hewitt provides more recent examples of changes in working time that were introduced amid vociferous resistance from scaremongers whose fears were subsequently proved unfounded. She notes that the CBI resisted reductions in hours worked in manufacturing because they would 'increase the costs of production and eat their way into profits'. The CBI feared that reductions in hours without pro rata reductions in wages would be met by reductions in employment. But in Britain most changes in working hours have been linked to changes to increase productivity, which have more than paid for the costs involved in reducing hours. The Institute of Personnel Management's (IPM) study in 1986 concluded that 'the reduction in the working week has had . . . at worst, only a marginal negative impact on costs'.[5]

The experience of ESI, an American computer company featured in Arlie Hochschild's *Time Bind*, bears out the IPM study's conclusion that reductions in working hours need not lead to lower productivity and high costs. ESI introduced reduced hours, and reduced salaries, for its plant workers and executives rather than make lay-offs. The company's vice-chairman, Doug Strain, discovered: 'First, productivity did not decline, I swear to God we get as much out of them at thirty-two hours as we did at forty. So it's not a bad business decision. But second, when economic conditions improved, we offered them one hundred per cent time again. No one wanted to go back!'[6]

For evidence that workplace change can be successfully introduced without adverse consequences for business, we can also look at the experience of countries like Sweden, Norway and Germany. Hochschild notes that the basic reforms of a time movement that are feared and seem so radical in the United States have already been tried with success in those three countries, each of which has maintained a thriving economy for decades, even though many sectors rely on a thirty-five-hour work week.[7]

But Scandinavia is not the family-friendly haven we are often told it is: work by Philip Hwang and his American colleague Linda Hass has shown that firms in Sweden are more family-friendly than firms elsewhere, but that traditional attitudes about gender and employee commitment continue to assert themselves and prevent the wide-spread take-up of flexible working policies, particularly by men. Nevertheless, the Swedish working environment is more advanced than that in the average British or American firm, and looks like heaven to those working for highly traditional firms in these cultures. Long hours are worked by fewer people than in the USA and the UK, and provisions for time off work are significantly greater. Linda Hass jokes that the Swedes are very critical of themselves, and fail to realize just how far their work culture has progressed: 'It's a matter of the half-full or half-empty glass. The Swedes see the Swedish glass as half-empty, whereas I see it as half-full. Believe me, Swedish firms are a lot better than American firms overall.'

Many will resist Germany's being held up as a role model for successful flexible working practices, seeing the country's recent economic misfortune as having been caused by its 'stakeholder' economy with its emphasis on worker involvement and protection. To such critics flexible working practices, like part-time working, will look like just one more element of an uncompetitive economic structure. But Germany's troubles have as much to do with the burdens imposed by reunification as they have with any fallibility in its economic model. And work-place practices such as flexible working hours, part-time jobs and job-shares need not go hand in hand with restrictive practices and regulations preventing firms from responding quickly and appropriately to market signals.

Both historical experience with changes in working time, and the contemporary experience of some European countries, suggest that flexible working is not something to be wary of. As Hochschild notes in relation to American companies, 'there is no proof that flexible hours are not in a company's long-term interest, and substantial evidence that they are'.[8] Not only are flexible working practices unlikely to represent a net cost to the economy, but there is every reason to believe that they would contribute a net benefit by enhancing the government's ability to respond to some of the pressing social and economic challenges currently confronting Britain.

Leveraging Flexible Working Practices for the Societal Good

Liz Bargh, chief executive of WFD and former director of the Opportunity 2000 campaign, believes that the imperative for changing working practices lies in a host of macro- and micro-economic forces.

> Large-scale forces such as globalization, the growth of the twenty-four-hour service culture and technological change, are demanding that we find more flexible ways of working; environmental concerns make conservation of scarce resources a priority, and highlight the illogicality of housing vast numbers of people in city-centre office blocks. On top of this, we have a polarized workforce in which for some work would be a godsend while others have more work than they can cope with. All of these things oblige us to seek another way of working, and of organizing work. The needs of the family constitute just one of many reasons to consider change.

Bargh mentions several of the many pressing societal challenges that render a rethink about the way work is allocated and carried out almost inevitable. In fact there are five important society-wide trends, some of which are likely to lead to the implementation of more workplace flexibility, and all of which should make the government respond by investing funds and energy in understanding, encouraging and rewarding the use of family-friendly working practices. These five trends are the polarization of employment, the changing nature of work, demographic trends, the growing appreciation of environmental issues, and the depletion of the nation's 'social capital'. Understanding the extent to which flexible working practices might both result from and constitute a response to some of these trends should persuade the government that family-friendly flexibility is to be embraced and encouraged rather than feared.

The Scarcity of Work and the Polarization of Employment

The scarcity of work is a theme addressed by several authors such as Jeremy Rifkin, Stanley Aronowitz and William DiFazio, and by the

Royal Society for the Advancement of Arts, Manufacturing and Commerce (RSA), which incorporated the theme within its position paper *Redefining Work*, published in spring 1998. Rifkin predicts the 'development of a virtually jobless world' in his book *The End of Work*, and Aronowitz and DiFazio prophesise that the restructuring of global capital and computer-mediated work will lead to severe unemployment and underemployment. All three writers suggest that there will not be enough work to go round in the future, and that the concept of the job, as we know it, will disappear.

Available evidence suggests that the advent of work scarcity on the scale envisioned by Rifkin is unlikely. The authors of a study published by the International Labour Office in Geneva insist that the credibility of Rifkin-like predictions is very limited, as they are based on doubtful generalizations extrapolating out to the whole economy job losses in a few large corporations, and failing to account for employment by small firms or the creation of new types of jobs.[9]

Nevertheless, a form of work scarcity is already a feature of the British economy, as is confirmed by a report produced by the Department for Education and Employment in spring 1997. During the decade 1984–94, say the authors of the report, family employment has become polarized: 'There has been an increase both in the proportion of 'work-poor' families (with no earners) and in the proportion of 'work-rich' families (with two earners)'.[10] A significant and growing number of children are growing up in situations of affluence, while around a third of all children live in households with no full-time earners.

The DFEE report speaks to the growing inequality in British society. But additionally, it illustrates the problem of too little work to go round. Given that those without work are often those with disadvantaged backgrounds and poor qualifications and skills, spreading the work between the 'work-rich' and the 'work-poor' is an exercise that is only easily carried out in theory. Those who exist at the very margins of society – the long-term unemployed, the homeless – will benefit little from measures designed to establish a better balance between work and life, and between workers and non-workers, within organizations. The policies needed to provide them with opportunities are different, and largely outside the scope of this book. However, that the work-poor group also includes skilled and qualified persons who are unable to find suitable work because they can't work standard hours (for instance, single mothers), and that the work-rich group includes many who do not wish to work as much as they do, suggests that any form of workplace change that renders working hours and contracts more flexible has the potential to benefit large numbers of people and to assist in the resolution of the work-scarcity problem.

The Changing Nature of Work

Like Jeremy Rifkin, William Bridges has witnessed the large-scale lay-offs made by large firms. But although Bridges accepts that jobs are disappearing, he insists that work is not. Work is simply taking different forms, and being parcelled out in different ways. This is no less of an upheaval than that predicted by Rifkin and others, but it is an upheaval that could have a happy ending, provided people can adjust to the new ways of creating, finding and doing work, and provided governmental institutions and policies can rise to the challenge of supporting them.

In *Jobshift* and his subsequent book *Creating You and Co.*, work transitions consultant William Bridges spells out his thesis that jobs are being replaced by new forms of work. There is nothing 'natural' about the job, he says. Before 1800 or so, no one ever had a job – they had work, instead. Jobs were created to meet the needs of the Industrial Revolution. They were the most effective way of getting work done in a world characterized by readily separated functions and areas of responsibility, linear work processes, long sequences of predictable activity, and discrete and relatively infrequent changes.

But jobs are not so effective today, says Bridges, because the way we are most productive has changed. Jobs are being replaced by temporary work, outsourced work, the use of consultants, cross-trained teams or self-managed telecommuters. These new work arrangements are arising not simply because of downsizing and corporate greed – though Bridges admits there is plenty of greed about – but because of a 'phenomenon that is transforming people's work lives beyond anything they could have imagined a decade ago'. That phenomenon is represented by six key factors: first, today's work increasingly involves the processing of knowledge rather than the manipulation of things; second, information and communications technology is undoing the concentration of people in time and space which industrial technology required; third, the pace of change has picked up remarkably; fourth, and in response to this third factor, companies are trying to 'build more flexibility, rapid-response customer focus and individual accountability into the organization'; fifth, the desire for flexibility is leading to efforts to 'de-integrate' or 'unbundle' the organization into separate elements; and finally, the force of the baby boom – 'the first generation of free agents' – is contributing to the movement away from fixed and standardized jobs.

In the environment created by these six factors, jobs have become dysfunctional in all but the slowest-moving organizations,[11] for they don't provide the necessary flexibility and adaptiveness. Jobs encourage people to do their jobs, but not to do 'whatever needs doing'; job structures encourage hiring; jobs 'obscure the larger picture and the ultimate goals of the collective effort'; and for individuals, jobs have become an overly large source of identity.

The new work environment described by Bridges requires a new worker, one who can find the work that needs doing and package up her individual attributes – desires, abilities, temperament, assets – in a way that enables her to secure and do that work. The new work environment also requires different things of institutions such as schools, colleges and unions, in addition to requiring some altogether new institutions, such as 'agencies' that coordinate the matching of organizational needs with individuals' offerings, providing some of the social contact and security that large organizations once did.

Bridges's vision of the future world of work may look far-fetched, but aspects of it are already evident in the decline in full-time jobs, in the growth in self-employment and part-time work, in the doubling between 1991 and 1995 of the proportion of white-collar workers on temporary contracts, and in the shortening length of job tenure.[12] In a speech at the Royal Society for the Advancement of Arts, Manufacturing and Commerce (RSA) in October 1997, Bridges insisted that we are presently too close to the changes to be able to discern them clearly,[13] but that a generation from now the things he talks about will seem obvious. The new realities of work are neither good, nor bad; they just are, and people will have to adapt to them. These realities are frightening in some ways, but profoundly liberating in others. They certainly create more scope for flexible work patterns and flexible careers than did the workplace of yesterday. In Bridges's work world, parents who work just eight months of the year or three days a week, and have a say in when, where and how they work, will not be in the minority. Theirs will be the standard pattern for a large sector of the working population. That this pattern of work will enable organizations to be more responsive and adaptable should be impetus for more of them to begin experimenting with it. And to the extent that this process of experimentation opens their eyes and ears to the possibilities represented by flexible working patterns in general, it will improve the environment within which family-friendly forms of flexibility operate.

The Demographic Pincer Action

Like the forces shaping the organization of work, those affecting demographics will both encourage and serve as a powerful rationale for greater workplace flexibility. At one end of the demographic spectrum, the ranks of the elderly are swelling and changing. At the other end, the young, new entrants to the workforce are becoming fewer in number and bringing markedly different motivations and demands to the work world than did previous generations. These demographic facts constitute a kind of demographic pincer action on existing workplace norms. They will force these norms to shift as surely as the macro-economic trends that Bridges documents.

The problem of an ageing population would not be solved by the reorganization and redistribution of work, but would certainly be greatly alleviated by it. And the problem is real indeed. Between 1993 and 2006, Britain will have seen a rise of 2.4 million in the workforce aged thirty-five to fifty-four, and a decline of 1.6 million in the workforce under thirty-five.[14] Forecasters predict that in Britain in the year 2030, 30 per cent of people will be aged over sixty (up from 21 per cent in 1990), and the number of working people supporting each pensioner will be 2.4 (as against 3.3 in 1990).[15] Organizations will worry about how to find enough employees, and governments will be concerned about how to fund the retirement of an ever-growing retired population. A reappraisal of age – the appropriate age for retirement, what kind of work, and how much of it, people can and should be doing at any particular age – is inevitable. That reappraisal bodes well for women, and men, who wish to slow down their careers by working part-time or taking short breaks in their thirties and early forties, then relaunch themselves on to faster career tracks in their late forties.

To a certain extent, the reappraisal of age and what it means is already under way. The idea that fifty is not old is catching on. In an article in *You* magazine entitled 'Recipe for Renaissance woman', the byline for which was 'Fab at fifty', Rose Gray tells us how fabulous it feels to have launched her successful restaurant, the River Café, at the age of fifty.[16] Another article, this one in *Good Housekeeping* entitled 'Old at forty, young at sixty: does age mean anything any more?', also sings the praises of the over-fifties: 'Today's dynamic fifty-somethings are happier and healthier than previous generations and highly satisfied with life,' says Marianne Heron. So why are we pushing them out of the workforce?[17] Gloria Steinem adds her voice to the chorus in her book *Revolution from Within* and an interview she gave to promote it: 'I am becoming more radical and rebellious with age,' she tells us in the *Sunday Times* of 15 May 1994. Her interviewer assures us that 'older women are in a position to make a difference, and Steinem, at sixty, is going on trying'.[18]

In *New Passages* Gail Sheehy argues that we need to shake up our preconceptions about what all ages mean, and what are appropriate behaviours and aspirations at any age. Having conducted thousands of interviews and charted the lives and dreams of men and women of all generations, she has concluded that there is a revolution going on in the life cycle. 'In the space of one short generation the whole shape of the life cycle has been altered. People today are leaving childhood sooner, but they are taking longer to grow up and much longer to grow old. That shifts all the stages of adulthood ahead – by up to ten years.' The life-cycle revolution means that people of fifty and sixty today don't think of themselves as old. They routinely believe that they are five to ten years younger than the age on their birth certificates. Fifty is what forty used to be, sixty is what fifty used to be. Not only do they not think of themselves as old, but they don't behave as if they are old. They are learning new things, taking on new challenges, exploring new sides of themselves. They are embracing their 'second adulthood' with energy and enthusiasm.

Health and physical capabilities are not as much of a hindrance to the enjoyment of a second adulthood as we might think. For instance, only 10 per cent of Americans of sixty-five and over have a chronic health problem that restricts them from carrying out a major activity. The other 90 per cent can take on both physical and mental challenges. And women in the UK today who reach the age of sixty can expect to live until eighty-two. For healthy women today, second adulthood may actually last longer than first adulthood.

Sheehy claims that many women in their 'flaming fifties' find themselves blazing with energy and accomplishment as never before in history. We now know that psychic prowess actually builds up in women as they age, and will be stronger at fifty than at forty or thirty. At the same time, many women develop a stronger sense of self and heightened confidence. If this is so, then our concepts of what women and men in their fifties can do within organizations must also be transformed. Organizations which, instead of writing off fifty- and sixty-year-olds, recognize what they have to offer and incorporate that recognition into their recruitment and working practices and career-path-planning will, like the women themselves, be the pace-setters of the future.

Sheehy is confident that organizations, government and society at large will have little choice but to seize the opportunities ensuing from a reassessment of age. 'The bottom line is that we are living longer, but most people are using up their assets faster. Is this any way for postindustrial societies to utilize their human resources? It is a problem that government, corporations, and private sector institutions are all going to have to address sooner or later,'[19] she says.

The need to change our perceptions of age so as to capitalize on the energy and talents of older people is reason enough to consider job and career structures capable of accommodating people's need to work less in their middle years and more in their fifties and sixties. But the ageing population provides another urgent rationale for the redesign of job and career structures. For while the young elderly will want and need to be active into their fifties and sixties, many in their seventies and eighties will need to be cared for. One in six employees in the UK has eldercare responsibilities, and half of these envision taking on additional caring responsibilities in the near future.[20] These people will be only marginally helped by the Labour government's plans to provide tax breaks for families who care for the elderly. All the tax breaks in the world won't help people whose careers are essential to them but leave little space for eldercare responsibilities. With so many in the working population responsible for the care of elderly people, and the simultaneous shifting of the burden of care from the state on to the individual and the family, the voices clamouring for flexible working arrangements that create the space for caring will soon become both more numerous and more ardent.

Added to these voices will be those of the younger generation, 'Generation X'. A series of reports published by Demos reveal that, while work remains central to the eighteen-to-thirty-four genera-tion, 'this has not led to the wholehearted acceptance of the traditional male work ethic with its emphasis on total dedication of time to the workplace'.[21] Generation X is looking for more out of work and out of life, and a better balance between the two: 37 per cent of women and 46 per cent of men in the age group say they are looking for a job that gives their life meaning; 80 per cent of mothers and 88 per cent of fathers say they want to spend more time with their family; 51 per cent of young single women and 48 per cent of young single men would like to take a year's unpaid leave; and 46 per cent of mothers in relationships would like to take unpaid leave during school holidays.[22]

A survey of business students at thirty colleges in ten countries similarly revealed that students put a balanced lifestyle above earning a competitive salary and the chance to climb the managerial ladder.[23] Janet Andre, an American business management consultant, hears young people saying that their personal life is as valuable to them as professional achievement.[24] David Cannon, author of *Generation X and the New Work Ethic*, argues that young graduates prefer to work for organizations that offer autonomy to taking roles in a hierarchical career structures.[25] And Barbara Moses, the Canadian author of *Career Intelligence: Mastering the New Work and Personal Realities*, believes that the 'twenty-somethings have watched their career-obsessed parents worship their work organizations and then be cast aside by them and are, as a result, more prepared both for working in the new economy, and to make new demands of it'.[26]

Several organizational leaders whom I interviewed stressed that the attitudes of the younger generation would be a force for change. Mrs Steve Shirley, founder and president of the FI Group, said organizations would need to take note of young people's healthier approach to balancing work and life. Irene Allen, co-owner and production director of Listawood, a computer mouse-mat manufacturer based in Norfolk, commented on 'the sea change in people's attitudes' that would shape workplace culture. Steve Beck, head of Gemini Consulting's Northern European operations, also suspects that organizations will need to respond to the new agenda set by the new entrants to the workforce: 'There is something very different about the way our younger employees think about work. They just aren't prepared to work eighty hours a week and give up everything else like we once were. We are going to have to find a way to deal with this if we are going to attract and retain these people and grow our business.'

Concern for the Environment

Environmental concerns may provide the same kind of impetus to workplace change as the need to provide better work opportunities for those in their fifties and sixties, to care for the elderly, and to respond to the demands of Generation X. However many people dispute the evidence that the ozone layer is thinning and the world climate becoming more unstable, one thing is abundantly clear to almost everyone: roads are becoming seriously congested, and air quality is deteriorating as a result. Liz Bargh is right when she says that, in the light of such signs of environmental degeneration, the concept of millions of people travelling to work in huge city office blocks every day makes little sense. As governments face up to the need to limit travel on congested roads and to halt the building of new ones, they will be inclined to support moves towards workplace flexibility that will free people to travel to work at different times, or to work partly from their homes.

Concern about road congestion and traffic-related pollution served as a major motivation for Oxfordshire County Council in implementing its homeworking and flexiworking policies. As a public-sector organization employing one in twelve of all employed persons in the county, they could not afford to be seen to be contributing to environmental destruction. In the future, more and more private-sector organizations may be forced, by a government intent on halting environmental damage, to take a similar view. Steve Shirley already sees environmental concerns as further justification for the flexible working policies that she first introduced as a means of enabling mothers to work.

Working from home is not always an unequivocally positive experience, as we saw in Chapter 8. But homeworking as one of a range of policies, and within a generally flexible and supportive work culture, is more likely to meet employees' needs than homeworking that is thrust upon them because of organizations' needs and without consideration of the constraints that some workers may face. And it would undoubtedly be an essential component of environmentally friendly working policy. If large numbers of employees were encouraged to work at home one or two days each week, and to stagger their arrival times on office working days, with some arriving at 9am and others at 10.30am, congestion on inner-city roads would soon lessen and the daily commute could become a relatively pleasant experience. When more employees are trusted to manage their own work according to flexible guidelines, to judge how much and when they need to be at the office, to communicate by phone and the Internet when it serves their purposes, both employee motivation and environmental protection will be served simultaneously.

Replenishing the Nation's Stock of Social Capital

Private capital, as amassed by organizations or individuals, is a body of assets accumulated over years of effort and value creation, which gives life to further sustained value creation, provides the capital-holders with protection against economic misfortune, and is handed down to future generations. Social capital can be described in similar terms, though the assets are different, and it is not private organizations or individuals who own and benefit from the capital, but society as a whole. The assets that make up social capital include a high level of social cohesion and a shared set of values and goals; strong and positive relationships, both within and between societal units; and a mentally healthy, educated and active populace. The list could fill chapters, for there are thousands of things that contribute to the long-term benefit of all members of a given society and could therefore be considered part of that society's social capital. The key is not to be able to articulate every one of these things, but to recognize that social capital exists, and is depleted or accumulated as a result of policy, action and accident.

Many in Britain fear that its stock of social capital is being depleted at an alarming rate. Indeed, there are signs of the withering social capital base everywhere – in rising rates of family breakdown and juvenile crime, higher levels of anxiety and depression among adults and young people, damage to social cohesion caused by the growing income disparity between rich and poor, and the increasing influence of technologically enabled, remote forms of communication and interaction at the expense of old-fashioned face-to-face contact. We struggle to find ways to stem the outflows from the social capital fund, to strengthen the bonds between individuals, their families and society as a whole. Governments wring their hands and look for solutions in policies aimed at strengthening the institution of marriage and supporting lone parents, and in such measures as tagging young offenders and fining their mothers and fathers.

Social capital will not be built up by a single initiative. But there is a growing appreciation of the role that organizations could play in creating an environment in which social capital can be accumulated rather than depleted. In his book *The Hungry Spirit* Charles Handy implores businesses to develop a sense of moral responsibility. Capitalism is a positive force in many ways, he says, for it creates markets that 'give wings to ideas' and provides the basis for efficiency, which is essential for the continued existence of society. But today's capitalism is largely missing the point in life, piling up riches we cannot possibly use and striving for efficiency, while one-third of the world's workers are unemployed or underemployed. Handy calls for a new philosophy that will make the market our servant rather than our master, and insists that corporations, because they are so large and powerful (in the list of the world's hundred largest economies, fifty are corporations[27]), have a major role to play in bringing this philosophy to life.

Handy's capitalism goes beyond capitalism as we know it today and is based upon the influence of corporations that are 'properly selfish'. It is also a capitalism which enables employees to bring their whole selves to work, to find more meaning in their work, and to balance that work with their need to connect with and be responsible to others – their families and communities. The risks to society of not embracing such a capitalism are grave indeed in Handy's view, and include the jeopardizing of democracy itself. But the benefits that could accrue to everyone, in the form of social capital and individual freedom and happiness, are immense.

Many of those active in the work–life field echo Handy's faith in the power of properly selfish organizational principles to strengthen society as a whole. They insist that businesses do have moral and social responsibilities, which include enabling their employees to balance work and life effectively, and that the moral/social case for workplace change is as powerful and relevant as the purely numbers-based business case. Hilary Simpson, principal personnel officer for Oxfordshire County Council, warns that adherence to the business case alone is anyway potentially dangerous: 'If you live by the business case, you could well die by it too. If your case is completely based on a recruitment argument, and the economic environment changes so that you don't need to recruit people, where does that leave you?' Leslie Chin of the work–life consultancy WFD insists that though the business case is real and compelling, 'the moral case should not be forgotten'.[28]

Some business leaders are themselves inspired by the wider implications for society of work–life balance initiatives within organizations. Steve Shirley is fully versed in the language of employee retention and productivity that is often used to justify work–life initiatives, but is adamant that the potential of employee empowerment and workplace flexibility to build social capital is as important as any immediate and concrete gains they bring to businesses. Employment practices which recognize people's whole selves and whole lives contribute to a healthier and more balanced social structure – one in which, among other things, stress is lower, divorces are fewer, families are stronger and children feel more secure. 'All of that is good for business in the end,' says Shirley.

In North America, a number of business leaders have publicly embraced the moral and socially responsible rationale for workplace change. The owner of Alby's General Store in Massachusetts, employing around fifty people, claims to see flexible working and employer-sponsored childcare as a moral obligation. Elliot Lehman, former chairperson of Fel-Pro, a US manufacturer of engine gaskets and chemical products, defines Fel-Pro's interest in family-friendly initiatives in terms of its commitment to the long-term health, education and welfare of children. The Little Tikes Company president claims that when a company demonstrates that it cares for its employees, and enables them to care for their families, 'the intangible benefits to the company are monumental'.[29]

Workplace change should not be seen as a panacea for society's problems, any more than should childcare or 'get tough on crime' policies. Nevertheless, it is important that we and our government recognize the potential benefits that would result from a concerted, sustained commitment to fundamental workplace change. For there is no doubt that workplace norms and practices that enable parents to reduce their working hours and accommodate their family lives more easily within them will take much of the stress out of family life, create more space for family members to build strong, secure relationships, and enable people to devote more time and energy to supporting their schools and communities. And it is strong family relationships – whether they be formed within traditional families or those headed by gay couples or single parents – and a sense of belonging and responsibility to a community that have been repeatedly found to militate against juvenile crime, mental ill health in children and community breakdown. It is family and community relationships that lie at the heart of social capital, and on which government initiatives must concentrate if the pool of social capital is to be enlarged. What better way to set about its enlargement than by providing encouragement, support and rewards for organizations that make progress in enabling employees to achieve a balance between work and the rest of their lives?

Talking direct to business: Flexibility as a tool for reducing the hidden costs of operations

Business and organizational leaders might find the link between flexible working practices and social capital or broad demographic trends intellectually interesting, but their behaviour and decisions are unlikely to alter unless a sound and immediately relevant business case – evidence that workplace change will generate tangible, measurable benefits which outweigh its costs – is put forward. It is the language of profits, costs, competitive advantage and efficiency that is used to judge business leaders; it is that same language that they will use in assessing the viability of family-friendly working practices. They will demand of a business case that it provide persuasive answers to two key questions: (1) will flexibility make my business less competitive? and (2) will flexibility be difficult to manage?

There will undoubtedly be costs associated with the introduction of flexible working practices, particularly in the short-term. These include the cost of efforts to identify employee needs and redesign jobs and processes, in addition to the costs associated with early-days inefficiency and hiccups. But the bulk of the evidence established to date suggests not only that there are few long-term costs associated with flexible working practices, but that there are long-term benefits in the form of less costly and more effective recruitment, lower employee turnover levels, reductions in employee stress and absenteeism, and enhanced individual and organizational performance.

Employers are increasingly willing to vouch for these benefits. In one survey of American employers, three-quarters claimed that family-friendly policies lower absenteeism, and two-thirds felt they improve worker attitudes. Some even felt that they enjoy reduced medical insurance costs as a result of lower stress levels.[30] AT&T's chairman wrote that family-friendly initiatives help the company to attract and keep the talented workforce it needs to win in the marketplace, and help employees to maintain a healthy balance between work and families which enables them to concentrate on giving their best to their customers. UK employers who have experimented with family-friendly policies vouch for the same kinds of benefits as American firms. In a 1992 survey of thirty-eight personnel managers of UK companies, over 70 per cent felt that flexible working helps in recruitment, reduces turnover, and generates high levels of productivity and commitment.[31] Lilly Industries' work–life programme brochure lists 'ten good reasons why work–life is the way forward', including improved morale among employees, retention of valuable skilled staff, reduced absenteeism, improved productivity, and a competitive edge from becoming the 'employer of choice'.

The employee-retention argument is the one most often put forward to justify flexible working. It is easy to attach hard numbers to higher retention levels, to persuade even the most sceptical that there are cost benefits associated with retaining more staff for longer periods. But, as we shall see later in this chapter, the benefits of improving employee retention are far greater than are captured by simple calculations of the hiring and training costs involved in replacing an employee, since they are linked to superior organizational performance in a way that is seldom recognized. And, just as the benefits of employee retention are often underestimated, so is the potential for flexibility to enhance effectiveness and creativity at both the individual and organizational levels. One can picture the benefits of flexible working practices as layers in a pyramid, with the cost savings resulting from more effective recruitment and lower turnover and absenteeism in the upper half, and the benefits of superior individual and organizational performance in a broad strip across the bottom. The benefits in the upper part of the pyramid are the easiest to spot and calculate, and are the first that many firms seek to capture. Those linked to the potential for superior performance are often missed by those whose attention is absorbed by daily business operations. They are less concrete and demand a greater leap of faith from those seeking to capture them, but they represent far more of what is potentially exciting and revolutionary about flexible working practices.

Flexibility as a Recruitment Tool

Companies with a recruitment problem, or seeking to gain competitive advantage through more effective recruitment, are likely to benefit from the implementation of genuinely flexible practices. On the basis of a study of US employees, the Families and Work Institute in America concluded that 'quality of work–life in some ways is just as important to workers as the traditional value of money'. The Institute notes that 60 per cent of employees considered the potential effect of their job on personal and family life to have been 'very important' to them in deciding whether or not to take that job.[32] In contrast, only 35 per cent rated salary/wage as a very important reason for joining their current employer. Carole Savage, London Business School MBA graduate, stated that her 1997 study involving 1,000 British working mothers similarly reveals that most want more flexibility and are willing to trade off money to get it. Several women I know have voted with their feet and their wallets, trading in highly paid positions in inflexible organizations for less well compensated jobs with flexible employers, or in their own businesses.

The fact that flexibility is sufficiently valued by employees to serve as a factor influencing recruitment is borne out by a survey of a hundred UK organizations carried out by Industrial Relations Services in 1990, which revealed that flexible working arrangements were considered the most effective aid to recruitment and retention.[33] Organizations such as Oxfordshire County Council recognize the value of flexibility as a recruiting tool. 'We can't always afford to pay the same salaries as private-sector organizations, so the fact that we are known to be a genuinely flexible employer gives us an edge, helps us to attract really high-quality people who would otherwise never consider working for us,' explained Hilary Simpson, the Council's principal personnel officer.

As William Bridges points out, the job culture is undergoing tremendous change, which may result in the replacement of 'jobs' by other means of organizing work. But for the time being, many firms in the UK and America are recruiting to fill jobs and finding it tough going.[34] Companies who recruit from the Generation X pool of potential employees are having a tougher time than others attracting the skills they need. Given the attitudes of that generation towards work–life balance, these employers could not fail to benefit from the introduction of flexible working practices. Even if new recruits have no need for part-time work or term-time working arrangements in the early phases of their careers, the fact that flexibility is on offer sends positive signals about company culture which will be factored into the job decision.

Retaining Knowledge and Skills

Employee retention is important, not simply because it lowers the costs of recruitment and training, but because it enables organizations to conserve knowledge and expertise. Flexible working practices are increasingly being recognized as effective means of improving retention levels, for men as well as women, parents as well as non-parents. IBM's vice president of workforce diversity, Ted Childs, noted that a 1996 survey of 7,500 IBM employees revealed work–life balance to be at the top of the list of factors cited as 'reasons for staying with IBM', whereas it had historically been a distant second to remuneration. Other American companies such as Corning and Dupont have implemented flexible working as a means of reducing what they saw to be punishingly high turnover rates.[35] Here in the UK both Midland and NatWest banks embarked in the late 1980s upon high-profile initiatives to improve retention through varied career-break and childcare-provision schemes.[36] Midland publicly attributes the fact that so many women now return from maternity leave – 82 per cent now as against 41 per cent in 1989[37] – to its childcare initiatives, but there is also evidence that the flexible work arrangements it has introduced have improved the bank's ability to recruit and retain staff. Glaxo Wellcome's flexible working and childcare support and advice schemes are held responsible for a rise in the rate of return from maternity leave from 40 per cent to 97 per cent over five years.[38]

Business cases commonly emphasize the cost savings derived from increased retention rates. The costs of replacement, training and downtime for a newly recruited employee vary across industries and businesses, but are never insignificant. A report published in 1993 jointly by Business in the Community and the Institute of Personnel Management estimated that the costs of replacing a junior manager earning £15,000 per annum in a UK organization, including the costs of recruitment, training, temporary cover and limited functioning of the new recruit, to be in the order of £7,000, or almost half the manager's annual salary.[39] Other case studies have estimated the cost of replacement to be as high as 150 per cent of annual salary.[40] Diana Good, the partner at London legal firm Linklater's & Paines charged with crafting and implementing a part-time policy for partners, explained that the firm had been persuaded to look at the part-time partnership option because of the high costs associated with the turnover of female lawyers. 'Over the past decade at least 50 per cent of those we have employed have been women,' explained Good. 'Yet just one in ten partners is a woman. Women were leaving in search of more flexibility just before consideration for partnership, which meant that we were recruiting for partnership from a talent pool that was significantly smaller than the one we started out with. Given the enormous amounts of money invested in lawyers in their early years, that is just not clever!'

The Linklater's & Paines example highlights the fact that the cost of turnover is represented not just by high recruitment and training costs but by the often incalculable cost of lost expertise. John Bateson, a senior vice-present with Gemini Consulting, insists that preventing this loss of expertise should be the primary aim of work–life-type measures: 'When you consider the enormous waste of talent, knowledge and experience which is represented by the fact that so many women leave corporate life, it becomes clear that we have no choice but to change the way we operate.' A Dupont study of women engineers highlighted just how great the cost of lost expertise could be: it revealed that it was the best performers, and therefore those with the most expertise, who were leaving in search of jobs with better work–family balance.[41] Such is the importance of the knowledge amassed by researchers at Glaxo that the loss of an individual is seen to represent the loss of 'what might have been'.

The value that employers place on retaining the skills and experience of particular individuals can outweigh many of the perceived inconveniences of flexible work arrangements. Peter Clark, head of legal services at Oxfordshire County Council and manager of two female lawyers who job-share, admits that managing a job-share is somewhat more problematic than managing a single job-holder. The handover of responsibility from one lawyer to the other takes time and is not always smooth, and the supervision of two lawyers rather than one is obviously more time-consuming for him. But Clark insists that he would much rather allow the women to job-share than lose them both. 'It's a real benefit to keep them – and there is no way they would still be here without this arrangement. In reality they each add a value equivalent to one and a half people because of their knowledge and experience.'

Frederick Reichheld, a director of the international consulting firm Bain & Company, calculates the true costs of turnover in terms of lost knowledge and expertise in *The Loyalty Effect: The Hidden Force behind Growth, Profits and Lasting Value*. Reichheld maintains that though accounting systems often mask the fact, 'inventories of experienced customers, employees, and investors are a company's most valuable assets'. Yet these assets are 'vanishing from corporate balance sheets at an alarming rate, decimating growth and earnings potential as they go': in a typical company customers defect at the rate of 10 to 30 per cent annually, employee turnover is between 15 and 25 per cent per year, and 'investor churn' is in excess of 50 per cent per annum. Companies Reichheld calls Loyalty leaders, on the other hand, see employees, customers and investors as assets. They choose them carefully, extend their productive lifetimes and increase their value. And through engendering high levels of loyalty from all three of their people-asset groups – employees, customers and investors – they generate superior, sustainable returns.

Reichheld provides compelling evidence of the links between loyalty and performance. US firms such as the Chick-fil-A restaurant chain, the State Farm insurance company and the Leo Burnett advertising agency have all generated superior returns based on strategies that emphasize customer, employee and investor loyalty. Leo Burnett, for instance, has the highest customer retention rate in its industry as well as the highest productivity rate. And 'if you wonder what getting and keeping the right employees has to do with getting and keeping the right customers, the answer is everything,' insists Reichheld.

There are several reasons why this is true. For one thing, it takes time to build solid personal relationships with customers. For another, loyal employees have greater opportunities to learn and increase their efficiency. For a third, the money these employees save their employers in reduced recruiting and training costs can be invested somewhere else – for example, in measures that will increase customer satisfaction. Finally, the same business philosophy and operational policies that earn employees' loyalty and boost their morale are likely to work for customers.[42]

'The true cash flow consequences of employee turnover far exceed managers' intuitive estimates,' says Reichheld. Employee retention is critical both for cost-efficiency and revenue growth. In one trucking company it was found that cutting driver turnover in half would lead to a 50 per cent increase in profits. In a stock brokerage, a 10 per cent improvement in broker retention would increase an individual broker's value to the firm by 155 per cent. And in one retail chain, the top third of stores in terms of employee retention were found to be the top in terms of sales productivity, producing 22 per cent higher sales per employee than stores in the bottom third.

Reichheld's analysis substantiates what some managers have asserted all along: that employee turnover damages businesses, so investments in reducing turnover are worth making. To the extent that the successful implementation of flexible working practices reduces turnover – and evidence suggests that it does – these practices can be seen to be directly responsible for improving businesses' long-term cost position and revenue-generation potential.

If the link between employee retention and business performance fails to make some in business sit up and take note, the Equal Opportunities Commission's stance on part-time working and job-shares might. In August 1997 the Commission stated that employers should make part-time working and job-shares available to senior staff or risk facing legal action.[43] Their warning came after Janet Schofield, a marketing support manager who was backed by the EOC, received £20,000 from Zurich Insurance Company after being refused a job-share when she returned from maternity leave. Schofield's victory, following hot on the heels of similar wins by Sarah Rolls over IPC Magazines and Kelly French over Bank of America, will force some corporate leaders to grudgingly accept flexible working practices even if compelling evidence of the relationship between employee retention and profits cannot inspire them.

Minimizing the Corporate Health Bill: Reducing Absenteeism and Stress through Flexible Working

Absence costs money. The Industrial Society estimates that absenteeism cost British businesses £13 billion in wasted salary bills alone in 1996.[44] (This conservative estimate does not take into account the costs of lost productivity, replacement staff, overtime bills or damage to morale.) The most frequently reported reasons for absence are cold/flu, stomach ache, headache, back problems, and stress/personal problems, in that order. Managers interviewed by the Industrial Society believe, however, that these reasons often serve to disguise the true causes of absence. At the top of the managers' list of probable reasons for absence are cold/flu, stress, and sickness of a family member/childcare problems.[45] Tony Morgan, chief executive of the Industrial Society, urges managers to create a climate of trust where questions of stress and family responsibility can be discussed openly. Only then, he says, will managers be getting to grips with the real causes of absenteeism and be able to take steps to reduce it.[46]

Stress is undoubtedly a major cause of absence. Stress shows up not just in high absenteeism costs, but in indicators such as lower morale and lower productivity. Work-related stress is more prevalent among parents than other groups of employees. The 1993 national study by the Families and Work Institute in America concluded that workers who have children exhibit higher levels of stress than workers without children.[47] The *Sunday Times* reported that stress costs businesses some £7–9 billion in sick pay, missed deadlines and poor performance,[48] much of which will be in addition to the £13 billion the Industrial Society estimates as the salary cost of absence.

It is not difficult to see how parenting responsibilities can cause both absence and stress. Family matters need to be attended to, whether both parents are working or not. Doctors' appointments need to be made and attended, sick children must be cared for, new childminders, nannies and nursery places have to be found when old ones disappear, and teenagers given advice at odd hours of the day and night. When both parents work full-time, these family matters will often be attended to on company time. For instance, each time an employee has to search for childcare or eldercare, they spend

276

approximately sixteen hours, 80 per cent of them during working hours.[49] Add to this the time spent on those things that positively nurture family life, and the cost to business of parents' parenting responsibilities soon mounts well beyond that represented by absence figures. It is time that is often squeezed hurriedly into the first or last half-hour of every day, or sneaked into a Thursday morning diary slot vaguely marked 'meeting – out of office'. Whatever the case, it represents time stolen from work and given surreptitiously to the family.

The fact that this time is taken on the sly means that it represents at once a cost to the employer and a cost to the parent. For when time for critical family matters is snatched, whatever is being attended to almost inevitably receives substandard treatment. (The parent screeches up to sports day at the last minute, and disappears before the last race is over; the sick child is given one day of parental care when she needs two.) And the parent, ever cognizant of depriving both their work and their family of adequate attention and time, feels a level of stress which cannot be measured, but which mounts day by day and exacts a lasting toll.

Whether it shows up in high absence levels or in lower levels of performance and morale, the cost of the work/family imbalance is high. Either organizations can ignore it, or they can take measures to minimize it. Like Tony Morgan of the Industrial Society, one human resources manager from a large public-sector organization believes it better to do the latter. 'People's home lives are getting more complicated. We can't hide from this. As a responsible employer you can either say that's not our problem, don't let it affect your work, or you can argue that looking after people makes business sense.'[50] Offering genuinely flexible working arrangements in one positive step that can be taken to minimize the cost of the work/family imbalance. Flexible starting-times mean that a parent with a sick child can take the time to find appropriate care for him or her and go into work later, rather than having to make an excuse and take the whole day off. The ability to work from home means that the parent can work while the child is resting or sleeping. And part-time working enables parents to squeeze many of their parenting tasks into their days off rather than stealing time from their work days. Even having a sick child need not result in absence, and thus cost to the employer: the part-time employee can care for her child in her own time, and rearrange her work days to fall later in the week. In return, she is freer to concentrate on work during the days when she *is* at work, thereby being more productive.

Where flexible working arrangements and reduced working hours contribute to an overall improvement in employee health as a consequence of reducing stress, the benefits to the employer may be greater still. Arlie Hochschild suggests that flexible employers may benefit from lower health insurance costs – not insignificant in a country like America where much of the bill for medical care is footed by employers,[51] or even in the UK, where many firms provide fully covered or partly subsidized private health care for their employees.

The benefits of lower health costs pale in comparison with other gains that could accrue from shorter working hours and more family-friendly arrangements. As Patricia Hewitt notes, 'Where long hours are worked regularly – as they are by many men doing manual jobs or working as doctors, managers or other professionals – the costs include the possible effects on employees' health and their own and other people's safety, as well as a possible loss of productivity.' Hewitt cites several studies linking long working hours with tiredness and high accident rates, including a study of the Clapham rail disaster which found that the senior technician responsible for the faulty wiring that caused the accident had been working a seven-day week for the previous thirteen weeks. A survey by the British Medical Association also found that doctors' long hours damage their effectiveness, and therefore patient safety. 'Doctors report that their accuracy in prescribing for patients is adversely affected by tiredness, and the BMA has argued strongly that cutting hours would substantially improve patient care.'[52] If shorter working hours can improve productivity and effectiveness for rail technicians and doctors, why not for lawyers, marketing executives and merchant bankers? How many poor defence cases, ill-conceived marketing plans and poorly constructed merger deals might have resulted from the excessively long hours that so many in law, business and banking regularly work?

The 'stick' of litigation may, in some cases, be a more powerful change catalyst than the 'carrot' represented by the potential of flexible working practices for reducing the corporate health bill. Corporations may be forced to pay directly for the stress engendered by the current conflict between work and personal life. In Japan, some two hundred families are suing firms they claim caused the deaths of their children by working them too hard.[53] Already, this has served as a warning to some corporations, who are introducing no-overtime days to make employees spend more time with their families. Here in the UK, employees have taken employers to court, and more may do so. A landmark personal injury case was brought by social worker John Walker against Northumberland County Council, after he suffered two nervous breakdowns as a result of a 'health-endangering workload' and was dismissed from the Council in 1988 on the grounds of permanent ill health. Walker was awarded £175,000 in damages, and the Council was declared 'in breach of the duty of care owed to [Walker] as his employer in respect of the second mental breakdown which he suffered as a result of stress and anxiety occasioned by his job'. An employment lawyer with the London firm Dibb Lupton Alsop noted that since the Walker case his firm had experienced a rise in the numbers of claims for compensation for work-related, stress-induced illness. The solutions often offered by experts to the problem of generalized workplace stress are the very same as those that would lessen the stress associated with the work–parenting conflict: job rotation, job-sharing, flexible working and homeworking.[54]

Flexibility for Superior Performance

Fred Reichheld's demonstration of the link between employee loyalty and organizational performance furnishes a strong rationale for the implementation of flexible working practices. But the link between flexibility and organizational performance is stronger and more multifaceted than that created by employee retention. Flexible working arrangements have been shown to encourage greater motivation, commitment and inventiveness in individuals, and to enhance organizations' ability to respond creatively and flexibly to business needs.

Higher levels of employee morale and commitment to business success were shown to result from family-friendly initiatives at Dupont. Announcing the results of a now much referenced study published in 1994, Dupont's president, John A. Krol, claimed that the results of the study clearly indicated that work–life programmes are a powerful tool to motivate people and encourage commitment to achieving business objectives.[55] The Dupont research had shown that employees who used or were aware of work–life programmes were the most committed employees in the company, and the least likely to feel overwhelmed or burned out. Those who used the programmes were 45 per cent more likely to strongly agree that they would go the extra mile to ensure Dupont's succeess than those who didn't use such services.

The work–life programmes at Dupont included a range of services in addition to flexible working options, and it was the entire package that generated such high levels of employee commitment. Other studies have shown a more direct link between flexible working arrangements, in particular, and employee morale and commitment. The Families and Work Institute's national study found that workers with more job autonomy and control of their work schedules are less burned out by their work, are more satisfied with their jobs, and take more initiative at work, in addition to being more committed to doing their jobs well, more loyal to their employers, and suffering from lower levels of stress than other workers. The study found that those workers whose managers and work environment accommo-dated their family commitments were similarly less burned out, more loyal and committed, and took more initiative. The study's authors concluded that worker empowerment is associated with greater job satisfaction, commitment to doing the job well and initiative on the job, as well as lower levels of stress; and that a 'constructive social climate at work' is an integral part of what makes companies work well.[56]

European studies bear out the conclusions of the national study conducted by the Families and Work Institute. The UK personnel managers surveyed by Isabel Boyer in 1992 confirmed that part-time managers are highly committed, and even more productive than full-timers.[57] 'Only on one measure of commitment can part-timers not match full-timers,' said Boyer basing the comment on her research. 'They work fewer hours.' Judith Gonyea and Bradley Googins of the Boston University Center on Work and Family point to an expanding body of literature confirming the connection between flexible work options and worker commitment, and claim that workers are more likely to think about their jobs in innovative ways and make contributions to their company when they perceive the organization to be supportive of them personally.[58]

The growth rate of Norfolk-based computer mouse-mat manufacturer Listawood has averaged 35 per cent per annum since the company was founded in 1989, hitting a remarkable 95 per cent in 1996. Irene Allen, who co-founded Listawood with her husband, Arthur, attributes much of the company's success to its flexible working arrangements, the effect of which has been to engender high levels of employee motivation and loyalty. That loyalty is valued at all times, but never more so than when the company needs employees to juggle their schedules or work extra hours to resolve a crisis or meet a particularly stringent delivery deadline. 'A little flexibility with respect to sports days and school outings and working hours is a very small price to pay for that sort of response from your staff,' said Allen in a speech she gave at a gathering of small businesses sponsored by the Royal Borough of Kingston in 1997. Flexibility has also played a major role in creating an empowered workforce. Allen delegates responsibility for quality, production, and health and safety to staff. Salespeople champion customer orders through production, and section leaders in the production units decide how they will meet each customer's scheduling and quality requirements. The idea of empowering people is central to the operation of the company, and empowerment has to go with flexibility, in Allen's mind; people cannot be made full partners in business decisions and success if they are treated like children when it comes to managing the balance between their work and personal lives.

As corporations and entire economies come to depend increasingly on 'knowledge workers' and as the quality and motivation of people outstrip the quality and productiveness of capital and plant in importance, the need to empower employees and provide conditions that maximize their motivation and inventiveness will only intensify. Knowledge workers are both more likely and more able to resist working-time routines; employers who can accommodate their needs for autonomy will benefit not just from lower turnover among these types of employees, but from their much increased contribution to the firms for which they work.

Flexible working practices which afford employees some level of autonomy do more than encourage personal commitment, creativity and initiative. They can also lead to a kind of *organizational* initiative and creativity. In its simplest form, this is represented by the creation of valuable roles that would be unviable as full-time jobs. Contrary to the belief that all jobs are naturally full-time, there are many that are better or as effectively done within reduced hours. If these roles are designed as full-time, resources are wasted; if, on the other hand, the absence of a full-time role prevents the role from being created at all, an opportunity to add value to the business, or resolve a particular problem, will be forgone. Neither represents a sensible or creative use of resources.

The mere fact of a part-time role being considered can lead to the creation of new and value-enhancing roles. These roles, and the business needs that they address, often fail to register on the radar screens of managers lost to the full-time operational mentality. Not until a valued employee requests a part-time role are line managers forced to consider business needs that lie beyond the traditional operational, and often short-term focused, roles that full-time employees carry out.

At Gemini Consulting, investment in the 'knowledge capital' that is the rootstock of the business was for a long time neglected, as consultants devoted all their time and energy to delivering immediate value to clients. No ambitious consultant with a traditional, full-time career in mind ever considered devoting himself to the capture, documentation and sharing of the knowledge amassed every day by project teams, and few senior vice-presidents would contemplate freeing up their most valuable resources for that task. But in the early 1990s the firm's leaders realized that it was critical that the firm invest in building and sharing its knowledge through the development of an effective knowledge management system. At the same time, I was looking for a part-time role. In the absence of any other candidates willing or able to step out of their full-time client-facing roles, I was given the task of designing and setting up the knowledge management system. I spent almost a year doing that, and another year coordinating its ongoing operation. If I had not been available and willing to take on a non-traditional, part-time role, the knowledge management system might not have received the level of investment required to get it off the ground. Thus a much needed, value-enhancing role was created to meet a business need that might have languished under-resourced for years had it not been for the coincidence of that business need with an employee's flexible working requirements.

Gemini soon became adept at creating flexible value-adding roles. Several part-time knowledge-building roles were created to support specific industry practices (consulting firms are often organized according to the industries they service), and a part-time manager was appointed to build up and manage the firm's business school faculty. In other industries and firms, a similar story can be told. The demand for flexible roles that lie outside traditional career structures can lead to the creative resolution of business problems and to formerly unacknowledged business needs being met. At one major investment bank, a woman works two days a week managing a small team of researchers who support the business-development teams in various parts of the bank. By happy coincidence, the role fits in with her desire for a two-day week and provides invaluable support to teams that might otherwise approach prospective clients with ill prepared or unconvincing proposals.

Gay Haines, whose company hat pin includes White Door, an executive placement firm specializing in the placement of experienced advertising executives on short-term or part-time projects within advertising agencies, believes that the consideration of short-term and project-based resources very often leads to greater creativity and business effectiveness. She cites one example of an agency that won and successfully serviced a consumer goods advertising account in Japan, despite not having the relevant talent or experience in house, because they were able to pull together a short-term 'dream team' from White Door's pool of talent. She also recounts how White Door's flexible and unusual resource base has enabled agencies to design new and effective roles or consider different sorts of experience than they otherwise would have. In one instance, a writer and film producer hired to do commercial direction, something that had never been contemplated or attempted before but which proved to be enormously successful.

Reduced hours and flexible roles also increase organizational creativity and flexibility by enabling firms to break free from the nine-to-five constraints on their ability to service customers, allowing both manufacturing and service firms to extend operating hours without necessarily increasing individuals' working hours. In the manufacturing industry, Patricia Hewitt points out in her book *About Time* the 'decoupling' of individuals' working hours from plant-operating hours has enabled employers to reduce the average working week while simultaneously achieving productivity gains.[59] In services, it represents the entire basis of operation for the hotel industry, and it has enabled the extension of operating hours in banking. As more work is conducted outside the confines of the eight-hour day and through electronic technology, the organizational responsiveness facilitated by flexible working will be increasingly valued. That the need for business flexibility can drive workplace flexibility, which in turn enables more women to succeed, is evidenced by the fact that at First Direct, the Midland Bank subsidiary which operates twenty-four hours a day and exclusively via electronic technology, 42 per cent of managers are women, compared with 23 per cent in Midland overall.[60]

At Granada Group, flexibility is implemented for the dual purpose of meeting business needs while enabling employees to make better use of their time. Granada's technology division, for instance, includes a group of engineers responsible for servicing customers' television sets. An analysis of this business revealed that customers are often frustrated by having to wait at home for service engineers to call, and engineers are frustrated by having to spend most of their day driving around, sometimes only to arrive at the customer's home and discover that the breakdown was simply a malfunction resulting from a misunderstanding of the operating instructions. The solution? Technology that routes all customer calls to an engineer, who spends time talking to the customer about the problem and, in many cases, enables him or her to fix it. The result? Both the customer and the engineer save time. The customer's time translates into goodwill and potential future sales for Granada. The engineer's time saved, in addition to the freedom to work from home which the new technology makes possible, turns an often tedious and restrictive job into one that is more flexibile and life-friendly.

Work by Rhona Rapoport, Lotte Bailyn and others sponsored by America's Ford Foundation attests to the link between flexible working practices which enhance work–life balance and organizational creativity and effectiveness. Their work has demonstrated that when individuals' requests for flexibility are ignored, or granted on a one-off basis without consideration being given to the organizational environment in which they operate, the 'systematic implications' of the requests for flexibility are ignored and 'institutional opportunities are missed'.[61] For example, when a sales manager and senior salesperson requested a job-sharing arrangement, they proposed revamping the management-development process so that a sales representative, working under the guidance of a sales manager, took on limited management duties. 'Such an apprenticeship model promised to be a significant improvement over the existing practice of "throwing sales people into management" with little training,' said Rapoport, Bailyn and the other authors of *Relinking Life and Work*. However, the company turned down the job-share proposal, and in doing so missed the opportunity to create a more effective management-development process.

In contrast, when requests for flexibility are used as opportunities to focus attention on sub-optimal management and work processes, significant organizational gains can be made. So, when a manager decided that his sales department's habit of working around the clock to complete customer proposals was wreaking havoc on people's personal lives, he stopped rewarding them for all-night working sessions and began, instead, to encourage them to develop better planning and problem-solving methods. He thereby simultaneously improved the work–life balance for his employees and the overall effectiveness of the sales department.[62] Problem-solving approaches like these, which have the dual objective of improving business performance while improving employees' work–life balance, can generate impressive returns. In the companies with whom they have worked, the Ford-sponsored researchers have seen sales teams exceed sales targets, administrative departments become more efficient, and engineering units improve productivity. According to Pat Nazemetz, Head of Benefits Compensation and Executive

Compensation and coordinator of the Ford study at Xerox, productivity rose by as much as 30 per cent in some Xerox Units, all while employees' lives became more balanced.

Flexible working practices encourages the recruitment and retention of people whose needs cannot be met within the context of full-time, long-hours careers. These may be women with small children, Olympic athletes who need time off for training, or lifelong learners who wish to study part-time. And many business leaders now recognize workforce diversity itself as a positive influence on organizational creativity and responsiveness.[63] Both British Airways and Glaxo Wellcome have seen evidence of higher creativity in working teams since implementing programmes to encourage diversity. NatWest's flexible arrangements constituted a response to the perceived relationship between the bank's ability to satisfy diverse customers, and the effective management and development of a diverse employee base.[64] A 1997 UK study which examined the differences between the way men and women approach design suggested that organizations should employ and retain more women in design and development if they were to maximize their ability to target female customers.[65]

Diversity may also contribute to a more functional management style within organizations. The national employee study conducted by the Families and Work Institute in 1992 found that workers' ratings of how well their supervisors manage work activity were strongly correlated with their ratings of these supervisors' skills in managing workers' diverse personal and family needs, suggesting that the competencies of good management go hand in hand with those required to manage diversity well.[66]

Confronting the Corporate Fear of Complexity

Many business leaders and managers fail to appreciate the benefits of flexible working. As Fred Reichheld asserts, they remain blinded by the flash of snapshot accounting which focuses attention and effort on many short-term costs and profits as opposed to the long-term sources of value-creation in a business.[67] But even those who accept that flexible working practices have the potential to enhance

business performance may stop short of advocating their implementation for fear of the complexity they may add to the business.
The widespread endorsement of flexibility as a means of improving
organizational performance will never be heard unless the corporate
fear of complexity can be moderated.

What is it about flexible working practices that business leaders and
managers believe to be complicated and difficult to manage? A large
majority of UK personnel managers surveyed by Isabel Boyer in
1992 believe that flexible working causes problems with promotion,
and management/communication difficulties.[68] The term 'manage-
ment/communication difficulties' covers a range of problems. Where
part-timers are concerned, the perceived difficulties include the
additional burdens that an individual's part-time working arrangement places upon others, the need to anticipate absences and
meeting-times, difficulties in meeting very tight deadlines, the fact
that part-timers often focus on the task at the expense of networking,
and the belief that promotion from part-time positions is rare and
difficult. Concerns about job-sharing have primarily to do with the
fact that handovers between job-share partners are often complex
and time-consuming, and that the success of the arrangement is
heavily dependent upon the temperaments of the partners and the
relationship between them.

To the list of management concerns with job-sharing listed by
Boyer's survey respondents should be added another that is frequently voiced: the belief that job-sharing destroys the accountability
that is essential to good management. If a job-sharing pair succeeds,
which one of them is ultimately accountable for that success and
therefore deserving of praise and promotion? Conversely, if the pair
fails to meet targets or deadlines, which one of them should be held
accountable? Who gets cautioned, demoted or fired as a result of a
failure to perform?

At first glance, the list of complications associated with part-time
working and job-shares looks overwhelming. But it is worth remembering that all forms of work organization and job design bring with
them advantages and disadvantages. Norman Fowler's job as shadow

environment secretary had to be split into two, and half of it given to a deputy, because his keeping the whole job would have invited conflict-of-interest charges. As mentioned earlier, the European Commission and the British Medical Association believe that the number of hours worked by junior doctors puts patient health and safety at risk. Labour government ministers want employers to offer young people a day per week of paid study leave because they believe many are becoming trapped in dead-end full-time jobs.[69] And the insistence that top jobs be filled by one person can mean that the full range of skills and experience required to do the job well are not brought to bear. For example, a *Harvard Business Review* case study of 1990 describes how the chief executive of a food company was having difficulties naming his successor because he recognized that the firm needed the talents of *both* the men he was considering. One adviser invited to comment on the case suggested that the interests of Winger Foods would have been better served by working out a plan to take advantage of both executives' skills and experiences.[70] He recommended a reporting structure which would enable one individual to report to the other without losing face. But job-sharing might have provided a better solution to the company's dilemma.

It is clear that even traditionally defined jobs create dilemmas and problems. But we deal with these matter-of-factly. The only difference between the challenges posed by flexible working and those posed by conventional job structures is that people are accustomed to dealing with the latter. Individuals and organizations will become used to managing the challenges of flexible working only through practice. Repeated experimentation with flexible options, and considered efforts to learn from each experiment, will not eradicate all the issues associated with flexibility, but it will make them manageable. Like the shortcomings of traditional job structures, these issues will come to seem like nothing more than the expected and unremarkable ups-and-downs associated with doing business.

It is already possible to point to measures that can mitigate many of the problems thought to accompany flexible working. There are ways to prevent part-timers being a burden to others, to smooth the handover process within job-shares, and to make job-sharing pairs accountable.

It is now recognized, for instance, that many of the problems associated with part-time working are caused by the way it is typically implemented. An individual working part-time is left to sink or swim in a sea of full-timers, with little thought having been given to the additional support she might need, or to the structural changes to other's jobs and to hers that are necessary to make her role viable. It is not surprising, therefore, that the individual working part-time is occasionally forced to dump work on her colleagues, fails to meet tight deadlines, or becomes focused on her core responsibilities while neglecting to build relationships with the members of her team. If, on the other hand, the responsibilities comprising a particular job are analysed, and some are formally left with the part-timer while others are allocated to a deputy or deputies, and if deadlines are set with the part-time position in mind and in consultation with the people required to meet them rather than imposed from above, the part-time arrangement is more likely to be a success than a burden.

There are also answers to management concerns about the need to anticipate part-timers' absences. If everyone is made aware of the days a part-time employee is working, in advance and regularly, meetings, dates and deadlines will be planned to accommodate these absences. It is when someone's part-time status is ignored or hidden that problems with absence arise – a meeting has to be rearranged because it was set for Friday when no one knew that the part-timer could not attend, for example. It is also important to realize that absence and unavailability are more facts of modern business life than problems to do with part-time arrangements. A consultant with two clients is necessarily unavailable to one of them for some of the week; a marketing manager is unavailable to attend the manufacturing workshop in Manchester if she is meeting suppliers in Düsseldorf. Even the most diligent of workaholics is unavailable to support staff or to make decisions when travelling for business, on vacation or on a training course. Yet we all cope with these sorts of absences because we are expected to. They are 'normal' absences. When a part-time manager cannot answer a customer's query on a Friday because she is attending her daughter's birthday party, however, it is not a 'normal absence'. People operating under the assumption that life is secondary in importance to work feel uncomfortable with it. They see absence as a problem associated with part-time working, when in fact it is a necessary side effect of people's multiple responsibilities both at work and in life.

The problems with promotion raised by Isabel Boyer's sample of managers are, like the absence problem, as much about mindset as they are about any barriers to promotion inherent in part-time working. In each organization, and each unit within it, there is a set of criteria for promotion. These criteria, whether officially acknowledged or not, specify the skills, experience and character necessary for promotion. They also prescribe a model of commitment which serves as an unofficial indicator of an individual's suitability for promotion. That model is almost invariably one of an employee working long hours, taking few career breaks and allowing his personal life to intrude only minimally into company time. However well a part-time employee demonstrates his eligibility for promotion based on the criteria pertaining to skills, experience and character, he will find it impossible to challenge an interpretation of commitment that he, by definition, cannot live out. To overcome this problem, an organization needs to acknowledge how the criteria pertaining to commitment influence promotion decisions, and to make a concerted effort to shift the perceptions and behaviours that allow this to happen.

As already noted, part-timers can also have difficulty fulfilling the skills and experience criteria for promotion. In an effort to make their part-time arrangement feasible, they may deselect themselves from certain project teams or decline to take on certain areas of responsibility. As a result, their experience will be amassed more slowly, and may well have persistent gaps within it. But these issues can be resolved by the application of different timelines to the promotion process. Rather than being expected to fulfil all the skills and experience criteria simultaneously and within a period of, say, four years, a part-time manager might be required to do so sequentially, and over a six- to eight-year period, becoming eligible for promotion at a later stage in his or her career. Such an approach to career management has been deployed with some success at Gemini. Consultants working three days a week or part of the year are expected to demonstrate the required range of promotion criteria during a series of assignments, and to take longer to be promoted to each level than full-time consultants. But the possibility of promotion does exist. Part-time legal associates at the London firm Linklater's & Paines will, similarly, be expected to have a flatter career trajectory than full-time associates, but will still be eligible for promotion to partner.

Like the difficulties associated with part-time working, those believed to accompany job-sharing are manageable. Management need not be cowed by concerns that the handover of responsibility from one job-sharer to the other will necessarily be messy and time-consuming, that relationships between them will be insufficiently strong to sustain the partnership, that job-sharing at senior levels leads to a lack of accountability. Successful job-sharing teams have demonstrated that these concerns can be overcome.

Susan Williams and Sue Osborn job-share as chief executives of the Barking and Havering Health Authority, a position they have held since early 1995. They both work thirty hours a week, with Williams working Mondays, Tuesdays and Thursdays, and Osborn working Tuesdays, Wednesdays and Fridays. They update one another and hand over responsibility in hour-long telephone sessions on Sunday, Monday, Wednesday and Thursday evenings. Technically speaking, the handovers are done in their own time, but neither is resentful of this. They see a rigorous handover process as fundamental to the job-share's success, and the sacrifice of a few hours of evening time as a small price to pay for an arrangement that affords both of them the opportunity to do challenging work at a senior level without losing their lives to that work.

Handovers between job-sharers are critical, but Williams and Osborn's case shows that they need not be problematic. Management fears that handovers will allow important details to fall between the cracks will be unfounded provided the job-sharers take their responsibilities seriously and are rigorously organized about the way they share information. Likewise with the management concern that job-sharing is over-dependent on the strength of the relationship between the sharing partners: strong relationships can be engineered if individuals are given some say in who they share with and work hard at keeping communication lines open.

Williams concedes that a strong relationship between sharing partners is essential, particularly at a senior level. She and Osborn know each other well, having job-shared together for twelve years – they held several positions together before the one at Barking and Havering Health Authority – and had worked together before their first job-share. They selected each other, and Williams maintains that this is necessary for job-shares covering anything other than the most routine work. 'I can't see how job-share registers which match people up can work unless the individuals have a say in who they will be sharing with,' she says. Emma Mathews, a lawyer who is one half of a job-sharing partnership in the Lord Chancellor's Office, also knew her partner before they began sharing, and agrees that a good relationship between partners is critical. Like Williams and Osborn, Mathews and her partner work hard at preserving that relationship. 'We work well together because we communicate well. But we also work very hard at not letting things get in the way of good communication because we are so keen for the share to be successful,' she says.

Another way to minimize relationship problems is to arrange job-splits rather than job-shares. In a job-share such as that of Williams and Osborn, parties are jointly responsible for the same set of tasks and areas and each covers a different part of the week. If a job is split instead, each party takes responsibility for a different set of tasks or areas. When partners do not know each other well, or have significantly different working styles, a job-split represents the best way for them to avoid conflict. However, the choice between job-share and job-split must also depend on the nature of the work to be done. In the legal department at Oxfordshire County Council, for example, the two job-sharing lawyers share the same case load because the cases tend to require immediate action from whoever is present on a particular day. Another job-share between two human resources managers in a consulting firm is structured more like a job-split, with one person taking responsibility for training, development and career management, and the other mainly overseeing benefits and compensation, and each taking on one or two special projects a year. This is effective because the work can be split into relatively discrete pieces and very little of it is so time-dependent that it cannot be put aside for a day or two.

Accountability is also less of a practical issue than sceptics make it out to be. For Williams and Osborn, for instance, the question of who is accountable for the efficient operation of the Health Authority is an easy one to answer: 'We are both accountable for everything,' explains Williams. 'If worst came to worst, and one of us was involved in something like defrauding the Authority, then both of us would have to go. That is the bottom line, and something you accept if you are job-sharing at this level of seniority.' As long as all parties agree on the rules affecting accountability, holding a job-share partnership accountable for its decisions and actions is no more of a problem than it is for any senior executive. When a job is split rather than shared, accountability is even less of an issue: accountability for decisions, actions or problems in a given area of the organization lies with the partner who has formal responsibility for that area.

Perfect accountability – as represented by one person being entirely and unquestionably answerable for the success or failure of a given plan or area of the business – is largely illusory in any case, having been dissipated by the gradual replacement of fixed job descriptions with team-based structures and fluid roles. When every individual is required to work with others to accomplish a significant task, and employees are expected to take the initiative in problem identification and resolution, it is impossible to take the accountability implied by job titles entirely at face value. When something goes right, it is likely that a team of people rather than one individual is deserving of praise. When something goes wrong, the actions and decisions of more than one individual are likely to be to blame.

At Gemini, as in most consulting organizations, most work is carried out in teams. Individual consultants have responsibility for particular aspects of client assignments, but are dependent on others, consultants and client-team members alike, to make both the overall assignment and their aspect of it a success. Our performance appraisal and promotion processes recognize and are shaped by this apparent contradiction between individual and group accountability. Individual consultants are appraised on their actions and abilities, and rewarded accordingly, but the influence of other people's actions and decisions is factored into that appraisal. This is no scientific process, but one that works well and fairly most of the time. And it is a process that would work well in the assessment of two individuals who are job-sharing.

Ultimately, concerns about the difficulty of assessing each job-share partner's performance, and determining who is accountable for what, are concerns about how promotion should be handled for job-sharing partnerships. Again, Williams and Osborn's answer is simple. In their case – a true job-share in which both partners have accepted joint accountability across the board – both of them would be promoted together. Only if one of them decided to stop job-sharing or working altogether, would the other be promoted at the expense of the first. Williams and Osborn have, in fact, benefited from several joint promotions during their twelve-year partnership.

Emma Mathews thinks her job-share at the Lord Chancellors' Office works brilliantly. Her employers clearly do too, as they have bent over backwards to accommodate her and her partner's changing needs in order to keep the two of them. Williams and Osborn's job-share is also testament to the fact that sharing is possible at very senior levels.

Yet, despite the success of job-shares like these, scepticism prevails in business and organizational circles. 'If people know us and our work they are prepared to accept that job-sharing at this level is possible,' says Williams. 'But people who have no practical experience of working with job-share teams are still incredibly wary of the whole idea. They just can't believe it is possible.' One of the reasons for this widespread disbelief is surely that examples of successful job-shares at senior levels are still rare. As more and more senior executives win the right to share, and news of their success spreads, the level of discomfort currently surrounding job-sharing will diminish. Until critical mass has been achieved and people talk about job-sharing arrangements with the same ease as they consider how best to construct project teams, job-sharers like Susan Williams, Sue Osborn and Emma Mathews will need to keep making the case for change, over and over again.

Countering Chaos Theory

Some managers' objections to flexible working practices are rooted not in a wariness of the specific complications they bring, but in a dread of the general havoc that would be wreaked by the imagined rush of simultaneous requests for part-time working that a flexible working policy would invite. Flexibility is fine for some, the argument goes, but if everyone worked that way, chaos would reign.

In fact, the opposite is true. The greater the number of employees wanting to work flexibly, the more successful and efficient each individual arrangement will be. Achieving critical mass is a key determinant of success. According to Marie Gill, Asda stores found that its shift-swap programme worked infinitely better when it was made official and employees had access to a greater number of people with whom to swap. And job-sharing arrangements are rendered significantly easier to manage when there are sufficient numbers of employees wishing to share for optimal job-sharing teams to be formed at every organizational level.

Even more importantly, the attainment of large numbers of employees wanting to work in a more balanced way opens the doors to the possibility of embarking on a structured approach to change management such as that tried by the Ford Foundation researchers in partnership with Xerox. Such an approach, which aims to re-engineer business processes with the dual objective of improving business performance and facilitating greater work–life balance, is the surest means of creating part-time jobs and job-shares that carry with them none of the 'management and communication' difficulties witnessed by many of today's managers.

History Lessons

It would be irresponsible to assert that implementing flexibleworking practices is anything other than a great challenge, to deny that change will bring with it a great many complications. But, as this chapter has attempted to demonstrate, the downsides of flexibility are outweighed by its enormous potential to reduce many of the hidden costs associated with existing working practices – both within organizations and in society as a whole – and to generate superior organizational performance.

Moreover, whatever challenges are associated with flexible working are dwarfed by those which American and European corporations have taken on over the past two decades. In response to the forces of globalization, the influence of technology and the competitive dynamics within industries, they have removed whole layers from their hierarchies, replaced many traditional jobs and functions with project groups and team-working, begun employing people on short-term contracts, and outsourced activities once regarded as core. Traditional jobs, as defined by organization charts and fixed job descriptions, have virtually disappeared, to be replaced by roles suited to leaner and more flexible structures. Organizations and their processes have been re-engineered and restructured, generating still more new skills requirements. A performance culture characterized by a focus on the measurement and rewards for individual and group effort is gradually displacing the annual pay round, and transferring risk from the organization to the individual. Along with the performance culture has come an emphasis on continuous learning and improvement. And as both jobs and the way they are rewarded have changed, so has the concept of management. Once synonymous with decision-making within a hierarchical organization structure, management is gradually being replaced by the concept of 'leadership', which is based on meeting the needs of others within a fluid organization.[71]

Juxtaposed with the upheaval in organizational structure, jobs, career paths and ways of working already seen in organizations, more flexible, family-friendly working practices look almost straightforward to implement. The building of career paths for part-time senior managers looks a less daunting task than the spawning of a performance-based culture in place of one based on collective bargaining and a job-for-life mentality. The creation of job-shares at chief executive level seems simple when measured against the re-engineering of entire businesses to meet the shifting demands of their customers.

Creating workplaces in which flexible working is genuinely possible will not be easy. But benefits will be enjoyed by those who seek change, and hidden costs will continue to be incurred by those who don't. The choice is plain and simple, for all firms, and for every individual with any influence within them: a future in which individuals can add value to the organizations while maintaining healthy, happy and balanced personal lives, or a future characterized by wasted talent and opportunity, declining mental and family health, and stress-related lawsuits run riot.

CHAPTER TEN

THE ORGANIZATIONAL CHANGE AGENDA

Situations can be modified. The net of rewards and constraints can be
rewoven. New tools can be provided. The people who are stuck can be offered
challenges. The powerless can be given more discretion, more influence
over decisions. Tokens can be provided with allies. And more . . .
self-perpetuating cycles can be interrupted.
ROSABETH MOSS KANTER, *Men and Women of the Corporation*, 1977

As corporations restructure and reinvent themselves, our findings
suggest that linking such change efforts to work–family concerns greatly
enhances their chances for success.
The Ford Foundation, *Relinking Life and Work: Toward a Better Future*, 1996

❖ ❖

EVEN THE MOST robust case for change will not convince everyone
that it makes sense to change the way working time is organized.
But there will be chief executives, managing directors and senior
managers reading this book who will have found themselves, at the
end of Chapter 9, intrigued by the concept of workplace flexibility,
energized by its evident potential to reshape work and family lives
to mutual advantage, and perhaps even committed to the idea of
embarking on some form of workplace change within their own
organizations. If they have reached that point, they will find themselves posing some important questions about what the change
process might look like. What are the key things to get right in such
a change process? What does the process of change look like, and
what is my role in it? How do we get started?

This chapter aims to answer these questions. Drawing on the
knowledge and experience of organizations active in the work–life
field, it identifies three key success factors for a change process and
outlines the specific actions implied by each. It is, if you like, an

introductory ABC for potential workplace revolutionaries: the leaders of organizations or organizational units who are in a position to launch work–life initiatives, as well as those who work closely enough to these leaders to be able to influence their thinking.

Making Change Happen: The Three Keys to Work–Life Balance

An understanding of what it takes to transform ordinary organizations into ones that recognize and accommodate employees' family commitments, and of why some organizations fail while others succeed, has been built up through the experience of experts working in the equal opportunities, work–family and work–life fields. Each of these experts can summarize the key factors determining the success or failure of change programmes.

Opportunity 2000, for instance, emphasizes five factors: senior management commitment, behavioural change, communication, organization-wide commitment to change, and a willingness to invest.[1] Val Hammond, chief executive of the Roffey Park Management Institute and the author of several Opportunity 2000 reports, lays particular emphasis on the need to change behaviour, and to bring the issues centre-stage within organizations rather than allowing them to languish on the periphery. Lisa Harker of the Child Poverty Action Group emphasizes the importance of overcoming internal resistance, gaining support at all levels, encouraging the take-up of schemes, and monitoring and evaluating progress.[2] Both WFD and the Families and Work Institute stress the need to move from efforts focusing on individual assistance to efforts that address cultural issues and management support and behaviour. The research team sponsored by the Ford Foundation, whose methods and results are arguably the most advanced, also stresses the criticality of addressing work processes and practices and, through them, culture.

The common threads running through the thinking of these individuals and organizations attest to a growing consensus about how change efforts need to be constructed if they are to have a significant and lasting effect upon employees' ability to achieve genuine work–life balance. The key success factors might now be summarized in three terms: (1) leadership commitment, (2) an emphasis on restructuring work and transforming culture, and (3) organization-wide involvement and ownership. The emphasis and specific language used by various experts in the field to describe these factors may well vary: some explicitly refer to behaviour as a manifestation and determinant of work processes and culture, while others speak about work and culture explicitly; some describe leadership commitment in terms of a willingness to invest resources in work–family change efforts, others in terms of a willingness to bring the work–family change effort centre stage; some accentuate the need to bring middle managers on board, others the necessity of involving men as well as women, thus highlighting the need for extensive organizational involvement and support. But the message is essentially the same, and was captured in wonderfully simple terms by MP Margaret Hodge, an advocate of work reform within the parliamentary context: 'You need to change the *work* itself. To do that you need strong *leadership* and a *critical mass* of support.'

1. Leadership commitment

It is no surprise that Opportunity 2000 puts leadership commitment first on its list of critical factors for successful change efforts, and that their members believe support from top management to be one of the most powerful forces for changing attitudes to, and perceptions of, women at work.[3] Opportunity 2000 research has shown that change programmes need to be, but seldom are, mandated from the highest level.[4]

A leader's commitment – of belief, support, energy and resources – is a precursor to the other essential elements of a change effort, something without which they become elusive, if not entirely unattainable. A minimal level of leadership support and endorsement is required for even the most halting steps, such as the distribution of a staff questionnaire to establish the need for work–family initiatives, to be taken. Much greater levels of support are required to move a company from the questioning and exploration stage to the point where resource is invested in the design, implementation, management and monitoring of initiatives.

How can that commitment be generated and demonstrated? Some leaders arrive independently at the conclusion that work–life issues are important: a surprising number of people recount stories of chief executives who suddenly become passionate about work–family issues as a result of watching their daughters begin to struggle with the irreconcilable demands of full-time work and mothering. Some leaders experience a slow awakening to the importance of work–family issues through repeated exposure to the topic at industry conferences, or at the best-practice forums sponsored by academic institutions and consultancies. Still others may be persuaded by the drip-drip effect of a valued human resources manager who persistently makes the case for change.

If a leader's interest in work–family issues is sparked independently, and grows steadily as a result of a daughter's experience or attendance at a series of sponsored workshops, so much the better. Senior and middle managers who are ardent about work–family issues need only to capitalize on that independently acquired enthusiasm, furnishing the necessary business cases and frameworks for action, and encouraging the leader to demonstrate his support clearly and repeatedly. If, on the other hand, a corporate leader shows little or no inclination towards supporting work–life initiatives, those around him must engage in the long, arduous, and potentially risky endeavour of persuading him. A passionately committed human resources manager must find ways to bring work–family issues to the leader's attention in such a way that they begin to connect with pressing business issues. Those lower down in the firm's hierarchy can also exert an influence. To the extent that they have the freedom to experiment, on a small scale, with initiatives that enable flexible working while also contributing to business success, and can subsequently bring these experiments to the attention of someone with influence, they too can be part of the lengthy process of engaging the attention and commitment of their organization's leader.

However leadership commitment is developed, it needs to be demonstrated loudly and clearly to the rest of the organization, and translated into tangible change efforts. Bold statements about the need to increase women's representation at senior level, or kind expressions of support for parents who struggle with the work–family balance, will not suffice. Leaders and their top teams have at their disposal five key mechanisms for demonstrating and leveraging their commitment: public statements of their vision and goals, business cases linking the work–life agenda to the business agenda, the investment of time and resources, the measurement of progress; and, perhaps most important of all, their own behaviour.

Leadership statements about visions and goals help to kick-start change initiatives and keep them uppermost in employees' minds. Opportunity 2000 members are asked to make statements of their goals and include these in their progress reports. Some leaders choose to make a commitment to equal opportunities or work–life balance a feature of letters to employees, presentations to shareholders or corporate value statements. AT&T's chairman wrote, in a letter to employees, that the 'way we address the family concerns of AT&T's people is an important issue for all of us – a competitive issue';[5] IBM's chairman John Akers wrote that 'the challenge to business is to provide employees with the flexibility they need to pursue and advance their careers while minimizing the impact on their personal lives';[6] and IBM's chief executive Lou Gerstner made a commitment to work–life balance a central feature of his acceptance speech at the 1995 Chief Executive of the Year Awards. In a policy leaflet, Oxfordshire County Council acknowledges its commitment to undermining the traditional separation of work and family life that lies at the heart of Western work culture, and describes the objective of its work–life initiatives as enabling employees to *integrate* work and family life rather than simply *combine* or *juggle* them. The provision of flexible working opportunities for mothers was at the heart of the FI Group's original vision and objectives, something which founder Mrs Steve Shirley was never reticent in stating publicly.

Repeated public statements of leadership support for work–life balance have more impact than single statements pasted boldly on the front pages of annual reports. Informal statements directed exclusively at employees can have a remarkably strong galvanizing effect. In the sales environment referred to in chapter nine, for instance, the sales team's habit of working around the clock to complete proposals for customers was broken when the team manager began to convey his disappointment with their behaviour rather than complimenting them on their commitment and willingness to get the job done. As a result of the manager repeatedly communicating his view that their way of working represented an inability to plan, the sales team began to recognize and reward new work habits such as planning ahead and anticipating problems.[7] In this way, a new informal reward structure, as conveyed by a simple change of language on the part of a senior manager, set the stage for the kind of structured review of working habits and processes that is fundamental to creating a work–life-friendly environment.

Irene Allen, founder and head of production for Listawood, the Norfolk-based manufacturer of computer mouse-mats employing around seventy people, many of whom work part-time, discovered that formal statements of values and objectives are important even in small organizations. In a speech she gave in 1997 Allen recalled the time when Listawood decided to start taking on more full-timers in order to be able to keep the factory open at three o'clock when most employees left to pick up their school-age children. They found that they ended up with a lot of employees who were used to clocking on and off, being told what to do, and avoiding responsibility. 'We hadn't explained to them exactly how we worked and what we expected of them,' said Allen. 'We realized that we actually had to start telling people about our culture.' Listawood joined Opportunity 2000 and set down a formal mission statement to communicate the company's commitment to flexibility, to treating people fairly and contributing to the community. Allen claims her staff loved it, and it made a real difference: 'We used the arguments contained in that original mission statement at all levels – from discussing the business plan at board level to whether we should have a carpet down in the smokers' room.'

Statements of support should be backed up by a business case linking work–family issues to core business objectives. This brings work–family issues to centre stage and communicates their relevance. The business cases for firms like British Airways, Midland Bank and Glaxo Wellcome are all linked to business needs such as the need to understand and match the customer base, the need to retain valuable skills, and the need to improve the corporate image.[8] Companies which recognize the full range of benefits accruing from flexible working practices, as outlined in Chapter 9, are increasingly constructing business cases that reflect that recognition.

The mere existence of a business case is not enough. More critical is the regularity and conviction with which the links between the business case and strategic business objectives are asserted. Only when a leader has a genuine belief that work–life programmes are essential to corporate competitiveness, and regularly conveys that belief, can the business case serve as a galvanizing force for the entire organization. Irene Allen talks often and with great enthusiasm about how integral flexible working practices have been to Listawood's rapid growth and profitability. At the BBC, the case for flexibility is firmly rooted in the corporation's unique role as a public service provider funded by public licence. Manager of HR Policy Development (Equality and European Employment Affairs) Dorothy May explains: 'Since we are broadcasting to a nation we are committed to reflecting the population in our workforce in a way that many other organizations may not need to be. That creates a very strong business case. And we are under scrutiny every single day, which is right and proper. This creates a deep commitment to diversity and the notion of work–life balance within the organization.'

For flexible working options to succeed, the business case and the leader's endorsement of it needs to acknowledge the specific significance of flexible working within the entire set of equal opportunities or work–life initiatives. Otherwise, efforts to create genuine flexible working opportunities, and careers based upon them, will remain secondary to initiatives that concentrate on getting people to work and enabling them to progress within the constraints of existing workplace norms and practices.

Statements of goals and business cases are worth little without an investment of time and resources in comprehensive change programmes. Here again, leadership commitment is key. A leader's willingness to invest resources – whether in the form of an equal-opportunities team or a project team tasked with exploring ways of restructuring work processes to be more flexible – will be critical to ensuring that a work–life change effort has impact. But the leader also needs to invest time – both his or her own, and that of the leadership team – if the invested resources are to generate real results. The largest equal-opportunities team in the world can have little impact if it exists in a 'managerial vacuum, unaided and neglected',[9] unrepresented at board level and thus unable to gain access to the time and attention of directors, conclude the authors of the Opportunity 2000 report, *Changing Culture*. The most spectacular success of a project team working in a small unit will have little impact on the rest of the firm's practices unless the leader and top team devote time and energy to spreading the word, and enabling the experiment to be repeated.

At IBM, Lou Gerstner's willingness to invest enormous sums in childcare support and work–life programmes sent a strong signal that he was serious about helping employees to balance their work and personal lives. Ted Childs, Vice President of Global Workforce Diversity at IBM, sees Gerstner's willingness to invest as a key reason for the progress IBM has made. 'Mr Gerstner allocated £50 million to dependent care when the company was under severe financial pressure. That is some signal of how important Mr Gerstner believes this is. He saw the linkage to productivity and morale, and he put his money behind it.' Childs maintains that money goes hand in hand with personal endorsement of the importance of work–life balance objectives: 'Since Mr Gerstner has been here, we have a commitment from senior management that goes right down to the core. Each year I brief the board on work–life matters, whereas before I could never gain access to that level.'

Further commitment to the change process is demonstrated by an insistence on progress being measured and tracked. Though by now something of a cliché, the old adage, 'You can't manage what you don't measure' still holds true. By insisting that measurement systems be put in place and that progress be reviewed regularly at senior levels, as in organizations such as Midland and British Telecom,[10] a leader at once signals his or her own commitment to a cause, and makes it impossible for people to avoid taking action to progress it.

Organizations must measure more than the numbers of women in each management grade, or the number of policies that have been put in place, or even the take-up rates of policies. These figures are important, but they tell only part of the story. To understand how well flexible working practices are enabling people to better balance home and work responsibilities, more sophisticated measures are needed. Evaluating the trends in working hours, for both full-timers and those with flexible arrangements; qualitative evaluations of how well flexibility is working; assessments of career progress for part-time workers – it is the inclusion of these sorts of indicators that will distinguish those who are deeply committed to work–life balance from those whose commitment is only superficial.

Perhaps the strongest of all signals that a leader is committed to enabling employees to achieve work–life balance is that leader's dedication to achieving balance in his or her own life. So long as top management members work excessively long hours, miss their children's sports days and take home briefcases crammed with work every weekend, even fully resourced change efforts and comprehensive measurement systems will have trouble making a dent in the prevailing work culture. A single message will come through loud and clear: work–life balance is fine for some, but if you want to succeed, you must put in the hours. Regardless of the fact that, in large organizations, only a minuscule number of individuals have the chance to make their way to the most senior levels of management anyway, the suggestion that long hours are necessary for success – of any kind – will infect the culture at every level.

There are few leaders who manage to practise what they preach in terms of work–life balance, but Gerry Robinson, the chairman of the Granada Group introduced in chapters 3 and 8, is one of them. He normally works from 10am to 6pm, frequently takes Fridays off and is often heard to say that he believes long working hours to be a sign of inefficiency. That attitude has a profound impact on the way Granada managers behave. Roger Maverty, head of Granada's technology division, says Robinson's attitude gave him the courage and determination to set firm limits to his own working hours. Peter Coleridge, commercial director for the hotels group, believes that Robinson's style of management creates an atmosphere in which results matter, but being there all the time and clock-watching does not.

Even if leaders cannot all manage to make the same pledge to balanced working as Robinson, they can make small, symbolic gestures that enable the first green shoots of an alternative to the long-hours culture to thrive. One manager I spoke to refuses to make or attend breakfast meetings, believing them to intrude into what should be family time. Another refuses to sanction early Monday morning meetings because these inevitably force people to prepare over the weekend. Still another walks around the office in the evenings telling people to go home. The managing director of one pharmaceutical firm was renowned for his ability to work reasonable hours, and his motto, 'I'll do today what needs doing today, and leave the rest until tomorrow' is still recalled within the firm. To the extent that leaders can make gestures like these, a culture based on work–life balance will be more likely to develop and thrive.

2. *Restructuring work and transforming culture*

Workplace culture is the dominant set of beliefs, assumptions and expectations underlying a firm's operations. It is characterized in more simplistic terms by the phrase, 'the way we do things around here'. In many ways this definition is best, for it captures the fact that culture is not entirely abstract, but lives in and is demonstrated by behaviour – by the way things are done.

As we saw in Chapter 8, there are aspects of workplace culture that are common to most modern organizations. One dominant paradigm defines that shared culture: the separation of work and family. 'Most institutions are still largely structured as if work and family are separate, with work supposedly the province of men and family supposedly the province of women,'[11] say the authors of *Relinking Life and Work: Toward a Better Future.*' Most employers 'still expect or assume that both female and male employees, regardless of their priorities or personal situations, will make work their top concern – over and above family, community, religion and other aspects of private life'. And most employers define the good, committed employee in terms that reflect their belief that work can and should be the priority in employees' lives.

The culture of any individual organization comprises those aspects that are common to most organizations, as well as those driven by its own particular history, environment and work processes. Work processes and workplace culture are inextricably linked: the way work is structured and carried out shapes the culture of an organization; in turn, the organizational culture reinforces work structures and processes, imbuing them with purpose, meaning and longevity. Not surprisingly, workplace cultures that are founded on the paradigm of work–family separation, and the connected assumption that commitment and value are demonstrated by the time spent at work, have work structures and processes that reflect these assumptions. Jobs are designed in such a way that only employees dedicating sixty hours a week can do them; project deadlines are set so that only round-the-clock working can deliver them on time; meetings are planned so that people must be at work by 7.30am, and work the night before to prepare; processes are designed so that a single employee's dedication of ten hours a day is required to make them operate smoothly; and careers consisting of full-time work for twenty years at a stretch are the only ones that lead to the top.

Assumptions about work–family separation and time shape work structures and practices, which in turn reinforce the culture of which those assumptions are a large part. A vicious and seemingly unbreakable cycle is thus set in place. Small wonder that part-time jobholders have difficulty getting their work done, or pursuing viable careers. Hardly surprising, either, that flexible working policies suffer from low take-up and effectiveness. No policy, or set of policies, stands a chance of creating genuinely flexible working practices so long as the connection between these basic assumptions and work remains solid.

Flexible working policies and tactical change efforts cannot sever that connection. They can only influence culture at the margins. The only thing that will transform cultures that are work–life-antagonistic into cultures that are work–life-friendly is an approach that simultaneously unearths the paradigm of work–family separation intrinisic to modern workplace culture and restructures the work processes and habits connected to that culture.

WFD, the Families and Work Institute, the Ford Foundation research team, and equal-opportunities managers within organizations that have travelled a long way down the work–life balance road on the back of policies and programmes, all now insist that the key to change lies in examining and restructuring the work itself, and through that process, beginning to dismantle the paradigms that underlie the work and create antagonistic work cultures. Change must begin at the policies and programmes level. Organizations like Xerox, IBM and Lloyds TSB, which have begun to experiment with work restructuring, began by introducing a wide range of policies covering flexitime, job-sharing, part-time work and parental leave. Such policies and programmes begin to legitimize alternative ways of thinking and working, create the space for further change, and give shape and definition to that change. But something more fundamental must fill the space created. Organizations that are serious about making genuine progress must move swiftly from the policies and programmes stage to the work-restructuring stage.

Each organization needs to undergo its own process of experimentation and learning in order to build the level of understanding of work–life issues that is required to sustain a fundamental, work-restructuring-based approach. Fiona Cannon at Lloyds TSB claims that the process of experimentation that the bank has been through has contributed to a deep understanding of the need for change at the level of work processes themselves, and a strong commitment to it. She doubts whether that commitment could have been generated in the absence of such a gradual and organization-specific learning process. But as more organizations experiment with work–life measures, and share their learning, the learning process for any individual organization can be short-circuited. Ford Foundation researcher Rhona Rapoport believes that, after a time, the learning from individual experiments will become part of conventional wisdom. It will then be possible for firms to jump-start their own change efforts, speeding through or skipping entirely the less useful stages in order to devote maximum energy to the stages that have greatest impact.

Once an organization has reached the conclusion that a restructuring of work is necessary, there are two levels at which it can be done: at the level of jobs, and at the level of large work processes and organizational units. Smaller organizations, or those that are wary of the change effort and want to proceed cautiously, might wish to begin at the first level, but will eventually be forced to take a move to the second level in order to impact the wider organizational culture. Large organizations may find that only an approach that takes into account entire work processes and large organizational groupings will have sufficient impact, even in the initial stages.

Restructuring jobs: the first step in restructuring work

What does it mean to restructure work at the level of the individual job? Simply stated, it means that rather than relying on individual employees to find ways of doing their full-time job on a part-time schedule in order to take advantage of policies that allow for flexible working, that job is broken down, analysed and reconstructed in such a way that it is explicitly designed to be a part-time job. For example, suppose a sales representative wants to work just five hours every day rather than the nine or ten that is standard in a company. A policy-centred approach would simply allow that individual to work the reduced hours, but would expect him or her to do the same job, perhaps making up the lost time in evening hours or in greater efficiency. Sales territories and sales targets would remain the same. A job-restructuring approach, on the other hand, would alter these things: the number of sales territories the individual would be expected to cover might be reduced, along with the monthly and annual sales targets. The surplus sales territory and target sales revenue would be allocated to another employee who also wanted a reduced working schedule.

The idea behind job-restructuring is that it retains the essential core of the job, thereby enabling the job-holder to build up the same kind of experience and demonstrate her performance against the same kinds of criteria as full-time job-holders. She might build up experience more slowly than full-timers, and have a slower career trajectory, but she can nevertheless acquire that experience and demonstrate the capabilities required for promotion to the next level within the firm.

A sales representative's job can be restructured through a simple reduction in the scope of the job and the targets applicable to it. Another means of restructuring jobs is what I call 'projectization'. A particular job is analysed and reconstructed as a series of projects, some of which can be done by the original job-holder and some by another individual. For example, a marketing manager might be in charge of a product launch in Europe, a product feasibility study in Asia, and an internal assignment aiming to manage the marketing department more efficiently. Each of these components of the job could be seen as distinct projects, and the marketing manager requesting a reduced work schedule could be assigned one or two of them instead of all three. Alternatively, if the timing of the projects allows, the manager could do the projects in sequence, on a three-days-a-week schedule, rather than doing them simultaneously on a full-time schedule.

Many jobs are not as simple to projectize as this. Even a job with a substantial project component is likely to comprise non-project elements such as ongoing responsibilities for staff management and administration. These make the division of jobs a good deal messier than in the above example. But they do not rule it out altogether. However imperfect a projectized job may be, it will still allow more genuine part-time working than an approach that simply asks the individual to get on with it, to somehow cope with doing a full-time job in three days. And, like the sales representative's job above, the projectized job allows for a build-up of experience and learning over time. While experience is accumulated at a slower rate than by a person doing three projects simultaneously for years at a stretch, it should nevertheless leave the job-holder in a strong position for eventual promotion.

Some jobs will be more easily projectized than others, and some industries more suitable for large-scale projectization. But the practice is becoming more common and more feasible throughout the corporate world, as William Bridges documents in *Job Shift* and *Creating You and Co.* More and more jobs consist of a series of discrete projects, and many projects are outsourced to external service providers. The key to making projectized jobs work for people who need time flexibility is to build their time requirements into the projectization decision, alongside all the other requirements, from the outset. Too often, project deadlines are set arbitrarily and, once set, make part-time working impossible. If the project deadline is set with a part-time schedule in mind, and the project team structured accordingly, the chances of a projectized job filling both the firm's and the employee's needs are significantly higher.

Where projectization is unfeasible, deputization (also mentioned in Chapter 9) offers an alternative means of restructuring jobs to be more doable on a reduced-hours basis. Deputization means allocating some of a senior person's job responsibilities to a more junior-level employee, or deputy, in order to allow the senior employee to work a reduced-hours schedule. This is really only the concept of a secretary taken a few steps further: managers have always delegated tasks like filing, letter-writing and meeting organization to secretaries. How much more of a leap in logic would it take for a sales representative to delegate responsibility for two emerging sales districts to a junior sales representative working under his or her supervision – as proposed by an individual in one of the Ford Foundation research team's client companies[12] – or for a marketing manager to hand over responsibility for certain products or certain aspects of product research to a junior marketing trainee? To a large extent, this already happens. Making it happen in the name of genuine reduced-hours working for senior people means doing it more, and more often.

At Oxfordshire County Council, deputization happens informally, and as a matter of course. Principal personnel officer Hilary Simpson explains that when an individual requests part-time work, a part-time job is often created by allocating some responsibilities to a junior who works closely with the more senior person. Simpson maintains that such a system has many advantages beyond its contribution to genuine flexible working: a deputy system provides good on-the-job training for junior employees, and valuable continuity when managers are ill or forced to resign suddenly. Deputization also takes place regularly in the Barking and Havering Health Authority headed by the job-sharing team Susan Williams and Sue Osborn (see p. 291). Williams explains that many people work part-time, and that those who choose to have great latitude to use part of their forgone salary to buy in the services of others, as needed, to help them get the job done.

Deputization works well at these two organizations because their culture is flexible enough to deal with it. There is no stigma attached to a manager who earns less than the norm for her grade or level of experience because she effectively shares her salary with a deputy. But such an accommodating culture cannot be taken for granted in all organizations. A corporate lawyer who asked for a three-day week and offered to use her forgone salary to hire a talented deputy was refused on the grounds that management could not accept a lawyer of her level working for what they saw as an inappropriately low salary. In that firm, salary was integral to position and status, not to mention job-grading and career planning. It was more than the management of the firm were willing to do to rethink grading systems in order to accommodate a talented individual's need for flexibility.

Deputization can only alleviate the overwork so often associated with part-time working arrangements if it takes place in the context of an organization that values work–life balance. In an organization where such balance is not valued, a manager's time freed up by a deputy will soon be absorbed by additional responsibilities that are gradually loaded on to her plate. Part-time managers need, themselves, to watch for this 'scope creep' and to actively resist it; and their managers, in turn, need to check their tendency to want to absorb what is easily misperceived as spare capacity, asking themselves, as they consider giving an individual a new task, whether that task might be better performed by someone else as part of an altogether new role. Failure to ask such questions is likely to result in the part-time manager being even more burdened than before she began to work part-time, doing more work herself and managing a deputy besides. If the burden becomes too great, that person could well resign. The irony is that the resignation is likely to prompt the restructuring of the job, the creation of one and a half or two jobs where there was one, which, if done earlier, would have prevented the resignation in the first place.

Thinking bigger: restructuring at the level of work processes and organizational units

Restructuring individual jobs works for a time, and works best in small organizations. Over the longer term, however, the restructuring of individual jobs, in the absence of a more broadly based approach, is suboptimal. As more employees request part-time positions, restructuring jobs on a one-off basis becomes messy, complicated and time-consuming. Even job-share registers that provide lists of employees wishing to job-share and jobs that are shareable, and begin to formalize and organize the job-restructuring process, eventually become unwieldy. Fiona Cannon operated a job-share register at Lloyds TSB for years, but came to the conclusion, in 1997, that such an approach was no longer serving the best interests of either the bank or its employees. In early 1997, Lloyds

TSB embarked on a change process that looked beyond individual jobs and registers of those jobs and aimed instead to restructure entire work processes and the jobs that comprise them.

The approach deployed by Lloyds TSB was crafted by the work–life consultancy WFD. It began with a feasibility study to establish how much and what type of flexibility was needed by the business and its employees. It then went on to redesign work processes and jobs which would deliver that kind of flexibility. The Ford Foundation-sponsored research team led by Rhona Rapoport offers another method for restructuring work processes. Theirs is founded upon the conviction that a key problem in today's workplace is its operating assumption that work and family life are separate – an assumption that leads to work being structured and carried out as if family life did not exist. Their methodology aims to overturn this assumption, bringing family life into the workplace and into the heart of the research process in a way that is constructive and conducive to improving both work–life balance and business effectiveness.

The Ford team's method has three key aspects. They begin by looking at work practices through a work–family lens. This means 'engaging people in a process of reflection on aspects of the work that make it difficult to integrate work and personal life. This process of reflection helps people make a link between individual experiences and systemic issues, such as how work is structured, how time is spent, and how employees demonstrate commitment and competence.'[13] Second, they seek to link what they have learned about the work culture and practices to a salient business need that the particular group is facing. This establishes a mutual agenda, one which aims to meet both business needs and work–family needs. Finally, they press for changes in the way work is carried out, challenging assumptions about 'unchangeable' conditions while encouraging 'out-of-the-box' thinking about work practices.

The Ford team applied this three-stage methodology in one sales and service operation, using the employees' work–family concerns to provide the energy and motivation for re-engineering and restructuring. Employees in the particular unit were under enormous pressure to achieve ever-increasing targets within an intensely competitive environment. Service workers were expected to be constantly available to customers, but they received little support from the organization. Individualism was the norm and collaboration within and across the sales, service and business operations areas was limited. Employees rarely shared information about customers, and were left to deal with problems on their own.

The intervention led to the formation of a cross-functional team responsible for selling, servicing and supporting a particular product line. The team restructured the ways the various functions worked together, with the dual goal of addressing work–family conflicts and improving customer service. The team soon began to collaborate in new and unexpected ways, with service helping sales identify sales opportunities, and sales helping service anticipate installations, removals and upgrades. And as cooperation improved, so did customer service and sales. Furthermore, the new team approach had an impact on the members' family lives, enabling them to provide coverage for one another and plan family time with greater certainty.

The Ford and WFD change methodologies both take as their starting-point the belief that work processes themselves – along with the assumptions surrounding them – lie at the heart of work–life imbalance and must therefore lie at the heart of any change process aiming to improve that balance. Both methods analyse the work being done and restructure it in such a way as to make it more conducive to work–life balance, whether that be by creating genuine part-time jobs or by enabling employees to provide cover for one another and plan family time. Both approaches help to connect work–family issues and bring family life into the realm of business discussions. In linking work and family life in this way, and legitimizing the pursuit of a work—life agenda alongside a business agenda, these methods help to overturn the assumption that work and home are the separate domains of separate people and that the balance between the two is of no concern to employers.

This process of analysis and restructuring also begins to overturn other assumptions that drive work processes and define the culture. As processes are pulled apart and put back together in different ways, some of the things once regarded as essential to effective business preparation are seen for what they are: bad habits which developed to support a particular inefficient process. Early-morning kick-off meetings and late-night debriefings become unnecessary within a newly re-engineered process; the reasons why two employees are unable to share responsibility for a particular job are forgotten when the process, and the job within it, are restructured; and the assumption that a manager needs to be on call five days a week, twelve hours a day, disappears when work is restructured to enable employees to make more effective decisions themselves, and to take managerial input at specific times.

The WFD and Ford team approaches demand the participation of large parts of an organization – men and women, parents and non-parents alike. Without the wholehearted involvement of a critical mass of employees, these methods stand little chance of overturning traditional assumptions and working practices. To be successful, all measures designed to improve work–life balance need to have relevance for and be supported by the organization at large.

3. Generating organization-wide involvement and ownership

Work–family initiatives have long been for and about women. Policies and programmes have been designed because mothers have needed or requested them; business cases have been built upon assumptions about the ability of work–family initiatives to reduce the costs of recruiting, and subsequently losing, female employees. But most experts agree that such initiatives can no longer be exclusively for and about women. They cannot even be just about work–family, but must instead be concerned with work–life. The effort to find new ways of working must be embraced by everyone, and be seen to benefit everyone. And communication processes need to reinforce the shared ownership and widespread relevance of the work–life agenda.

It is key, says Opportunity 2000, to look for areas of flexibility that make business sense and that do not treat work–life balance as just a women's issue. Opportunity 2000 research confirms that, while successful equal-opportunities initiatives must include specific policies aimed at women, extensive cultural change is best promoted by a strategy focusing on issues of diversity and development – and with that, work–life balance – for all. USA-based academics Judith Gonyea and Bradley Googins maintain that the perception of work–family programmes as primarily of benefit for working women can have negative consequences, such as discrimination against women, and the association of a stigma with the take-up of policies.[14] At Oxfordshire County Council, where 57 per cent of all employees work part-time, work–life initiatives are deliberately posited as being for everyone because, as Hilary Simpson stresses, to do otherwise would lead to resentment and charges of unfairness. Likewise, at IBM and Xerox, both men and women have the right to flexible work.

The Families and Work Institute believes that the shift from designating work–family initiatives for mothers and fathers, to recognizing that 'helping all employees create more balance between their work and personal lives is a necessary part of creating an effective workplace',[15] signifies a firm's transition from stage two to stage three of their four-stage categorization. Many stage-three companies, says the Institute, change the terminology they use in accordance with new thinking – referring to work–life programmes rather than work–family programmes. Leslie Chin of WFD also sees the term 'work–life' as being more appropriate in the light of the increasing recognition of the importance of balance for *all* employees, and for the business as a whole.

Establishing the breadth of work–life initiatives – their relevance to mothers, fathers, employees with eldercare responsibilities and those with significant commitments to community and charity work – is essential if a sense of fair play is to be preserved and women are not to be sidelined, or 'mommy-tracked'. Breadth is also the key to shifting the fundamental assumptions and cultural norms that underlie work structures and processes. One, two or even hundreds of women working part-time cannot shift them; neither can any effort that fails to confront the way most people work within the organization. Policies designed for women or employees with family commitments imply that most employees do not have such commitments, and marginalize rather than normalize different ways of working.[16] Without a critical mass of employee involvement and support, work–life initiatives cannot hope to confront the fundamental cultural barriers that make the difference between a few part-time jobs, floating like boats in a hostile sea, and a workplace where work–life balance is genuinely valued and achievable.

Depth is as important to work–life initiatives as breadth. Not only must initiatives involve and benefit a broad spectrum of employees, they must be supported by and relevant to the different levels within the hierarchy – front-line employees, mid-level supervisors and senior managers. The support of middle managers could be the most pivotal of all: one of the barriers to change most commonly cited by work–life experts and the leaders of work–life initiatives within organizations, is the failure of middle managers to support the initiatives. One Opportunity 2000 manager commented that mid-level management is 'the chewing gum' in an organization – 'where all the policy sticks'[17] – or doesn't, as the case may be.

Echoing this view, the Families and Work Institute insists that gaining mid-level management support, and changing its behaviour, is essential to creating sustainable change. Mid-level managers are the ones who must implement policies and initiatives within organizational units and work processes, finding ways to create and accommodate flexible roles; and it is their daily responses to employees' work–life conflicts that determine whether the organizational culture is inherently receptive, or inherently hostile, to the value of work–life balance.[18]

At IBM, Ted Childs and his team work hard to generate widespread acceptance of flexible working practices. Childs seeks out disbelievers to persuade them of the benefits of flexibility. 'I tell them that there is nothing for them to lose,' he says. 'If an employee works their forty hours in a compressed period of time, what does it cost the manager? If they work less than forty hours, and get paid less, where's the cost in that?' Maria Ferris, who works alongside Childs, acknowledges that there are still pockets of the organization that remain sceptical about the value of flexible working, but these are becoming fewer and fewer.

Overcoming the resistance of middle managers and securing their commitment to change is primarily a matter of convincing them that there is something in it for them. The construction of a robust organization- or business-unit-specific business case is key to demonstrating what that something is. The Ford Foundation-sponsored teams' methodology is essentially about constructing such a business case. It links the work–life imbalance suffered by employees to issues confronting the business, and demonstrates how both sets of problems can be resolved through the redesigning of working processes and the breaking down of assumptions. IBM's practice of insisting that managers discuss the results of staff work–life surveys with their teams, and specify how they will respond to them, represents another means of establishing the relevance of work–life initiatives to middle managers.

Paradoxically, though breadth and depth are critical to the success of work–life initiatives, it is equally important that those initiatives not be 'broad-brush' in conception or implementation. They should not be managed entirely at the organization-wide level. Organization-wide policies and initiatives need to be made relevant and activated within smaller units – work teams, departments, divisions and business units. According to Rhona Rapoport the Ford research team that worked with Corning, Tandem and Xerox found that the best results were achieved when experiments were carried out at very concrete levels within manageable units, and the experience and learning then shared between units and across the entire organization. Those efforts that tackled the issue by working only at the organization-wide policy level, or by launching organization-wide initiatives but failing to devote resources to specific, unit-based experiments, were not as successful. This is not to say that organization-wide awareness and endorsement of initiatives is irrelevant: indeed, it is necessary to create the context within which unit-level initiatives can flourish. An 'outside-in, inside-out approach' – one which establishes two-way links between the wider organizational context and concrete change inside individual work units – is most likely to succeed.

Generating involvement and support through communication

Communication, communication, communication – as crucial to a major change effort as is location, location, location to successful retailing. Communication needs to flow both ways – from the top of the organization to the bottom, and vice versa. Joanna Foster, chairperson of the BT Forum, an organization whose mission is to understand and promote the value of organization-wide communication, maintains that open communications represent the foundations upon which work–life efforts can be built: 'by encouraging open communication, listening and negotiation, people and organizations can shape the future of work to create a better balance between work and family life',[19] she says. Bottom-up communications, in particular, are the starting-point of any effective change programme, and their absence is a sure recipe for the misguided formation of policy and action plans. Employees need to be asked about what work–life issues they face, and what they need to resolve them, before policy initiatives are crafted. They need to be consulted regularly during the formation of policy initiatives and action programmes – should even be the driving force behind them. And their input needs to be regularly sought during and after the implementation of any initiative or programme.

The importance of upward communication is stressed by Opportunity 2000 campaigners, who discovered that action plans and policies are often created in the name of female employees but with little input and involvement from those employees themselves. The campaign's fifth key success factor – which they call 'sharing ownership' – was added in 1996 to reflect this finding. A failure to seek honest input is undoubtedly one of the reasons for the prevalence in the United States of so many 'family-friendly' benefits – such as lactation rooms, nursing stations and sick-child day-care facilities – that seem to be so out of touch with mothers' and fathers' real needs.

Upward communication can take the form of formal surveys and focus groups, whose output is then channelled up to senior management levels. But even more important is giving people permission to talk, on an informal basis and in small groups, about their families, the work–life issues they face, and what they feel about them. The Ford Foundation researchers found that this form of upward and lateral communication was essential to their approach to workplace restructuring, and led to some quite remarkable results: 'By giving people permission to talk about their feelings and their personal dilemmas in the context of redesigning work, a surprising level of energy, creativity, and innovative thinking gets released.'

The liberating, creativity-enhancing effect of honest, open communication, such as that encouraged by the Ford team's change process, can almost certainly be attributed to the increased personal relevance that communication lends to a given change programme. Employees can see both that their needs are being taken into account and that there is a concrete pay-off for them if a given change effort succeeds. They will feel more incentive to invest energy and creativity in a change effort that simultaneously aims, for example, to improve customer service *and* to deliver real benefits to employees in terms of work–life balance, than they would in an effort directed at creating value exclusively for the organization.

When top-down and lateral communications highlight the links between work–life initiatives and business objectives, they reinforce the relevance of work–life objectives in the minds of those who are asked to support them but who may have no need for better balance themselves. Communications of all forms – management briefings, staff magazines, annual reports, departmental briefing meetings – can be deployed to convey the relevance of work–life efforts to business performance.

Performance assessments provide an invaluable opportunity to communicate the links between work–life objectives and business performance. Even those who fail to read company newsletters or work–life policy documents invariably sit up and take note when a connection is made between the implementation of these policies and assessments of their own performance. For work–life initiatives to gain a firm foothold within organizations, the set of criteria against which managers are judged needs to be broadened to include the extent to which those managers support a balanced work culture and specific work–life initiatives. They can be asked: How effectively do you retain valued employees and capitalize on their talents? Have you identified forms of flexible working that benefit both the organization and the individual? What specific steps have you taken to implement the firm-wide work–life policy? What steps do you take to encourage employees to be open about their need for flexible working, and to encourage take-up?

Backing up managers' self-assessments there needs also to be an independent means of evaluating how well certain departments and managers perform. Databases can supply information about the numbers of women in management, or the numbers of employees working flexibly, both of which can serve as a starting-point for understanding how well managers are doing. Regular staff surveys and informal focus groups, such as those deployed by IBM, can be used to generate more qualitative information, establishing how receptive different parts of the organization are to work–life initiatives and to what extent these are being undermined by a culture of long working hours. Compulsory 360-degree feedback processes, requiring that managers seek formal feedback from their employees, can generate insights into how individual managers behave and the extent to which they are supportive of initiatives. Such comprehensive feedback processes are not without their problems, not the least of which is employees' unwillingness to be honest for fear of retribution. Nevertheless, implemented in a wider climate of openness, and given unequivocal support from the top, such processes can have an impact.

All of these mechanisms – personnel statistics, self-evaluations, formal surveys, focus groups and feedback processes – serve to communicate the importance of work–life goals to the organization and to measure the true extent of managerial commitment to these goals. Just as the willingness to measure progress is an important signal that a leader and the top team are committed to real change, so the active integration of measures within the managerial performance-evaluation process helps to encourage widespread management 'ownership' and support. The adage that you can't manage what you don't measure applies equally to people and their management behaviours as it does to revenues and costs.

Work–Life Re-engineering in the Small Company

Almost 30 per cent of British workers work for firms employing fewer than nine people, and some 50 per cent work for firms with fewer than a hundred employees.[20] The kind of structured workplace re-engineering recommended by WFD and the Ford Foundation research team might seem hopelessly impractical to these employees. Ted Childs recalls being asked how IBM's programmes, designed for an organization with 200,000 employees and enormous wealth, could possibly serve as role models for small organizations employing just a hundred people. Childs refused to concede that work–life issues were any less relevant to small firms, or that work–life initiatives were impractical and unaffordable: 'No matter how many employees you have, if you're an employer, your common denominator is that your employees are your greatest asset. And to the degree that they have distractions and are not focusing on you, your company is suffering.'[21] As we saw in Chapter 9, as a result of traditional working practices firms do indeed suffer from the hidden costs of high absenteeism, stress and turnover and suboptimal levels of initiative and creativity. Small firms will suffer no less than large ones.

Work–life re-engineering in small companies will necessarily be done in a less formal way and with much less fanfare than in large firms. And there are aspects of small business operations that will act as barriers to work–life balance. Small firms' resources are frequently so stretched that one individual's reducing her working hours can have dramatic implications for the other employees, and for the output of the firm. And the fact that employees in small firms often form close relationships and depend upon one another's support can make them reluctant to demand changes that might upset the equilibrium of these relationships. But, equally, there are aspects of the small-firm environment that make it more conducive to work–life balance, and work–life re-engineering as a means of achieving it, than that of larger firms. Business processes are necessarily simpler and easier to re-engineer. And the close relationships between employees can encourage the kind of open communication and cooperation that are necessary for restructuring efforts to succeed.

Jill, who works for a small marketing consultancy employing fifteen people, explained that she was loath to refuse responsbilities that forced her to work more than her agreed three days a week because 'there are so few of us, and I know that if I refuse to do the work, it will end up on the plate of someone who works right alongside me – someone who cannot afford to be overworked any more than I can'. Jill's close working relationship with her colleagues, and her sense of responsibility towards them, incapacitate her from taking control of her own work situation to create a better work–life balance. Certainly, it is difficult to simply refuse work in an environment like the one Jill describes. But there is another side to the close relationships and intimate working environment of a firm like this. They enable open communication and cooperative efforts to flourish. So, while it might not be acceptable for Jill to refuse work, it is both acceptable and possible for Jill and her colleagues to work together to find a way of restructuring the work so as to ameliorate all of their situations. It is also easier for them to gain collective access to the managing director of the firm, and to communicate to her both the issues the consultants are facing and their proposals for dealing with them, whether these be changing team structures, hiring more junior team members or changing the way assignments are managed.

Employees of small firms, or of small independent departments within larger organizations, can undertake, on a purely informal basis, the kind of three-step process the Ford research team recommends, and they often do. Journalist and author Maureen Freely, mentioned earlier, who also teaches at Warwick University, realized that she and her colleagues had been pursuing a Ford-like approach for some time. 'We were all struggling to cope with family responsibilities within inflexible work lives. Last-minute childcare emergencies were a problem for everyone. At one point we started talking to one another about it, being very open, and thinking about ways we could help each other. I offered to cover for one guy in certain situations, and he did the same for me. We all started working in this much more cooperative way, and it really did ease the burden.' Two Gemini consultants told me a similar story: they had been part of a team which had established 'work–life contracts' for every team member. These contracts specified each team member's weekly personal objectives, whether they be leaving once a week to attend a wife's antenatal class or finding time for exercise. The team members worked together, supporting and covering for each other as necessary, to ensure that each was able to fulfil their particular contract.

The small working environment is one in which the cooperative, holistic, work-centred approach can more easily be deployed. It is also an environment in which leadership commitment to change can be generated on the basis of personal relationships. Lucy Daniels of WFD has found that the impetus for implementing more flexible working practices in small firms often comes from the company owner's relationship with a key employee and her keen appreciation of how valuable that employee is to the firm. Leadership commitment to change thus springs out of opportunism, but is no less powerful as a result.

Change in small firms is very likely to be driven by such opportunism. But, once the first flexible arrangement has been put in place and other employees come forward with their own demands, a somewhat structured, work-centred approach will generate the best results. In fact, the same key success factors apply to small firms as to large: leadership commitment, a work-centred approach, however informally organized; and organization-wide involvement and ownership.

In early 1997 Lucy Daniels began working alongside Bruce Macdonald and Sheila West at the Royal Borough of Kingston on a special project called Striking the Balance, which aims to spread understanding of flexible working among small businesses in Kingston. The project offers a free consultation to every business that participates, and assists each in developing a strategy that meets both the organization's business goals and the personal needs of its employees. At a seminar to launch the project, West and Macdonald brought in Irene Allen, the founder of Listawood, to speak about her own company's experience with flexible working. The response from the other small-business leaders was wildly enthusiastic. Allen's sharing of her experience did much to dispel the scepticism and fear of small-company managers. More events and projects like the one of which her speech was a part would go a long way towards changing small-business working culture.

The Organizational Change Agenda: What Role for Government?

Some organizations will pursue a work–life agenda out of a self-interested desire to retain the best talent or enhance the creativity of their teams. Others will embark on work–life efforts in order to gain public relations kudos, or as part of a broader image-making campaign. But there will be many organizations that hesitate, remaining sceptical about the case for change, or being unable to generate the impetus for action despite an intellectual commitment to it. How to persuade these organizations to take the plunge, or even to take their first uncertain steps towards a future in which work–life balance is a genuine business objective.

If recalcitrants and sceptics are to be persuaded to embark on work–life efforts, and those firms that are already committed to the work–life cause are to be encouraged and supported in their efforts, government, and through it, the community, must get involved. Says Arlie Hochschild, 'A time movement would need to find its center *outside* the corporation, however important it may also be to co-operate with advocates of family-friendly policies inside the company.'[22] She calls for a broader social movement which includes policy-makers and elected officials who are prepared to demand family-friendly reforms. Rhona Rapoport also insists that the work–life movement within corporations be boosted by changes within the community, many of which cannot get off the ground without government support and funding. Work–life activists in the UK such as Peter Moss and Jeremy Lewis argue for a state role in encouraging family-friendly employment practices in Europe, though Lewis warns that enacting tougher anti-discrimination legislation, which reinforces cultural assumptions that work–life balance is a woman's issue, is the wrong way for the state to exert its influence.[23]

The avenues open to a government that wishes to encourage the work–life revolution are innumerable. A good starting-point will be the Labour government's commitment to the EU's forty-eight-hour-working time directive. The directive cannot hope to have an impact on working hours for those who regularly work longer hours than they are contractually obliged to because their workloads and company cultures demand it. Nevertheless, government commitment to the directive would legitimize the efforts of those working towards work–life balance within corporations, and create a platform for those efforts.

The government could play a still stronger, more positive role. It could fund a public campaign in support of work–life balance, much like the Swedish government's crusade for gender equality. Government funding could also be supplied to local authorities that commit to local work–life balance schemes such as the Striking the Balance project in the Borough of Kingston. A portion of the monies that firms invest in work–life experiments, like those undertaken by the Ford Foundation, could be made tax-deductable, as could some part of the cost associated with hiring work–life consultancies. Tax incentives should also be extended to firms that can demonstrate that they have specific measures in place for responding to the needs of employees with caring responsibilities. True, it would be difficult for any government agency to discern how well these measures work – whether they create genuine flexibility, or flexibility in name only. But a limited set of measures, attached to tax advantages, would encourage a positive climate within which even sceptical organizations could begin to experiment with flexibility.

The very least we should expect from a government is that it should be vociferous in support of work–life balance. Ministers should be aware of what the term means, and be able to articulate a strategy for improving work–life balance that is more comprehensive than a call for better childcare provision. Ministers and backbenchers alike should be encouraged to articulate points of view on workplace change and the value of work–life balance, and to use their influence within their constituencies to promote both. Merely by speaking out about the importance of balance and popularizing the notion that workplace change is both desirable and possible, government representatives can contribute to a higher level of employee confidence, thus generating the bottom-up pressure for change that will influence the environment within which firms operate.

The political climate that exists in early 1998 is as conducive to the work–life revolution as any we could hope for. Tony Blair's Labour government was swept into power on a wave of popular conviction that there is more to life than self-interest and profit – that there is such a thing as 'society', after all. The government has embraced that conviction while remaining sympathetic to the fundamental precepts of capitalism. It appears to share the belief of Charles Handy, author of *The Hungry Spirit*, in the power of markets, in addition to the 'doctrine of enough' which he believes is essential to humanize those markets and render them agents of the greater good.

But Blair's government needs to be proactive specifically in support of work–life balance. In addition to granting tax breaks for people who care for the elderly, it needs to encourage firms to enable people to spend time caring without entirely forgoing their jobs. To its commitment to more childcare provision to assist single parents in returning to work should be added efforts to persuade employers to favour the flexible working arrangements that would enable single parents to balance their home and work responsibilities more easily.

Government action is even more critical to the future of those on the margins of the economy, those who stand to gain little from changes in the workplace itself. The long-term unemployed and unemployable need to be supported in their efforts to become skilled, active members of the workplace. A discussion of the range of measures which must be brought to bear to improve the lot of the 'underclass' is largely outside the scope of this book, but is hopefully a firm priority for the Labour government's social exclusion unit. A workplace revolution which transforms the lives of working people would seem fruitless if it did not take place alongside an effort to bring more people within arm's reach of the benefits it has to offer.

The government should use every mechanism available to it to foster the workplace revolution, because it has so much to gain from the social capital which that revolution would build. The size of the government purse can only be enhanced by a reduction in the costs associated with prevailing working patterns, costs which range from income support for lone parents to some of the £330 million a year spent on legal aid for matrimonial and family proceedings. But it is within organizations themselves that much of the investment in change must take place. A certain amount of capital will flow naturally to them, in the form of healthier, more motivated and creative employees and the lower costs of attrition and stress. But much of the social capital will be built up over the longer term, and will be shared among those organizations that do not invest in change as well as those that do. Government involvement is necessary if firms which invest early and substantially in workplace change are to capture their fair share of the social capital early on. Only with government support and incentives will enough firms be willing to invest in the kind of change that will generate such enormous benefits for us all.

Who are the Leaders of the Workplace Revolution?

There are organizations at every point on the spectrum of change in today's work world. Many are doing nothing at all to further the cause of work–life balance, and refuse to condone part-time working, job-sharing or flexitime in anything other than the most routine of jobs. Others pay lip-service to flexibility, but appear to be taking only the most halting of steps towards its implementation. A few are genuinely committed to change and making significant progress. They are workplace revolutionaries in the making, and some among them figure as examples throughout this and the previous chapters. Each one illustrates one or more of the important dimensions of a successful workplace change effort.

At Asda stores, for example, it is the extent to which work–family balance is connected to core company values, and thus to core business objectives, that stands out. Two of these values – 'We are all colleagues – one team' and 'We hate waste of any kind' – lie at the heart of Asda's endeavours to help employees balance work and family life, and have inspired a wide range of flexible working arrangements including term-time-only working, study leaves, shift swaps, a family-hours rota, leaves of absence and career breaks. 'Most businesses say that the customer comes first,' explains employee relations manager Marie Gill, 'but here we say our colleagues come first because we believe that if you get that right everything else follows. And, if you hate waste, that doesn't just apply to produce. It applies to people's time and talent.'

According to Marie Gill, ex-chief executive and current chairman Archie Norman's strong support for Asda's values and for the family-friendly emphasis that derives from them is a key reason for the success of flexible practices within Asda. The same is undoubtedly true at Listawood, the £3.5 million-turnover manufacturer of computer mouse-mats. Having depended upon women working during school hours to get the company started, co-founder Irene Allen sees flexibility as integral to Listawood's success, and cannot conceive of operating any other way. 'Swimming galas, sports days, helping at the school, we all took time off to do it because we were working in that community, and each of us had different commitments which we all respected and that's what we did. I didn't think this was unusual ... If people asked me for time off for family reasons, I always said yes,' said Allen in her speech to small-business leaders in Kingston.

Like Archie Norman and Irene Allen, Granada's Gerry Robinson is a role model of the type of leadership that is essential to making flexibility a reality within organizations. His singular dedication to working sensible hours and achieving a healthy balance between work and life is rooted in a belief that good management is not about time but about taking responsibility for making the right decisions. And making the right decisions requires that a manager gain perspective by spending enough time outside the organization. Robinson's beliefs and behaviour have a huge effect on behaviour throughout Granada. IBM's leader Lou Gerstner is also a strong role model, being passionately committed to supporting employees in balancing their work and private lives. But IBM is also exceptional for the sheer weight and comprehensiveness of its work–life efforts. Its commitment of £50 million to a dependent-care fund in 1995, the wide range of flexible working arrangements on offer – flexitime, flexiweeks, summer hours, telecommuting, permanent part-time working – and the large-scale staff surveys deployed to better understand employees' evolving needs for support and flexibility, all testify to IBM's seriousness about work–life balance.

Oxfordshire County Council's total dedication to supporting its employees in achieving work–life balance is similarly impressive, though the council has less money to invest in childcare support than a giant like IBM. Council employees benefit from up to forty-five weeks' paternity leave, extended maternity leave, compassionate leave (ten days paid), flexitime, part-time and job-sharing options, career breaks, a number of nurseries and a holiday play scheme. More importantly, the council encourages take-up of these flexible working policies, and is dedicated to making them work. Eighteen per cent of management positions are part-time, and managers are supported in their attempts to craft part-time solutions rather than being left to squeeze full-time jobs into three or four days a week.

The public sector throws up many workplace revolutionaries in addition to Oxford County Council. The BBC has a wide range of flexible working arrangements in place and seems to have succeeded in creating widespread cultural acceptance of flexibility, and in minimizing the stigma normally associated with part-time working. The Barking and Havering Health Authority is distinctive not simply because it is headed by two job-sharing chief executives, but because flexibility is encouraged throughout the organization, and people are empowered to do what is necessary to make part-time working effective. The Lord Chancellor's Office, where Emma Mathews works as an appeals lawyer, is no less worthy of the title 'workplace revolutionary'. There are several part-timers and job-sharing pairs in the department of twenty. And the Royal Borough of Kingston impressed me not just with the flexibility within its own operations – a large number of people job-share, for instance – but also with its efforts to support local businesses in understanding and implementing flexible practices.

White Door, the subsidiary of the London firm hat pin which coordinates the supply of talented advertising and communications professionals – many of them parents wanting more balanced lives – to companies on a short-term or part-time basis, struck me as living proof of the possibilities for introducing alternative working models even within fast paced, creative industries, and as an example of the kind of agencies that William Bridges believes will spring up to coordinate work in the future de-jobbed world.

Flexibility is a core part of the strategy for organizations like these, and each is making genuine headway in the battle to shift the outdated assumptions about working time that make balancing work and private life so difficult. At the same time, no one of them would claim to have got things completely right. The long-hours culture is still in evidence in pockets within Oxfordshire County Council, for instance, and part-time working arrangements are still rare at senior management levels in Granada. These organizations are at the forefront of the workplace revolution, but even for them, the resilience of traditional working practices and culture proves difficult to overcome.

What is likely to be necessary to overcome resistance in these and most other organizations, particularly the largest among them, is a more formal attempt to restructure work processes and workplace culture. IBM's Maria Ferris claims that the real gains are in job design: 'We are looking at how to design jobs so that flexibility is a possibility.' Several initiatives have been undertaken to identify barriers to work–life balance and flexibility that lie in the work itself. The management of one factory, for instance, organized an ACT – accelerated change team – which held sessions to identify issues and barriers to change. Several recommendations were made by the team, all of which were accepted during the sessions: the team's finding that a particular report that was rarely read or referred to yet nevertheless absorbed 212 hours of employees' time each month and led to many a late-night working session, resulted in the elimination of the report.

Others are coming round to the view that rethinking how work actually gets done is the key to changing the balance between work and life. Like IBM, the BBC is considering launching an effort to redesign certain aspects of operations to make flexibility work more effectively for both the corporation and its employees. When Rhona Rapoport visited the UK in the autumn of 1997 to describe the work-restructuring which she and her research team had done in partnership with the Ford Foundation and several large US companies, she received a number of calls from UK organizations interested in doing something similar.

Two organizations, mentioned earlier, have already gone down the work-restructuring track ahead of the pack. Xerox, in the US, and Lloyds TSB here in the UK, have embarked upon large-scale projects to restructure work processes and, with them, the assumptions and roles that act as barriers to work–life balance. The Xerox experiment, begun in 1991, has already generated significant results in terms of improved business performance and better work–life balance for employees. The Lloyds TSB project was still in its very early stages at the time of writing. But both projects were undertaken in organizations that had discovered that the creation of a truly flexible and balanced workplace culture required a more fundamental approach than that represented by the policies and programmes they had long had in place. These organizations are the true leaders of the workplace revolution.

Collaborative-action research with the Ford Foundation and Xerox

The Ford Foundation is an American organization with a 'long-term commitment to promoting women's advancement, children's healthy development and an equitable society'.[24] The Foundation began exploring issues of work–life integration in the mid-1980s, and by 1988 had developed a new initiative whose purpose was to enable men and women to achieve a better balance between their work and personal lives. The Foundation chose the workplace as the focus of their initiative because of their belief that workplaces affect large numbers of people and are amenable to change. Within the workplace, their focus was not discrete work–family programmes, but 'the assumptions underlying how work is done in the organization, including the work cultures and structures'.[25] They began looking for organizations that would partner them in experimenting with a collaborative-action research approach to bringing about work–family integration.

Xerox, one of three companies that agreed to work with the Ford Foundation, had a reputation for being a leader in the work–family area. Since the 1980s, the firm had provided subsidies for childcare, in addition to having implemented many flexible working policies such as part-time working and leaves of absence for a range of purposes. But despite having these policies in place, Xerox still found they were having trouble retaining valued female employees. And, says Pat Nazemetz, head of benefits compensation and executive compensation, flexible working was still marginalized. To a certain extent, this had been the wish of managers and employees alike, who had expressed a desire to negotiate flexible arrangements on an individual basis. But, as more and more people came forward to ask for flexibility, managers found themselves unable to cope with it on an individual basis, and other employees found themselves picking up the slack from part-timers who were struggling to make their arrangement work within an increasingly overworked environment. 'We were working at the margins, but by 1991 it was becoming clear that a more systemic, organic solution was needed,' says Nazemetz.

A research team consisting of a group of academics based at the MIT Sloan School of Management and Xerox employees began the four-year experiment in 1991. Working with different units within Xerox, the team deployed the three-stage research method outlined in Chapter 10. They began by looking at work practices through a work–family lens, established a link between what they learned about work culture and practices and a specific salient business need, and finally pressed for change in these work practices in order to enable employees to meet this business need in addition to their own need for work–life balance.

The research team's case study of the changes at one specific site illustrate both the approach and the results achieved. That site was a sales and service operation with some six hundred employees. This operation comprised three functions: sales, service and administration. The sales organization was arranged in different product lines and customer groups; the service technicians were organized by geography; and administrative workers processed all orders and scheduled installations. The operation enjoyed a company-wide work–family benefits programme which allowed for flexitime, compressed work weeks, job-sharing and other provisions. But such provisions were rarely used, and work–family issues were rarely, if ever, openly discussed. Nevertheless, those issues simmered under the surface, and were frequently discussed in an informal and behind-closed-doors way.

The research team followed the three-step approach. Stage one, looking at the work through a work–family lens, began with interviews with more than sixty men and women at all levels across the three functions within the operation. The team focused not only on work–family issues, but on people's ability to do what needed to be done within the job and still have time and energy for outside interests. The interview process made it legitimate to discuss work issues alongside work–family issues, and soon enabled people to draw connections between the two. The interviews, and indeed the entire process, afforded the team an opportunity to 'engage and challenge people's assumptions about the roles of men and women, and the unspoken rules of the workplace'[26] which lay at the heart of both work ineffectiveness and work–life imbalance.

During the interviews the research team learned about the significant business issues affecting the operation. These included the deterioration of customer relations, with a consequent decline in revenues. The operation had responded to this issue by adopting a new selling strategy – one which required close partnering with customers to diagnose their needs, as well as a high degree of collaboration and coordination among the Xerox functions. Through the interview process, it became clear that this strategy of customer focus was being undercut by the same work practices that made it difficult for employees to integrate work and personal concerns. Employees were rewarded for individual achievements rather than knowledge sharing and cooperation; communication was poor; sales targets were introduced without consultation with the service function, and service technicians were expected to respond to calls at two hours' notice. All of this contributed to a competitive, stressful atmosphere in which it was impossible to plan work effectively, let alone plan to accommodate family needs. A culture of blame prevailed, with service technicians blaming sales representatives for wreaking havoc with service schedules, sales representatives holding service technicians responsible for poor customer relations, and administrative staff blaming both groups for being slow to provide information.

The research team was able to hold up a mirror that showed the connections between business issues and work–family concerns: cross-functional collaboration was not a reality, the individualistic culture meant that people were reluctant to help each other – and as a result, everybody's work took more time and was difficult to plan.

The researchers proposed that a cross-functional group be established to sell to, service and support one significant customer. This group would serve as a pilot for developing the kind of collaboration that was required throughout the operation. The research team also believed it would make work more predictable and less stressful and time-consuming, which would benefit employees' family lives. Initially, this idea was greeted with great scepticism and resistance, but through a process of discussion management was persuaded to support a pilot exercise with a part of the operation named the Offset Group – a seventy-five-person unit that had suffered poor customer service for years.

A team consisting of three managers from service, two from sales and one from administration was initially formed, and increasing numbers of the Offset Group were involved as the nine-month experiment progressed. The research team worked with the Offset group to design and implement the cross-functional structure and cooperative process they had envisioned. The researchers saw their role as supporting the group's effort and asserting the dual agenda whenever possible. They were specifically called upon to help sales managers to figure out how part-time work could be managed within the new structure and process, and by service managers to benchmark alternative work schedules.

The results achieved by the Offset Group were remarkable. Sales exceeded targets, customer satisfaction improved, and group members reported feeling more supported, more in control of their work and work–family issues, and less stressed. The benefits achieved by the Offset Group soon spilled over into the rest of the six-hundred-person operation, as employees began to appreciate the gains to be made from connecting work issues to work–family concerns. The service groups developed a scheduling system whereby employees could trade weekend work for days off in the week to cope with staff cuts and twenty-four-hour call contracts; the management of the sales function endorsed the moving-back of starting-times for all morning meetings and the earlier ending of all afternoon meetings, and an alternative sales schedule.

These benefits were so significant, and began to accrue within such a short time, that the traditional re-engineering trap – an increase in effort and stress in the name of creating a process which required less of both – was avoided. Re-engineering efforts normally involve such enormous commitments of time and effort on the part of employees that they can face years of overwork and stress before any efficiency benefits are seen. And often, by then a whole new set of business issues has arisen and a new re-engineering effort launched. At Xerox, employees initially resisted the change effort because they feared being dragged into something that would add still more stress to their working life. 'Sounds like a great idea, but I don't have time to contribute,' said many who were asked to participate in interviews and meetings. But, says Rhona Rapoport, once the experiment began, the employees reaped benefits so quickly that sceptics were soon brought on board.

The Offset Group pilot project succeeded where other attempts at cross-functional cooperation had failed. The research team attributes the largest share of the pilot success to a single reason: 'The members of the group and the others who knew of its work came to believe that the group would make a real difference to the company and that it would also give them more control over their lives at work and at home, and make both more manageable. This connection to their personal lives, we believe, engaged their creativity and energized them to make the group successful.'[27]

Experiments in other parts of the business produced similarly spectacular results. Work–life balance improved and productivity increased in a product-development group, for instance. The group was under a lot of pressure to introduce a new product into the colour-copier market. Until the Ford experiment took place, they were 'throwing time at the problem', working from 8am until midnight and many Saturdays. People were demoralized and exhausted from working permanently in crisis mode. The collaborative-action research approach put the spotlight on the unconstructive habits and behaviour of the group and enabled them to restructure their time. One simple change involved the introduction during each day of periods of enforced quiet time – for personal work – and collaborative time. The boundaries between these periods were rigorously enforced, causing people to be very disciplined about what they did when, and how much time they spent talking over problems with, or making demands of, others. As a result of these and other measures, the group launched a new product on time and within budget for the first time in years.

The success of the Xerox experiments was undoubtedly due to the fact that they embodied all three key success factors outlined in Chapter 9: they were driven by a work-centred approach – one which aimed to change the prevailing culture by addressing specific business issues and work structures and processes; they benefited from high-level management support and commitment, as demonstrated by the fact that management gave the go-ahead to such an intense research project and supported it with organizational resources and time, and by the subsequent willingness of Xerox's chief executive to communicate the project's results widely, both within and outside Xerox; and, finally, the experiments were inclusive – they sought involvement and support from a wide range of employees, and were explicitly designed to involve and benefit both men and women, people with and without families, managers, sales people, technicians and clerical staff alike.

One of the main points gleaned by the Ford Foundation research teams during their work with Corning, Tandem and Xerox was that an approach that worked within specific units to change work structures and processes within those units was far more effective than one that attempted to address the work–life issue on an organization-wide level through organization-wide directives, policies and programmes. Stubborn and tenacious work cultures require tenacious change processes to transform them – processes rooted in the daily work of specific organizational units.

The criticality of a work-centred approach is stressed by Rhona Rapoport, as is the importance of senior management support. Considerable senior management support was necessary to launch the experiment in the first place, but additionally, ongoing senior support helped create a climate of safety and minimize risk. The success of the process was based on people having explicit permission to talk about their feelings and personal dilemmas in the context of redesigning work, and management needed to give that permission. Upper management also had to signal their faith in the process to help others believe that cultural change was possible, and to provide support to lower-level managers who were tasked with bringing about change. 'In concrete terms,' wrote the team, 'that means getting some sign from senior managers that they are willing to suspend, if only temporarily, some of the standard operating procedures that the work groups have identified as barriers both to work–family integration and to productivity.'[28] And, once initial experiments had been completed, senior management needed to spread the word and reinforce the connection between work–family issues and business performance.

Ongoing management support is essential if initial experiments like the Offset Group pilot are to become part of an ever-growing work–life movement. 'Lasting change requires an infrastructure, a process for carrying the lessons learned and the methodology used to other parts of the organization,'[29] say the authors of *Relinking Life and Work: Toward a Better Future*. Multiple points of diffusion exist, and need to be used. And, as people spread the word about initial experiments, they need to be encouraged to emphasize the process as much as the end result. For it is the process itself that is most enduring, and that must be absorbed into the organization's culture and habits. The 'process of ongoing enquiry that connects work to family and community, links work–family issues to the way work is accomplished, and does so in a manner that is equitable for both men and women', is what will effect genuine transformation within an organization, and within the corporate world as a whole.

Keeping the process alive means consistently reasserting the dual agenda, continually putting work–family issues on the table alongside work issues. The research team members admits that this is difficult, and that they should have done it to an even greater extent than they did. Nazemetz and her team are working hard to ensure that the legitimacy of the dual agenda is maintained. They have combined the learning from the Ford work with other research about how to create an empowering work environment, and made that available in the form of a 'toolkit' to managers and teams across Xerox. The principles that underpin the collaborative-action research – trust, teamwork, a sense of ownership, giving teams the resources they need to do their job properly – are constantly reasserted in this toolkit, and in the case studies that support it.

'The trick,' says Nazemetz, 'is to keep communicating about this stuff . . . We keep saying to people, if you do this, you *will* get better business results.' Xerox chairman and Chief Executive Paul Allaire went on record to assert the link between work–life balance and business results at a chief executives' summit in New York City in September 1997.

> The bottom line is this: people who have a say in how the work gets done have a greater sense of control over their lives. Workers with this sense of empowerment are more efficient, productive and satisfied on the job. Companies that treat employees with respect – as key members of the team – are repaid in the dividends of employee motivation, productivity and commitment to quality . . . A 'family-friendly' culture is just one of the approaches we use at Xerox to unleash the full creativity of our employees.

Allaire's speech contributed to the all-important cross-fertilization of ideas that will launch Xerox-like experiments with flexibility in other corporations. Allaire also facilitated this cross-fertilization at a personal level. He was accompanied at the Chief Executives' summit by a job-sharing pair from one of Xerox's sales teams. At a round-table discussion, the chief executive of an engineering firm revealed that two of his engineers had asked if they could job-share and he had said no. Allaire insisted that this man meet the two Xerox job-sharers, who then spent half an hour talking to him, explaining how job-sharing might work in his own company. 'If you get that kind of thing happening often enough,' says Pat Nazemetz, 'you can begin to challenge the myths.'

Creating a living, ongoing process that continues to generate results for both the business and the employees also requires that the benefits that are generated and publicized be 'captured by families'. Rapoport warns that unless employees are legitimately able to take the time that is freed up by the process, and actively do so, the benefits will all be absorbed by the firm and the energy that this method unleashes will dissipate, triggering anger and mistrust within the organization. To a certain extent, the very fact of keeping a dual agenda on the table acts as a deterrent to the benefits being absorbed entirely by the organization. But without a conscious effort to maintain that dual agenda, bolstered by organizational infrastructure and policy, there is no guarantee that work–life balance will improve. Rapoport also warns that workplace change, on its own, is no panacea. Attitudinal changes within the family and community, encouraged by company and social policy, are needed to cement the benefits of workplace change.

Even with processes like collaborative-action research and the unerring support of a chief executive like Paul Allaire, the benefits of work–life experiments are not easily achieved. But Pat Nazemetz is optimistic: 'Nothing will happen overnight, and there will be setbacks. The change in workplace culture will happen on a slow, evolutionary basis, and critical mass will be hard to achieve. But one day, we will wake up and realize that we have that critical mass, that fifty per cent of employees are challenging traditional working practices and achieving balance. Then there will be no stopping the changes.'

Lloyds TSB: forging work–life balance from flexibility with a hundred different faces

Lloyds TSB is the UK-based financial services group that resulted from the merger of the Lloyds and TSB banks in 1995. In terms of 1996 revenues (£6.7 billion) it is just two-thirds the size of Xerox, but in terms of number of employees (82,000) it is roughly the same. Also like Xerox, Lloyds TSB has a history of being family-friendly. It is one of ten core members of Employers for Childcare, a forum of major UK employers that lobbies the government to develop a national policy and strategy for childcare – Lloyds TSB equal-opportunities manager Fiona Cannon chairs the forum. The company provides for employees' childcare needs in a variety of ways, including subsidized nursery facilities, and flexible working options such as job-shares have long been common. Non-standard working patterns have been introduced in parts of the business, such as call centres and branches providing extended hours of service. The bank's Information Systems group, experienced in flexible working, teleworking and remote systems access since 1992, launched an initiative to help other parts of the bank implement such practices in 1995.

With so many flexible arrangements negotiated by individuals on a one-off basis, and so many experiments with flexibility in different parts of the bank, the problem at Lloyds TSB was not a lack of flexibility, but a lack of consensus about what flexibility actually meant. To some managers it meant non-standard shifts to cover extended operating hours; to some employees it meant a three-day week or term-time-only jobs. And a manager's idea of flexibility was often employee's nightmare, and vice versa. 'We had no common language with which to talk about flexibility,' said Fiona Cannon. 'People were often talking at cross-purposes. And everyone seemed to feel that flexibility wasn't really working. Managers felt it was too often designed to meet only staff needs, while staff often felt it was designed to suit the bank.' To use terminology later adopted by WFD – the consultants who assisted the bank, *flexible resourcing* (flexible-hours arrangements introduced by the employer) often seemed to be at odds with *flexible working* (arrangements originated primarily by staff for their own benefit).

Numbers tell part of the story of how well flexibility was working for individuals. While reduced-hours working was common among support staff (29 per cent worked reduced hours in September 1997), it was still rare in the ranks of management: just 1.4 per cent of middle managers and .5 per cent of senior managers worked reduced hours. Though the bank had been successful in introducing flexible working practices, it remained to be seen whether part-time employees could enjoy career success, responsibility and seniority.

By May 1997 it was apparent that Lloyds TSB, like Xerox, had gone as far as it could with an approach to flexibility based on making incremental changes at the margins of the business. Something new had to be done to make flexibility work for the bank and its employees. That something, as recommended by Cannon to the senior management team, began in the spring of 1997 with a study conducted in conjunction with WFD. A small team of consultants and Lloyds TSB employees began a feasibility study to analyse previous experience with flexibility, indentify the success factors and the barriers that emerged from these experiments, and recommend a way of developing the appropriate flexibility strategy for the business.

A key objective of this feasibility stage was to understand the different definitions of flexibility which existed throughout the business, and to forge a greater level of consensus about what flexibility could and should mean. Perhaps more importantly, the team aimed to uncover the myths and assumptions that might have been generated by previous efforts to implement flexibility – myths such as 'Job-sharing is impossible', or 'Flexitime can only work for managers with no direct reports.' The WFD consultants believe that the power of such myths cannot be diffused unless they are understood and dealt with directly.

During the course of the feasibility study, the work team interviewed managers from across the organization, reviewed reports covering existing flexible arrangements within the bank, conducted some benchmarking of ten organizations with flexible working arrangements designed to meet both business and employee needs, and built a high-level business case for change. The outcome of the feasibility study was widespread understanding of the case for genuine flexibility and a commitment to proceed to the next stage of the project, which the team were in the process of designing in late

1997. Fiona Cannon believes that the answer to meeting the needs of both the business and its employees will lie in some form of job-restructuring that creates job 'modules'. These modules would then be combined in different ways to form half-time or full-time roles, as required. Cannon is convinced that almost every job can be modularized, and therefore done in a non-traditional way. 'I don't see why even the most senior jobs couldn't be restructured,' she says emphatically.

Looking Ahead

The workplace revolution at Lloyds TSB is far from complete. In fact, like the change process at Xerox, it has barely begun. The researchers who worked at Xerox believe that major organizational change takes somewhere between eight and ten years.[30] Pat Naze-metz at Xerox believes that something as fundamental as a change in the meaning and organization of work takes longer than that. Like Nazemetz, I believe we need to think in terms of several decades rather than several years. We should not expect Xerox, Lloyds TSB or any of the other firms featured in this chapter to represent work–life balance perfection next year, or even ten years from now.

What we can expect is that in firms like these, the workplace revolution will proceed, slowly, surely, doggedly; that every year their employees will notice differences in their ability to balance work and private life, and that other firms will take inspiration from them and begin to follow suit. Firms like these are the leaders of the workplace revolution. They long ago recognized the difference between the superficial adoption of work–life language and pro-grammes, and genuine commitment to work–life balance, and have opted for the latter. Though very much aware of the difficulties that lie on the road ahead, they are resolutely marching down it.

William Bridges believes that, a generation from now, the idea of a de-jobbed world in which individuals make their own careers and in which flexible working is the norm will seem pretty obvious. Pat Nazemetz at Xerox is similarly convinced that a generation or two will make an enormous difference to the state of the work–life movement. She predicts that we will one day look up to find that the world of work has completely changed, and that most people are working in a life-friendly way. Given the initial successes achieved at Xerox and Lloyds TSB, the interest in structured workplace change shown by firms like IBM and the BBC, and the advocacy of leaders like Listawood's Irene Allen and Granada's Gerry Robinson, there is every reason to share in her optimism.

CHAPTER ELEVEN

✣

STARTING FROM WHERE WE ARE

Between stimulus and response, there is space. In that space is our power to
choose our response. In our response lie our growth and our freedom.
STEVEN COVEY, *First Things First*, 1994

There is that within all of us which cries out for a better and fairer world.
Where better to start than where we are? . . . if you want to change the world,
you have to start with your own life.
CHARLES HANDY, *Hungry Spirit*, 1997

✣ ✣

NOT ALL OF us work for companies like Xerox or Lloyds TSB.
Many people works for organizations which, though cognizant of
the difficulties that many working parents face, are yet to develop
the will to change the work culture and practices that contribute to
those difficulties. Still others, like the female legal compliance
director in Chapter 8, work for organizations whose corporate head
remains resolutely buried in the sand, and for managers who respond
to the raising of work–family issues with petulance. And not all of us
are in positions of leadership allowing us the latitude to begin to
affect the working culture and practices of such organizations.
Though perhaps managers of small teams or even substantial
departments, we feel ourselves as much the prisoners of corporate
cultures as the people we manage.

But are we? Are we all really helpless prisoners, powerless to
instigate change? Or have some of us, more of us than we may
realize, sufficient authority and influence to be able to affect, if not
the wider corporate culture, then our own working lives, and the
working lives of those around us? The answer, undoubtedly, is yes.

Certainly, those with little education and few marketable skills
will find it more difficult to effect transformations of their working

lives. But even the relatively unskilled and powerless have a voice in those organizations where leadership sensibilities have been raised to work–family issues. At Asda, the views of employees earning just a few pounds an hour in part-time jobs are solicited and acknowledged in the crafting of working arrangements which better reflect and accommodate their personal responsibilities.

Many of us lie somewhere between the two extremes within organizational life. We are neither leaders with the ability to initiate fundamental change, nor the hapless victims of poor opportunity and corporate misfortune. Many of us are acknowledged as people whose experience and talent are of value to the organizations we work for. We manage projects, small teams, large departments, even entire divisions. We have some capacity to start the workplace revolution, if only one that brings change to our own working life.

Work–life advocates, however, maintain that individual action is no panacea. 'It is problematic when work–family issues are viewed as individual concerns to be addressed only through flexible work practices, sensitive managers and individual accommodations. This approach often fails the individuals involved and it may lead to negative career repercussions,' warn the authors of the Ford Foundation report, *Relinking Life and Work*. Individualized arrangements can also be problematic for organizations. The logistics of managing a number of flexible arrangements, each negotiated separately and without regard for the work environments and processes of which they are part, can become overwhelming. And, when change is seen exclusively in terms of individual accommodation, opportunities for greater productivity and innovation are missed. 'Even when individuals defy cultural norms and use their personal situations to suggest innovations in the way work is done, and even when such changes benefit the entire organization, the systemic implications of the innovations are ignored and the institutional opportunities are missed.'[1] The opportunities to embrace innovative work practices, to rethink the criteria for effective management or for the use of time, go unnoticed as managers and the individuals they manage become enmeshed in the daily struggle of trying to make an individual flexible arrangement work within an environment that is inherently hostile to it.

But organizations cannot make the leap from corporate dinosaur to advocate of systemic workplace change overnight, even if they learn from others how to short-circuit the route. Most organizations are likely to *begin* their work–life experiments with individuals or small groups. Equally, individuals will be unable to wait patiently for a systemic approach to take root. They need some form of work–life balance immediately, however imperfect and potentially negative in its wider consequences it may be.

How to resolve this dilemma, to reconcile the fact that individual action is probably necessary, with the realization that it is also insufficient and even potentially negative in some of its repercussions? How to place individually crafted flexible arrangements within the context of the need for fundamental systemic change? What advice can be offered to women and men who need flexibility now – advice that will also take into account our understanding of the need for an approach that addresses the nature and structure of work itself?

The only way to release ourselves from this Gordian knot is to capture some of the principles of systemic organizational change within a strategy for accommodating individual needs. Just as we understand that leadership commitment, a systemic, work-centred approach, and widespread involvement and support are all essential to implementing organization-wide change, so we need to recognize the role of these success factors in the crafting of individual solutions. What this means in practice is that, rather than negotiating part-time working arrangements that leave job responsibilities and performance expectations intact, individual's need arrangements that involve some fundamental restructuring of personal priorities and/ or work responsibilities. It also means that, in crafting individual solutions, it is important to generate managerial support and commitment not just to the merits and mechanics of a particular arrangement, but to the principle of work–life balance. If a systemic, work-centred approach is taken, and managerial support for both the flexible arrangement and the principles underlying it is sought and gained, the arrangement is more likely to work for the individual concerned. Individual solutions that acknowledge the wider context and that shake up an organization's belief systems and behaviours in even a small way, do not deter that organization from capturing the benefits of a systemic approach, but rather scatter the vital seeds from which a systemic approach can evolve.

In outlining a personal-change strategy which acknowledges the importance of systemic change and organizational commitment to work–life balance, this chapter encourages individuals to focus on changing their own working lives while keeping one eye on the big picture. What follows is a statement of *five principles* that women, and men, need to keep firmly in mind as they embark upon their pursuit of a more balanced life.

1 Choose Your Time

Most women I spoke to when preparing this book agreed that timing, while not being everything, is certainly important. Those who had taken steps to restructure their working lives had waited until they had achieved significant professional success and standing before doing so. They encouraged others to do the same. 'I certainly would not advise a young marketing assistant to request part-time status within six months of starting her first job,' said one. 'You need to build up a solid set of skills and a reputation so that you are bargaining from a position of strength,' said another. 'Make yourself valuable,' said a third. In part, such advice acknowledges the fact that intense and uninterrupted experience and learning in the early years may be necessary for individuals to amass the knowledge, skills and confidence to succeed at managerial levels. It also reflects an appreciation of the realities of corporate politics, which are such that requests made by seasoned, highly valued employees will be looked upon with a good deal more favour than those coming from junior and, to some extent, more easily dispensable employees.

In the future, advice such as this may prove unnecessary. Once workplace norms and cultures have begun to accommodate new definitions of jobs, commitment and careers, it may be possible for individuals to build promising careers on the back of flexible working arrangements entered into during their early years as twenty-something management trainees. But for now, advice to 'choose your time' is wise. Deferring your request for flexible hours until you have amassed solid experience increases your chances of getting what you need and reduces the risk of your suffering as a consequence.

But timing cannot protect you entirely from negative consequences. There is simply no way of attempting to restructure your working life without accepting some risk to yourself and to your career in the process. When Rosa Monckton, president of jewellers Tiffany & Co., approached her bosses in New York about reducing her work week from five days to four, then to two, she could not be certain that they would react positively, or even that they would allow her to stay on. When Sheila Cook moved from full-time to part-time status in BBC radio, she could not be sure that she would not end up covering the most mundane stories, or be pushed aside to make way for a younger, more eager and harder-working journalist. When I requested a part-time position after my first daughter was born, I had no foolproof assurance that I would be given one, or that I would not have permanently blotted my copybook.

So restructuring your working life means taking a risk. It is that simple. Depending on where you work, the risk you take will be slight or it will be significant, but it will never be non-existent. If you place yourself at the vanguard of a change movement, you cannot escape risk – which is why many will choose not to rock the boat.

Elizabeth Perle McKenna found that although more than half the women she interviewed for her book *When Work Doesn't Work Anymore* felt that work wasn't working, more than two-thirds of them had done absolutely nothing about it.[2] The cautious will opt to toe the corporate line, return to work full-time within weeks of giving birth, refuse to mention children at the office, work long hours, and accept every travel assignment and promotion that comes their way. But in choosing to jeopardize nothing in their work environment, they are likely to jeopardize things far more precious in their personal lives. They condemn themselves, in the words of Charles Handy, to live in the boxes they have made for themselves or that others have made for them. In the process, they often sacrifice family, relationships and that all-important source of strength – the opportunity to be comfortable in their own skin.

The risk, and the fear it engenders within us, has to be accepted.

If we accept and acknowledge the fear, it can even become a positive force – a sign that we are growing and a signal to move ahead rather than retreat. Advertising executive Carole Reay not only felt positive about pushing through her own and others' fear of change – she felt a sort of obligation to do so: 'The way I look at it, I have a pretty comfortable life. I don't have to risk my life to feed my children or protect them from the ravages of war, like so many women across the world. So the very *least* I can do is be brave about this – about confronting a definition of work and a way of working which is making me and other women like me miserable.'

2   Take Personal Stock

The transformation of one's working life is impossible without the transformation of one's self and one's values. Most women accept this on some level. A recognition that their values have somehow shifted is often what activates their desire to change their working lives in the first place. But it is important to recognize the extent to which a reshaping of work life involves a dramatic shift in values and world view. A failure to grasp the depth of the change required of the self is likely to lead to a half-hearted and ultimately unsuccessful attempt at restructuring work life.

One woman's story illustrates the danger of changing one's work life without also taking stock of one's personal life and values. Jennifer was a senior manager in the corporate division of a bank. She decided, after the birth of her second child, that she could no longer tolerate the pace of her life or the absences from her children. She requested, and was granted, the right to work four days a week, to leave the office by six on those days, and to continue her work as required in the evenings. Unwilling to face the fact that this arrangement would be likely to call for a significant restructuring of her job and the way she did it, Jennifer ploughed stoically on with the same title, staff, responsibilities and list of performance criteria. For a few weeks she managed to get home by six most evenings, and to take Fridays off. But before long she found that she was staying at the office late into the evening, and spending large parts of her

Fridays on the telephone, or dashing into the office for meetings. And she was more exhausted, bad-tempered and stressed-out than ever. Clearly, Jennifer's part-time arrangement was not working.

Much of the blame for this failure should have been shouldered by her corporate bosses, who had conceded that she could work part-time provided she got the job done and didn't let her performance suffer. Jennifer's own naive belief that she could perform exactly as before in fewer working hours and without additional support was also responsible. But more significant than her naivety was her failure to confront her own deeply held values and aspirations. Jennifer found herself breaching her own deal because she could not stand to be absent from key meetings, or to ask people to rearrange them for her; she could not bring herself to delegate or leave undone a report that she felt might place her in a positive light with her bosses; and she was unwilling to let go of the mental timeline she had long carried around inside her head – which determined that she would be director of the division by the time she was thirty-six. For all that she wanted a saner life and more time with her children, she still valued the definition of the 'professional and committed manager' and 'career success' that had determined her behaviour for the previous eight years. In terms that Gerry Robinson of Granada might use, she was still controlling every aspect of her job rather than learning how to assume responsibility through other people, and was still wedded to 'ambition' as opposed to a 'work ethic'. She had what author William Bridges would call the *wish* to change her life, but not the *desire*. Like many of us, she was afraid of 'desire' because achieving it takes such an enormous effort and threatens to mess up life as it presently exists.

Jennifer had embarked upon a quest to change her working life without giving enough consideration to her innermost desires, aspirations and priorities. She thought she wanted to shift the balance between work and home, but applied only a half-hearted effort to achieving it because she neither understood, nor was willing to let go of, the things that drove her to give everything to work. She had not accepted that the restructuring of her working life would require an overhaul of her own vision of what her life would look like, how her career would progress, and how her own personal standards and identity would be defined. She had not taken personal stock.

Elizabeth Perle McKenna points out that many women cling to their original life agendas – agendas formed during years of education within traditional institutions and male-dominated work environments, and, for some, years of unbridled commitment to the feminist vision of equality. 'We see that the consequence of holding on to our original agenda is decreased happiness, but we are unable to draw up a new one yet ... but work will never work unless we change the way we value success and the way we judge our progress towards it. If we don't start with our values, all alteration will remain cosmetic,' she warns.

Quoting American journalist Dorothy Thompson, Perle McKenna reminds us that 'one cannot exist today as a person – one cannot exist in full consciousness – without having to have a showdown with oneself, without having to define what it is one lives by, without being clear in one's own mind what matters and what does not matter.' Perle McKenna encourages women to 'have a showdown' with themselves, to take stock of where they are, what they like about it and what they don't, and to act upon the insights that emerge. Creating a balanced life, one in which work and personal life exist comfortably alongside one another, is impossible in the absence of this stock-taking process. Our own definitions of personal identity, success, power and career need to shift as much as the organizational definitions of these things must.

Stock-taking does not take place in a vacuum. We do not discover ourselves by introspection alone but through what we do and how we live. To become what Charles Handy calls an inner-directed person, or to 'live from the inside out' as Perle McKenna puts it, one may have to experience years of being 'sustenance-driven' (that is, driven by the need for financial and social security) and 'outer-directed' (motivated by a search for esteem and status as the outward symbols of success). But by cultivating self-awareness, by learning from our experience, by listening to our inner voices, we can search for purpose in ourselves and our lives, and create a balance between work and life that furthers that purpose.

Steven Covey, founder of the Covey Leadership Center in Utah and the author of several books including *First Things First*, believes that if people listen to their inner voices and develop their conscience, independent will and creative imagination, they can craft a personal vision – a principles-based vision that 'taps into the core of who we are and what we are about', clarifying purpose and giving direction. Without such a vision, people can become trapped by external images of who they should be and how they should spend their time, trapped into living their life according to a paradigm of urgency rather than a paradigm of importance.[3] Most people's lives, like Jennifer's, are so dominated by the paradigm of urgency – the urgency of this meeting, that phone call, or the next promotion – that they are unable even to wonder at what their personal priorities are, let alone organize their lives in order to devote more time to them. With a vision, they are able to say no – peacefully and confidently – to the less important things in their lives.

The beginnings of a vision were what helped Carole Reay to recognize the extent to which her existing working life and working persona denied so many parts of her, and to take the important steps towards changing both. Armed with her vision, Carole is likely to have a great deal more success in changing the structure of her working life than Jennifer. Carole's honesty and vision will enable her to work wholeheartedly towards changing her present work situation, even if that means withstanding the disapproval of colleagues, accepting a new definition of power and influence, performing an entirely new role within her firm, or even doing a new type of work altogether.

Anyone who is serious about creating a better balance between her work and her personal life must establish a vision that includes a new definition of professional competence and how that is built and demonstrated, as well as a different perspective on her career, what it looks like, how it is to be built, and over what period. She must redefine the desired pace of her life, as well as the goals. This is what Handy means when he talks about 'embracing the doctrine of enough'. Unless a person develops a clear sense that there is such a thing as enough – enough money, status, professional recognition –

as well as a sense of what his or her own personal level of 'enough' is, he or she will forever be trapped by the doctrine of 'more, better, bigger, faster, richer'. The desire to maximize the material and external symbols of success will dwarf any desire or effort to create space and time for the things one values most.

'Enough' is a doctrine that can and needs to be applied at several different levels within our lives. It is perhaps easiest of all, though not easy in itself, to say 'enough' to what the Japanese call the *chindogu* of life – all the useless things we may be tempted to buy. It is harder to say 'enough' to the pace and degree of professional success and career progress. But the doctrine is perhaps most difficult to apply where power is concerned. Many people are reluctant to change their working lives for fear of relinquishing power – the power to make decisions, economic power, even the power to command dinner reservations that comes from a prestigious business title. But we must say 'enough' to power – and indeed, redefine the very concept – if we are to stand a chance of creating a sustainable work–life balance for ourselves.

It has become axiomatic that enabling women to attain more power within organizations, politics and society would be a wholly positive achievement. In *Fire with Fire: The New Female Power and How it Will Change the Twenty-first Century*, Naomi Wolf encourages women to relinquish their fear of power – a fear that she attributes to a dread of being criticized and of having too much. What Wolf fails to acknowledge is that when women demonstrate reluctance to seize power, they may be influenced less by a fear of having too much than by a fear of *giving up* too much – too much time with the children, too much connectivity with family and community, too much of themselves. And while this fear makes women reluctant to take hold of power as traditionally defined, it is evidence of a wholly different sort of power: power within the self. Power within the self does not give people direct control over others. What it does give them is the power to do what is necessary for their own growth, to create joy and satisfaction in their own lives, to give time to those things that they value. Attaining power of this kind can mean decreasing one's dependence on traditional symbols of power and success – large staff and a large budget, a corner office with a view, a fancy business title, an awe-inspiring career record, an envy-inspiring salary. That, in turn, requires inner strength, self-awareness and confidence in life's wider purpose.

Poet Ralph Waldo Emerson described success as laughing often and much, winning the respect of intelligent people, earning the appreciation of honest critics, appreciating beauty, and 'knowing that even one life has breathed easier because you have lived'.[4] His was a success arising from excellence, effort, giving, and leaving a legacy. Anyone contemplating a change in their working life that will take them off the mainstream career track – by working part-time, job-sharing, or simply committing to leave the office by five every day – needs to let go of a careerist view of success and craft a personalized version of Emerson's philosophy, instead. Those of us who wish to achieve balance will have to trade off some career success and power as we have traditionally defined them. We will need to accept that our careers will look different than we once might have imagined – slower-paced and with a flatter trajectory, more disjointed, punctuated with unforeseen breaks, twists, turns and forgone opportunities.

Opportunities must necessarily be forgone even in a perfect world. Though many jobs are doable on a flexible basis, some are not. Some jobs simply could not be shaped to fit in with the needs of a nursing mother or the timing of the school day. Says Dorothy May of the BBC, 'Even in a perfect world, you probably couldn't go sailing up the Amazon to make a historical documentary with a three-week-old baby in tow.' In fact, May recalls as a 'complete disaster for everyone concerned' an instance when a BBC documentary-maker took her newborn on an excursion to the West Indies. For May, the key is to enable parents to turn down particular assignments which are genuinely incompatible with parenting responsibilities, or to take career breaks as and when they are necessary, without such actions relegating them permanently to a secondary career track. 'People need breaks and accommodation, but then they need to be able to get back on to the mainstream career track,' she insists.

Even when opportunities for challenging work and promotion are

not sacrificed, conventional notions of success and power are likely
to have to be abandoned. Susan Williams, who shares the chief
executive role at Barking and Havering Health Authority with Sue
Osborn, claims that letting go of established notions of power and
success is essential to being comfortable with job-sharing. 'You've
got to share power to do this, and you can't worry about accredita-
tion or individual recognition. We are task-oriented and motivated
by the satisfaction of the job being well done. ' Emma Mathews, the
job-sharing appeals lawyer in the Lord Chancellor's Office, has let
go of the ambition and desire for power that once drove her. Other
things now motivate her – the ability to keep in touch with the 'real
world', having an income to call her own, the self-esteem that comes
from making an impact in a case.

For Susan Williams, the sacrifices she has had to make in order
to job-share at a senior level have been 'absolutely worth it'.
Mathews is similarly certain: job-sharing has enabled her to keep
her foot on the career ladder, and kept her choices open for the
future. Both women have adopted a broad and long-term view of
life. In Charles Handy's terms, they view it not as a horse race but
as a marathon, in which it is possible to choose one's pace and in
which there is ultimately no winning or losing, only the taking part,
and the getting better.[5] Experiencing life and career as a marathon
is not tantamount to an endorsement of what the Americans have
termed the 'mommy track', a slower career path running parallel to
the mainstream track, effectively preventing women from ever
reaching positions of seniority. When jobs are genuinely restructured to make part-time working possible, performance is assessed
relative to new objectives; entire teams and departments, like those
at Xerox, are involved in working to achieve better work–life balance,
and career paths multiply to reflect the different experience of those
whose learning is garnered more slowly and in non-traditional ways;
flexible working arrangements look less like stops on a mommy track
than like parts of a complex workplace mosaic in which people
progress in different ways and at different speeds, but progression is
denied to no one.

However, the workplace will not accept the marathon principle
unless we do. Until we undergo personal transformation – taking
stock of ourselves, and our visions of power and success and career

as the embodiment of these things – we cannot expect transformation in the workplace. As Dorothy Thompson might have said, we are not in a position to have a showdown with the workplace until we have had a showdown with ourselves.

3   Understand What You Need

Not all efforts to change working life require the same degree of personal transformation to inspire and sustain them. For some people, the smallest amount of change would make a difference to their lives. The balance they have struck between work and life works well most of the time, but they need something to ease the pressure a little. A publisher I spoke to fell into this category. 'Just the ability to come into work an hour later every day would change my life enormously,' she said. Others need more than this. Five-day weeks, even with an hour shaved off the start of each day, do not allow them the space to be the parents they want to be or that their children need. These women need part-time jobs, job-shares, or frequent career breaks. Some need these things for a short period, others for ever. Delivering what they need is impossible in the absence of job- and career-restructuring. There are yet others who need such a fundamentally restructured work life that they cannot envision creating it within the confines of the organization they work for. They need to move to other, more family-friendly companies, or to go into business for themselves.

It is important to be honest with yourself about what it is you really need. Only you know what is not working in your life, and only you can decide what is necessary to fix it. There is no point in seeking an agreement to start work an hour later every day if what you really want is the flexibility to attend school meetings and concerts during the day, work at home when a child is ill, or be home with your children after school. Understanding and accepting your needs – whether they be for change at the margins, fundamental job-restructuring, a new work environment or total independence – is the first crucial step to meeting them.

4 Adopt a Systemic Approach to Getting What you Need

Peter Senge, the renowned organizational learning expert and author of *The Fifth Discipline*, defines a system as 'a whole whose elements "hang together" because they continually affect each other over time and operate toward a common purpose', and systems-thinking as 'a way of thinking about, and a language for describing and understanding, the forces and interrelationships that shape the behaviour of systems'. Systems-thinking recognizes that there are interdependencies within any 'system' – that any action taken in one part of the system will have an effect somewhere else; it acknowledges that lasting change results from redesigning entire systems rather than isolated parts within them; it also accepts that the 'easiest way out [of a problem] will lead back in',[6] and that the greatest leverage for change lies in changing behaviours and attitudes.

Systems-thinking enables organizations to learn more effectively by maximizing individuals' understanding of the system of which they and their job are part. In organizations adept at systems-thinking, individuals consider the impact of their behaviour and decisions on other parts of the organization, and build this into their plans; they look for fundamental solutions to problems – 'systemic' solutions – rather than quick fixes; they address the roots of problems that lie deep in attitudes and behaviour.

Senge and his colleagues at the Center for Organizational Learning at MIT's Sloan School of Management have seen many organizations improve their learning ability, and their performance, through the application of systems-thinking principles. The Ford Foundation applied the same principles in their efforts to improve work–life balance at Xerox. But the principles of systems-thinking are not just for organizations: they are equally relevant to individuals, particularly individuals who are part of a system (an organization) and who want to change their daily existence within that system.

Whatever an individual needs in terms of a changed working life – change at the margins, a restructured job, or a role outside her current organization – she will need some amount of systems-thinking to make that change stick. A systems-thinker will acknowledge the wider system of which she is part and the influence that system will exert upon her ability to work differently, and will steel herself against the inevitable organizational pressure to revert to old habits; she will seek fundamental change, rather than the quick fix represented by a boss's proposal that she solve her 'time problem' by working from home once a week; most important of all, she will attempt to change, not just the structure of her working life, but the behaviours and attitudes – particularly her own – that underlie that structure. If the principles of systems-thinking are woven into the effort to change working life, that effort stands a far greater chance of succeeding than one which, like Jennifer's above, skirts around the thorny issues of attitudes and behaviour, and attempts to maintain the smooth surface of the former working life intact.

Change at the margins

Penny, an in-house lawyer, needed peripheral change – she wanted to create more flexibility within her working day without challenging the concept of the five-day, full-time week. She described her philosophy as being one of 'just doing it'. Gerry Robinson's, too, has been a 'just do it' approach. He did not seek a formal restructuring of his job, or official sanction for his leaving work at a reasonable time every day. He just did it, throughout his career. And when MP Margaret Hodge was leader of Islington Council in London, she just did it, too: she left work at three o'clock every day to be with her children, and resumed work at seven in the evening.

But the 'just do it' philosophy is not as simple as it seems. A certain amount of systemic thinking is required to make even this philosophy work. When Margaret Hodge decided that she wanted to spend more time with her children, she did it by restructuring her working day and being completely honest about having done so. Not for her the odd dash home under the guise of attending a dental appointment or letting a plumber into the house. Hodge stated clearly that she was structuring her working day to allow for a four-hour break between three and seven o'clock. Council meetings were scheduled for before three or after seven, and she made sure she got her work done by working late into the evening when her children were asleep. Her position as leader of the Council gave her the freedom to construct a working day that suited her. But many in positions of leadership do not take advantage of such freedom. What distinguishes Hodge is her absolute conviction that what she was doing was right for her family, her life and ultimately her work – a conviction that enabled her to withstand many a snide comment or disapproving look. Her example is testimony to the importance of a systemic approach to change – one that restructures work and is supported by strong beliefs and behaviour consistent with them.

Because systemic thinking takes into account the wider system and the effects of individual actions upon it, it highlights the trade-offs of any particular action. Margaret Hodge was and is aware of the trade-offs she was making when she sought a balanced life. Many of her contemporaries from her days with Islington Council are now cabinet ministers, while she is an MP of just three years' standing. But she has no regrets. While raising her children she managed to gain enough experience and exposure to enable her to become an MP. It is a job she loves because it gives her 'an opportunity to change the world in small but significant ways', and she still has plenty of time to gain the promotions she would now like. She may yet have access to great amounts of conventional success and power, but she will have attained it through a marathon approach to life, and has, in addition, the reassurance of knowing that she did the best by herself and her children in the process.

Even now, despite the fact that her children are young adults and she has more freedom to work as she pleases, Hodge has not relinquished her conviction that it is possible to be effective while challenging some of the conventions of work life. As chairperson of a select committee, she decided that the traditional meeting time of 1am to 1pm and 3.30pm to 10pm every Tuesday was inefficient, and asked the committee to sit from 10am to 4pm over three days of one recess instead. This was unheard of, and shocked many traditionalists within her committee. But others quietly applauded her for it, and she is sticking with her decision. She has gone further still, inviting the disapproval of her colleagues by suggesting that job-sharing should be possible for MPs.

Margaret Hodge knew how to reorganize her time so that more of it was available to her family, and she was brave enough to do it. Others may need more help to escape the grip of the 'more, better, faster' philosophy – an approach to managing work and time that takes account of priorities and values. Steven Covey offers one such practical method. Whereas many time-management methods are like sophisticated diary planners aiming to help people do more, faster, Covey teaches that effective time management must, instead, be like a 'gardening process – identifying what's important and focusing our effort to help it grow'. He advises people to think deeply about the needs and principles in their lives in order to shift from 'urgency thinking' to 'importance thinking'. He then helps them to develop a framework in which they can organize their time to focus on these needs and principles and translate their personal 'mission statement' into the fabric of daily life.

That framework is an organizing process that takes about thirty minutes at the start of each week. To put it into practice you need to start by connecting with what's most important in your life, and this means writing a personal 'mission statement'. This reinforces the importance of 'first things first' in your mind, and helps you to put them first in the week. Next, identify your different roles – at work, in the family, in the community or in other areas of life – and set yourself one or two important goals for each role. You then need to schedule the week around these priorities. To demonstrate how scheduling in priorities first makes more of the time available, Covey describes an experiment with a jar, sand, water and different-sized rocks. If the sand, gravel and water are placed in the jar first, few big rocks can be fitted in, but 'if we know what the big rocks are and put them in first,' says Covey, 'it's amazing how many of them we can put in – and how much of the sand, gravel and water fits in between the spaces.' Without a clear concept of what the big rocks are, the week is easily filled by the 'flood of activities ... that constantly clamour for our attention'.

Once the week has been planned around the 'big rocks', it will be necessary to exercise integrity as you then navigate through the week's unexpected opportunities and challenges. The final step is then to evaluate the week – to learn from living so as to avoid repeating the same mistakes week after week.

Covey's process rests on methods and tools that seem complex and artificial at first, but in the end his process is not a matter of tools but a way of thinking[7] – a way of thinking that most of us have to learn. Learning it changed the life of my friend Graeme. After we did our MBAs together in 1986, he returned to Australia to become a management consultant with McKinsey, spent several years as marketing manager for an airline, and finally became marketing director for a bank. Graeme gave a hundred per cent to his career; he also tried to give the same amount to his family. In 1996, the strain of doing too much got to him, and he found himself virtually incapacitated by exhaustion. He continued to work, but slept the rest of the time, sometimes spending the entire weekend in bed. His wife Bettina finally issued an ultimatum: change your life or live it on your own. After much soul-searching, Graeme enrolled in one of Steven Covey's courses.

Covey's methods helped Graeme to define his personal mission, and to begin to reflect it in his weekly diary. Whereas previously he had started every week with an over-full agenda and had attempted to squeeze everything in to please everyone, he now spent a half-hour every Sunday planning his diary to give priority to the things that truly mattered, putting first things first. Before long, he discovered that by making time for the things that were important to him, and being clear about what he needed to do as opposed to what he used to be persuaded into doing, more space opened up in his weekly diary and the pressure eased. He discovered what Arlie Hochschild calls the 'hidden pockets of inefficiency'[8] that existed within his long work day, and began eliminating them.

Restructuring your job

Re-prioritizing and focusing were enough to help Graeme create the space for work and family within his life. As leader of Islington Council, Margaret Hodge was able to balance work and family by rearranging her work hours. Her solution required immense amounts of energy, for it meant making up the four hours lost in the afternoon by working late into the night. But it worked for her. For many of us, however, re-prioritizing and rearranging work times within the constraints of the existing job will not be enough. We need to fundamentally restructure our jobs so that they can be done in two, three or four days a week. Steven Covey's approach can help us to define and articulate our vision, values and priorities. But we may discover that we need more than what Covey can offer in order to translate these things into our daily lives. Having gone through his evaluation process, at the end of several weeks we may conclude that the only way to stop making the same mistakes, to change our contract with work, is to change the nature of that work itself.

Parents at Work advises individuals as to how to go about restructuring their working life, in addition to advising organizations on how to create the conditions in which such restructuring can take place. One message comes through loud and clear from Parents at Work publications: do your homework before approaching your manager.[9] If taking personal stock gives you the strength and conviction to embark upon and sustain an effort to change your work life, doing the necessary homework is what will enable you to take the first practical steps towards it.

Doing your homework is all about making a strong case for change. That case needs to respond to these three key questions. What sort of flexibility do you need? How can that be achieved? How will it impact your immediate manager and the firm as a whole? Answering the first question is not as simple as it seems. Though you may be certain that your existing working arrangements are making you miserable, you may have difficulty envisioning exactly what sort of flexible arrangement will meet your needs. Is it fewer hours, different hours, less work, different work or less travel that you want? Or is it all of these things? Further complicating the picture is the fact that your needs are likely to change with each passing year, and with the birth of each child.

However difficult it is to be precise about the sort of flexibility you are asking for, you must form some view of it. Simply saying to your manager that you need something different, and placing upon him or her the onus of figuring out what sort of arrangement will work, and how, is a sure-fire way of maximizing resistance to your suggestion. Somehow, you need to come to some initial conclusion about what you are looking for from a flexible arrangement, and what specific form the arrangement could take.

There is a range of options to consider. The Parents at Work *Guide to Flexible Working* lists flexible hours (flexitime), part-time working, job-sharing, working from home, term-time working, annual hours (that is, so many hours a year) and employment breaks. In considering which of these options might best suit your needs, you need to be simultaneously considering the way in which each option could be implemented. If you decide, for instance, that you need to work a three-day week, you must think about how your existing job could be restructured to fit in with this schedule. If you can't see how it would work, you need to research other jobs, which you would be qualified and happy to do and which would fit in with the schedule.

The methods for restructuring jobs that were outlined in Chapter 10 are worth remembering here. Projectizing and deputizing jobs – what Parents at Work refers to as creating 'multiple-occupancy jobs' – can be an effective way of restructuring jobs to fit shorter and different schedules. Chances are that if you analysed your present job, you would find that it could be divided into a series of projects, some of which could be carried out by you and some by another part-timer. Or, you might find that by employing a talented deputy, you could retain oversight of most of your existing responsibilities while hiving off some day-to-day responsibility to the deputy.

Some jobs require nothing as complicated as projectizing or deputizing to make them doable on a part-time basis. They can be made to fit a reduced-hours schedule simply by halving the targets normally set for full-time employees. Sales people can be allocated fewer customers, or fewer territories, as is the case with a Lilly Industries sales team consisting of entirely part-time sales people. One book editor felt that reducing targets, such as the number of authors to manage, would make part-time work feasible in publishing.

Conversely, some jobs cannot be made to fit within a reduced-hours schedule. Some require an all-or-nothing commitment for a definable period. Dorothy May's example of the documentary film-maker on the Amazon comes to mind here, as do some jobs in corporate finance and law. For these types of jobs you may need to propose a different sort of flexible arrangement, one based upon working every other project or case, rather than being obliged to work them back to back. This way, a part-time schedule would be achieved in the form of a month off for every two or three months on. Janet, a lawyer who has been tasked with crafting a flexible working strategy for her firm, believes that this could be the answer for that particular firm's corporate legal practice. The on-off method of organizing work time will do little for the parent who wants a regular, everyday presence in her children's weekday lives, but it could work well for families with older children, and is surely better than a schedule that consistently absents a parent from home for sixty or seventy hours a week, year in, year out.

If you have trouble envisioning how your job could be restructured to fit in with a reduced-weekly-hours or yearly-hours schedule, look for examples of how similar jobs have been restructured in other firms, or even other industries. Tapping into the available evidence that flexibility works is an essential part of the homework. Examples from other firms within or outside your industry build your confidence and credibility, and will help to dispel any scepticism that your manager might feel. However and wherever you find the relevant parallels – whether through your own networks and industry association, or by contacting organizations like Opportunity 2000, Parents at Work or New Ways to Work – the key is to go to your manager armed with as much information as possible.

The case for change should not be just about you and your job. It should also take into account the organization and its needs. In addition, it should address the needs of your immediate manager, and how these might be affected by a restructuring of your job. You have to build a business case for change that highlights the potential benefits of your flexible working on several levels. Benefits to the organization include all those outlined in Chapter 9: lower recruitment costs, higher staff-retention levels, lower costs of absenteeism and stress, higher morale and productivity, and greater individual and organizational creativity. You need to draw on data specific to your firm to describe these benefits in a way that is convincing and relevant. Much as the Ford Foundation research team identified pressing business issues that served as the 'hooks' for their work–life efforts in companies like Xerox, so you need to identify a hook for your own request for a new working arrangement. Find a problem that it will help solve, or a way that it will enhance business performance.

Depending on who your manager is and how he feels about flexibility, you may need to spell out what he specifically has to gain from it – what his own personal hook is. It may be that he has been having trouble filling particular vacancies, and that the possibility of flexible working would help attract more and different applicants. Or perhaps he has a problem training and preparing new talent to fill more senior management posts, in which case the creation of deputy positions to support part-time roles like the one you are proposing would represent a way of managing the promotion process. The extent to which you can create a hook based on your manager's particular problem or needs will greatly influence the likelihood of your crafting a work arrangement that suits you.

For all the benefits that flexibility may represent for you and the organization, it will also create some difficulties. Organizations are systems and, as already noted, changes in one part of a system usually have repercussions elsewhere within it. You cannot foresee and solve all the complications that might be created by a change in the way you work, but do consider the possible repercussions on your immediate working environment, and propose some initial thoughts on how these might be dealt with. If a change in the way you work will necessitate changes in the way those around you work, do some research into how they are likely to respond to that. Surfacing and addressing potential complications in advance can only strengthen your case. If you fail to anticipate them, or sweep them under the rug, they will end up sabotaging your efforts to create a sustainable new working life.

Getting out

If you work for an organization that is completely antagonistic to the balanced-life philosophy and refuses to be persuaded by your business case, you have two choices open to you: take your case to court, as have individuals working for IPC Magazines and Oddbins, or leave. (Chances are that even if you do fight your case in court, and win, you will end up leaving the firm because the legal battle will inject a level of discomfort into your relationship with the firm that will be hard to shake off.) Even if you work for a relatively flexible firm, you may find that you want a degree of flexibility too great to be accommodated. Getting out may be the best or only option open to you.

If going it alone is unappealing or impossible, you need to direct your job search towards firms known to be more family-friendly than the one you work for. Despite the availability of various directories of family-friendly firms, such as the membership lists of Opportunity 2000 and Parents at Work, and Scarlett MccGwire's book *Best Companies for Women*, this is no straightforward matter. Such directories, in addition to the informal lists you might acquire through your personal networks, can only be a starting-point for your job search. Once you have identified family-friendly firms that you could and would like to work for, you need to set about investigating just how work–life friendly they are in practice.

The only way to establish how well a given firm might accommodate your needs is to ask questions. Hal Morgan and Kerry Tucker, authors of *Companies that Care*, recommend that prospective employees begin asking questions even at first interview stage. Initially, they advise asking relatively safe questions, such as how women have progressed within the firm, what the general benefits are, how the review process works, and the extent to which the firm is involved in the community. Questions like these can give you a sense of the firm's attitude to its employees, and the extent to which it feels responsibility to stakeholders other than shareholders. Morgan and Tucker even suggest that, if you are serious about wanting some form of flexible or part-time arrangement, you make this clear at the outset, and convey confidence in your ability to contribute on these terms.

If you and the firm decide to proceed with further interviews, you can then ask some tougher questions. Ask to see the employee handbook, request details about flexible policies and the numbers of people who make use of them, and ask whether you can talk to a few employees about what it is like to work for the firm. When putting this kind of question about the opportunities for flexible working, continue all the while to express interest in other aspects of the firm's strategy and operations; your aim is to come across as someone who will be interested in the intrinsic values of the job and in contributing to the success of the firm, but who is also committed to a balanced life.

It is not inconceivable that you will be able to start a new job in a new firm on a flexible basis. I know of several women who secured senior positions with new employers as part-timers. These women had sufficient experience and talent to be seen as highly valuable recruits, and they played that for all it was worth. One day it will be possible for those whose talent is less startling, or whose experience is more sketchy, to be hired on a flexible basis. Flexible work will be the norm rather than the exception, and the employee who commits herself to slaving away from dawn until dusk will be an object of curiosity rather than admiration.

Increasing numbers of men and women opt not for a flexible arrangement within an enlightened firm, but for total independence. They start their own businesses, or become what Charles Handy calls 'portfolio careerists', people who exchange full-time employment for independence, amassing 'a collection of different bits and pieces of work for differing clients'.[10] Women now choose the independent option more often than men. During the 1980s, women's self-employment rose by 81 per cent compared with 51 per cent for men.[11] Now one in four self-employed people are women, and twice as many new businesses are being set up by women as by men.

If you have an idea for a new business, and can generate funding to get it off the ground, becoming an entrepreneur may be the best option for you. And though starting your own business is likely to demand more of your time in the early stages, it can provide greater freedom later on. Emma Bridgewater, for instance, was able to cut back to a part-time schedule after years of running her pottery design and manufacturing company full-time.

'Going portfolio' or 'creating you and co.', as William Bridges calls it, is one way of starting your own business when access to funding is limited, or when the business idea consists of you rather than a product or service. As we saw in Chapter 9, Bridges insists that the workplace is steadily being de-jobbed, and that many of us need to focus our efforts on becoming different sorts of workers – essentially portfolio workers building our careers 'around a strategy for finding the work that needs doing in order to provide what a customer wants or enhance a client's ability to provide what a customer wants'.

Bridges offers practical advice as to how to create 'you and co.', your own portfolio business. 'Each of us has some unique combination of motivation, capability, style, and incidental advantages that represents work that fits us, the work we were made for',[12] he says.

The key is to understand what that unique combination is. Bridges uses the acronym DATA, standing for desire (what truly motivates you? what taps into your innermost desires for your life?), abilities, temperament, and assets (characteristics, experiences, areas of expertise, or possessions that give you advantages over rivals), to represent an individual's 'unique combination'.

Understanding your own DATA is the first essential step to finding your life work. Bridges provides practical tools to help people uncover their DATA, and to proceed with the other necessary steps towards creating 'you and co.': finding your market, or markets, turning your DATA into a product for that market and building a business plan for the marketing and delivery of that product.

An individual's market can, and often does, include some part of the organization she already works for. It may not be necessary to break all ties with your employer in order to create a new working life for yourself. If your current job cannot be restructured to be more flexible, you may be able to create work for yourself within your organization by applying Bridges's principles. Understand what you have to offer, look for a 'market need' for that offering within your company, and write a proposal for how you should go about meeting that need.

This form of internal portfolio working is actually practised in far more organizations than we might realize. 3M, the technology company whose products include reflective sheeting, surgical tapes and the ubiquitous Post-It® note, is a 'de-jobbed workplace' that encourages workers to create their own work. If employees have ideas, they are encouraged to form small groups, develop and test those ideas, then sell them within the organization. Gemini Consulting actively encourages people to understand their own DATA – though we refer to it differently – and to apply that DATA to meeting the firm's or a client's needs. Lawyer Janet believes that the concept of employees marketing their own particular sets of attributes and abilities within a firm accurately reflects how many firms operate, though they may be unaware of the fact:

A law firm is made up of individuals who apply their talent and experience to solving problems. They are, essentially, free agents. Yet so many at the top persist in hanging on to the idea that they 'own' their employees, and that unless these employees are working flat out, all the time, for them, there is something wrong. If we could convince senior people to accept the notion that they are buying services from individuals, some of whom may do three assignments a year for them, others of whom will work back-to-back assignments as per the traditional model, there would be a lot more scope for work flexibility within this profession.

Like the small business, the portfolio career can be difficult to manage. 'I've had a portfolio career and I don't recommend it . . . I think Charles Handy should be shot,' jokes TV News London chief executive Roz Morris. Maureen Freely, who combines fiction-writing, teaching and journalism in her own portfolio, agrees that the portfolio career has its drawbacks. The income can be insecure, and the various parts of the portfolio often sit uneasily alongside one another, creating periods of stress and chaos. Charles Handy was only partly right when he said in *The Empty Raincoat* that, for portfolio workers, the 'price tag now goes on their produce, not their time'. As with the owner of a small business, the link between 'produce' and time spent is so direct for a portfolio careerist that some feel compelled to work most of the time. But for others, the portfolio career affords them a welcome, and even necessary, opportunity to control their working lives.

William Bridges believes that the security and stability we associate with 'jobs' are increasingly illusory, in any case. The long-term employment contract is becoming a thing of the past, and jobs as we know them are disappearing, to be replaced by more flexible ways of getting work done. 'In this world, portfolio or freelance workers may in fact have greater security than people with "jobs", who can easily lose those "jobs",' he said in a speech to the RSA in October 1997. Freelancers don't have all their eggs in one basket, and they have learned how to create work for themselves by seeking out market needs and applying their own personal resources to meeting them. Bridges maintains that, as de-jobbing increases within the economy, the launching of a portfolio career will be not simply an attractive alternative for some, but a necessary response for most.

There is a far higher level of comfort and security associated with portfolio-working when there is a second family income backing it up. But there *are* sole or main breadwinners who have successful portfolio careers. One friend of mine, Catherine, is a single mother who was accustomed to earning a substantial salary as a strategist with a large consulting firm. She left because she wanted a new challenge, but soon found that the choices open to her in the corporate world were impossible to combine with her role as a single mother to two young children. So she 'went portfolio' as a business strategy consultant. She has never regretted her decision, despite the fact that her income is lower and less secure than she was used to. Now, she can choose the work she wants to do, and set her own ground rules for doing it. She has not yet been lured into the trap of maximizing her income by accepting every job that comes along and working ridiculously long hours. The value she places on a balanced life, and time with her children, the recognition of which came after many years of painful soul-searching, gives her a steely-minded determination to control her work life rather than be controlled by it.

Independence – whether as a portfolio worker or as the owner of a small business – provides more scope for the control of one's time and effort. But it can be another form of trap unless you are very clear – as Catherine is – about what you are trying to achieve through it. A clear sense of priorities, and a systemic approach to crafting a new work life, are as important for the entrepreneur and portfolio worker as they are for employees of organizations.

Many who work independently impose the same constraints upon themselves as were previously placed upon them by organizations. The work is always there waiting to be done, and they are the ones responsible for doing it, so they spend all their time working. Or they feel insecure about their income stream, so they are tempted to maximize income, thereby maximizing the time they spend on work. It is difficult to turn the taps off, to refuse work and money. I know one portfolio careerist who is among the most discontented mothers I know. She consistently says that she wishes she could spend more time with her boys, but just as consistently fails to do so. Despite the fact that she and her husband live well, and could afford to scale back their living standards in exchange for a reduced workload, she finds it difficult to make the decision to do so. She never turns down work, or sets deadlines that would enable her to pace herself differently. Her treadmill is all the worse because it seems to be of her own making.

This woman is trapped partly because she has failed to fully take stock of her life – to acknowledge her priorities, and to make herself comfortable with the trade-offs that are required to live them. Without taking stock, it is almost impossible to resist the lure of work when you work independently. So direct is the link between the amount of work you do and the money you make that it is difficult to opt to work less, or differently.

Difficult but not impossible. Mark set up his corporate communications business in 1994 after years of working for communications and promotions agencies. Once he and his wife had had their fourth child, he felt he needed to work very differently in order to support her at home and play a significant role in the daily care and raising of his family. Over the past four years he has created a very successful and profitable small business that employs one other full-time consultant, and freelancers as required. He has also succeeded in turning upside-down his former working habits. He no longer thinks in terms of hours worked per day but in chunks of work that need to be done in a given week or month. So he builds into his week his key commitments to his family – which include driving the two older children to school and occasionally picking them up, attending school functions and concerts, helping the children with their homework, and looking after the young twins while his wife gets a much needed weekly break. He then schedules work around these commitments. Some days he works from 5am until 8.30am, then again from 10.30 until 4pm, and finally for a couple of hours in the evening. Others he works from nine until seven. If he has to miss a half-day's work in the week and he has an important deadline, he makes up the time at the weekend. He travels to his London office from Oxfordshire only once or twice a week, and spends the rest of the time meeting with clients or working from home, making extensive use of the Internet for communicating with his employee and his freelance consultants.

Mark is supported by a wife who stays home full-time, which makes his juggling act less fraught than it might be in a dual-career household. And he probably works around fifty hours a week, albeit in a very unconventional schedule. Nevertheless, the way he has

succeeded in shaping his working life around his personal commitments, and resisted the temptation to work and be available to
clients all the time, is a testimony to the fact that work–life balance
is possible for the entrepreneur. What is required, and what Mark
has, is the unswerving conviction that personal time and time with
family are important and worth preserving.

5   Build Support

For the owner of a small business or the portfolio careerist, the
things most likely to sabotage a flexible arrangement are a failure of
conviction and of self-discipline. If you take with you to your new
work situation all the old corporate baggage – the work ethic which
equates long hours with commitment, the assumption that clients
need you to be available twenty-four hours a day, the association of
success with an ever-increasing salary – it is unlikely that you will
gain from independence much flexibility or freedom.

But if you choose to try to work flexibly within an organization,
the perceptions and responses of other people may be as much of a
threat as your own inability to shed conventional assumptions and
behaviours. Support for your case for working differently is something you must build, from the outset and continuously.

The quality of the thinking you put into your proposal for a
different working option, and into the business case in particular,
goes a long way towards building support. But you need a relatively
sympathetic and supportive ear to put that case to. If that ear is not
your immediate boss's, it may be that of the manager of another
division, or of the firm's human resource manager. You need,
somewhere in the organization, a mentor – someone who will listen
to you, support you, and assist you in persuading the organization to
give you what you need – and if you cannot find one, then the
chances are that you face greater problems than that of having to
propose a new way of working.

For some, putting a proposal to a mentor may be a simple matter.
For others whose mentor may be organizationally remote from them
or less well versed in the rationale for flexible working, the proposal
may need to be leaked gradually and subtly before it can be made

formally. Only you can judge how gradual should be the process of convincing someone to support your case. One lawyer claims she spent several years building up the support of a couple of key partners within the firm for her working part-time. She did it during informal conversations, and by exposing them to new information that would serve as a rationale for change, and finally through a formal proposal for a 'trial run'. The trial run was successful, and she continues to work a nine-to-four day. Not all of us could afford to wait so long for a change in the way we work, but we can learn from this woman the importance of a carefully planned and paced persuasion strategy testing the waters and preparing the ground with one or two key individuals before placing the formal case on the table.

Seeking a mentor to champion your case, and working with that mentor to persuade the organization to accept your proposed working arrangement, is only the first step in building support. As important, in the long run, will be the extent to which you build support in the organization at large, not just for your particular case, but for the principle of flexible working and work–life balance. Here is the point at which individual action meets systemic organizational change: you can leverage your individual arrangement to further the cause of work–life balance in general by, first, continuing to do the job well and, second, by being seen to be both an example of flexibility and a spokesperson for it.

I always have mixed feelings when a manager tells me that so-and-so is so good that people really aren't aware that she works part-time. Good for so-and-so, I think, but too bad for everyone else. For unless the link between strong performance and flexible working becomes more obvious to people, flexibility will forever be viewed with scepticism by large parts of the corporate world. Worse, the barriers to work–life balance will remain entrenched within the corporate culture. The assumption, particularly, that people should give priority to their work life over anything else, will remain intact.

If the work world is really going to change, then the individuals who are beginning to change it need to be honest. This doesn't mean that at every opportunity they need to shout from the rooftops about their three-day week. But it does mean that they should not attempt to hide it. The more comfortable a person becomes being perceived as a part-timer who also has talent, adds value, and is committed to her career, the more readily others will associate flexible working with these qualities.

Starting from Where We Are

This chapter is no step-by-step guide to creating a flexible working arrangement. No such guide can be written at this point, because all efforts to transform the assumptions that dominate our own and others' thinking about work are so new and experimental. Ultimately, these efforts are aiming to change attitudes, but those attitudes are not easily shifted by snappy ten-point change checklists.

What this chapter does offer is a statement of principles which will, hopefully, serve as inspiration for considered action. And one principle stands out from the others: the need to take personal stock. Unless you do this, unless you confront your fear and come to terms with your values and your feelings about power and success, no number of useful hints can help you create and sustain a flexible working arrangement. Taking stock gives you a sense of your personal power, and it is this power that will sustain you through the effort to craft a new way of working. We all have more power than we think we have, says Susan Jeffers, psychologist and author of *Feel The Fear And Do It Anyway*. 'You have the power to create what you need. Given commitment, clear goals and action, it's just a matter of time.'[13]

It is not just the educated middle class, and well positioned within organizations who have the power to create what they need. 'To say, as some do, that inner direction, or self-expression and control of your own life, is only possible for middle-class, middle-income and middle-aged individuals is to be ridiculously patronizing,'[14] writes Charles Handy. 'The young and the poor may not find it easy, but to allocate them automatically to the ranks of the Sustenance Driven [driven exclusively by the need for financial and social security], is to assume that they have no wish to be responsible for their own future, however difficult that might be.'

William Bridges agrees. When once asked whether the de-jobbed world and the flexible portfolio career would benefit the haves at the expense of the have-nots, he was adamant that it would not. 'The haves are the ones who have benefited from the "job" culture, and many of them will have more trouble relinquishing those benefits to pursue new ways of working than will those who have been excluded from the job culture.' Bridges recalls speaking to a group of disabled individuals, and having been prepared for a high level of antagonism towards his ideas. Instead, he found them amazingly responsive. They felt that in the new world in which people's individual DATA and ability to apply that to problem-solving were what counted, they would be discriminated against far less than in the 'job culture'.

For those truly on the margins of society, those without jobs or working for pitifully lower wages and under poor conditions, the issues they face today are primarily ones of sustenance: how to earn enough to pay the rent and put food on the table. Talk of working options that might enable them to enjoy life, fulfil goals and spend more time with their families will be all but irrelevant until they are in a position of being able to worry about anything but where the next meal will come from. They need subsidized childcare, training, better working conditions and better protection more than they need choices about *how* they work. But for anyone who is working and earning more than they need merely to survive, and who has skills that are transferable, there is some choice. There is choice about where to work, how to work, how much to work. Whether employed at a checkout till at Asda, or as managing director of a large firm, an individual can exploit his or her own personal power to affect his or her working life.

Those with the most power and choice have, at the same time, the most to lose from change and the most to gain. They could also have much to regret if they decline to change their working lives. Every woman needs to ask herself how she would want to look back on her life. If looking back and seeing Superwoman, making appointments with her children and buying seventy Christmas presents in October horrifies her, then she needs to generate from that horror the will to use her personal power to change her life, and the place of work within it.

Changing your working life will not be painless. Writing in the mid-nineteenth century, English historian Henry Thomas Buckle, reminds us why.

Every new truth which has ever been propounded has, for a time, caused mischief; it has produced discomfort, and often unhappiness; sometimes disturbing social and religious arrangements, and sometimes merely by disruption of old and cherished associations of thoughts. It is only after a certain interval, and when the framework of affairs has adjusted itself to the new truth, that its good effects preponderate; ... but at the outset there is always harm. And if the truth is very great as well as very new, the harm is serious.[15]

The 'new truth' is that life has changed, and that work needs to be flexible enough to accommodate that life. Whatever profound discomfort organizations suffer as a result of coming to terms with this truth, and however disturbing this truth might be to us as individuals, we cannot escape it. Change will come, and it starts from where you are. Take stock, be brave and take the leap.

REFERENCES

❖

INTRODUCTION

1 M. Vaughan, 'More witless propaganda to crush the spirit', *Herald*, 6 February 1997

2 'For modern parents, choices come guilt edged', *Daily Telegraph*, 8 February 1997

3 B. Hugill and R. Brooks 'BBC row over working mother "facts"', *Observer*, 9 February 1997

4 B. Hugill and R. Brooks [Int., 3]

5 B. Hugill and R. Brooks [Int., 3]

6 G. Russell, 'A mother's place is in the home', *Sunday Telegraph*, 3 November 1996

7 R. Abrams, 'In defence of working mothers', *Guardian*, 29 October 1996

8 K. Gyngell, 'The price of feminism', *Mail on Sunday*, 7 March 1993

9 E. Currie, 'You can have it all', *Options*, March 1992

10 L. Purves, 'Farewell superwoman', *The Times*, 4 February 1997

11 J. Brannen et al., *Mothers, Fathers and Employment: Parents and the Labour Market in Britain, 1984–1994*, Department for Education and Employment, Norwich, 1997

12 'A mother's place', *New Generation*, June 1997

13 B. Littlejohn, 'It's a love-hate thing, listening to little me', *Guardian*, 30 January 1988.

14 L. Grant, 'Maze that's lost its way', *Guardian G2*, 26 August 1997

15 E. Perle McKenna, *When Work Doesn't Work Anymore: Women, Work and Identity*, 1997

16 D. Greenberg, 'Working mother to working mother', *The Herald*, South Carolina, 4 October 1996

17 H. Kirwan Taylor, 'Warring Mothers', *Tatler*, November 1994

18 C. Crewe, 'The mother of all jobs', *Telegraph*, 12 October 1997

19 J. Bone and J. Bale, 'Pepsi chief quits to watch her boys play football', *The Times*, 25 September 1997

20 S. Moore, 'Superwoman flies into the public eye', *Independent*, 24 January 1997

21 B. Toner, 'Motherhood – what you think', *You*, 4 May 1997

22 C. Kennedy, 'Tomorrow's world for women', *human resources*, November/ December 1996

23 P. Morgan, *Who Needs Parents? The Effects of Childcare and Early Education on Children in Britain and the USA*, Institute of Economic Affairs, 1996

CHAPTER ONE

1 R. Coward, *Our Treacherous Hearts: Why Women Let Men Get Their Way*, 1993

2 K. Figes, *Because of Her Sex: The Myth of Equality for Women in Britain*, 1994

3 A. Katz, *The Juggling Act*, 1992

4 E. Gillibrand and J. Mosley, *When I Go To Work, I Feel Guilty: A Working Mother's Guide to Sanity and Survival*, 1997

5 C. Jardine, 'Calm down, Mum, I'm managing OK without you', *Daily Telegraph*, 31 July 1996

6 A. Stone, 'Bye bye baby: on mother guilt and poverty', in *Child of Mine*, ed. C. Baker Kline, New York, 1997

7 A. Neustatter, 'Who's minding the baby?', *You*, 24 November 1996

8 S. Orbach, *What's Really Going On Here?: Making Sense of Our Emotional Lives*, 1994

9 D. Crittenden, 'The mother of all problems', *Saturday Night*, Vol. 111, No. 3

10 G. Greer, *The Female Eunuch*, 1970, 1991

11 K. Millet, *Sexual Politics*, 1971, 1977

12 S. de Beauvoir, *The Second Sex*, New York, 1952, 1989

13 M. Freely, *What About Us? An Open Letter to the Mothers Feminism Forgot*, 1995

14 P. Leach, *Children First: What Society Must Do – and Is Not Doing – for Children Today*, 1994

15 A. Roiphe, *A Mother's Eye: Motherhood and Feminism*, 1996

16 M. Freely [1, 13]

17 C. Hoff Sommers, *Who Stole Feminism?: How Women Have Betrayed Women*, New York, 1994

18 A. Roiphe [1, 15]

19 A. Rich, *Of Woman Born: Motherhood as Experience and Institution*, 1977

20 C. Shraft and E. Schappell in C. Baker Kline ed. [1, 6]

21 R. Coward [1, 1]

22 E. Perle McKenna, *When Work Doesn't Work Anymore: Women, Work and Identity*, 1997

23 A. Oakley, *Housewife*, 1974

24 A. Roiphe [1, 15]

25 A. Pearson, 'Mother Nature is an old bag', *Evening Standard*, 5 February 1997

26 P. Yates, 'Mothers should not work', *Options*, February 1992

27 L. Purves, *How Not to Be a Perfect Mother*, 1994

28 P. Sykes, *Parents Who Teach: Stories from Home and from School*, 1997

29 A. Burgess, *Fatherhood Reclaimed: The Making of the Modern Father*, 1997

30 P. Leach [1, 14]

31 A. Roiphe [1, 15]

32 A. Burgess (1, 29]

33 R. Shore, *Rethinking the Brain: New Insights into Early Development*, New York, 1997

34 C. Gorman, 'Sizing up the Sexes', *Time*, 20 January 1992

35 T. Radford, 'Genes say boys will be boys and girls will be sensitive', *Guardian*, 12 June 1997

36 T. Radford [1, 35]

37 A. Fausto Sterling, *Myths of Gender: Biological Theories About Women and Men*, New York, 1985

38 S. Kitzinger, *The Complete Book of Pregnancy and Childbirth*, New York, 1980, 1989

39 C. and P. Hill, *Your New Baby – How to Survive the First Months of Parenthood*, 1995

40 D. Hutton, 'Babies on the brain', *Vogue*, April 1994

41 P. Leach [1, 14]

42 M. Jackson, *The Mother Zone*, Toronto, 1992

43 L. Purves [1, 27]

44 C. Gilligan, *In a Different Voice: Psychological Theory and Women's Development*, 1982, 1993

45 L. Brooks, 'All mod cons', *Guardian* G2, 9 October 1997

46 S. Orbach [1, 8]

47 M. Freely [1, 13]

48 'A to Z of the movers', *Guardian*, 26, 27, 28 May 1997

CHAPTER TWO

1 N. Walter, 'Hard Labour', *Guardian*, 28 May 1997

2 R. Abrams [Int., 7]

3 M. Vaughan [Int., 1]

4 A. Roiphe [1, 15]

5 J. Adler, 'It's a wise father who knows . . .' *Newsweek*, spring/summer 1997

6 M. P. Dunleavey, 'Take our sons to the laundromat – please', *Glamour*, May 1997

7 B. Clement, 'Working mothers feel the strain of dual role', *Independent*, 25 March 1992

8 T. Apter, *Professional Progress: Why Women Still Don't Have Wives*, 1985, 1993

9 S. MccGwire, *Best Companies for Women*, 1992

10 *Daily Mail*, week of 13 July 1997

11 M. Henwood et al., *Inside the Family: Changing Roles of Men and Women*, Family Policy Studies Centre, 1987

12 S. Stacey, 'Wife, mother, breadwinner: is the effort killing you?' *Sunday Times Stress manager*, 1 June 1997

13 *Daily Mail*, 15 February 1992

14 P. Hewitt, *About time: The Revolution in Work and Family Life*, 1993

15 P. Hewitt [2, 14] and D. Coyle, 'At last, the true value of housework is revealed', *Independent*, 7 October 1997

16 P. Hewitt [2, 14]

17 E. Ferri and K. Smith, *Parenting in the Nineties*, Family Policy Studies Centre, 1996

18 P. Hewitt [2, 14]

19 M. Henwood et al. [2, 11]

20 D. Cohen, 'FATHERHOOD: It's what men really want', *You*, 15 June 1997

21 L. Shapiro, 'The myth of quality time', *Newsweek*, 19 May 1997

22 E. Ferri and K. Smith [2, 17]

23 M. Henwood et al. [2, 11]

24 *Report of the All Party Parliamentary Group on Parenting and International Year of the Family UK Parliamentary Hearings*, 1994

25 R. Holliday, 'Don't laugh girls but ... Sadly, men are still behaving badly', *Evening Standard*, 5 June 1997

26 J. Brannen et al. [Int., 11]

27 A. Hochschild, *The Time Bind: When Work Becomes Home and Home Becomes Work*, New York, 1997

28 A. Burgess [1, 29]

29 L. Harding, 'The women who made COSMO', *You*, 16 February 1997

30 A. Oakley, *Housewife*, 1974

31 A. Roiphe [1, 15]

32 P. Brook, 'Superwoman goes home', *Saturday Night*, Vancouver, Vol. 111, No. 5, June 1996

33 A. Devlin, 'Prisoner: cell block hell', *Guardian G2*, 19 August 1997

34 C. Gilligan [1, 44]

35 J. Gray, *Men Are from Mars, Women Are from Venus*, 1993

36 T. Radford [1, 35]

37 S. Ruddick, 'Maternal thinking' in J. Treblicott, ed. *Mothering: Essays in Feminist Theory*, 1983

38 A. Burgess [1, 29]

39 J. Adler [2, 5]

40 M. Phillips, *The Sex Change State*, The Social Market Foundation, 1997

41 M. Freely [1, 13]

42 E. Ferri and K. Smith [2, 17]

43 E. Perle McKenna [Int., 15]

CHAPTER THREE

1 M. Haran, *Having It All*, 1991

2 J. Finch, 'Up up and Away', *Guardian G2*, 20 November 1997

3 C. Kennedy [Int., 22]

4 H. Bellingham, 'Some superwoman', *Daily Telegraph*, 22 January 1997

5 B. White et al., *Women's Career Development*, 1992

6 J. Smith, 'You're a woman who juggles her life? Big deal!', *Evening Standard*, 11 September 1996

7 J. Smith [3, 6]

8 N. Caine and C. Norton, 'Domestic service sweeps back in two-salary homes', *Sunday Times*, 5 January 1997

9 N. Horlick, *Can You Have It All?*, 1997

10 A. Hochschild [2, 27]

11 P. Leach [1, 14]

12 S. A. Hewlett, *When the Bough Breaks: The Cost of Neglecting Our Children*, New York, 1991

13 P. Brook [2, 32]

14 L. Shapiro [2, 21]

15 L. Shapiro [2, 21]

16 L. Harding, 'Don't fall for the quality time trap', *You*, 24 August 1997

17 P. Leach (1, 14]

18 S. Kelly, 'Time to go home', *Daily Telegraph*, 12 August 1996

19 L. Purves [1, 27]

20 S. R. Covey, *Seven Habits of Highly Effective People*, New York, 1994

21 H. Gurdon, 'You can't do everything with the time of your life', *Daily Telegraph*, 28 August 1995

22 S. R. Covey and A. R. Merrill, *First Things First*, New York, 1994

23 A. Hochschild [2, 27]

24 K. Berridge, 'What we need is a wife', *Sunday Times Women and Money*, 23 November 1997

25 C. Crewe [Int., 18]

26 Parents at Work, *Time, Work and Family*, 1995

27 P. Brook [2, 32]

28 A. Hochschild [2, 27]

29 P. Morgan [Int., 23]

30 E. Galinsky et al., *The Changing Workforce: Highlights of the National Study*, Families and Work Institute, 1993

31 Parents at Work [3, 26]

32 J. Brannen et al. [Int., 11]

33 J. Gardner, *Gender, Care and Economics*, 1997

34 P. Hewitt [2, 14]

35 S. Horrell, 'Household time allocation and women's labour force participation' in M. Anderson et al. eds. *The Social and Political Economy of the Household*, 1994

36 L. Purves [Int., 10]

37 A. McFerran, 'Doing business the family way', *Independent Tabloid*, 3 December 1996

38 A. McFerran, 'Relative values', *Sunday Times* magazine, 9 June 1996

39 L. Harding, 'I want my child to feel more secure than I did', *You*, 21 January 1996

40 S. A. Hewlett [3, 12]

41 L. Shapiro [2, 21]

42 A. Hochschild [2, 27]

43 R. Tait, *Roads to the Top: Career Decisions and Development of Eighteen Business Leaders*, 1995

44 J. Finch [3, 2]

45 A. Kirwan Taylor, 'When the juggling stops', *Vogue* September 1995

46 P. Brook [2, 32]

47 E. Perle McKenna [Int., 15]

48 C. Gilligan [1, 44]

49 S. Maxwell Magnus, 'Work, work, work . . .', *Guardian G2*, 23 July 1997

50 I. Katz, 'Woman on top of her game', *Guardian G2*, 23 Oct 1996

51 E. J. Pollock 'This is home; this is work: for Connie Duckworth, there's the job and there's her family, and they never overlap', *Wall Street Journal*, New York, 31 March 1997

CHAPTER FOUR

1 M. Cleave, 'People say that mothers are happy with the present arrangements for children. If they were I'd shut up', *Sainsbury's Magazine*, August 1994

2 D. Lepkowska, 'Schools chief in nursery row forced to quit', *Evening Standard*, 29 April 1996

3 P. Morgan [Int., 23]

4 F. Abrams, 'Nursery crimes? Not guilty', *Independent*, 26 April 1996

5 J. Freedland, 'Childcare report backs working mums', *The Times*, 5 June 1996

6 C. Hall, 'Children in day-care "are brighter"', *Daily Telegraph* 4 February 1997

7 H. Harman, *Getting Welfare to Work*, 1996

8 A. Roddick, 'Blaming mother is the strategy of children of all ages', *Independent*, 9 February 1997

9 H. Wilkinson et al., *Tomorrow's Women*, Demos, 1997

10 M. Linton, 'Ministers rue "gaps" in child care', *Guardian*, 29 August 1996

11 P. Morgan [Int., 23]

12 N. Caine, 'How to cut the costs of childcare', *Sunday Times Money*, 16 November 1997

13 P. Morgan [Int., 23]

14 P. Morgan [Int., 23]

15 'Mothers spurn chance of full time daycare', *Sunday Times News*, 9 November 1997 and M. Freely, 'Lies damned lies and working mothers', *Guardian G2*, 11 November 1997

16 P. Leach [1, 14]

17 I. Breugel, letter to editor, *Guardian*, 4 June 1997

18 P. Leach [1, 14]

19 P. Moss, '"Employee childcare" – Or services for children, carers and employers', *Employee Relations*, Vol. 14, No. 6, 1992

20 L. Hanna, 'Flexible friends – "family-friendly" work schemes', *Guardian*, 20 April 1993

21 [2, 24]

22 H. Harman, *The Century Gap*, 1993

23 R. Fowler, 'Working mothers at bottom of heap', *Independent*, 29 August 1996

24 S. Bevan et al., *Who Cares? The Business Benefits of Carer-friendly Practices*, Institute for Employment Studies, 1997

25 T. Marshall, 'Infant care: a day nursery under the microscope', *Social Work Service*, No. 32, 1982

26 P. Moss [4, 19]

27 G. Greer [1, 10]

28 R. Coward [1, 1]

29 A. Oakley [2, 30]

30 P. Morgan [Int., 23]

31 F. Abrams [4, 4]

32 H. Harman [4, 22]

33 K. Figes [1, 2]

34 'Majority of working mothers believe child learns more in day-care', *Working Mother*, New York, 17 March 1993

35 'Talent at two years old', *Guardian*, 25 April 1996

36 C. Jardine, [1, 5]

37 R. Shore [1, 33]

38 J. Herring et al., *Day-care and the Children Act: An ABC for Providers*, Day-care Trust

39 P. Leach [1, 14]

40 E. Melhuish and P. Moss, *The Day-care Project*, Thomas Coram Research Institute. Also in E. C. Melhuish, 'Research on day-care for young children in

the United Kingdom' in E. C. Melhuish and P. Moss, *Day-care for Young Children: International Perspectives*, London: Tavistock/Routledge, 1991

41 C. Norton, 'Too young to go to nursery?' *Sunday Times*, 4 January 1978
42 P. Leach [1, 14]
43 P. Moss and H. Penn, *Transforming Nursery Education*, 1996
44 A. Hochschild [2, 27]
45 T. Marshall [4, 25]
46 P. Leach [1, 14]
47 S. Faludi, *Backlash: The Undeclared War Against Women*, 1991, 1992
48 K. Figes [1, 2]
49 A. Burgess [1, 29]
50 P. Morgan [Int., 23]
51 P. Morgan [Int., 23]
52 T. Marshall [4, 25]
53 P. Morgan [Int., 23]
54 P. Morgan [Int., 23]
55 K. Figes [1, 2]
56 C. Kelleher, letter to editor, *The Times*, 29 April 1996
57 P. Leach [1, 14]
58 P. Morgan [Int., 23]
59 P. Leach [1, 14]

CHAPTER FIVE
1 K. Gyngell, 'The danger of becoming a career woman at any cost', *Mail on Sunday Femail*, 28 April 1996
2 A. Gerrie, 'Taking the rearing view – full-time mothers', *The Times*, 12 February 1992
3 *Full-Time Mothers Newsletter*, spring 1997
4 H. Kirwan Taylor, 'Mother Courage', *Tatler*, September 1995
5 D. Goodman, letter to editor, *The Times*, 29 April 1996
6 L. Dillner, 'A child of our time', *Guardian*, 3 December 1996
7 'Education – placing the blame for the fall in reading standards', *Independent*, 20 February 1992
8 L. Burrows, 'Spare the job, mother, and save the child', *Sunday Telegraph*, 27 October 1996
9 G. Russell [Int., 6]
10 M. Phillips [2, 40]
11 P. Morgan [Int., 23]
12 Unsworth, 'Join on, no girls', *Sunday Times* magazine, 16 November 1997
13 J. Coles, 'Hugs, tears and men only in promised land', *Guardian*, 4 October 1997

14 T. Unsworth [5, 12]

15 V. White, 'Mothers up in arms', *Irish Times*, 23 February 1993

16 L. Burrows [5, 8]

17 K. Gyngell [Int., 8]

18 K. Gyngell [5, 1]

19 The information in the last three pages derives from A. Fuligni et al., *The Impact of Parental Employment on Children*, Families and Work Institute, New York, 1995

20 M. Rutter and D. J. Smith eds., *Psychosocial Disorders in Young People: Time Trends and Their Causes*, 1995

21 A. Fuligni et al. [5, 19]

22 C. Dodd, 'Mummy why do you have to go to work?', *Independent*, 22 April 1996

23 L. Purves [Int., 10]

24 R. Shore [1, 33]

25 A. Fuligni et al. [5, 19]

26 R. Shore [1, 33]

27 L. Hoffman, 'The effects of maternal employment on the academic attitudes and performance of school-aged children', *School Psychology Review*, Vol. 9, No. 4, 1980

28 B. Hugill and R. Brooks [Int., 3]

29 Department of Education and Science Study

30 A. Fuligni et al. [5, 19]

31 R. C. Kessler and J. A. McRae, 'The effects of wives' employment on the mental health of married men and women', *American Sociological Review*, Vol. 47, 1982

32 R. C. Kessler and J. A. McRae [5, 31]

33 A. Fuligni et al. [5, 19]

34 A. Fuligni et al. [5, 19]

35 E. Ferri and K. Smith [2, 17]

36 M. Phillips [2, 40]

37 E. Ferri and K. Smith [2, 17]

38 E. Ferri and K. Smith [2, 17]

39 A. Burgess [1, 29]

40 E. Ferri and K. Smith [2, 17]

41 P. Morgan [3, 29]

42 P. Morgan [3, 29]

43 A. Burgess [1, 29]

44 H. Wilkinson, [4, 9]

45 A. Burgess [1, 29]

46 Y. Roberts, 'Once upon another time', *Guardian G2*, 4 November 1996

47 D. Eyer, *Mother Guilt: How Our Culture Blames Mothers for What's Wrong with Society*, New York, 1997

48 Information in this and the previous two paragraphs from D. Utting et al., *Crime and the Family: Improving Child-rearing and Preventing Delinquency*, 1993

49 Dr T. Dalrymple, 'It's the most miserable human existence I have encountered anywhere', *Sunday Telegraph*, 27 October 1996

50 *The Big Story*, Carlton Television, 20 November 1997

51 D. Utting et al. [5, 48]

52 D. Utting et al. [5, 48] and *Khaleej Times*, 7 April 1992

CHAPTER SIX

 1 Full-Time Mothers, *Full-Time Mothers: A Child's Need, a Mother's Right*

 2 P. Morgan [Int., 23]

 3 B. Dineen, 'Eternal dilemma for working woman', *Yorkshire Post*, 4 November 1996

 4 A. O'Connor, 'Mum is free to go on working . . .', *Guardian*, 4 September 1996

 5 A. Gerrie [5, 2]

 6 P. Yates [1, 26]

 7 D. Keane, 'Mothers don't have to work', *Mail on Sunday*, 3 December 1995

 8 M. Marrin, 'Why we should stand up for housewives', *Sunday Telegraph*, 15 March 1992

 9 M. Freely [4, 15]

10 C. Hakim, *Key Issues in Women's Work: Female Heterogeneity and the Polarisation of Women's Employment*, 1996

11 D. J. Swiss, *Women Breaking Through*, New York, 1996

12 P. Leach [1, 14]

13 [2, 24]

14 Woman of the Year Lunch, *The 1996 Woman of the Year Lunch Survey Report*, October 1996

15 J. Brannen and P. Moss, *Managing Mothers: Dual Earner Households After Maternity Leave*, 1991

16 J. Brannen and P. Moss [6, 15]

17 H. Wilkinson [4, 9]

18 AGE Melbourne, 18 February 1993

19 Woman of the Year Lunch [6, 14]

20 J. Brannen and P. Moss [6, 15]

21 E. Perle McKenna [Int., 15]

22 C. Handy, *The Hungry Spirit*, 1997

23 P. Brook [2, 32]

24 C. Gilligan, 'Restoring the missing text of women's development to life cycle theories' in *Women's Lives*

25 A. Woodham, *Good Housekeeping*, May 1994

26 K. Muir, 'Let's face it, infants stink and so does motherhood', *The Times*, 26 May 1995

27 P. Vincenzi, 'Invisible mother syndrome', *Good Housekeeping*, January 1996

28 B. Toner [Int., 21]

29 R. Miles, 'Should mothers work? No', *Mail on Sunday*, 3 August 1997

30 A. Roiphe [1, 15]

31 E. Perle McKenna [Int., 15]

32 K. Figes [1, 2]

33 J. Gardner [3, 33]

34 A. Kwitney, 'The Eternal Now' in C. Baker Kline ed [1, 6]

35 D. Keane [6, 7]

36 J. Robinson, letter to editor, *The Times*, 18 June 1997

37 M. Richardson, 'Staying at home', *The Times*, 21 June 1997

38 E. Ferri and K. Smith [2, 17]

39 A. Fuligni et al. [5, 19]

40 D. Hutton, 'The parenting trap', *Vogue*, March 1996

41 A. Roiphe [1, 15]

CHAPTER SEVEN

1 P. Yates [1, 26]

2 H. Kirwan Taylor [5, 4]

3 'Keeping mum at home', *Scotsman*, 10 February 1997

4 'Mums on the run', *Guardian*, 3 February 1997

5 L. Slater, 'Wouldn't you rather be at home?' *Telegraph*, 20 January 1997

6 S. MccGwire [2, 9]

7 'Maternity arrangements '95: part 2', *EOR*, No. 64, November/December 1995

8 M. Marrin [6, 8]

9 *Guardian*, 4 October 1996

10 K. Figes [1, 2]

11 A. Holdsworth, 'Age of the flexible woman', *Telegraph*, 28 February 1992

12 P. Leach [1, 14]

13 K. Labich, 'Can your career hurt your kids?', *Fortune*, New York, 20 May 1991

14 L. Shapiro [2, 21]

15 B. Coloroso, *Kids are Worth It*, Toronto, 1995

16 [2, 24]

17 P. Brook [2, 32]

18 S. MccGwire [2, 9]

19 C. Hogg and L. Harker, *The Family Friendly Employer: Examples from Europe*, 1992

20 W. Hirsh et al., *Beyond the Career Break*, Institute of Manpower Studies Report 223, 1992
21 Full-Time Mothers [6, 1]

CHAPTER EIGHT
 1 R. Tait [3, 43]
 2 A. Hochschild [2, 27]
 3 S. Bevan et al. [4, 24]
 4 'Maternity arrangements'95: part 1', *EOR*, No. 63, September/October 1995
 5 J. Gallagher and K. Wilson, 'Branson's Virgin told me: abort your baby or lose your job', *Mail on Sunday Femail*, 1 September 1996
 6 N. Bunyan, 'Victory for driver who left work to see daughter born', *Daily Telegraph*, 3 September 1996
 7 S. Orbach, 'Pregnant – not fat', *New Generation*, September 1997
 8 C. and P. Hill [1, 39]
 9 S. A. Hewlett, *A Lesser Life: The Myth of Women's Liberation*, 1987
10 S. A. Hewlett [8, 9]
11 A. Hochschild [2, 27]
12 L. Brooks, 'Helen Fraser', in 'Fifty most powerful women in Britain', *Guardian G2*, 27 May 1997
13 O. Craig, 'Cheating our children', *Sunday Times*, 25 May 1997
14 K. Berridge [3, 24]
15 Editor's note to 'New and expectant mothers at work – a guide for employers', *City of London Working Mothers Group Newsletter*, February 1995
16 C. Mock and A. Bruno, 'The expectant executive and the endangered promotion', *Harvard Business Review*, Cambridge, January–February 1994
17 L. Purves [1, 27]
18 S. Bird, 'Baby blues: a journal', in C. Baker Kline ed. [1, 6]
19 A. Campbell, 'The complete guide to working from home', *Good Housekeeping*, July 1996 and S. Simmons, *Flexible Working: A Strategic Guide to Successful Implementation and Operation*, 1996
20 N. Pandya, 'Working at home not domestic bliss', *Guardian*, 2 November 1996
21 C. Hogg and L. Harker [7, 19]
22 L. Bennets, 'Nora's arc', *Vanity Fair*, February 1992
23 A. Campbell [8, 19]
24 L. Purves [1, 27]
25 S. A. Hewlett [8, 9]
26 P. Hewitt [2, 14]
27 J. Brannen et al. [Int., 11]
28 [7, 7]

29 D. Rowan, 'Industry's crèche economy', *Guardian*, 12 November 1997

30 S. MccGwire [2, 9]

31 'What price part-time work?', *Essentials*, June 1996

32 P. Hewitt [2, 14]

33 I. Boyes, Flexible Working for Managers, 1993

34 'Part-time workers – in from the periphery', *IRS Employment Trends*, No. 531, March 1993

35 I. Boyes [8, 33]

36 J. Brannen et al. [Int., 11]

37 H. Harman [4, 22]

38 L. Haas and P. Hwang, 'Corporate culture and men's use of family leave benefits in Sweden', *Family Coordinator*, Vol. 44

39 R. Syal, 'Mothers in wave of job loss claims', *Sunday Times News*, 23 June 1996

40 E. A. Stannard, 'Powerful women and a crack at the glass ceiling', letter to editor, *Guardian*, 31 May 1997

41 I. Boyes [8, 33]

42 R. Rapoport et al., *Relinking Life and Work: Toward a Better Future*, The Ford Foundation, United States, 1996

43 S. MccGwire [2, 9]

44 A. Roddick [4, 8]

45 D. Rowan [8, 29]

46 C. Power, 'It's just a job', *Newsweek*, 19 May 1997

47 C. Simkin and J. Hillage, *Family-Friendly Working: New Hope or Old Hype?*, Institute of Employment Studies, July 1992

48 C. Cooper and S. Lewis, *Beyond Family-Friendly Corporations*, Demos, 1995

49 H. Wilkinson et al. [4, 9]

50 J. Fierman, 'Are companies less family-friendly?', *Fortune*, 21 March 1994, (European issue)

51 D. J. Swiss [6, 11]

52 A. Hochschild [2, 27]

53 J. Fierman [8, 50]

54 A. Hochschild [2, 27]

55 D. E. Friedman and A. A. Johnson, *Moving from Programs to Culture Change: The Next Stage for the Corporate Work-Family Agenda*, New York, 1996

56 F. Schwartz, 'Women as a business imperative', *Harvard Business Review*, March–April 1992

57 Leslie Chin's presentation to *Striking the Balance Transnational Seminar*, Royal Borough of Kingston, 19–21 June 1997

58 L. Harker, 'The family-friendly employer in Europe', in S. and J. Lewis eds. *The Work–Family Challenge: Rethinking Employment*, 1996

59 *Striking the Balance Transnational Seminar*, Royal Borough of Kingston, 19–21 June 1997

60 C. Hogg and L. Harker [7, 19]

61 H. Morgan and K. Tucker, *Companies That Care: The Most Family Oriented Companies in America, What They Offer, and How They Got That Way*, New York, 1991

62 A. Hochschild [2, 27]

63 S. Lewis and K. Taylor, 'Evaluating the impact of family-friendly employer policies: a case study', in S. and J. Lewis eds. [8, 58]

64 J. Lewis, 'Work–family reconciliation and the law: intrusion or empowerment?', in S. and J. Lewis eds. [8, 58]

65 *Guardian*, 25 June 1997

66 'Women fear family–friendly jobs will bar career success', *City of London Working Mothers Group Newsletter*, February 1995

67 P. Hewitt [2, 14]

68 P. Brooks [2, 32]

69 A. Hochschild [2, 27]

70 R. Tait [3, 43]

71 L. Buckingham, 'Still the same old boy's club', *Guardian*, 4 October 1997

72 K. Berridge [3, 24]

73 J. Brannen et al. [Int., 11]

74 Oxford, Lilly Industries, Midland Bank

75 A. Hochschild [2, 27]

76 E. Perle McKenna [Int., 15]

77 D. J. Swiss and J. P. Walker, *Women and the Work/Family Dilemma: How Today's Professional Women are Finding Solutions*, New York, 1993

CHAPTER NINE

1 P. Hewitt [2, 14]

2 A. Katz [1, 3]

3 A. Hochschild [2, 27]

4 A. Hochschild [2, 27]

5 P. Hewitt [2, 14]

6 A. Hochschild [2, 27]

7 A. Hochschild [2, 27]

8 A. Hochschild [2, 27]

9 E. Lee et al., *World Employment: National Policies in a Global Context*, International Labour Office, Geneva, 1996

10 J. Brannen et al. [Int., 11]

11 Ideas in this paragraph and from the previous two are from W. Bridges, *Creating You and Co: Be the Boss of Your Own Career*, 1997

12 H. Wilkinson and G. Mulgan, *Freedom's Children*, Demos, 1995

13 William Bridges' speech to the Royal Society for the Encouragement of Arts, Manufacture and Commerce, 6 October 1997

14 *Towards 2000: A workplace agenda for the next half decade*, GHN Limited, 1995

15 J. MacGregor, *Pensions in the 21st Century*, Centre for Policy Studies, 1996

16 R. Stark, 'Recipe for a renaissance woman', *You*, 12 May 1994

17 M. Heron, 'Old at forty, young at sixty', *Good Housekeeping*, May 1994

18 L. Jardine, 'Still angry after all these years?' *Sunday Times Style & Travel*, 15 May 1994

19 G. Sheehy, *New Passages*, 1996

20 S. Bevan et al. (4, 24]

21 C. Cooper and S. Lewis [8, 48]

22 H. Wilkinson and G. Mulgan [9, 12]

23 A. Daniels, 'Students put home life before high flying', *Guardian*, 22 October 1997

24 E. Perle McKenna [Int., 15]

25 H. Wilkinson and G. Mulgan [9, 12]

26 S. Whittaker, 'It's a new era on the job front', *Gazette*, Montreal, 13 September 1997

27 C. Handy, [6, 21]

28 Leslie Chin [8, 57]

29 H. Morgan and K. Tucker [8, 61]

30 A. Hochschild [2, 27]

31 I. Boyer [8, 33]

32 E. Galinsky et al. [3, 30]

33 H. Morgan and K. Tucker [8, 61]

34 H. Morgan and K. Tucker [8, 61] and 'Employers fight to fill graduate jobs', *Guardian*, 30 September 1997

35 H. Morgan and K. Tucker [8, 61]

36 [9, 14]

37 H. Morgan and K. Tucker [8, 61]

38 [9, 14]

39 H. Morgan and K. Tucker [8, 61]

40 H. Morgan and K. Tucker [8, 61] and A. Hochschild [2, 27]

41 A. Hochschild [2, 27]

42 F. Reichheld *The Loyalty Effect: The Hidden Force Behind Growth, Profits, and Lasting Value*, New York, 1996

43 'Job share boost for senior staff', *Financial Times*, 28 August 1997

44 Industrial Society, *Maximising Attendance*, Managing Best Practice Series Vol. 32, 1997

45 Industrial Society [9, 44]

46 Industrial Society [9, 44]

47 E. Galinsky et al. [3, 30]

48 R. Rees, 'Someone will pay for this', *Sunday Times*, 18 May 1997

49 S. Bevan et al. [4, 24]

50 S. Bevan et al. [4, 24]

51 A. Hochschild [2, 27]

52 P. Hewitt [2, 14]

53 *Sunday Times*, 4 May 1997

54 R. Rees [9, 48]

55 *Dupont Corporate News* (press release), 1994

56 E. Galinsky et al. [3, 30]

57 I. Boyer [8, 33]

58 J. Gonyea and B. Googins, 'The restructuring of work and family in the United States: a new challenge for American corporations', in S. and J. Lewis eds. [8, 58]

59 P. Hewitt [2, 14]

60 [9, 14]

61 R. Rapoport et al. [8, 42]

62 R. Rapoport et al. [8, 42]

63 J. Gonyea and B. Googins [9, 58]

64 [9, 14]

65 *Opportunity 2000 News*, spring '97

66 E. Galinsky et al. [3, 30]

67 F. Reichheld [9, 42]

68 I. Boyer [8, 33]

69 J. Carvel, 'Study deal for young workers', *Guardian*, 9 December 1997

70 H. Levinson and N. Stone, 'The case of the perplexing promotion', *Harvard Business Review*, January–February 1990

71 [9, 14] and P. Simpson, *The Internal Labour Market*, RSA, 1997

CHAPTER TEN

1 T. Mitchell, *Opportunity 2000 Campaign Fifth Year Progress Reports 1996*, 1996

2 L. Harker [8, 58]

3 M. Bogan ed., *Changing Culture: Achieving a Balanced Workforce*, 1996

4 M. Bogan ed [10, 3]

5 H. Morgan and K. Tucker [8, 61]

6 H. Morgan and K. Tucker [8, 61]

7 R. Rapoport et al. [8, 42]

8 [9, 14]

9 M. Bogan ed. [10, 3]

10 M. Bogan ed. [10, 3]

11 R. Rapoport et al. [8, 42]

12 R. Rapoport et al. [8, 42]

13 R. Rapoport et al. [8, 42]

14 J. Gonyea and B. Googins [9, 58]

15 D. E. Friedman and A. A. Johnson [8, 55]

16 S. Lewis and K. Taylor [8, 63]

17 M. Bogan ed. [10, 3]

18 E. Galinsky et al. [3, 30]

19 'Home alone', *People Management*, 26 September 1996

20 DTI small firms statistic in *Small Firms in Britain*, DTI, 1995

21 H. Morgan and K. Tucker [8, 61]

22 A. Hochschild [2, 27]

23 J. Lewis [8, 64]

24 R. Rapoport et al. [8, 42]

25 R. Rapoport et al. [8, 42]

26 R. Rapoport et al. [8, 42]

27 R. Rapoport et al. [8, 42]

28 R. Rapoport et al. [8, 42]

29 R. Rapoport et al. [8, 42]

30 R. Rapoport et al. [8, 42]

CHAPTER ELEVEN

 1 R. Rapoport et al. [8, 41]

 2 E. Perle McKenna [Int., 15]

 3 S. R. Covey and A. R. Merrill [3, 22]

 4 C. Handy [6, 21]

 5 C. Handy [6, 21]

 6 P. Senge et al., *The Fifth Discipline Fieldbook*, 1994

 7 S. R. Covey and A. R. Merrill [3, 22]

 8 A. Hochschild [2, 27]

 9 I. Pilia and L. Daniels eds., *The Employees' Guide to Flexible Working*, Parents at Work, 1995

10 C. Handy, *The Empty Raincoat*, 1994

11 H. Wilkinson et al. [4, 9]

12 W. Bridges [9, 11]

13 S. Jeffers, *Feal the Fear and Do It Anyway*, 1987

14 C. Handy [6, 21]

15 Henry Thomas Buckle in G. Seldes, *The Great Quotations*, New Jersey, 1983

BIBLIOGRAPHY

❖

M. Anderson et al., eds., *The Social and Political Economy of the Household*, 1994

T. Apter, *Professional Progress: Why Women Still Don't Have Wives*, 1985, 1993

C. Baker Kline ed., *Child of Mine*, New York, 1997

S. Bevan et al., *Who Cares? The Business Benefits of Carer-friendly Practices*, Institute for Employment Studies, 1997

M. Bogan ed., *Changing Culture: Achieving a Balanced Workforce*, 1996

J. Brannen et al, *Mothers, Fathers and Employment: Parents and the Labour Market in Britain, 1984–1994*, Department for Education and Employment, Norwich, 1997

J. Brannen and P. Moss, *Managing Mothers: Dual Earner Households After Maternity Leave*, 1991

W. Bridges, *Creating You and Co: Be the Boss of Your Own Career*, 1997

A. Bruno and C. Mock, 'The expectant executive and the endangered promotion', *Harvard Business Review, Cambridge*, January/February 1994

A. Burgess, *Fatherhood Reclaimed: The Making of the Modern Father*, 1997

B. Coloroso, *Kids are Worth It*, Toronto, 1995

C. Cooper and S. Lewis, *Beyond Family-Friendly Corporations*, Demos, 1995

R. Coward, *Our Treacherous Hearts: Why Women Let Men Get Their Way*, 1993

S. R. Covey, *Seven Habits of Highly Successful People*, New York, 1994

S. R. Covey and R. Merrill, *First Things First*, New York, 1994

L. Daniels and I. Philia eds., *The Employees' Guide to Flexible Working*, Parents at Work, 1995

S. de Beauvoir, *The Second Sex*, 1952, 1989

D. Eyer, *Mother Guilt: How Our Culture Blames Mother's For What's Wrong With Society*, New York, 1997

S. Faludi, *Backlash: The Undeclared War Against American Women*, 1991, 1992

A. Fausto Sterling, *Myths of Gender: Biological Theories About Women and Men*, 1985

E. Ferri and K. Smith, *Parenting in the Nineties, Family Policy Study Centre*, 1996

K. Figes, *Because of Her Sex: The Myth of Equality for Women in Britain*, 1994

M. Freely, *What About Us?: An Open Letter to the Mothers Feminism Forgot*, 1995

D. E. Friedman and A. A. Johnson, *Moving from Programs to Culture Change: The Next Stage for the Corporate Work-Family Agenda*, New York, 1996

A. Fuligni et al., *The Impact of Parental Employment on Children*, Families and Work Institute, New York, 1995

E. Galinsky et al., *The Changing Workforce: Highlights of the National Study*, Families and Work Institute, New York, 1993

J. Gardner, *Gender, Care and Economics*, 1997

E. Gillibrand and J. Mosley, *When I Go To Work, I Feel Guilty: A Working Mother's Guide to Sanity and Survival*, 1997

C. Gilligan, *In a Different Voice: Psychological Theory and Women's Development*, 1982, 1993

J. Gray, *Men Are From Mars, Women Are From Venus*, 1993

G. Greer, *The Female Eunuch*, 1970, 1991

I. Haas and P. Hwang, 'Corporate culture and men's use of family leave benefits in Sweden', *Family Coordinator*, Vol. 44

C. Hakim, *Key Issues in Women's Work: Female Heterogeneity and the Polarisation of Women's Employment*, 1996

C. Handy, *The Empty Raincoat*, 1994

C. Handy, *The Hungry Spirit*, 1997

M. Haran, *Having It All*, 1991

L. Harker and C. Hogg, *The Family-Friendly Employer: Examples From Europe*, 1992

H. Harman, *Getting Welfare to Work*, The Labour Party, 1996

M. Henwood et al., *Inside the Family: Changing Roles of Men and Women*, Family Policy Study Centre, 1987

J. Herring et al., *Day-care and the Children Act: An ABC for Providers*, Day-care Trust

P. Hewitt, *About Time: The Revolution in Work and Family Life*, 1993

S. A. Hewlett, *A Lesser Life: The Myth of Women's Liberation*, 1987

S. A. Hewlett, *When the Bough Breaks: The Cost of Neglecting Our Children*, New York, 1991

C. and P. Hill, *Your New Baby – How to Survive the First Months of Parenthood*, 1995

J. Hillage and C. Simkin, *Family-Friendly Working: New Hope of Old Hype?*, Institute of Employment Studies, Brighton, July 1992

W. Hirsh et al., *Beyond the Career Break*, Institute of Manpower Studies Report 223, 1992

A. Hochschild, *The Time Bind: When Work Becomes Home and Home Becomes Work*, New York, 1997

L. Hoffman, 'The effects of maternal employment on the academic attitudes and performance of school age children', *School Psychology Review*, Vol. 9, No. 4, 1980

C. Hoff Sommers, *Who Stole Feminism?: How Women Have Betrayed Women*, New York, 1996

J. Hopkins, 'Facilitating the development of intimacy between nurses and infants in day nurseries', in *Early Child Development and Care*, Vol. 33, 1988

N. Horlick, *Can You Have It All?*, 1997

Industrial Society, 'Maximising Attendance', *Managing Best Practice Series*, Vol. 32, 1997

O. James, *Britain on the Couch*, 1996

M. Jackson, *The Mother Zone*, Toronto, 1992

S. Jeffers, *Feal the Fear and Do It Anyway*, 1987

A. Katz, *The Juggling Act*, 1992

R. C. Kessler and J. A. McRae, 'The effects of wives' employment on the mental health of married men and women', *American Sociological Review*, Vol. 47, 1982

S. Kitzinger, *The Complete Book of Pregnancy and Childbirth*, New York, 1980, 1989

P. Leach, *Children First: What Society Must Do – and Is Not Doing – for Children Today*, 1994

E. Lee et al., *World Employment: National Policies in a Global Context*, International Labour Office, Geneva, 1996

S. and J. Lewis eds., *The Work–Family Challenge: Rethinking Employment*, 1996

T. Marshall, 'Infant care: a day nursery under the microscope', *Social Work Service*, No. 32, 1982

'Maternity arrangements '95: part I', *EOR*, No. 63, September/October 1995

'Maternity arrangements '95: part 2', *EOR*, No. 64, November/December 1995

S. McGwire, *Best Companies for Women*, 1992

E. C. Melhuish and P. Moss, *The Day-care Project*, The Thomas Coram Research Institute.

E. C. Melhuish and P. Moss, *Day-care for Young Children: International Perspectives*, 1991

K. Millet, *Sexual Politics*, 1977

T. Mitchell, *Opportunity 2000 Campaign Fifth Year Progress Reports 1996*, Business in the Community, 1996

P. Morgan, *Who Needs Parents? The Effects of Childcare and Early Education on Children in Britain and the USA*, Institute of Economic Affairs, 1996

H. Morgan and K. Tucker, *Companies That Care: The Most Family Oriented Companies in America, What They Offer and How They Got That Way*, New York, 1991

P. Moss, '"Employee childcare" or services for children, carers and employers', *Employee Relations*, Vol. 14, No. 6, 1992

P. Moss and H. Penn, *Transforming Nursery Education*, 1996

A. Oakley, *Housewife*, 1974

S. Orbach, *What's Really Going On Here?: Making Sense of Our Emotional Lives*, 1994

Parents at Work, *Time, Work and Family*, 1995

E. Perle McKenna, *When Work Doesn't Work Anymore: Women, Work and Identity*, 1997

M. Phillips, *The Sex Change State*, The Social Market Foundation, 1997

L. Purves, *How Not To Be a Perfect Mother*, 1994

R. Rapoport et al., *Relinking Life and Work: Toward a Better Future*, The Ford Foundation, United States, 1996

F. Reichheld, *The Loyalty Effect: The Hidden Force Behind Growth, Profits and Lasting Value*, New York, 1996

A. Rich, *Of Women Born: Motherhood as Experience and Institution*, 1977

A. Roiphe, *A Mother's Eye: Motherhood and Feminism*, 1996

Report of the All Parliamentary Group on Parenting and International Year of the Family UK Parliamentary Hearings, 1994

M. Rutter and D. J. Smith eds., *Psychosocial Disorders in Young People: Time Trends and their Causes*, 1995

F. Schwartz, 'Women as business imperative', *Harvard Business Review*, March/April 1992

P. Senge et al., *The Fifth Discipline Fieldbook*, 1994

G. Sheehy, *New Passages*, 1996

R. Shore, *Rethinking the Brain: New Insights into Early Development*, The Families and Work Institute, New York, 1997

P. Sykes, *Parents Who Teach: Stories from Home and from School*, 1997

D. J. Swiss, *Women Breaking Through*, New York, 1996

D. J. Swiss, and J. P. Walker, *Women and the Work/Family Dilemma: How Today's Professional women are Finding Solutions*, New York, 1993

R. Tah, *Roads to the Top: Career Decisions and Development of Eighteen Business leaders*, 1995

Towards 2000: A workplace agenda for the next half decade, Business in the Community, GHN Limited, 1995

J. Treblicott ed., *Mothering: Essays in Feminist theory*, 1983

D. Utting et al., *Crime and the Family: Improving Child-rearing and Preventing Delinquency*, 1993

B. White et al., *Women's Career Development*, 1992

H. Wilkinson et al., *Tomorrow's Women*, Demos, 1997

N. Wolf, *Fire with Fire: The New Female Power and How It Will Change the Twenty-first Century*, 1994

All texts are published in Britain unless otherwise stated.

INDEX

❖

Abrams, Fran, 116, 121
Abrams, Rebecca, 4, 5
Abramsky, Jenny, 197
absenteeism, 270, 276–8
Adams, Rebecca, 51
Adler, Jerry, 159–60
advertisements, 207–8, 221
after-school clubs, 199–200
ageing population, 260–3
Allaire, Paul, 339–40
Allen, Irene, 264, 281–2, 303, 304,
    325, 329–30, 344
Alleway, Lynn, 5
Allott, Annabel, 55, 65
Apter, Terry, 55, 109
Asda, 295, 329, 346
attachment question, 146–8
Australia, 176
awards, 76
Axtens, Kirstie, 55, 239

Bailyn, Lotte, 228, 285
Bargh, Liz, 70, 233, 256, 264–5
Barking and Havering Health
    Authority, 291–2, 312, 331, 356
Barnardo's, 104
Barnes, Brenda, 12, 196
Barnes, Carole, 197
Bateson, John, 273–4
BBC, 2–3, 5, 167, 201–2, 304, 330–1,
    332, 344, 349, 355
Beauvoir, Simone de, 27, 28

behaviour problems, 91–2, 137–8
Belgium, 106
Belsky, Jay, 120, 122, 130
Bennis, Nora, 142–3
Bevan, Sally, 80
The Big Story, 164, 165
biological differences, nurturing,
    37–46, 68
birth, 215
Blair, Cherie (Cherie Booth), 75, 197
Blair, Tony, 328
Body Shop, 230–1
Bonny, 170, 186, 203
Boots, 230, 240
Boyer, Isabel, 280, 287, 288, 290
brain: development, 151–2, 192;
    gender differences, 40–1; quality
    care and, 117–18
Brannen, Julia, 60, 175
breastfeeding, 43–4, 95, 217–18
Bridges, William, 181–2, 249,
    258–60, 271, 311, 331, 343, 351,
    368–9, 370, 376
Bridgewater, Emma, 12, 89, 368
Bright, Jon, 162, 164, 165
British Airways, 286, 303
British Social Attitudes (BSA), 59, 60,
    63
British Telecom, 305
Broadcasting Complaints
    Commission, 101
Brook, Paula, 65, 86, 94, 98, 178,
    199, 241

Brown, Tina, 96, 97, 98
Bryant, Diane, 216–18
BT Forum, 320
Buckle, Henry Thomas, 377
Burgess, Adrienne, 38, 39–40, 45, 58, 59, 62, 64–5, 68, 121, 158–9, 161
Burrows, Lynette, 4, 6, 141, 143
Business in the Community, 208, 273
Buzan, Tony, 43

Camilleri, Tracy, 32, 154–5, 202
Cannon, Fiona, 112–13, 132, 242, 245–6, 251, 309, 313, 341, 342, 343
capital, social, 266–9, 328
career breaks, 194–5, 200–3
Cassani, Barbara, 93, 98
CBI, 254
Channel Four, 101
Child Poverty Action Group, 101
Child Support Agency, 108
childcare *see* day-care
children: after-school clubs, 199–200; attachment question, 146–8; behaviour problems, 91–2, 137–8; and delegation, 84–6; delinquency, 16, 138, 143, 161–5; disconnection of parents from, 85–7; effects of day-care, 113–26, 128–31; effects of parental absence, 89–93; Few Short Years myth, 189–204; gender differences, 39; illness, 277–8; fathers' importance to, 53–4; intelligence, 2, 16; maternal love, 17, 27–48; mental health, 140, 148–50; need for mother, 35–7; quality time with, 15, 74, 78, 79–82, 88; resilience, 89; self-esteem, 91, 93; separation from, 26; social development, 147–8; time spent with mothers, 144–6; underachievers, 151–5
Children Act (1989), 118

Childs, Ted, 305, 318, 323
Chin, Lesley, 267, 317
Chodorow, Nancy, 53–4, 65, 66
Clark, Peter, 273
Cohen, David, 61
Coloroso, Barbara, 198
communication, and organizational change, 319–22
competitiveness, and flexible working, 252–5
complexity, corporate fear of, 287–95
confidence, loss of, 201, 203
Conran, Shirley, 77
Conservative Party, 108, 252
Cook, Sheila, 196, 201–2, 349
Cooper, Cary, 59, 75–6, 233
Coopers & Lybrand, 230
Corasaniti, Mary Ann, 120, 122
Cotton, Marcia, 229
Covey, Steven, 82, 83–4, 352, 361, 362–3
Coward, Ros, 24, 28–9, 33–4, 35, 94, 114
Cox, Charles, 75–6
Crace, John, 58
creativity, organizational, 282–7
crime, 138, 142, 161–5
culture, workplace, 242–6, 307–8
Currie, Edwina, 5, 6, 75

Daily Mail, 58–9
Daily Telegraph, 5, 75, 159
Dalrymple, Theodore, 163–4
Daniels, Lucy, 150–1, 324–5
day-care: after-school clubs, 199–200; costs, 118–19; Day-care Dream, 15–16, 101–33; day-care as nursery education, 126–8; effects on children, 113–26, 128–31; public policy on, 131–2; quality care, 117–18; tax allowances, 112; time of entry into, 120; time spent in day-care, 119–21, 129–31; at work, 104, 112–13

Daycare Trust, 101, 106–7, 127
delegation, 84–6
delinquency, 16, 138, 143, 161–5
demographic pincer action, 260–4
Demos, 105, 107, 159, 176, 233–4,
    263
denial, working mothers, 94–6
Denmark, 108, 119
Department for Education and
    Employment (DFEE), 70, 257
Department of Education and
    Science (DES), 153
Department of Social Security (DSS),
    110
deputization, 311–13, 364
Despatches, 101
Dex, Shirley, 107
Dinnerstein, Dorothy, 53–4, 65
domestic service, 76–7
Douglas, Carolyn, 131
Drummond, Maggie, 200
Duckworth, Connie, 96–7
Dupont, 280
Dwyer, Kevin, 198

Early Years and Family Network, 154
Earthmother myth, 1, 6, 12–13, 14,
    16, 137–44, 167–70
education, nursery, 126–8
Ehrenreich, Barbara, 182
elderly, care of, 263
Elizabeth II, Queen, 75
emotional honesty, 46–9
employee retention, 270, 272–6
Employers for Childcare, 132, 341
'empty-nest syndrome', 181
'enough', doctrine of, 354
environmental concerns, and
    workplace change, 264–5
environmental influences, child
    development, 40, 42
Ephron, Nora, 221
Equal Opportunities Commission,
    276

Erdrich, Louise, 179
Ermische, John, 153
ESI, 254
Essex University, 3, 87
European Union (EU), 239, 326
Evening Standard, 58, 76
Exell, Richard, 109–10
exhaustion, 96
extended family, 114–15
Eyer, Diane, 161

Faludi, Susan, 3, 28, 121, 125
Families and Work Institute, 62, 146,
    147, 149, 150, 151–2, 236–7, 238,
    239, 249, 271, 277, 280–1, 286,
    299, 308, 317, 318
Family Policy Studies Centre, 54–5,
    63, 156, 162–3
fathers: disconnection from children,
    85–7; gender differences, 38–46;
    65–70; house-husbands, 55–7, 58;
    involvement in family life,
    159–61; New Father myth,
    14–15, 50–72; nurturing impulse,
    38–42, 44–5; paternity leave, 211,
    219–20; reactions to childbirth,
    34–5; as sole earners, 156–9;
    VSMs (virtually single males), 241,
    242; and wife's employment,
    141–2, 155–61
feminism: and child's need for its
    mother, 35; denial of mother love,
    27–30; denigration of mother care,
    113–14; support for day-care, 104;
    and women's guilt, 24
Ferris, Maria, 332
Few Short Years myth, 189–204
Figes, Kate, 24, 116, 121, 125, 126,
    182
finances, 175–8
Finland, 108–9
flexible working: American
    companies, 234–5; career breaks,
    194–5, 200–3; changing jobs,

366–73; and competitiveness,
252–5; cost savings, 269–71;
deputization, 311–13, 364;
employee retention, 270, 272–6;
and family rhythm, 246–8; fear of
complexity, 287–95; Few Short
Years myth, 192–4; homeworking,
208, 220–4, 265; improved
performance, 280–7; job-
restructuring, 3010–13, 362–6;
job-sharing, 231, 285–6, 288–9,
291–5, 313, 356; leadership
commitment, 300–7, 324–5; part-
time work, 7, 109, 153, 192–4,
204, 224–34, 282–3, 289–91,
311–13; personal-change strategy,
345–77; portfolio careers, 368–72,
376; projectizing, 310–11, 364; as
a recruitment tool, 271–2;
reducing absenteeism and stress,
276–80; self-employment, 368;
time movement, 250–1; work-life
initiatives, 316–44; and workplace
culture, 307–8; *see also* work;
working mothers
Ford Foundation, 236, 237, 247, 285,
286, 295, 299, 308, 309, 312,
314–15, 316, 319, 320–1, 322,
324, 327, 333–9, 346, 358, 365
Fortune magazine, 18, 235
Foster, Joanna, 90, 233, 320
Fowler, Norman, 158, 287
France, 106
Fraser, Helen, 216
freelance workers, 370
Freely, Maureen, 10, 30–1, 46, 48,
68, 69, 77, 111–12, 186, 251, 324,
370
Friedan, Betty, 170, 174
Fukuyama, Francis, 142
Fuligni, Alison Sidle, 146
full-time mothers, 165–6; contented
full-time mothers, 170–3; day-care
issue, 107; Earthmother myth, 1,
6, 12–13, 14, 16, 137–44, 167–70;
Few Short Years myth, 189–204;
identity, 178–81; mental life,
182–5; public debate about, 2–7;
time spent with children, 144–6;
unwilling full-time mothers,
173–5
Full-Time Mothers, 8, 138–9, 167,
203

Galinsky, Ellen, 146, 236, 237, 239
Gallup Poll, 55
Gardner, Partridge, 70
Gemini Consulting, 231, 232, 245,
273–4, 282, 290, 293, 369
gender differences, 38–46, 66–8
Generation X, 263–4, 272
genetics, gender differences, 41, 42,
68
Germany, 106, 254, 255
Gershuny, Jonathon, 87–8
Gerstner, Lou, 302, 305, 330
Gibson, Mary, 85
Gill, Marie, 329
Gillibrand, Eileen, 24, 25–6
Gilligan, Carole, 46, 47, 66–7, 95,
178
'glass ceiling', 10, 64
Glaxo Wellcome, 273, 274, 286, 303
Good, Diana, 273
Goodman, D., 140
Gordon, Jack, 61–2
government, organizational change
agenda, 325–8
Granada Group, 285, 306, 330, 331,
344
Grant, Linda, 9–10
Gray, John, 66–7
Greer, Germaine, 27, 28, 113–14
guilt, 14, 23–7, 33–4, 37–8
Gurdon, Hugo, 83
Gyngell, Kathy, 5, 16, 139, 143, 145,
168

Haines, Gay, 186, 283
Hakim, Dr Catherine, 170
Hammond, Val, 70, 233, 299
Handy, Charles, 177–8, 266, 327,
    349, 352, 353, 356, 368, 370, 375
Hanna, Lynn, 109
Haran, Maeve, 12–13, 64, 74, 94, 96,
    97, 169, 178–9, 187
Harding, Louette, 56–7, 58, 80
Harman, Harriet, 103, 106, 107, 116,
    117, 125, 126–7, 199
Harvard Business Review, 18–19,
    216–18, 237, 288–9
Hass, Linda, 221, 254–5
Henricson, Clem, 162, 164, 165
Henwood, Melanie, 59
Hewitt, Patricia, 109, 225, 240, 250,
    254, 278–9, 284
Hewlett, Sylvia, 79, 91, 215–16, 222
Hill, Christine, 43, 196, 214
Hochschild, Arlie, 63, 84, 86, 92,
    120, 234–6, 239, 241, 243, 250,
    253, 254, 255, 278, 326, 362
Hodge, Margaret, 199, 251, 300,
    359–60, 362
Holdsworth, Angela, 197
Holmes, Paddy, 15–16, 101
homeworking, 208, 220–4, 265
Hopkins, Dr Juliet, 39, 123, 129
Horlick, Nicola, 4–5, 63, 78, 98, 192,
    225
Horrell, S., 88
house-husbands, 55–7, 58
housework, 59–60, 62–3, 76–8, 174
Howard, Michael, 164
Howarth, Peter, 58
Hughes, Penny, 12, 169
Hutton, Deborah, 43, 187
Hwang, Philip, 68, 254–5

IBM, 201, 240, 245, 272, 302, 305,
    308–9, 317, 318, 319, 322, 323,
    330, 331–2, 344
identity, 178–82

Independent, 6, 62, 106
Industrial Society, 276, 277
Institute of Child Health, 104
Institute for Employment Studies,
    209
Institute of Manpower Studies, 200
Institute of Personnel Management,
    254, 273
'invisible-mother syndrome', 179–80
Irish Mothers Working at Home
    Association, 142
Italy, 119
ITV, 164

Jackson, Marnie, 44–5, 219
Jacobson, 130
James, Oliver, 91
job-restructuring, 310–13, 362–6
job satisfaction, 178
job-sharing, 231, 285–6, 288–9,
    291–5, 313, 356
Joseph Rowntree Foundation, 156

Katz, Adrienne, 250
Keane, Dillie, 168, 184
Kelleher, Colette, 127
Kelly, Ruth, 50, 52, 71
Kelsey, Linda, 12, 64, 98, 169, 197
Kessler, Ronald, 155–6
Kingston, Royal Borough of, 325,
    326, 331
Kirby, Jill, 8–9, 139, 167
Kitzinger, Sheila, 42
'knowledge workers', 282–3
Knox, Heather, 209
Kraemer, Sebastian, 68
Kwitney, Alisa, 183

Labour Party, 101, 102, 108, 165,
    199, 239, 252, 263, 288, 326,
    327–8
Lawrence, Frances, 4, 161
Lawrence, Philip, 4, 51, 161
Leach, Penelope, 29, 38, 44, 68, 79,

80, 101, 107, 108, 117–18, 127,
131, 174, 197, 198
leadership commitment, 300–7,
324–5
Lee, Peter, 154
Lee-Potter, Lynda, 196
Leigh, Rosemary, 229
Levant, Ronald, 91
life agendas, 351–2
life-cycle revolution, 261–2
Liley, Ruth, 139
Listawood, 281–2, 303, 304, 325,
329–30, 344
Lloyds TSB, 112, 132, 245–6, 295,
308–9, 313–14, 332, 341–3, 344
London Weekend Television, 230
lone mothers: day-care issue, 106,
108; employment, 107, 108
Lord Chancellor's Office, 292, 294,
331, 356
love, maternal, 27–48

McClaren-Thompson, Sue, 229
MccGwire, Scarlett, 55–6, 193, 200,
229–30, 366–7
McKenna, Elizabeth Perle, 34, 94,
177–8, 245, 349, 352
McRae, James, 155–6
Magnus, Sharon Maxwell, 95
Managed Mothering myth, 15, 17,
73–100
Marrin, Minette, 168, 195
Marshall, Trudy, 111, 120, 122, 123
Martian values, 67
Maslow, Abraham, 181
maternity leave, 96, 193, 210, 214,
215–17, 219, 273
Mathews, Emma, 292, 294, 331,
356
May, Dorothy, 304, 355, 364
media, polarized viewpoints, 8–13
Melhuish, Edward, 23–4, 117
mental health, children, 140, 148–50
mentors, 373–4

middle managers, resistance to
change, 318–19
Midland Bank, 231, 232, 272–3,
284–5, 303, 305
Miles, Rosalind, 181
Millet, Kate, 27–8
MIT Sloan School of Management,
333–4, 358
Modern Times, 5
Monckton, Rosa, 79, 96, 178, 187,
349
morale, and flexible working, 280–2
Morgan, Patricia, 4, 15, 102, 106,
115, 121, 128, 130, 133, 141, 156,
168, 192
Morgan Grenfell, 4, 230
Morris, Roz, 173, 196, 215, 370
Mosley, Jenny, 24, 25–6
Moss, Peter, 11, 60, 64, 69, 103, 112,
113, 118–19, 127–8, 130, 131–2,
175, 233, 249, 326
mothers: biological influences,
37–46; child's need for, 35–7;
denigration of mother care,
113–14; emotional honesty, 46–9;
gender differences, 38–46, 65–70;
maternal love, 27–48; separation
from children, 26; *see also* full-time
mothers; lone mothers; working
mothers
Mothers, Fathers and Employment, 70
myths, 13–17; Day-care Dream,
15–16, 101–33; Everyone an
Earthmother, 167–70; Few Short
Years, 189–204; the Guilt Thing,
14, 23–7; Managed Mothering,
15, 17, 73–100; New Father,
14–15, 50–72

Nang, Dr Philip, 37
nannies, 77, 84–5, 130
National Childbirth Trust, 9
National Children's Bureau, 101,
118, 122, 123

NatWest, 272–3, 286
Nazemetz, Pat, 285, 333, 339, 340, 343–4
needs, personal-change strategy, 357
Netherlands, 108
Neustatter, Angela, 130
New Father myth, 14–15, 50–72
New Generation, 9, 103
New Ways to Work, 365
Newsnight, 8–9, 167
Newsweek, 18, 80, 232
Norman, Archie, 329, 330
North, Alison, 8–9
Norway, 233, 254
nurseries, staff:child ratios, 118
nursery education, day-care as, 126–8

Oakley, Annie, 35, 65, 114, 174
O'Brien, Margaret, 153
Opportunity 2000, 71, 208, 233, 299, 300, 302, 303, 305, 316, 318, 320, 365, 366
Orbach, Susie, 26–7, 48, 86, 196, 211, 218, 249
Osborn, Sue, 291–3, 294–5, 312, 356
Oxfordshire County Council, 265, 272, 274, 293, 302, 312, 317, 330, 331

Panorama, 2–3, 5, 6, 8, 51, 52, 125, 139, 151, 153, 191–2
Parenting in the Nineties, 54–5, 60, 62, 65, 156, 159, 186
Parents at Work, 71, 86, 87, 139, 210, 231–2, 239, 363–4, 365, 366
parliament, 48–9, 50, 72
part-time work, 7, 109, 153, 192–4, 204, 224–34, 282–3, 289–91, 311–13
paternity leave, 211, 219–20
Penn, Helen, 118–19, 131–2
Perry Pre-School Project, 115–16, 128–9
personal-change strategy, 345–77

Phillips, Melanie, 141, 156–7
Pichaud, David, 60–1
Piper, Anne Marie, 65, 95
Plant, Sadie, 47
Poris, Michelle, 146
portfolio careers, 368–72, 376
Powell, Sarah, 2, 3
power, personal-change strategy, 354–6
pregnancy, 42–3, 210, 211–17
projectization, 310–11, 364
Promise Movement, 141–2
promotion, 290–1, 294
Pruett, Dr Kyle, 68
Purves, Libby, 7, 36, 45, 81, 82, 90, 151, 221–2

quality care, 117–18
quality of life, 82–4
quality time, 15, 74, 78, 79–82, 88

Rapoport, Rhona, 228, 236, 237, 285, 309, 314, 319, 326, 332, 336, 338, 340
Reay, Carole, 25, 61, 95, 176–7, 240, 251, 350, 353
recruitment, flexibility and, 271–2
Reichheld, Frederick, 274–5, 279, 286
Reinach, 170, 186, 203
Rethinking the Brain, 151–2, 153
Richardson, Joely, 90
Rifkin, Jeremy, 256, 258
risk, personal-change strategy, 349–50
Roberts, Dr Ian, 104, 121, 124–6
Roberts, Yvonne, 4, 5, 39, 86, 91, 95–6, 97, 161, 176, 251
Robertson, Anne, 122
Robinson, Carolyn, 226
Robinson, Gerry, 86, 241, 306, 330, 344, 351, 359
Robinson, Josephine, 184–5

Roddick, Anita, 24, 63, 90, 103, 230–1
Roddick, Justine, 90, 93
Roiphe, Anne, 27, 29–30, 31, 35, 38, 53–4, 65, 181, 188
role reversals, 15
Rolls, Sarah, 226, 275
Rose, Philippa, 216
Ruddick, Sarah, 68
Russell, C., 120
Rutter, Michael, 148–9

Sarch, Yvonne, 15, 75
Savage, Carole, 13, 227–8, 271
Scardino, Marjorie, 63
school runs, 88–9
Schwartz, P., 122
Scott, Belinda, 191
Self magazine, 119
self-employment, 368
Senge, Peter, 358
Shapiro, Laura, 80
Sheehy, Gail, 261–2
Shirley, Steve, 223, 264, 265, 267, 302
Simpson, Hilary, 267, 271, 312, 317
single mothers *see* lone mothers
Skuse, David, 41, 42
small companies, work-life initiatives, 322–5
Smith, David J., 148–9
Smith, Joan, 76
social capital, 266–9, 328
society, breakdown of, 142–3
Sommers, Christina Hoff, 31
Spain, 119, 238
Stannard, E., 227, 228
Steinem, Gloria, 10, 70, 261
Sterling, Anne Fausto, 41
Stewart, Alison Clarke, 80
stock-taking, personal-change strategy, 350–7
Stogdale, Valerie, 12

stress: and absenteeism, 276–8; and length of working hours, 278–80
Striking the Balance, 325, 327
Sunday Express, 52, 59
Sunday Telegraph, 163, 209
Sunday Times, 58, 277
Superwoman myth, 1, 6–7, 12–13, 14–16, 74–100
support, personal-change strategy, 373–4
Sweden, 70, 108–9, 119, 120, 130–1, 233, 238, 254–5, 326
Swiss, Deborah, 234, 239, 248
Sylva, Kathy, 117
systems-thinking, personal-change strategy, 358–9

Tait, Ruth, 92, 209, 251
Tatler, 139–40
tax incentives: day-care, 112; organizational change, 327
Taylor, Frederick, 84
Taylor, Helen Kirwan, 16, 93–4, 98, 140, 191
technology, 149, 174, 247–8, 285
Thatcher, Margaret, 65, 75
Thomas Coram Research Unit, 60, 64, 103, 118, 119, 121–2, 123, 233
Thorpe, Philippa, 84, 216, 242
3M, 369
Tiffany & Co., 349
time: length of working hours, 18, 132, 243, 253–4, 278–80, 326; speeding up domestic life, 92; time management, 83–4, 360–2; 'time movement', 250–1; time spent in day-care, 119–21, 129–31
The Times, 58, 61–2, 76, 140, 184–5
timing, personal-change strategy, 348–50
Tomorrow's Women, 105, 107
Toynbee, Polly, 3, 6
Tyler, Val, 221

underachievers, 151–5
unemployment, 155, 328
United States of America, 112,
    115–16, 117, 141–2, 215–16,
    234–9, 253, 320
Utting, David, 162–3, 164, 165

Vandell, Deborah Lowe, 120, 122
Vaughan, Margaret, 51
Venusian values, 67
Vincenzi, Penny, 179–80
Violato, C., 120
Virgin Airlines, 210
VSMs (virtually single males), 241,
    242

Walker, Judy, 248
Walter, Natasha, 110, 176
Walters, Julie, 63
Weiser, Gill, 221
WFD, 246, 299, 308, 314, 315, 316,
    322, 341, 342
What About the Children?, 140
Whille, 130
White, Alice, 198
White, Barbara, 75–6
White Door, 284, 331
Williams, Bridgit, 180
Williams, Susan, 291–3, 294–5, 312,
    356
Wilson, Peter, 91–2, 148, 149
Wolf, Naomi, 10, 28, 31, 354
Wolfendale, Sheila, 24
Woman of the Nineties Award, 76
work: absenteeism, 270, 276–8;
    changing nature of, 258–60;
    childcare at, 104, 112–13;
    demographic pincer action,
    260–4; employee retention, 270,
    272–6; environmental concerns,
    264–5; family-friendly, 207–48;
    'glass ceiling', 64, 110; length of
    working hours, 18, 132, 243,
    253–4, 278–80, 326; and men's

position in society, 140–2; morale,
    280–2; need for change, 17–19,
    47, 70–2, 99–100, 249–97;
    organizational change agenda,
    298–344; organizational creativity,
    282–7; polarization, 257–8;
    promotion, 290–1, 294;
    recruitment, 271–2; scarcity,
    257–8; and social capital, 266–9,
    328; workplace culture, 242–6,
    307–8; *see also* flexible working;
    working mothers
Working Mother magazine, 218, 235
working mothers: ambivalence, 34;
    attachment question, 146–8;
    blame for social ills, 2–4, 140–4,
    161–5; breadwinners, 56–7, 58–9;
    career breaks, 194–5, 200–3; and
    change in the workplace, 71–2;
    and child's mental development,
    151–5; child's need for, 35–7;
    Day-care Dream, 15–16, 101–33;
    delegation, 84–6; disconnection
    from children, 85–7; effects of
    absence on child, 89–93; effects on
    fathers, 141–2, 155–61; Few Short
    Years myth, 189–204; guilt, 14,
    23–7, 33–4; homeworking, 208,
    220–4, 265; identity, 178–9,
    181–2; Managed Mothering myth,
    15, 17, 73–100; need to work,
    168–70; new babies, 216–20; New
    Father myth, 50–72; pregnancy,
    210, 211–17; public debate about,
    2–7; quality time, 15, 74, 78,
    79–82, 88; reasons for working,
    175–8; *see also* flexible working;
    work

Xerox, 230, 245, 286, 295, 308–9,
    317, 319, 332, 333–40, 341, 343,
    344, 356, 358, 365
XL for Men, 63

Yates, Paula, 5, 36, 168, 191
You magazine, 13, 56–7, 58, 61, 62,
  261

Young Minds, 148, 150
Ypsilanti study, 115–16, 117, 125,
  127, 128